THE INVENTION OF "RACE"

THE
INVENTION OF "RACE"

THE COLUMBIAN TURN IN MODERN CONSCIOUSNESS

BY

A.A. HUEMER

LANDER, WYOMING
AGATHON BOOKS
MCMXCVIII

Publisher's Cataloging-in-Publication Data
Huemer, A.A.
 The invention of "race:" the Columbian turn in Modern
consciousness / by A.A. Huemer.--1st ed.
  p.   cm.
 Includes bibliographical references.
 ISBN   0-9662443-7-0   (paperback)
 1. "Race"--Consciousness   I. Title.
 2. Ideology, Propaganda, etc.
 3. Logic--Reasoning, etc.
 4. Philosophy--*Philosophia*, etc.
  Library of Congress Catalog Card Number: 98-84028
305.8---Hue

For Mariette, whose support made this work possible, and for Belinda who knew that this book would be published.

ACKNOWLEDGMENTS

I wish to give my thanks to those persons who have assisted and encouraged this project. To Henry S. Kariel for teaching me the virtues of well-crafted writing, of intellectual and spiritual strength, and of playfulness. To Manfred Henningsen for guiding me toward philosophia. To his teacher Eric Voegelin for guiding him so well. To Lewis Hanke, Thor Heyerdahl and Lynn White, Jr. for quietly fomenting a revolution in the understanding of history. To Kiyoshi Ikeda for most honestly explaining to me the institutional limitations of a grant program dedicated to the investigation of institutional racism, and for encouraging me to continue with this project at an early stage when I was tempted to abandon it entirely. To Barry Fell for the correspondence we have shared sporadically over the past few years; for his subtle encouragement of this work, and for letting me know that I was not 'off the track'. To mi ate, Petaga Yuha Mani, for helping me to find a place to pray. To L.J. Matthys for a mountain of newspaper and magazine article clippings, some of which have been indispensable to completing this study. To Muriel James for reading an early, incomplete draft of this manuscript, and for making some suggestions which have been incorporated herein. To Aaron Whyne and Leonard Wilson for proof reading and early research assistance. And to misun, Peter V. Catches for several patient proof readings of this manuscript. To all of you I offer my deepest thanks.

CONTENTS

PREFACE xi

PART I   THE ANCIENT WORLD--THE WORLD LOST

CHAPTER I   The Legacy of Rome 1
             A history of rhetoric and War

CHAPTER II   The Education of the Barbarians 27
             The continuation of Roman traditions

CHAPTER III Spain and the Modern Age 53
             The founding of the "race" idea

CHAPTER IV   The World Before "Race" 93
             Ancient societies in the Americas,
             the crossroads of the world

PART II   THE MODERN WORLD--THE WORLD TODAY

CHAPTER V   The World Today--
             The United States of America 183
             "Race" and politics in a Modern setting

CHAPTER VI   The World Today--A Word of Caution 293
             Revolutionary movements and national liberation

CHAPTER VII The World Today--A Warning 313
             The possibility of genocide

EPILOGUE 353
BIBLIOGRAPHY   A list of references cited 387

Pardon me friend, if what I'm sayin' don't seem right
But that's the only chance I get now, both day and
night.
Hey, pardon me sir, if what I'm sayin' brings you down,
But that's the only way to show you, that I'm a clown.
Hey, I'm quite sure you'll understand,
I'm quite sure you'll understand.

--Cocker and Stainton

PREFACE

Reason is the most powerful and significant blessing which the Great Mysterious Spirit that is All has bestowed upon our human species. Indeed, the other animal beings of this earth also have powers each of their own: thus is an antelope swift and a bison strong; so does an eagle soar away and up, and disappear into the sun. But it is through Reason that we humans continue with the objective of our lives, which is *to learn*[1]. For ages beyond our memory, humans have employed the tool, speech, to evoke their blessing. And ever as the languages of our forbearers sought to express most accurately the world[2] about them, so much more closely was their vision directed toward the Truth. Thus our ancestors were able to learn, for their words were a constructive tool of their Reason. And so, countless aeons ago, cultures--or what are now more commonly called ethnicities or nationalities-- were devised among all of humanity as the Ancients counseled their Wisdom. Many have been the nations of humankind, and many are the languages which we speak. Yet, as we say and do things differently, we are as ever, always alike. We all remain

---

[1]

By *learning* I mean the lifelong process of becoming aware, of increasing the dimensions of one's consciousness, of openness to new information.

[2]

The natural planet earth. Nothing else is intended by my use of this word.

blessed by Reason, we all reason--learn--through language[3], and we are one in that it is our culture's language which sets our course as we seek to look toward the Truth.

But what if the tool, language, is misshapen and twisted, so that it no longer seeks to express most accurately the world about? What if any tool is misshapen? If a knife were to have a handle which too closely resembled its blade, its wielder would be as likely to be cut as the object under its edge. If a language seeks to conceal or change what is about in the world, then reasoning in that language will not move toward the Truth. Such reasoning will go in this or that particular direction, but in the end will always remain founded upon a desire for untruth. The culture of such a language will have misdirection and mispurpose, for it will have ceased to foster learning in our particular human way which consists of exalting our blessing, Reason. By misdirecting language and perverting Reason, the connection with the Spirit within and the Sprit without is severed[4], and the blessing is cursed, though not abated. Such a culture might accomplish colossal, yet dreadful achievements.

The chapters which follow intend to explain with clarity just how such misshapen reasoning has overtaken and besieged the minds of all humanity over the past few millennia[5]. More

---

[3]

Is it possible to imagine learning accomplished by human beings without the use of language? Is it possible for human beings to even *think* without the use of language symbolized?

[4]

For an excellent discussion of the relationship between Reason, the sacred, and the earthly, see: Eric Voegelin, "Reason: The Classic Experience," *The Southern Review* (Baton Rouge: Louisiana State University, April, 1974), Volume X, Number 2, pp. 237-264.

[5]

The process of derailment referred to here began circa 2000 years ago for some, 500 years ago for many more, and even more recently for some.

precisely, it will be shown that it is at the very base of our common human relation where untruth has built an impediment to our practice of reasoning. The effects of such a system of delusional thinking,[6] *enculturated*, are dangerous and powerful.

As I have stated, I hold that all of our human species are always alike. We are one, and our relation in that oneness is that of siblings. This is not so common a statement as it may seem at the moment.

In Ancient times, and since the dawn of humanity, the sibling relation of our species has served well our mutual health and prosperity. By three or four thousand years ago, humanity-- whose common ancestors three or so million years earlier had been a highly endangered and extraordinarily feeble species--had grown to the point that cultures were neighboring up against one another the whole world 'round. As neighbors, they retained their unique, distinctive language and culture identities, and as neighbors, they learned from one another. Over the world, various culture mythologies tell of that time, "a time long, long ago, when there was a Golden Age, and all who were strangers met as brothers."

Now, however, it is not the same. It is not said in the same way any more. One does not any longer hear that "all of humanity are siblings." It is now held that: "all races are equal." That such a seemingly subtle, yet nonetheless massive distortion has occurred in the base of our relations with our sisters and brothers may, I believe, easily be shown. I have become convinced that the transposition of our common family relationship follows a lengthy and a very discernable course of development. Two thousand years ago, in his official chronicle of what at that time was the world's bloodiest war of conquest ever,

---

[6]

False opinions about matters of fact.

Julius Caesar, wishing to make a *certain* point, spoke only the good about Rome, and described only the bad in its enemies, the Gauls. The Gauls were not a "race," however, but "Gaul" *was* a Roman invention.

The tradition of grammatical laws of speech which guided Julius Caesar's Latin language to its mark was taken up by a Spaniard named Nebrija, early in the year 1492. Presently, by convention, that is also known to be the same year in which "Columbus the navigator discovered a New World, peopled by New Men." Twenty one years later, in 1513, the word "race," in its sense of human population categories, was introduced for the first time ever into the dictionaries of five Modern languages: Spanish, Portuguese, English, French and Italian. The advent of "race" to other languages postdates *this* introduction.

Now there are various "races" upon this earth, though the exact number seems impossible to say, for the criteria of "race" vary so. Yet every individual human being on this world now knows, or is made to know just which group of "race" they belong to. For many, it has become a matter to be encoded in the laws. All of us now know that in the past, enormous suffering has been inflicted upon some "races" by certain other "races," but that in spite of all of that, all "races" are now equal--or almost so. I submit that it is not by chance that this widely-proclaimed equality finds all of our species sharing an equally fixed, nervous gaze upon our "races'" stockpiles of nuclear weaponry, and the plodding, methodical elimination of ecosystems--of our very 'ground of being'--from this earth. The 'equality' of these shared viewpoints are but a reasonable byproduct of the misdirection of language, and distorted reasoning by which we all have been seized.

It is in the hope that we shall be able to withdraw our gaze from the searing light of that nuclear fire, that we shall remember how to live in harmony upon our ground of being, and turn our selves toward a more loving light that I have discussed the ideas and past events in what follows below. I had originally considered subtitling this discourse: Concomitant Patterns in Modern Societies, but now a wiser council has prevailed. In the interest of clarity I have found it prudent to abandon those fires which burned within me throughout my earliest inquiry into the matters to be discussed here. The intention of what follows is to gently guide the revelation of a course of past events which have often been ill considered and ignored. That which stands nearer to and that which stands farther from the direction of Truth shall become evident to each as we proceed. My desire is to disclose the purpose--an unchanged purpose--for which the idea of the "racial" classification of humans was invented, five hundred years ago. As we view and consider that purpose in action, we may justly weigh the deeds excused by reasoning misdirected, and perhaps we may find something to learn.

PART I

THE ANCIENT WORLD--THE WORLD LOST

Our ship left the stream of Oceano, and passed into the open sea.
Soon it came to the island of Aiaia, where Dawn has her dwelling
and her dancing lawns, and Helios his place of rising.
                              --Homer

I'd rather be a sparrow than a snail
Yes I would.
If I could,
I surely would.
I'd rather be a hammer than a nail.
Yes I would.
If I only could,
I surely would.
Away, I'd rather sail away
Like a swan that's here and gone.
A man gets tied up to the ground,
He gives the world its saddest sound.
Its saddest sound.

> --P. Simon

CHAPTER I
The Legacy of Rome

Life is inseparable from violence. The crust of our earth, a being whom we do not ordinarily consider to live, has since its very beginning been the stage for violent activity on such a huge scale as the upheaval of mountain ranges, the movement of continents, massive earthquakes, volcanic caldera eruptions, and destructive collisions with comets, asteroids and meteorites from the vastness of space beyond. Yet as we humans experience time, such events seem rare, and the violence which they bring to our lives seems odd and unexpected. We are shocked when such violence touches our lives. On the other hand, as we live our lives from day to day, we tend to overlook the violence which we ourselves do so that we may live. Nonetheless, we must continually be party to the slaughter of those of our fellow beings, the animals, whose flesh we deem most suitable for our meat. Nor is the harvester of the field exempt from the scream of the lives cut short by his scythe.

There is nothing new or unusual in this. For millions of years humans--including our earlier hominid[1] ancestors--have scavenged and hunted so that they might eat. Whether banding together to steal the kill of a hunting or another scavenging species, or as the ages passed, learning to master the hunt for themselves, or even later on, tearing into the earth with the plow after slashing and burning the forest into a bed of fertile ash, humans have with violence taken what they must in order to survive. In this necessity to bear and withstand violence for the sake of life, we humans are like the other predatory species of animals and plants[2] with which we share this earth. And as with other animals, we humans have for a very long time[3] known the violence of fighting amongst ourselves.   This has usually occurred, as it does among our fellow animal beings--both predatory and vegetarian--over a rivalry for the possibility of mating. Sometimes such struggles have resulted in death for one or both of the combatants.[4]   Indeed, Modern scientists of humanity, the anthropologists, have learned that even among the least warlike of peoples, such as the Inuit, or the Greenland

---

[1]

Paleoanthropologists are still debating the age of the hominid genus from which our species arose. Current estimates are at circa one and one half million years ago, with predecessors as early as three and a half million years ago.

[2]

To be predatory is to be disposed to exploit or prey upon others. It is a feature so common to the biological realm that even certain species of plants may be found which subsist through carnivorous predation or violent exploitation of others.

[3]

In some cases, lesions discovered on the unearthed remains of *Homo erectus* or our 'cousin' species *Homo sapiens neanderthalensis*, appear as if they could only have been the result of inter-human strife.

[4]

It is noteworthy that throughout the animal kingdom, such deaths are clearly the exception to the rule.

Eskimo, homicide is not an uncommon experience. As in most Ancient human cultures, however, the repeating or multiple homicide perpetrator is virtually unknown[5].

There is another form of violence done by some humans and some of the animals while suffering from the most extreme hardships of starvation, and that is cannibalism, eating the flesh of one's own species.

Among humans, in the past, there have also been a few cultures in which our brothers and sisters have devoured their own kind as a ritual of their spirit. And this is something different from the first form of cannibalism. Such people as these often terrorized the nations which lay beside them, and sometimes drove them mad.

When madness has arisen among nations from this or some other cause, such as envy or greed, the nations have turned to warfare. In warfare the nations have indulged in a devouring violence among warriors. Warfare has existed among humans for a long, long time. For example, over 4,390 years ago, by force and intrigue, Sargon of Akaad proclaimed himself Emperor of the World. Some 1,500 years later the Assyrians began to violently subdue the lands which are now known as Egypt, Sudan, Ethiopia, Jordan, Israel, Syria, Cyprus, Iraq, Kuwait, and parts of Turkey, Iran, and Saudi Arabia. The process endured for some two hundred and twenty five years.

From at least this age, from time to time, there have come and gone short-lived nations which have sought to dominate neighboring and outlying nations by force of arms. And there has

---

[5]

In a great many Ancient tribal societies one act of homicide might result in the perpetrator's banishment from society for a certain regulated period of time. Repeat offenders might face death. For examples of this principle see: Karl N. Llewellyn and E. Adamson Hoebel, *The Cheyenne Way: Conflict and Case Law in Primitive Jurisprudence* (Norman: University of Oklahoma Press, 1941), pp. 132-165.

at least as long been warfare for the feud and revenge, or for the sake of a hostage, or in self-defense. But warfare, although it is one means by which our species devours its own kind, does not ordinarily appear to us to be yet another form of cannibalism. Perhaps this is because warfare has for so long a time been mostly the business of *warriors*.

But *once* there was a nation which slaughtered unknown millions of men and women, young and old, simply for the sport of it--for the sake of public entertainment--as well as for the lust to possess vast territorial realms, or in other words, for the practicality of it. This is yet another form of cannibalism: devouring one's own kind for the sake of pleasure or usefulness. This is cannibalism for fun and profit. It is a kind of human violence entirely different from all the rest, in both its scale and its motives. Before the advent of the empire-builders we shall consider in this context--for at least *hundreds* of thousands of years--cannibalism for pleasure and profit had been unknown among human cultures, and although there had been warfare for thousands of years, the families within nations had always been distinguished from their warriors-at-arms. The empire-builders we shall soon consider were the first of our species to bring mass-scale slaughter into human experience.

Although violence is inseparable from life because it is a part of the very process of life, violence apart from the life process--violence done for another reason than to live--is an extreme rarity among our fellow beings on earth, the animals.

There is no species of great cat, no pack of wolves so whimsical as to spend all of their days and nights simply hunting down and killing victims one after the other, leaving their hunting ground littered with rotting, uneaten corpses. But there is a kind of exception to this in the behavior of victims of the mammalian disease rabies. In its final stage rabies destroys the brain of its victim. A large, rabid carnivore can easily kill and maim at random, for no apparent reason. Such creatures are utterly unpredictable, very dangerous, and appropriately, are called mad. They end their lives immersed in violence and pain, and have become voided of joy, which is yet another inseparable portion of life.

Although research scientists in California have for a couple of decades been measuring anxiety readings obtained from plants using lie detector equipment, Modern minds are too well-conditioned to easily perceive the existence of an emotion such as joy--or its opposite--within a plant, a worm, a fish, or a salamander. However, if we consider the warm-blooded creatures which by convention are thought of as being 'higher', and therefore more like ourselves, we may easily observe the flow of joy in their lives in the same kinds of contexts in which we most often experience it in our own human existences.

When stroking a cat, upon feeling and hearing it purr, we know that it is happy. A dog, reunited with its special human friend after a long separation, has no difficulty in expressing its joy and love. After feasting well, a lion basking in the sun with its eyes closed displays its pleasure for all the world to see. Wolves feeding and nurturing their young, baboons grooming one another, a playful colt, otters during even the dreary business of the hunt for food--all display various aspects of joy, pleasure and love in contexts similar to our own[6].

But as I have said, there may be no species of animal to be found which devours and destroys its own or any other species simply because it derives pleasure from destroying. As we have

----

[6]

A skeptic who denies that creatures other than humans can have authentic emotions and feelings might profit from the experience of visiting a zoo of the old-fashioned, obsolete kind, where animals are kept in cramped and uncleaned cages. There the skeptic can attempt to convince himself that the animals are not discontented, unhappy and neurotic.

seen above, the rabid beast can destroy without any apparent cause. But all such creatures are mad, sick and suffering, and they know no pleasure derived from any source. In our own species there emerged an exception to this.

I mentioned earlier that once there was a nation which took for its national pastime a peculiar joy in the spectacle of bloody murders enacted before the massed public. This was no passing fancy, either. That cannibalistic "sport" which we shall soon investigate endured for well over six hundred years--well over twice as long as the Assyrian madness--and cost untold millions of human lives. How shall we know such a nation? How shall it be called? Shall it be known as *madness*?

This may be so, but for the sake of our own wakeful awareness and that of our posterity, we must seek to understand the process of disease which led an entire nation to indulge itself in the madness of mass-cannibalism. To do this we shall first have to know them by their own name for themselves: they were Rome, the culture which most contemporary historians agree was the source point of our present-day Modern societies.

According to legend, Rome was founded over 2,740 years ago by the twins Romulus and Remus. Out of a dispute over Romulus' supposed cheating in a contest to decide the city's site, Remus was slain by his twin. Then, since a city needs a population as well as a location, Romulus established a sanctuary for murderers and other criminals on the Capitoline Hill, and thereby Rome's numbers began to grow. Next, Romulus contrived to kidnap a number of women from the nearby nation of the Sabines. Thusly he pressured the Sabine King into merging his throne with Rome. The Sabine King was then murdered by Romulus, and Rome had grown once again.

From that time forward, "The Romans were pre-eminently men of war. The only choice they had for centuries was to conquer or be conquered. Possibly war was their most natural expression; certainly it was the price they must pay for being a nation[7]."

The Latin historian Livy, writing 800 years after Rome's founding, observed that from its earliest days until his own time, Rome had been continuously at war with its enemies. Who were Rome's enemies? The list of Rome's enemies included all of its immediate neighbors, whoever they might be at any given time. They were the Etruscans to the north, the neighboring Sabines, the Samnites to the east, Greeks and Phoenicians to the south; then the Celtiberians in Spain, Cisalpine Gauls further north in the Italian Alps, Carthaginians in North Africa, and the Gauls of what is now France. These nations and leagues of nations (and many other) fell before the Roman short sword before Roman culture underwent a most significant transformation during the period of history known as the Middle Ages of Europe, beginning roughly some sixteen hundred years ago.

The notion, mentioned above, that Rome perpetually had no choice but to destroy or be destroyed--that its neighbors on all sides were actually deadly menacing enemies--is a particularly Roman self understanding which has been handed down to us over the ages, and is now accepted as if it were genuinely the truth.

Yet if one were to be able to travel backward in time and ask an Etruscan about Rome, one might be told something like: "They intend to wipe every trace of us from the face of this earth." Of course this is just speculation. But it is curious that today we know very little about the Etruscans. They seem to have simply

---

[7]

Edith Hamilton, *The Roman Way to Western Civilization* (New York: Mentor Books, 1957), p. 109.

vanished, leaving hardly a trace at all. Although they are considered to have made a significant contribution to Roman culture, it is impossible to clearly understand the nature of that contribution, for Roman writings about Etruscans are pointedly hostile and one-sided. On the other hand, it is also curious that little survives of the literature of the Etruscans, for they lived in an age and in a part of the world where written language was conventionally known to have been widely used for over two millennia[8]. The surviving fragments of Etruscan writing which have mostly been found in their tombs, have still not been adequately deciphered, and this is in part because of the sudden and total destruction of their cultural continuity.

Further, it is curious that with the exception of the Greeks and Egyptians, every other enemy of Rome's also came to an abrupt and total cultural end at the time of its conquest by Rome. So complete was the erasure of the Celts of Gaul that until recently they were thought of as having been extremely rude, barbaric peoples who had no literature. That is now known to be untrue on all accounts[9]. Perhaps Egypt and the Greeks were spared the usual fury of Roman conquest because of the close interrealtion of their peoples, and in particular, because Rome claimed that Greek culture was the standard for its own society.

---

[8]

The great antiquity of incipient, or developmental writing and notation techniques is a subject which I will take up later, in the fourth chapter below, along with the subject of global, universal human spread of written languages at a much earlier date than is commonly accepted.

[9]

Thanks largely to excavations and research conducted in Ireland, Spain, Portugal, northern Europe and North America, the Celtic nations are now known to have been master iron workers of their age, far-ranging seafarers, and very literate people, rather than simply "children of the forest."

Today, Rome's claim of Greek culture is broadly accepted, and we know, for example, that Rome adopted the gods of the Greeks and gave them Latin names[10]. It is common these days to speak of the Greco-Roman culture which was the foundation of our own Modern societies[11]. On closer examination however, the identification of Rome with the Greeks appears to be more like a Roman self-justification achieved after the fact of Rome's subjugation of the Greek nations, rather than a clear-cut reality. There are actually enormous and significant differences between their cultures.

To begin with, unlike Rome, the Greeks were not a single state, but rather, were a number of small nations mostly occupying the peninsula of Greece. Over the course of their histories these nations were sometimes allied with one another, and sometimes engaged in warfare with one another. But they never erased one another from the land as Rome did with its neighbors on the Italian peninsula. The Greeks were never efficient conquerors and empire builders as were the Romans, although the Greeks were most formidable warriors. Even when the Macedonians (who unlike the Romans did have a Greek culture) under Philip and his son Alexander, conquered their way eastward to the Indus River and beyond into India, their methods were strikingly different than those of the Romans. Philip and Alexander conquered armies on the battlefield, and then their victories were formalized by marrying their generals--and finally Alexander himself did so--into the noble families whose armies

---

[10]

The Romans characteristically adopted foreign gods when they found that it might serve a particular practical purpose of their own. I will discuss this further in the second chapter below.

[11]

Especially in such important cultural institutions as legal systems, it would be almost impossible to find a single Modern nation in the world today which has not been deeply affected by Ancient Rome.

they had defeated. In the end, what Alexander achieved 2,300 years ago was to bring more knowledge of Greek culture to the nations east and southeast of Macedonia, and to bring better knowledge of those distant cultures back to the Greeks.

After the death of Alexander it did not take a very long time for his empire to begin to fall back apart into smaller culture groups which mostly resembled those which had existed before he had arrived. Nothing similar ever occurred in the case of those nations which were subjected to military conquest by Rome. Indeed, all of the nations on earth were in some way or other, sooner or later, touched by the Roman Empire, and nothing has ever been quite the same since then.

There are other distinctions which belie the supposed derivation of Roman culture from those of the Greeks. The Greeks were extremely creative artistic peoples. Their sculpture is varied and original, and is still admired to this day in museums around the world, as well as in Greece, where much of it remains. Rome's artists were short on originality, and for the most part copied the works of the Greeks. The art of Rome is often very lifelike--excessively so, some say--and is just as often described as being cold. Roman architecture was very rude and simple for several hundred of Rome's early years, and it only began to show sophisticated qualities after the conquest of the Italian peninsula had been completed by Rome, and as it absorbed and copied, unacknowledged, the design and structural forms of the nations it had destroyed. But the spirit behind the gaudy pastel colors with which the Greeks painted their buildings and temples is absent in the uniformly red tile roofed, stark white marble and stucco, and concrete of Roman architecture.

The Greeks were also peoples of learning who sought knowledge in all fields simply for its own sake. They built a mechanical clock, and put it in a temple. They made complex steam-powered mechanical devices such as the "walking tripods" of the oracle at Delphi, yet they considered such things to be mere curiosities, and useful only, for example, as stage props in plays. They studied the natural world about them, and the heavens above; they studied their own language, history, politics and ethics, and they studied the immortal soul. Our Modern word philosophy is derived from the Greek term *philosophia*, meaning the love of wisdom. The Romans cared little for these things--especially philosophy--which made the Greeks the peoples they were, save when they had practical applications to meet ends desired by Rome.

So of all the learning of the Greeks, the Romans eagerly adopted only practical technology, the concept of civil laws, and the related Greek study of persuasive speaking known as rhetoric.[12]

For their part, the Greeks paid little attention to Rome, except as it menaced them. Twenty two hundred and seventy years ago the Greeks and Rome were engaged in indecisive warfare, but still, Greeks wrote little about Rome until long after Rome had conquered them--through 'diplomacy'--some one hundred and fifty years later. How then shall we know of Rome if all of its neighbors and enemies are silent on the subject due either to their utter destruction by Rome, or because they deemed Rome to be unworthy of mention?

If we turn to the literature of Rome in order to discover what Rome was, we do indeed find a first significant clue. We might surmise that Romulus (although reared by a wolf) and his successors were not illiterate. In Romulus' time reading and writing were known and used by cultures all over the earth. But from Romulus' time and for the following five hundred years, with only one exception, no Roman literature has survived. It is

---

[12]

Specifically, rhetoric is the theory and practice of eloquence, spoken and written, which aims at expounding the rules which should govern all prose composition or speech *designed to influence the judgements or feelings* of people.

as if Rome had conquered itself, and wiped out all records of its past existence just as it had done to the 'enemies' it obliterated, excepting the Greeks and Egyptians. What did happen was indeed something of the sort.

Cato was a great Roman patriot who lived roughly 2,150 years ago. As a military man Cato had fought against the Carthaginian generals Hannibal and Hasdrubal during Rome's second war with that Phoenician nation, and he lived long enough to see the preparations made for Rome's third and final conflict with Carthage, in which the latter was utterly destroyed. The most significant aspect of Cato's career however, was in his capacity as one of the first Roman masters of the study of rhetoric[13]. In that office he was known as Cato the Censor of Morals. And from that lofty position, Cato personally oversaw and directed the destruction of all Roman literature which had existed before his own time.

Apparently Cato the rhetorician thought that Rome's earlier records would have an *improper* influence over people's feelings and judgements where Rome was concerned. The only bit of writing which Cato deemed worthy of survival from before his time was a fragment of a treatise on agriculture in North Africa. In light of the Roman obsession with practical knowledge it is easy to see why he did so. After Rome had destroyed Carthage and taken over much of North Africa, Roman farms in North Africa produced the grain which fed the Roman armies that completed Rome's conquests to the north, south, east and west.

The only literary works surviving from Cato's own time-- excluding some of his own speeches--are the comedies of the playwrights Plautus and Terence. Their works contained no political material (as was common for theatrical works of the time

---

[13] One of Cato's most renowned speeches was entitled: "Carthage Must be Destroyed."

in other countries), were set in Greek locales, and were peopled by caricatures of Greek people. There was nothing in the works of either Plautus or Terence that a censor could construe as being guilty of "diminishing the Majesty of the Republic[14]."

If Cato's task of changing the historical record in order to properly influence posterity evokes an image of the labors of Winston--the protagonist of George Orwell's novel *1984*--in his job at the Ministry of Truth, then we are prepared to see how Rome was truly unique--how it was the first nation of its kind ever on this earth--and how it stands at the beginning of a particular tradition which leads directly to the cultures of the Modern Age. From Cato's day onward, the rigorous study of rhetoric formed the base of every learned Roman's education.

One hundred years after Cato, a fully-developed Roman literature emerged, beginning with the speeches and letters of another grand master of rhetoric, Cicero[15]. During this period Caesar's commentaries on his campaign in Gaul were written, and not long afterward, Livy wrote his voluminous history of Rome. This brief time ushered in the golden age of Roman literature. But so polished, so persuasive is the rhetorical style of Caesar's and Livy's works that an experienced, critical reader might only *begin* to suspect that their reports are somewhat biased, and often contain material (such as quotations) which was simply fabricated by the author.

---

[14]

This was the Roman legal wording of condemnation when a person had committed the crime of offending the State.

[15]

Cicero wrote a great many letters on political subjects to his friends. Their preservation gives us our first view of criticism of the Roman state. Whether Cicero intended the letters to be preserved or not is a topic well worthy of investigation and debate.

Although the Etruscans, Samnites, Sabines[16], Carthaginians and Celts were rather thoroughly erased and therefore cannot tell us their story of Roman conquest, there are other sources available to tell us something about these peoples. And as we look at some of those other sources we can see that the official Roman version of their wars is not simply biased, but downright distorted.

For example, the Carthaginians who Rome so bitterly despised and who they characterized so rhetorically were also described by the Athenian, Aristotle. Aristotle was a philosopher, a man who allowed Reason to guide him toward the Truth. Aristotle was also the tutor of Alexander the Great, and we have already seen how substantially the conquests of Alexander differed from the annihilation that was Roman conquest. Of Carthage, Aristotle wrote:

> Many of the Carthaginian institutions are excellent. The superiority of their constitution is proved by the fact that the common people remains loyal to the constitution; the Carthaginians have never had any rebellion worth speaking of, and have never been under the rule of a tyrant[17].

We must contrast this with what we know of the Roman's own government.

By their own rhetorical accounts, Rome established the rule of civil law (their civil law was itself partly devolved through their study of rhetoric), and this ruling concept has been handed down to the Modern world of today. By their own admission, Rome also suffered many civil wars which were as bloody as any of their conquests, and Rome knew the rule of many tyrants, and they

---

16

One small fragment of the Sabines *was* admitted to Rome, and these founded a clan of Romans a little over 2,200 years ago.

17

Richard McKeon, ed., *The Basic Works of Aristotle* (New York: Random House, 1941), p. 1171. [*Politics*, Book II: Chapter 11.]

often experienced the political assassination of rulers and of the friends and families of rulers. So powerful, however, is the perspective-altering influence of Roman rhetoric, that without another form of government with which to compare theirs, such as, for example, that of the Carthaginians, we might not realize that there was something quite distinctive about Roman political life. If we were to allow the power of Roman rhetoric to tamper with our ability to reason, and to stop our questioning and our search for yet more information, we might read their self-description and say, as the rhetorician intended: "Yes, that is the way politics has always been."

I have already briefly mentioned in a note above something of the lost civilization of the small tribal nations of the Celts of Gaul, Britain, Ireland and Scotland, and something also of the Celtiberians of Spain[18]. Because the Romans were careful to destroy the monuments of the Celts along with the historical records which these conveyed, there is little which the Celts--the Celts of Gaul in particular--can tell us directly about either themselves, or the darkest hours of their histories[19]. In his commentaries on his military campaign in Gaul, however, Julius Caesar attributes a most interesting speech to a Celtic nobleman, Critognatus. This tells us yet more about Rome. Critognatus allegedly delivered his oration before a council held within the besieged Celtic fortress at Alesia not long before it fell to the Romans. These are the words which Caesar gives his Gaul to

---

[18]

See note 9, above.

[19]

The most extensive examples of the Celtic Ogam style of writing have to date been discovered in Ireland (which was never conquered by Rome until the time of Saint Patrick), Portugal (Rome's last Iberian conquest) and in North America. Recent archaeological excavations of Celtic tombs (which the Romans did not have the foresight to destroy) have begun to bring to light examples of Ogam inscriptions from the rest of the Celtic world.

speak with:

> What counsel, then, have I to offer? I think we should do
> what our ancestors did in a war that was much less serious
> than this one.   When they were forced into their
> strongholds by the Cimbri and Teutoni, and overcome like
> us by famine, instead of surrendering they kept themselves
> alive by eating the flesh of those who were too old or too
> young to fight. Even if we had no precedent for such an
> action, I think that when our liberty is at stake it would be
> a noble example to set our descendants. For this is a life
> and death struggle, quite unlike the war with the Cimbri,
> who, though they devastated Gaul and grievously afflicted
> her, did eventually evacuate our country and migrate
> elsewhere, and left us free men, to live on our land under
> our own laws and in possession of our rights. The Romans,
> we know, have a very different purpose. Envy is the motive
> that inspires them. They know that we have won renown
> by our military strength, and so they mean to instal
> themselves in our lands and towns and fasten the yoke of
> slavery on us for ever. That is how they have always
> treated conquered enemies. You do not know much,
> perhaps, of the condition of distant peoples; but you need
> only look at the part of Gaul on your own borders that has
> been made into a Roman province, with new laws and
> institutions imposed upon it, ground beneath the
> conqueror's iron heel in perpetual servitude[20].

Although the candor of the speech which Caesar wrote and
attributed to Critognatus seems remarkable regarding the
motives for and expected result of Roman conquest--especially so,
since we know that the Celts *were* exterminated politically and
their resources appropriated--what is even more remarkable is

---

[20]

S.A. Handford, translator, Julius Caesar, *The Conquest of Gaul* (New York:
Penguin Books, 1951), pp. 226-227.

Caesar's use of a rhetorical formula which was still in use over 1,900 years after his time. This is the conqueror's description of an enemy who has been singled out for annihilation as *a noble savage.*

Caesar presents the classic formula for the noble savage who is ultimately quite ignoble because he has the potential for, or is reputed to actually practice cannibalism. This is also the noble/ignoble savage who practices human sacrifice (a charge which Caesar makes elsewhere, and a charge which Tacitus, for example, later on makes against the Germans in his *Germania*). And here we see for the first time something which occurs over and over again almost to the present day: the conqueror which accuses its victim of cannibalism is itself guilty of a form of cannibalism so terrible as to be almost beyond imagining.

I have mentioned above that Rome was cannibalistic, and that this was a cannibalism beyond that caused by an emergency of severe starvation, beyond ritual cannibalism[21], and beyond the cannibalism of common warfare. I have said that Rome partook of a fourth kind of cannibalism--cannibalism for fun and profit[22].

Let us first consider cannibalism for fun. About 2,260 years ago, Rome devised its own unique form of public entertainment, a spectacle of murder enacted before the massed public. It was known as a "sport" by them and was called the gladiatorial games. These "games" consisted of armed combat to the death between individual "warriors" and groups of "warriors" by the tens, hundreds, or even thousands. The "games" were performed in

---

[21]

This form of cannibalism often does not even entail the murder of a victim, but rather, may consist of the ceremonial, symbolic eating of the remains or ashes of a deceased relative.

[22]

Cannibalism may not only be defined as the eating of human flesh, or the appetite of a species which eats its own kind, but also as the activity of a species which devours, or *wastes* it own kind.

gigantic stadia. The Coliseum in Rome, for example, held 80,000 spectators, and the Circus Maximus, where Roman citizens watched deadly chariot races and other lethal diversions, could accommodate 260,000 viewers.

Everywhere Rome conquered it built the stadia--on the average large enough for 20,000 spectators--and introduced the gladiatorial spectacle. Only in Athens, did the conquered Greeks reject the gladiators by twice, as the spectacle was about to begin, appealing to Reason. On the first occasion, a respected devotee of *philosophia* rose from the midst of the audience just as the butchery was about to commence, and cried out: "Athenians, before you admit the gladiators, come with me and destroy the altar to Pity[23]." With one voice, the people denounced what was about to begin. On Rome's second attempt to force the gladiators upon them, the Athenians' response was the same.

Who were the gladiators? For the most part, they were prisoners of war who were forced into the arena under the threat of certain death. But Rome never had nearly enough prisoners of war to feed to the arena, and so persons condemned to die for such crimes as "diminishing the Majesty of the Republic," or at a later period for "Christianus," were sent to the gladiatorial "schools" to learn how to kill one another and hold on to the hope that if one was skillful or lucky enough, one might meet death later and not sooner, or perhaps even ultimately win one's freedom[24]. Yet these prisoners still did not provide enough bodies

---

[23]

Hamilton, *op. cit.*, p. 108.

[24]

Just a few decades ago, the nations of the world were shocked to learn that the tyrant of Uganda, Idi Amin, tortured the prisoners in his jails by offering them the same twisted hope for life. At that time, documented stories by eye witnesses surfaced about political prisoners who were "forced" to beat their fellow prisoners to death with hammers while guards watched. But never have the nations of the Modern world, which proudly proclaim their

to feed Rome's hunger for human flesh, and so masters sold those of their slaves who displeased them to the "schools." Eventually *volunteers* also came forth from among the Roman citizenry, and these, more often than not, were ambitious glory-seekers who arranged to participate in rigged "contests."

What was the nature of the "contests" of the circus and the arena? There were wild animal "hunts:" in one, two hundred lions and lionesses were killed; in another, five thousand animals were slaughtered--a mix which included elephants, bulls, tigers and panthers. The unexpected death of a "hunter" would only add to the excitement. There were "contests" between dwarfs, and between dwarfs and women. By means of hidden canals, the circus was flooded, and naval "battles" were fought. Twenty four ships were on one occasion involved in such a spectacle, and aboard them, nineteen thousand human beings fought to victory or death. Over four hundred years after the gladiatorial spectacle had begun in Rome, the son of Marcus Aurelius--who has often been considered to have been Rome's wisest ruler--boasted of murdering two thousand "opponents" using only his left hand. In the latter days of the Empire, one emperor was reported to have been unable to take a meal unless he had first witnessed the bloodshed of the arena.[25] Thus did a wise father raise his son. Thus did an Emperor exemplify the virtues to his State. Thus, for well over six hundred and fifty years, did Rome consume the flesh of unknown millions of human beings.

Roman heritage, ever expressed their revulsion at the similar perversions of Rome.

[25]

This report would seem unbelievable if we did not know of a similar means by which the Spaniard Francisco Pizarro had stimulated his appetite 462 years ago in the courtyard square at Caxamalca, Peru.

Let us next consider cannibalism for profit. Warfare, a form of cannibalism which we do not commonly recognize as such, is, I have said, for a variety of causes, a very ancient human occupation. Sargon of Akaad was on intimate terms with envy. He may have been the first person in the world to overthrow what the Ancients considered the most perfect form of government possible--the dynastic true monarchy of a God-King or Titan. Sargon found it necessary to subject the ruler he overthrew to public humiliation. During the brief two hundred and twenty five years when the Assyrians ran amok in the Fertile Crescent region, they earned a reputation for ferocity in battle. No doubt they were intimate with the political execution of rival heads of state, but still, they were not exterminators of humankind. The Ancient Israelites were the first people ever to proclaim that by the direct authority of Almighty God Himself, they had been promised the ownership of a country already belonging to somebody else[26]. But when the time came when they did occupy Canaan, they did not find it necessary to hound the Canaanites into extinction.

Rome, however, in its conquests as in the spectacle of the gladiators, introduced something entirely different, something never before known in human existence. Rome brought Total War into the realm of human experience. Although we are confounded by the rhetoric which we now commonly call ideology, we still have some idea of what Total War is in our own day and age. What was Total War in Roman times, when it first began?

Caesar had his Gaul Critognatus speak truly indeed concerning the result of conquest by the Romans[27]. Roman Total

---

[26]

See for example: *Genesis*, 17, and *Exodus*, 6.

[27]

And Caesar's was an accurate portrayal of motives as well. The fertile lands of North Africa fed Rome's armies for centuries after Rome's destruction of

War resulted in the complete disappearance of the Etruscans and the Samnites, and the elimination of all but one small clan of the Sabines. There are also some statistics and data available to us.

During the course of Rome's first war with Carthage, the Carthaginian navy was effectively destroyed. Carthage's losses amounted to 334 ships, each of which carried a crew of 400 men. This totals up to 133,600 Carthaginian dead in naval engagements alone. At the time of Rome's third and final war with the Carthaginians, the population of the city of Carthage was 750,000. After Rome captured the city, it was burned, and then the remaining rubble was leveled, so that not one stone was left standing upon another. Then the soil of the devastated area was sown with salt. All that is known of the fate of the three quarters of a million Carthaginian men, women and children is that a very small number of them managed to escape to Carthage's trading colonies further south, on the west coast of Africa, to the Canary Islands, and still further westward, across the Atlantic Ocean.

Julius Caesar's body count for his campaigns in Gaul was 1,192,000 Celtic men, women and children killed. Another one million were carried off into Roman slavery, and few of these were suitable as household slaves. Most of these slaves were condemned to death by torture--either as "players" in the "games" of the arena, or chained to the oars of a Roman galley

---

Carthage, up until the time when Rome's misuse of that soil created the desert which exists there to this day. The elimination of allied Celtic and Phoenician sea-traders left that enterprise free for Roman monopoly. The heavily timbered forests of conquered Gaul were quickly cut down to feed Rome's shipbuilding needs. The larger fur bearing animals of the forests of Gaul--such as the European bison--were quickly exterminated to feed Rome's fur trade with the east. The iron mines of Gaul and tin mines of Britain were important sources of military metals which Rome did not wish to bother about trading for. The silver and gold resources of other nearby lands could not be ignored by Rome.

until they perished, or never to see the light of day again, laboring until death in the bowels of a Roman mine. Hundreds of thousands of Britain's Celts were sent into Roman slavery after their conquest as well.

These staggering losses of human life occurred in a world which was much less populous than our own. By conventional present-day estimation, there were one hundred million human beings on earth in Rome's time. Although this estimate is based upon the uncritical acceptance of the rhetorical proposition that the western hemisphere was hardly inhabited, the figure may be near to the truth for the eastern hemisphere world of the African and Eurasian continents. Given such numbers to ponder, we may be able to perceive that life for the Roman state meant death for a most significant proportion of the entire world's human population.

Some other powerful images of Rome's hunger for human flesh in War are available. They often come right out of the official Roman records. When the rebellion of slaves and gladiators led by Spartacus was crushed around 2,070 years ago, the survivors of his army of 100,000 were brought to the Imperial City for punishment. Their crucified corpses lined over a mile of the main road into the city. Once, when a friend of the Greek historian Plutarch "visited a battlefield which had established an emperor on the throne [of Rome], he found [Roman] bodies piled up sometimes as high as the eaves of a little temple there[28]."

Never before was there a nation like Rome. There could hardly be a clearer reflection of a nation's soul than the spectacle of the gladiators which Rome so boldly paraded before the world. But the world--at least the Modern world--has not seen, let alone judged that soul. Symptomatic of that oversight are the remarks of a respected contemporary scholar, an excellent and fastidious

---

[28]

Hamilton, op. cit., p. 188. Parenthesized material is *my* addition.

researcher who read the works of the Romans in their own original Latin language. After writing a page and a half of text describing the Roman style of torturing captive human beings to death before the Roman public in the gladiatorial arena, the scholar concluded:

> To pass from this contemplation, from the way Rome was pleased to amuse herself, to the consideration of what she really did in the world, is to make a startling transition. The Romans did not trample all nations down before them in ruthless brutality and kill and kill in a savage lust for blood. They created a great civilization. Rome's monumental achievement, never effaced from the world, was law[29].

This is precisely why we must begin with Rome, and nowhere else, in order to understand the *origins* of the mass mental derangement from which we now suffer, and which we shall know as the "race" system. Rome entered the temple of Reason--the human mind--with rhetoric, and began a process of destruction and defilement which has never been questioned-- that is to say, subjected to self-examination--let alone reversed, to this very day. The Roman masters of rhetoric made a frighteningly practical discovery about human psychological behavior. They found that if their rhetoric--their grammar, as they later called it--properly proposed the laws of speech, and that if these were reflected in the speech of the laws, they could, by controlling language, control the very thoughts and thereby the behavior of human beings, be they friends or foes.

The rhetorical Romans had discovered, for example, that by habitually calling the bloodbath of the gladiatorial area a "sport," and by conducting that spectacle in what was deemed to be a

---

[29]

Hamilton, op. cit., p. 111.

lawful manner, most Roman citizens--even some of the gladiators themselves--would actually come to believe that it really *was* a sport.

Need we ponder for a very long time in order to begin to imagine the consequences of calling murder "play," and *believing* that it *actually is* play?

When Rome exported its innovation, Total War, to Gaul and Britain and North Africa, the political equilibrium existing between countless small nations--tribal and city-state--was upset as never before. This destruction set in motion population migrations and wars of conquest far outside of Rome's immediate sphere of influence. Eventually, it was such movement by distant warring peoples that helped to topple the Imperial Roman state.

Even so, Rome--and its posterity--never recognized the full impact of the fact that Rome's actions as a nation among nations had a wide range of unanticipated consequences. In its style of Total War, Rome had invented (but never acknowledged) *ethnocide*[30], the extermination of entire nations, and Rome had set a precedent for future states to come. Rome had in fact set many precedents, physical and mental. Roman consciousness, influenced by the needs of the rhetorical habit, was not capable of calling wars of extermination what they truly were. So Rome convinced itself--and the historians of its posterity for the succeeding two thousand years--that it had invented world peace, *Pax Romana* they called it, and based upon the highest principles of 'international law' is how they said it stood[31].

---

[30]

In present Modern times, when human mentality is encumbered with the false idea of "races," the concept of ethnocide has been completely eclipsed by a spurious notion of "genocide." This severely impairs our ability to fully appreciate the significance of the extermination of entire nations.

[31]

Rome was careful to insure that its declarations of war against enemies it had subjected to intolerable provocation followed the strictest letter of

In a similar vein, Rome's destruction of Phoenician and Celtic sea power not only disrupted a nearly two thousand year-old tradition of trade between the Americas and western Eurasia and Africa, but it also created an imbalance in maritime power that led to the emergence of piracy on the high seas in the Mediterranean and eastern Atlantic. A couple of hundred years later, after Rome had succeeded in suppressing this piracy, the claim of rhetorical Rome was not that Rome had solved a problem which Rome itself had created, but rather, that Rome was the founder and protector of the high law of the seas.

This then was the legacy of Rome: a legacy of lies accepted as if they are the truth. This is the greatest "gift" of Rome to all the world: the terrible secret of political thought control, achieved through the deliberate misuse of language and the debasement of Reason.

To be sure, the architectural and engineering achievements of Rome were most impressive: gigantic stadia and circuses to house the bloody spectacle of Roman "sport," water powered grain mills to grind the flour which fed Roman armies, thousands of miles of paved roads to lead those armies to their conquests, and the system of aqueducts which carried water to grand fountains, to enormous public baths, and to the gladiatorial arenas to wash away the caked and stinking human blood.

Roughly 1,500 years ago the last emperor of the Western Roman Empire (almost two hundred years earlier, the emperor Diocletian had divided the Empire into halves; the western half ruled from the city of Rome, and the eastern half ruled from Constantinople) was deposed in favor of the Gothic invader Odoacer. Traditionally, the date of that event, 476 A.D., is given as the end of the over twelve hundred years' life span of the Roman state.

Roman law and legal procedure. Thulsly, for example, was Carthage lawfully obliterated.

But, because of the awesome power of Roman rhetoric, it was not, as we shall see in the following chapter, the end of Roman culture. During the historical epoch known as the Middle Ages of Europe, Roman culture and institutions underwent a profound transformation, yet they emerged with their power to control the human mind enhanced rather than diminished.

We don't need no education.
We don't need no thought control.
No dark sarcasm in the classroom.
Teacher leave them kids alone.
Hey! Teacher! Leave them kids alone.
All in all its just another brick in the wall.
All in all you're just another brick in the wall.
                              --R. Waters

CHAPTER II
The Education of the Barbarians

The Christian warriors who gave the mighty Roman Empire the final push which toppled it over were known by their own tribal nations' names as the Goths, Ostrogoths, Visigoths and the Vandals. They had much in common with one another. All of them spoke Germanic languages and possessed Nordic, or Teutonic cultures. These Teutons were never a single nation however, but like the Greeks and the Celts and the Phoenicians, they were a language-culture group comprised of a number of small nations which were sometimes allied with one another, and which sometimes warred with each other. The Teutons shared, as did the Celts and Phoenicians, a hearty contempt for Rome.

It is conventionally believed that Teutonic culture is of more recent origin than that of the Celts, and that they originated in Scandinavia, gradually moving into the area of present-day Germany, displacing and sometimes merging with the older Celtic populations. The age, however, of Teutonic culture may be far greater than previously suspected. Ancient inscriptions left by seafaring Nordic traders near the site of present-day Toronto,

Canada, have pointed to the presence of this culture group along the shores of the Baltic Sea of western Eurasia, well over 3,600 years ago.[1]

Perhaps it seems surprising to learn that as well as language and culture, the Teutons shared a spiritual way which was derived from the teachings of Jesus of Nazareth. But there should be no surprise in this at all. By the fourth century of the current era (C.E., or A.D. by present convention), news about the Way of Jesus had traveled to Africa, throughout Eurasia, and to the Americas.[2] Diverse Christian communities had come into being in all of these places. Thus did the Teutonic nations receive the Way of Jesus as taught by the Greek, Arius. But the history of Christianity as we know it today is not revealed in the histories of many widely separated, culturally diverse communities. Rather, it is told in the history of the development of one large, powerful, centralized administrative organization.

The history of Christianity is, in this important sense, the story of the transformation of the Roman Empire. To understand that transformation is to understand the preservation of the Roman cultural tradition of rhetorical mentality. To understand that preservation is to understand the grounds from which the "race" idea was able to issue forth.

Rome did not lose control of its vast empire in a day. The process took centuries. The process took long enough, indeed, for Romans to figure out how to reclaim, in the end, the grasp on power which they ever craved so mightily.

---

[1]

Barry Fell, Bronze Age America (Boston: Little, Brown and Company, 1982), *passim.*

[2]

For a discussion of early Christians in America, see: Barry Fell, Saga America (New York: Times Books, 1980), pp. 164-191.

During the reign of emperor Marcus Aurelius--three hundred years before Odoacer siezed the Western Emperor's throne--a series of devastating, depopulating plagues began to sweep across the Western Empire[3]. For centuries the Western Empire[4] was so besieged. So severe was the depopulation of Roman Gaul, that some nations of the Teutons, including some of the Franks and the Alamanni were invited to migrate to the region and resettle it. Thirty two years after the death of Marcus Aurelius, the emperor Caracalla issued the *Constituto Antoniniana* which bestowed Roman citizenship upon all new free subjects of the Empire.

In this way did the western Franks--whose name means "free men" in Latin--and some tribes of the other Teutonic nations begin to gain intimate knowledge of the secrets of Roman culture. It has been common among historians to suppose that this extension of Roman citizenship to "barbarians" from outside of the Empire was an important factor in undermining the Empire's cohesion. But might not the opposite be equally possible?

When first they met, Rome and all of the Teutonic nations were the bitterest of enemies. With the passage of time, however, Roman emperors and generals began to hire mercenary soldiers from among the German nations in ever increasing numbers. This is just what had happened to the Celts whom Rome had marked for extermination centuries earlier. The end result in the case of the Teutonic nations was different, however.

---

[3]

For the most part the origin and nature of these scourges is unknown, but among them was an outbreak of the "social" disease herpes, which became so severe that the Senate passed a law banning kissing on the mouth.

[4]

Although the Roman Empire was not formally split into Western and Eastern divisions until the reign of Diocletian, in 286 A.D., the western and eastern portions of the lands embraced by the Roman Empire had been culturally distinct for tens of centuries.

Many of the Teutons who were 'advanced' to Roman citizenship by the Edict of Caracalla were, as I have said, former mercenaries, and hence, they were already somewhat familiar with Latin culture and appreciative of Roman institutions. Although "true Romans" never considered any "barbarians" to be their equal, the Roman naturalized Teutonic nobility--including the western Franks, the Visigoths and the Ostrogoths--strongly identified themselves with Roman culture.

Theodoric, an Ostrogoth, became allied with the emperor of the Eastern Roman Empire at Constantinople. He deposed the Goth, Odoacer, and ruled Italy from 493 to 526, as an independent kingdom subject to the Eastern Roman emperor. The reign of Theodoric was notable for his efforts at preserving Roman culture. His own daughter, who subsequently became regent in Italy, was educated in both Greek and Latin. The Visigoths who ruled briefly in southern France and in Spain up until their conquest in 711 by armies marching under the banner of the Islamic faith, also sought to adopt and to preserve Roman culture.

In most cases, rule was accomplished in the independent kingdoms which had once constituted provinces of the Western Empire by staffing Roman offices with "barbarian" personnel.[5] In some cases, the Teutonic conquerors established dual systems--they themselves using a Germanic language and their own system of laws, and their Roman subjects continuing in their use

---

[5] Philip Levine, "The Continuity and Preservation of the Latin Tradition," in Lynn White, Jr., ed, *The Transformation of the Roman World: Gibbon's Problem after Two Centuries* (Los Angeles: University of California Press, 1966), p. 225. Levine observes that: "Many of the existing political, legal, and administrative institutions were simply taken over by these barbarian invaders...."

of Latin language and institutions. In either kind of approach to the administrative aspect of conquest however, the conquerors assisted their Roman subjects in preserving the Latin cultural system.

But this was not uniformly the case with German nations which invaded the Roman dioceses[6]. A number of these nations, including the Ostrogoths--who were subject to the Hun[7] ruler Attila--attacked both the Eastern and Western Empires seeking the destruction of all things Roman. The Vandals with similar intent invaded Gaul, then Spain, and finally Roman North Africa in 429. There they established their rule over nearly all of the former Roman possessions. The Vandals persecuted everything that was Roman, and are well remembered for their attacks upon Roman Christians in North Africa. In 455, they attacked the city of Rome itself.

But from that time onward, the reign of the first Vandal king, Genseric, was conducted in peace up to the succession of his son Hunneric, in 477. The Vandals, who did indeed persecute Roman Christians were, however, Christians themselves, and they did not persecute all Christian groups. The favorite project of Genseric, continued by his successors, was the restoration of Ancient Carthage's maritime culture. It is perhaps because of this attempted restoration, more than anything else, that the rhetorical Roman mind created and bequeathed to posterity the word "vandalism." Roman revenge upon the Vandals was had in

---

[6]

Dioceses were the administrative land divisions of the later Roman Empires.

[7]

The origins of the Huns, a confederation of tribal nations, may first have been to the west of China. During the fourth and fifth centuries C.E. their attacks created a severe strain upon the Roman Empires. The Huns, however, as did the Celts and the Teutons, sometimes also provided mercenary soldiers in the service of Rome.

534, when the general Belisarius, in the employ of the Eastern Roman emperor Justinian, reconquered the lands the Vandals had held for the previous one hundred and five years[8]. A little more than a century after that, Islamic armies began the war which finally (about fifty years later), near the beginning of the eighth century, released North Africa once and for all from Roman rule.

However, during the centuries when the Teutonic and Huns' nations were alternately destroying and helping to preserve Roman culture and institutions, some Romans were busy devising their own best self defense. Conventional history tells us that during those years the Roman soul underwent a tremendously profound change, becoming, we are led to believe, the opposite of what it had been for nearly one thousand years. The first landmark of this great change is the Edict of Milan, a law issued by the emperor Constantine I in 313, which granted freedom of worship to all religions within the jurisdiction of Roman law. Not long afterward, during the reign of the emperor of Theodosius I, which began in the year 379, Rome's traditional state religion was decreed banished, and Roman Catholic[9] Christianity became the official state religion of Rome. Curiously, Christian Rome did not halt the gladiatorial bloodbath until about a decade after Theodosius' reign had ended.

More than merely curious, however, is the manner in which Rome coopted the Way of Jesus and converted it into a vehicle for preserving some of the worst elements of Roman culture, making of it, in the long run, an excuse for the bloodiest conquests ever

---

[8]

During the period of Belisarius' campaigns, Italy was also reconquered, becoming a province of the Eastern Empire. The reign there of the Ostrogoths was ended in 555.

[9]

The word *catholic* means *universal.*

in the history of the world. Those conquests, at the dawn of the Modern age, far surpassed in ruthlessness and terror anything ever imagined in the old Roman Empire.

Jesus of Nazareth was born into the heart of a quarter of the globe which had been tormented by ever-increasing Roman terror for almost half a millennium. His simple message was one of love: of love for God, of God's love for humanity, of love between ourselves and our brothers and sisters; and it was a message of forgiveness: of God's forgiveness for humanity, of forgiveness between our brothers and sisters, and our forgiveness for God. This was a powerful antidote to the cynical lesson in unrelenting hatred which the overpowering mechanical force of Rome's military might had imposed upon much of humanity. As I mentioned earlier, Jesus' apostles very quickly spread this good news throughout very nearly the entire earth, from India and China, to America. His warning to avoid the path of the gentiles (meaning the Romans), to give unto Caesar his due--which is to say, to let Caesar be the owner of hatred, envy and greed upon this earth--was embraced by peoples the world over. Given such an enormous loving spiritual force, it is not surprising that Jesus was executed by Romans, as was Spartacus before him, upon the traditional Roman instrument of public execution, the cross.

Given the terrifyingly efficient rhetorical abilities of Roman culture, it is not at all surprising that Roman Christians blamed Jesus' murder not on their own Roman predecessors, but on someone else--the Jews--and almost succeeded in making the charge stick, as they also nearly did in their attempt at separating Jesus from his own Jewish identity.[10]

---

[10]

Needless to say, many otherwise well-intentioned persons who have been indoctrinated in Roman Christianity still believe that Jews, not Romans, murdered Jesus; they fail to grasp the significance of the fact that Jesus conceived of himself as a Jew.

Unfortunately, the fate of the many far-flung communities of early Christians was, as was that of Jesus himself, bound to the desires of Romans. Although the first Christians in Rome were almost entirely slaves and foreigners, with the passage of time more and more established Roman families became Christian converts. Rome, after all, was by tradition a nation which in times of emergency and stress was accustomed to adopting foreign gods as a practical measure of solution. Following the reign of Constantine I, there was only one Roman emperor who was not a Christian. This change in the composition of Rome's Christian community was reflected by a radical change in the collective personality of Roman Christians.

Most of the early non-Roman Christian communities had considered the church to be nothing more or less than the *ecclesia*, the community of the faithful gathered under their head, Jesus Christ. The equality of all members of such groups was one of their primary characteristics. In some of these Christian churches women commonly attained the priesthood, in others, all members would take turns in rotation, playing the roles of clergy and laity. The active continuation of spiritual experience played a crucial role in all such communities of the faithful. Such experiences commonly took the form of spiritual healing, speaking in tongues, gnosis--the personal knowledge of mystical insight, the gift of prophecy, and the performance of miracles. Such spiritual experience was, at that time, something which was considered an open possibility available to any church member.

As increasing numbers of prominent Romans became Christians, and as Roman state persecution of Christians diminished correspondingly, Romans sought to fit the new religion into the familiar form of their old cultural institutions. This is how the Roman Catholic and Eastern Orthodox Christian church organizations emerged. Within the Eastern and Western divisions of the Empire, the term for the old Roman administrative territorial units, called *dioceses*, was adopted by the new state Church of Rome for its own purposes of administration. At the head of each diocese was a bishop who had the exclusive power of ordaining deacons and priests. With the passage of time the principal cities of the Empire, bishopric seats of power called *sees*, assumed a position of great prominence in Rome's new state religion.

These sees were at Jerusalem, Rome, Antioch, Alexandria and Constantinople, and their bishops came to be known as patriarchs, or *popes*, from the Latin word for father. Early on, the Pope of the see of Rome assumed the title of *Pontifex Maximus*, which had also been the title of the head of Rome's old pre-Christian state religion. Roman Christians used the word *church* to designate not only the community of the faithful, but also the building where worship was practiced, and the administrative organization of the religion as well.

After Constantine I had made the open practice of Christianity safe for Roman citizens, they built their church buildings after the pattern of the old pre-Christian Roman basilica, a practice which continued for centuries afterward in Italy. Also dating from Constantine's reign was the central importance of the Pontifex Maximus in the city of Rome. Gradually this Papal primacy spread throughout Italy, and eventually throughout most of western Eurasia. Thus the aspects of Roman Christianity which came to assume predominant importance in the world began to slowly emerge as the primacy of the Roman Church organization was advanced, from the third through the fifth centuries.

While most of the Ancient cultures in Rome's part of the world had preferred to commemorate the dates of the deaths of great persons, Roman Christians found it convenient to celebrate the birth of Jesus as well. They assigned him a birthday which coincided with their old pre-Christian festival of the Saturnalia, a time when they were accustomed to exchanging gifts and going to raucous parties. It is likely that this choice of a birth date for Jesus was also useful to the Romans at a later time in converting the German nations to Catholicism, for it also coincided with the traditional Celtic and Teutonic celebrations of the Yule.

There was, in particular, a singularly useful tool which Roman Christians employed in universalizing their religious institution: that most deadly of Latin instruments, Roman rhetoric. As early as the latter half of the second century, Roman Christians were beginning to apply their training in rhetoric and its associate, grammar, to the cause of their new faith. At about that time Minucius Felix and Tertullian, two Roman lawyers recently converted to Christianity, composed argumentative treatises in favor of Christian conversion[11]. Both of their works conformed to the classic Latin style of rhetorical instruction. Indeed, through the fifth century, Roman Christians and non-Christian Romans alike received traditional Latin schooling in grammar, Roman literature, and rhetoric. Two centuries after Minucius Felix and Tertullian, Ambrose and Jerome demonstrated in their works how effectively Latin rhetoric could serve Roman Christianity. The work of their contemporary, Augustine, who held the chair of rhetoric in Milan however, "...provided a firm philosophic basis for the continuity of the Latin tradition in the now predominantly Christian context[12]."

Such Latin continuity was expressed through the use of the Latin grammar written by Aelius Donatus--Jerome's instructor--for more than the next one thousand years as the standard for initiating the young into the Latin tradition. Roman rhetoricians and grammarians had become quite unselfconscious of the

---

[11]

Levine, *op. cit.*, see especially his discussion of Christian rhetoricians on pp. 216-224.

[12]

Ibid., p. 222.

destructive consequences of their linguistic habits at least as early on as the middle Latin period, and so Donatus' grammar included in its introduction the customary invocation to the effect that 'language is a most effective tool in service of the Empire'. And as Latin-schooled Roman Catholic Christians looked about them, empire is indeed what they saw. It was at first, an empire of the spirit.

Universal Roman Christianity sometimes confronted 'opponent' Christian groups singly, one at a time. The differences between Roman Christianity and the Christianity of Arius--which was followed by the German nations--were the focus of the Nicene Council, convened by the emperor Constantine I. In 325, the Council anathematized Arianism. The problem of Arianism persisted for the Roman Church however, until the conversion of Clovis, a Frankish king, from Arianism to Catholicism in 496. The quarrels between the Popes of Alexandria, Constantinople and Rome led eventually to the former sees' splitting from Roman Christianity in the fifth and eleventh centuries, respectively[13]. But there were many other Christian groups to which Rome opposed itself.

Many of these diverse groups were, from the middle of the second century, lumped together by the Roman Christian organization under the single heading of *Gnosticism*. Soon, under the reign of Roman bishop Irenaeus, they were labeled heretical and declared to be outside of salvation. Throughout the third century, the Roman Church vigorously opposed such 'heretics'. After the fourth century conversion of the emperor Constantine I, the *Orthodox*, as first defined by Irenaeus, gained military support. Shortly after this, the penalty for heresy

---

[13]

As time has passed, the Coptic Christianity of Egypt and Ethiopia, and Eastern Orthodox Christianity have lost the more severe aspects of Roman culture, placing a lesser emphasis, for example, on rhetorical vigor.

increased in great measure. So intense became the pressure upon Gnostics and other small groups of early non-Roman Christians, that by the fifth century they were either non-existent, forced into exile, or in hiding.

Toward the climax of this period of suppression, at the beginning of the fifth century, an extensive collection of writings of many non-Roman early Christians were cached by followers of a Coptic Christian order. These books were sealed in a large red earthenware jar, and buried for safekeeping beneath a boulder at the cliff at Nag Hammadi in Upper Egypt. The collection was not seen again until its rediscovery in 1945. The surviving 52 gospels and other writings have, since their rediscovery, revealed the broad scope of censorship exercised by the Roman Church hierarchy in its compilation of the approved official version of the New Testament.[14] The recently rediscovered gospels, written contemporaneously with, or even earlier than the recognized gospels, portray a fuller and deeper measure of Jesus than the Roman version does.

For example, in the *Gospel of Thomas*, Jesus counsels:

> If you bring forth what is within you, what you bring forth will save you. If you do not bring forth what is within you, what you do not bring forth will destroy you.[15]

In the *Gospel of Philip*,

> ...the companion of the [Savior is] Mary Magdalene. [But Christ loved] her more than [all] the disciples, and used to kiss her [often] on her [mouth]. The rest of [the disciples were offended] ...They said to him, "Why do you love her

---

[14]

Unfortunately, a large portion of this collection was destroyed during the two weeks it lay in a kindling pile next to the oven in a Bedoin home.

[15]

Elaine Pagels, *The Gnostic Gospels* (New York: Random House, 1981), pp. xiii-xiv, and 152.

more than all of us?" The Savior answered and said to
them, "Why do I not love you as [I love] her?"[16]

The *Gospel to the Egyptians* was known as "the [sacred
book] of the Great Invisible [Spirit]."[17] In the *Gospel of Mary*,
Levi speaks to mediate a dispute between Mary Magdalene and
Peter:

Peter, you have always been hot-tempered. Now I see you
contending against the woman like the adversaries. But if
the Savior made her worthy, who are you, indeed, to reject
her? Surely the Lord knew her very well. That is why he
loved her more than us.[18]

According to *On the Origin of the World*, God
Boasted continually, saying to (the angels)..."I am God, and
no other one exists except me." But when he said these
things, he sinned against all of the immortal ones....[19]

In *Thunder, Perfect Mind*, a feminine deity declares:

...I am the first and the last.
I am the honored one and the scorned one.
I am the whore and the holy one.
I am the wife and the virgin...
I am the barren one,
        and many are her sons....
I am the silence that is incomprehensible...
I am the utterance of my name.[20]

The authoritarian, male-centered, hierarchical organization

---

16   *Ibid.*, p. xiv and 77.

17   *Ibid.*

18   *Ibid.*, pp. 77-78.

19   *Ibid.*, p. 34.

20   *Ibid.*, p. xvi.

promoted by Roman Christians could have never justified itself in such a diverse body of scripture. And so, in a Catonian act of censorship, the larger body of the sacred books--the allegedly 'heretical' ones--were purged.

As the Roman monopoly over Christianity grew, so too did the effectiveness of Roman missionaries increase. Although the Roman Empire never succeeded in conquering Ireland, the last Celtic outpost on the Eurasian side of the Atlantic, the mission of Patrick, bishop of the Roman Church, did succeed in converting the Irish to the Empire's state religion. Patrick's mission commenced twenty years before the fall of the Western Throne, and continued until 492. Among his notable achievements was the banishment of all serpents from the Isle. Although there never actually were snakes in Ireland, this is an appropriate symbol for the conversion he accomplished, given the significance of serpent symbolism in the Roman scriptures, as well as the common, world-wide use of the serpent as a symbol of the Ancient, pre-Christian form of monotheism now often known in the vulgar vernacular as 'sun worship'.

From the start the Irish showed great aptitude for establishing a learned monastic tradition which excelled in the training of a cadre of missionaries in service to the Roman Church. Throughout the sixth, seventh and eighth centuries, the Catholic missionaries of Ireland, and their students in England kept the faith of Rome strong in the lands which had once comprised the Western Empire. The travels of the Irish monks were extensive in the cause of their mission.

Brendan's journey was among the more famous, even though it was, in a manner of speaking, less than successful. In the mid-sixth century, following the northern route of Ancient maritime commerce, he undertook a voyage to North America.

Upon returning, however, he reported not converts, but that he had visited the "land promised to the saints." For many centuries afterward, the tale of his travels was a favorite among the literate in the western Eurasian kingdoms.

Boniface, a missionary from England who was tutored in the Irish school served the Church of Rome in the mid-eighth century. He ministered first among the Franks, bringing their Catholicism into line, and then among the Frisians--a people never subdued by Rome--who had just been conquered using a new style of highly mobile combat invented by Charles Martel, a Frankish Mayor of the Palace.

The Christianity of the Franks was a matter of great concern to Roman Christians. The threat to the catholicism of their church which had been posed by Arian Christianity was ended among the German nations by Colvis' conversion in 496. The Franks were truly a power worth reckoning with in the early Middle Ages. Shortly before his conversion, Clovis had, betraying a treaty with the Alamanni, consolidated extensive new realms into his kingdom. In the early sixth century practically all of Gaul became the possession of the Roman Christian Franks led by Clovis, and it eventually became known as France, after the name of these Teutonic conquerors.

Although the empire of spirit embarked upon by Romans converted to Christianity had fared very well during the centuries following Constantine's reign, since the fall of the Western Throne, Romans had known little of the earthly power which, after all, was their great passion. The city of Rome had been ruled from that time and for the following three hundred years, by a succession of foreigners. First came the Goths, then the Ostrogoths, then the Byzantine (the Eastern) Empire, and finally the Lombards, who ruled northern Italy until about 756.

However, the interrelationship between the monastic Irish missionaries, the Catholic Franks, and the Pontifex Maximus of Rome eventually returned temporal power to the hands of those who, by culture, were Romans. And that power, once grasped, was never again released.

At around the beginning of the third decade of the eithth century, Charles Martel's[21] armorers came up with a remarkable technical innovation. They added stirrups to the saddle of a heavy cavalry horse. Although the stirrup may have been in use in other parts of the world for some time[22], its use in westernmost Eurasia was completely new. It was a measure of Martel's military genius that he appreciated the full potential of the stirrup. By seating an armored warrior on an armored horse, Martel invented what came to be known as shock combat. His knights, as the warriors were called, were capable of carrying a heavy lance at the rest position, one handed, and, held in the saddle by their stirrups, they could impale an enemy on the lance with the full momentum of themselves and their charging horses. So great, in fact, was the force of impact, that the victim tended to get stuck on the end of the lance, a situation which, in the heat of battle, was much to the discomfort and disadvantage of the knight. And so a baffle arrangement was added near the tip of the lance to keep it from penetrating its victim too deeply. The new weapon was called the winged lance.

Martel's field test of his new military technology in Frisia was, needless to say, a smashing success. The marshy terrain which had protected the Frisians against ethnocide for centuries could not defend them against a highly mobile force of cavalry which possessed a military technology never before seen on earth.

---

[21]

He was also known as Charles the Hammer.

[22]

For a rather complete discussion of this subject see: Lynn White, Jr., *Medieval Technology and Social Change* (New York: Oxford University Press, 1962), pp. 14-28.

No doubt the Roman Pontifex was impressed by Martel's inventiveness as well as by the continuing Frankish loyalty to Catholicism and support of its missionary activities.

The eighth century was a time when Romans felt their way of life most severely threatened on nearly all sides by the advance of powerful armies marching under the banner of a new religion, Islam. Considering that the majority of the military successes of the Islamic forces during the first century of the new faith's existence had been mostly in lands once comprising the Roman Empire, Romans must have felt that the teachings of the prophet Mohammed were directed against them in particular. All the more threatening was the fact that the prophet Mohamed had embraced the teachings of the Old Testament and of Jesus, just as the Romans had. Even more frightening was the realization that--unlike the Romans--the Islamic conquerors did not seek to persecute or exterminate faiths which differed from their own.

So, the greatest boost to Charles Martel's prestige in the eyes of the Roman's Church came in 733, not long after his field test of shock combat in Frisia. In October of that year Martel turned his new battle technique against an army of Saracens and defeated them decisively near Poitiers, driving their Islamic forces back into Spain, a position from which they never again successfully advanced. Rome's appreciation of Martel's victory was so bountiful that the Pope scarcely complained when the Franks confiscated vast tracts of Church land in France, in order that they might support the increased number of heavy war horses which their new cavalry technique necessitated.

Charles Martel's successors intensified the bond between Rome and the Franks. On the invitation of Pope Stephen II, Martel's son, Pepin III, invaded the kingdom of the Lombards in northern Italy in 777. Pepin gave the lands he conquered to the Pope, establishing the Papal States, one of which, the Vatican, still exists today. In return for Pepin's aid, the Pope conferred upon him the title of King of the Franks. Pepin's son

Charlemagne confirmed the Donation of Pepin in 774, and he extended the Frankish empire from the Pyrenees in Spain, to an eastern frontier running from the Baltic to the Adriatic seas. On Christmas day in the year 800, by their mutual agreement, Charlemagne was crowned first Emperor of the new Holy Roman Empire, by Pope Leo III, in the city of Rome.

The Frankish fascination with practical engineering, usually for military ends, closely paralleled the similar concerns of Roman culture, and just as often was accompanied by unforseen consequences. Charles Martel's introduction of mounted shock combat brought into being more than just the Medieval knight and the associated Age of Chivalry. The new form of battle he introduced was so compellingly successful that no nation wishing to survive could afford to do without it--in a matter of centuries it had been adopted throughout westernmost Eurasia, and in Byzantium, Syria and Egypt. It also resulted in a broadening of the distance between social classes[23], and the creation of feudalism, the final stage of incipient Modernity[24].

---

[23]

The development of the chimney and fireplace flue during the ninth to eleventh centuries also tended to accentuate class divisions. Prior to this time all members of a household in northwestern Eurasia lived, ate and slept together around a central fireplace in a great hall which had a simple louvered smoke hole in the roof above. After the perfection of the chimney, the lord and lady separated themselves from the commoners who served them. For a fuller discussion of this see: Lynn White, Jr., *Medieval Religion and Technology: Collected Essays* (Los Angeles: University of California Press, 1976), pp. 270-272.

[24]

Historians have for some time realized that the development of the agricultural and trade societies of Antiquity was a very extended process, and that thousands of years before there were fully agricultural societies, there were *incipient* (or developmental) agricultural societies. Similarly, we might understand the Modern Age more deeply if we view it as the result of an extended *process of development*, and not simply as a phenomenon which *sprang forth suddenly* during the Renaissance. Given such a broader

The increased emphasis on cavalry in battle placed new demands on the Frankish nobility. Nobles were expecetd to maintain war horses for military campaigns, and those unable to do so either pooled their resources, or found themselves descending into the peasantry; a composite group made up of Celtic remnants left after Caesar's conquest, other early Teutonic immigrants, and Frankish commoners. Eventually, the increasing demand for war horses led the peasantry into a new relationship with the land.

The cavalry needed *oats* to feed its mounts, and because of this, the peasant's independent square field was gradually replaced by a more efficient long strip field. The heavy wheeled plow was introduced, and eventually three-field crop rotation was established. Peasants were forced to combine their resources in order to support the new agricultural demands placed upon them, and this gave birth to the manorial system. Under this new form of agricultural organization which utilized new techniques and new implements, it soon became evident that one man could do the work formerly done by four men on the same amount of land. The peasant had become the feudal serf, producing oats for his lord's horses, and some surplus to boot. The attitude of the peasant farmer of being one with the land--a part of nature--had become transformed into the serf's version of his lord's perspective: that of a coercive master of the natural world.

Because one man could do the work of four on the land, there was a surge of unemployment among farming people. But because of the new military technology's demands there were sometimes jobs to be found in newly growing towns and cities working for an armorer, harness maker, cobbler, or in the mines. And because of the success of the new style of farming a very

---

view of things, Rome would, with justice, emerge as the first incipient Modern society. Certainly the Modern opinion of Rome as the primary foundation of civilization is consistent with such a perspective.

significant surplus of oats began eventually to be grown. This surplus went to human consumption, and from the tenth to the fourteenth century, the population of northwestern Eurasia grew steadily larger. Towns and cities became ever larger, and in these, a new merchant class began to appear. The outward success and prosperity of this new way of life made possible by mechanical devices led to an obsessive fascination with power technology.

In the centuries following the collapse of the Western Roman Empire, water power mills became very widely used in western Eurasia. Shock combat was introduced in the mid-eighth century. The heavy wheeled plow and the new agricultural system which accompanied it diffused throughout the region from the eighth to the tenth centuries. After that, horsepower began to be applied where only oxen had been used before. Early in the eleventh century, Eilmer of Malmesbury, an English monk, successfully flew the first 'hang glider'. (He actually glided six hundred feet through the air, but because of a design flaw, his flight ended in a crash in which both of his legs were broken[25].) Windmills began to come into use in the late twelfth century. This was also when a new, more powerful crossbow was devised. (The wounds from this weapon's bolts were so terrible that Pope Innocent II banned its use on all but the Moslem infidels. The ban did not stick. In faraway India, the new weapon came to be known as the *parangi*, meaning the "Frankish" bow.) Early in the fourteenth century a practical solution to the problem of constructing a mechanical clock was discovered, and their use became widespread. (The use of mechanical clocks was especially pronounced in Gothic cathedrals, where pipe organs and clocks

---

[25]

For the details of this and other early experiments in manned flight, see: Lynn White, Jr., "Eilmer of Malmesbury, An Eleventh Century Aviator; A Case Study of Technological Innovation, its Context and Tradition," in White, *Medieval Religion..., op. cit.*, pp 59-73.

were architecturally united in an assemblage which--including the elaborately structured building itself--was considered to be a symbol of "the world.") At approximately the same time, gunpowder and cannon began to come into vogue, and within another century's time the technique of corning gunpowder to produce reliable ignition was devised. Then, early in the fifteenth century, the principle of the crank began to be applied to all sorts of mechanical devices. Technology was on the *move*.

All of this innovation was, however, in the context of the Ancient Roman engineer, a practical man who used very clever practical knowledge to solve practical problems. It was not as important to know *why* something worked, as it was to know simply that it *would* work. For the first six centuries of the Middle Ages the new Roman--the Catholic Christian--societies of western Eurasia showed no interest in science as the Ancient Greeks had known it. Indeed, this was actually a continuation of Ancient Rome's disdain for such matters.

From the seventh through eleventh centuries, the Greek concept of science had been kept alive and even improved upon considerably in the Islamic societies of Spain, North Africa, and the Middle East. It was through the Islamic cultures that *science* came to the attention of western Eurasia in the late eleventh century, *via* what is known as the Saracen Connection. Yet in the Catholic Christian nations, the newly-rediscovered mode of inquiry was science twisted by *cant*[26]. During the four centuries when the present-day scientific movement was taking shape-- roughly from the mid-thirteenth to the mid-seventeenth centuries--every major scientist in western Eurasia also considered *himself* to be a theologian of the Roman Catholic Church.

---

[26]

Cant is yet another word for rhetoric.

Throughout the course of the Middle Ages, this was one theme which remained extraordinarily consistent: the persuasive power of Roman rhetoric. There was no education, no literacy for the majority of western Eurasia's population. The masses were simply indoctrinated from the pulpit; they would learn no more than they were to be told. The thin upper crust of the new Roman aristocracy continued, until the Modern epoch, to be carefully trained according to Donatus' formal Latin style. They learned to uncritically accept such propositions as 'language is a tool of empire'. There was no room left in their controlled thoughts for considering that language might instead be the servant of Reason.

War was also a constant companion of Medieval society; War between rival kings and nobles, War between rival kingdoms and city states, War with the Slavs, generalized War with Islam, War with the Mongols, the eight Crusades in the Middle Eastern Holy Land between the eleventh and thirteenth centuries, War to drive the Islamic Moors from Spain, and War with the Turks. Even so, because of the successes of the new agricultural system, and the outburst of clever technological innovation, the mood in Medieval societies was generally one of optimism and prosperity, and of a forceful domination of the natural world.

All of that was to change with the dawn of what historians would later call a new age, the Renaissance. That period, between 1300 and 1650, was viewed at the time as an epoch of rebirth of the classical civilizations of Ancient Greece and Rome. There can be no disputing the magnificence of the artistic, scientific and technological achievements which emerged from western Eurasian--especially northern Mediterranean--societies during those times. But there is another side to this period which is of the greatest importance: the spiritual, psychological side.

Medieval historian Lynn White, Jr., has written that:

The vast creativity of the Renaissance and its unrivaled talent for innovation, its instinct for beauty and for intellectual adventure, are glorious blossoms rooted in a slime stinking far worse than anything that can be identified in the earlier centuries of the Middle Ages or in more modern times[27].

White contends that the period "was the most psychologically disturbed era in European history[28]. How did this come about?

Early in the fourteenth century, death returned to western Eurasia with a vengeance not seen since the days of the old Roman Empire. Famine, disease and War of unrelenting proportions were visited upon those lands for the next three and a half centuries. Things began slowly at first, with universal crop failures in the north from 1315 to 1317--entire villages were vacated, never again to be resettled. Famines in the south from the 1330ˢ through the 1340ˢ carried off untold tens of thousands. But this was nothing compared to what was yet to come.

Late in 1347, bubonic plague, also known as the Black Death, struck at Caffa in the Crimea. The new disease spread rapidly westward through the continent, all the way to Iceland, killing one person out of three. As many as 25,000,000 people may have perished in the disease's first sweep, and the plague kept returning periodically until 1665.

The Wars of the Renaissance were as bad, if not considerably worse than what the Roman Empire had first brought into the world. By the fourteenth century, the feudal armies of western Eurasia had become transformed into exclusively mercenary

---

[27]

Lynn White, Jr., "Death and the Devil," in Robert.S. Kinsman, ed., *The Darker Vision of the Renaissance: Beyond the Fields of Reason* (Berkeley: University of California Press, 1974), p. 25.

[28]

Ibid., pp. 25-26.

forces. When these soldiers for hire were not properly paid, as they often were not, they turned ferociously upon the countryside about them, plundering, murdering and looting, and most frequently indulging in systematic torture to extract information about the location of valuables.

Lynn White, Jr., observes that:

This dreadful epoch opened in 1338 with the outbreak of the Hundred Years' War between England and France. The battlefield was France, which had been the heart of medieval Europe, and France was devastated and depopulated hideously. One reason that the cultural primacy in Europe passed briefly to Italy in the fifteenth century was the wrecking of the chief center of northern vitality. Similarly, large parts of Germany and eastern Europe were scorched by the Hussite wars that blazed for decades, anticipating in their brutality the religious wars that broke over Europe in the sixteenth century.

The wars of religion were not hostilities between religions; they were cruel civil wars in which neighbors murdered one another. Except in England, Catholics generally backed centralized government, whereas Protestants were fighting for local autonomy. In France, for example, a high proportion of the nobility and the self-governing burgher cities, fearing the growth of royal power, became Calvinist, as did the Netherlanders who resented Spanish Hapsburg domination. In the long run, centralized government and Catholicism won most of the battles and lighted most of the fires of execution. Protestantism was not simply contained; it was exterminated over wide areas which it had once controlled. The culmination of the ghastly process was the Thirty Years' War, from 1618 to 1648, which reduced the population of Germany by at least one third. Only toward the middle of the seventeenth century did governments conclude that mercenaries must be replaced by highly disciplined standing armies, salaried in peacetime as well as during war. Not even in our own century have the terrors of war in Europe matched those of the Renaissance[29].

In response to these centuries of intense, unending terror, the Catholic Roman mind snapped. The epidemic of masochism of the flagellants followed the plague. After Pope Innocent IV decreed in 1252 that his Dominican inquisitors could employ torture to extract confessions from accused heretics, the popularity of torture exploded across the region. Within a few hundred years there was a proliferation of ingenious new machines for inflicting unbearable pain upon human beings. Torture in the public square, followed by execution, if necessary, became a common form of mass public entertainment. Any spectator who dared to protest against such sadistic, or to be more precise, *cannibalistic* cruelty, was sure to be whipped. Commoner and noble alike became fascinated, obsessed by death and the process of the decay of human corpses. Necrophilia, the sexual enjoyment of dead bodies, became rampant.

During this period it began to become very acceptable for people to focus mass hatred on groups of persons who first, were relatively defenseless, and second, who could seemingly easily be identified as "others." It became proper to mark out such groups for extermination. The persecution of lepers, and especially of Jews became legion. In the fifteenth century, demonic possession and witchcraft began to become sporadically epidemic here and there across the region. Once identified, such persons were also subject to merciless persecution. The false accusation became widespread during these times, and such accusations were most often granted credibility. The age of the witch hunt had begun in earnest, and its terror extended even as far as North

---

[29]

Ibid., pp. 27-28.

America, where the first witch burning there occurred in 1407, in the Norse colony in Greenland. If one disliked one's neighbor, it was easier to get that person burned at the stake, or quartered, than it was to make an effort toward getting along.

In these times of widespread psychological perversion and mental illness, a great many leading social figures were deeply touched by madness. *Gilles de Retz* was exemplary of this. In the first half of the fifteenth century, he gained recognition as one of the greatest nobles of France. He was a close companion of Joan of Arc. He was also a pederast of incredible cruelty. Over the course of his lifetime he kidnaped, sexually abused, tortured to death, and then cut into pieces scores of young boys. Toward the end of his life he purchased his seat in heaven by endowing, in apparent sincerity, a Roman church dedicated to the Holy Innocents--the little children.

The Renaissance was a crucible of madness from which flowed our own Modern Age. If we honestly wish to understand where we now are and how we got there, it would be a serious mistake to underestimate the importance of the effect which the sustained traumatic terror of the Renaissance had upon the collective consciousness of the Medieval nations which had already been conditioned for well over a thousand years into complete submission to the demands of Roman rhetoric.

The temple of Reason had been destroyed, and the rubble was scattered so far that none should know that it had ever existed. The conditions were right for the emergence of the first Modern state, and they were right, as well, for the emergence of the constant companion of all Modern nations: the fifth, most horrible cannibalism ever. The conditions were right for the invention of the cannibalistic mandate of ethnocide, the concept that there are "races" of human beings.

The sex police are out there on the streets,
Make sure the pass laws are not broken.
The race militia has got itchy fingers,
All the way from New York back to Af-Africa.
Cuddle up baby, keep it out of sight,
Cuddle up baby, slip it out of sight,
Cuddle up baby, keep it out of sight,
Undercover, undercover, undercover,
Keep it out of sight,
Under cover of the night.
--Jagger and Richards

Chapter III
Spain and the Modern Age

For almost five hundred years, the tale of Columbus' egg has been the subject of a jolly joke among historians, grammarians and intellectuals. As one version of the story goes, Columbus was in that fateful meeting with the future backers of his inventive enterprise. But things were not going well for his cause. So Columbus proposed a demonstration to sway opinion in his favor. He drew forth an egg from his purse, and challenged the assemblage to stand it on end.

No doubt the two Catholic Sovereigns found the test to be beneath their dignity, and declined to try it. But they watched with amusement as the Bishop of Avila tried, and tried, and failed. Then the royal treasurer tried, but did not succeed. The chancellor tried. The royal mineralogist took his turn, but could not stand the egg on end. The cosmographer tried. A clever lawyer sprinkled some salt on the table, and making a little mound of it, sought to balance the egg thereon. But still the egg would not stand. And so it went. Finally it was Columbus' turn. He declared that, after the manner of a wager, if he should succeed with the egg, then all would see why his plans for the Western Lands must be supported. Then having acquired his audience's consent, he grasped the egg by the sides, and smashed it, blunt end down, upon the table before him. The egg truly did stand up upon its crushed-flat end. "You see," he said, "its easy once someone shows you how."

It's no joke. Columbus had done two things: he had demonstrated the power of words to skirt reality, giving it an interpretive twist with a certain purpose; and he had symbolized the physical impact his new ideas would have upon the earth.

Columbus' enterprise was a long time in the making. According to his own account, he first put to sea at the age of fourteen, commencing with his study of navigation. He traveled extensively throughout the Mediterranean, down the west coast of Africa, and in 1477, to Iceland and a "hundred leagues beyond[1]"--which would have put him in the Norse colony on Greenland. The latter voyage was common enough throughout the fifteenth century. At least as early as the second decade of the 1400s, western Eurasian, in particular, English pirates based in North America were raiding the Norse colony across the Davis Strait from them. Pope Nicholas V discussed one of these raids in a 1448 Papal letter to the two Bishops of Iceland.

From the nearby pagan[2] coasts came thirty years ago a fleet of barbarians which attacked the local people in a cruel assault[3]....

---

[1]

This is according to the record of Columbus' son, Ferdinand, and also according to the account of Bartholomé de las Casas, a Dominican who perhaps accompanied Columbus on his fourth voyage (las Casas' father was a companion of Columbus on an earlier voyage).

[2]

The word *pagan*, is commonly understood as meaning "not Christian," but in actuality it most specifically denotes "a dweller in the country."

[3]

Quoted in Thor Heyerdahl, Early Man and the Ocean: A Search for the Beginnings of Navigation and Seaborne Civilization (Garden City, New

Of course, Greenland is a part of North America, or Turtle Island, as many of its Ancient nations knew it. (Greenland is the turtle's head.)[4] Although the Norse established several short-lived colonies on the North American mainland, the most famous of these being in what they called Vinland, the center of their North American activity was their Greenland colony. From there, they kept the Ancient northern route of western Eurasian and North American trade open from at least the year 1000 to nearly 1500, about which time the colony dissolved.

The Norse colony on Greenland was a full participant in the Medieval life of western Eurasia. Following the conversion of the Norwegian king Olav Trygavson to Catholicism, Roman Christianity quickly became the religion of all the Norwegians. The first Roman Catholic priest to visit North America since Brendan, accompanied Leif Eirikson to Greenland in the year 1000. In 1112, Greenland received its first visiting bishop, Erik Gnupsson. The Iceland annals record that Bishop Gnupsson also sailed further west from Greenland to visit the Norse colony of Vinland. From 1126 onward, Greenland had its own resident bishop, and soon there were even two.

The point of departure for the Ancient southern route of trade between western Eurasia and Africa and the Americas lay off of the west coast of Africa. Columbus investigated this area between 1482 and 1484. Throughout most of the Middle Ages, this route had been kept open by Islamic and African nations' traders. This was the route which Columbus followed when he embarked upon his famous inventive voyage of "discovery" in 1492.

York: Doubleday & Company, Inc., 1979), p. 143.

[4]

The resemblance of the North American continent to the alligator snapping turtle (*Macrochelys temmincki*, a North American species) is indeed remarkable. To verify this, consult an atlas and a herpetology text.

It is extremely likely that Columbus began to hear tales of the Western Lands from the very first time he put to sea. Knowledge of the Americas--and how to get there from Africa, Iberia, Scandinavia and Britain--was fairly common in those days. This was especially so among the Moorish, Basque, Portuguese, Norse and English seamen who inevitably numbered among Columbus' shipmates.

Although there is no way of knowing exactly when Columbus first formulated his plan for trans Atlantic conquest, because he never quite admitted on the public record that such was what his plan was, he first approached the Portuguese king, the English king, and the city of Genoa for support during the period of his African Guinea coast voyages. All of these potential sponsors, however, found his plan to be impractical. A few years later, in 1486, Columbus had his first meeting with the Catholic Sovereigns Isabella and Ferdinand.

The research which went into Columbus' plan was rigorous and thorough. Not only had he already visited North America by the traditional northern route, visited the traditional southern route point of embarkation, and made intensive inquiries of his fellow seamen, but he had also read every available literary account of the Americas.

His study of classic and Medieval Latin sources was exhaustive. He knew of Eratosthenes' mathematical estimation of the earth's circumference, made some 2,200 years ago, with an error of less than one percent. He read Seneca, a Spanish Roman in touch with the Ancient seafaring traditions of Iberia's Basques, Carthaginians and Celtiberians. Seneca, who until his execution had been the principal minister of the emperor Nero, had written: "Spain will soon be linked with the Indies across the Atlantic Ocean[5]." Seneca knew perfectly well that the *Epeiros* (the Roman

---

[5]

Quoted in Fell, *op. cit.*, p. 138.

name for the Americas) blocked the path to the Indies, for as a merchant trader he had most probably grown wealthy on profits from the Spanish trade with the Americas. But he very strongly suspected the existence of an easy portage to the Eastern Ocean.

The Ancient Romans indeed traveled all over the world, from the Americas to China. Roman artifacts, coins and Ancient Latin inscriptions have been discovered at various sites in the Americas; Roman trade goods have been unearthed in the seacoast cities of Thailand; and Latin history records that the emperor Marcus Aurelius dispatched a fleet of traders to China, "going around Arabia and across the Indian Ocean."[6] Rome, in defense of its trade monopoly--a monopoly made possible by the extermination of the Celts of Gaul and the Carthaginians--erected a wall of protective rhetoric, however. Rome propagated the idea that the earth is flat.

Columbus studied much more about the Americas than just the accounts of learned Greeks and Romans. He read about Brendan's sixth century voyage, he read Adam of Bremen's *Geography of the Northern Lands*, written in about 1070, which accurately chronicled the Norse activity in Greenland and Vinland, he studied the Ancient *Portolano* maps, and he read Cardinal Pierre d'Ailly's *Imago Mundi*, which restated Seneca's case for a westward route to the Indies. It is very unlikely that he did not know of the first prince of Orkney, Henry Sinclair's,

---

[6]

Quoted in Stan Steiner, "China's Ancient Mariners," in *Natural History* (New York: American Museum of Natural History, December, 1977), p. 59.

voyage to Nova Scotia in 1398. That expedition had been led by Admiral Antonio Zeno, a Venetian, and the brother of Messire Carlo Zeno, the most famous naval commander of his time[7]. Columbus was also entirely familiar with Marco Polo's *Travels*.

Of the greatest use to Columbus, however, were his close ties with the Vatican, which gained him detailed knowledge of the Americas and of some of the nations to be found there[8]. This intelligence came about directly because of the Norse colony in Greenland. The Norse were prolific traders whose trade routes extended from China to the Americas. With their conversion to Catholicism, everything they knew about the world was absorbed and preserved by the Vatican. It would be foolish to discount the Norse-Church connection. To do so would entail a conviction that the Church had somehow forgotten all about the existence of its Greenland parishes. In fact, quite the opposite was true, as very close ties were maintained between the Vatican and Greenland for almost five hundred years. For about two hundred and fifty of those years, the Greenland colony had been paying a Crusader's tax to the Church, a custom followed by all Catholic nations. But because of the unique conditions on the Greenland colony, the Pope ruled that the Norse settlers there could pay their tax in *naturalia*--timber, furs, and ivory--instead of the customary payment in gold. An inventory of a Greenland Crusader's tax compiled by Archbishop Erik Valendorf of Norway

---

[7]

Frederick J. Pohl, *The Sinclair Expedition to Nova Scotia in 1398: A pre-Columbian crossing of the Atlantic definitely dated as to year, month, and day of landing* (Pictou, Nova Scotia: Pictou Advocate Press, 1950), pp. 7 and 17.

[8]

Columbus, writing of his own education, states that he had a great deal of intercourse with ecclesiastics; and the encouragement which he was given by two learned Franciscan monks at the convent of Santa Maria de la Rábida in 1484, is, for example, very well-known.

included "the skins of black bear, beaver, otter, ermine, sable, wolverine, and lynx."[9] None of those creatures were to be found in Greenland.

The centuries of intensive Norse trade with America are notable because of the intelligence about that land--"the land promised to the Saints"--which they generated for the Vatican. Even more notable is the inescapable fact that throughout all of their trading activities in the Americas, the Norse, who were very knowledgeable about the geography of the world's northern hemisphere, never for a moment thought that they were in the Indies.

Columbus also had at his disposal the Medieval recalculation of Eratosthenes' figure for the earth's circumference which was made by the Arab Scholar, Alfraganus. Alfraganus set the length of a degree of longitude at 56 and two thirds Arabic miles, which yields, as did Eratosthenes' calculation, a reasonably accurate figure for the earth's circumference. The only major literary references for travel to the Americas which Columbus *did* in fact lack were those of the Chinese, Phoenicians, Celts, and the Americans themselves.

But in 1486, their Catholic Majesties were not yet ready to back Columbus' proposal, for at that time Spain was involved in a War with Grenada, the last Moorish outpost of Islam left on the Iberian peninsula. During the next few years, the Spanish Kings alternately encouraged and discouraged Columbus. Then, in December of 1491, he was invited by Their Majesties to the camp of Santa Fé on the outskirts of Grenada to watch the triumph of the Spanish army. Grenada fell on January 2, in the year of 1492, a year which better than any other may serve to mark the commencement of the Modern Age.

There are a number of good reasons for marking the opening

---

[9]

Quoted in Heyerdahl, *op. cit.*, p. 138.

of the Modern Epoch in 1492, in Spain. Spain had been politically united in 1469 by the wedding of Isabella of Castile and Ferdinand of Aragon. They reigned jointly from 1479, until Isabella's death in 1504. Reorganizing their kingdoms, they established absolute royal power, limited the privileges of the high nobility, and encouraged the advancement of the middle class, in particular bestowing royal protection upon lawyers. By 1492, with the fall of Grenada in January, and the banishment of all Jews from Spain that March, social and political conditions had created a suitable national mood of aggressive self-confidence from which there could emerge an irrepressible urge in Spain for a glorious new War, a new Holy Crusade which could bring millions of new converts into the fold of Catholic Rome, and which could also, incidentally, bring vast amounts of pearls, gems, and gold and silver bullion into the Royal and Papal treasuries. All that was needed in order for such a campaign to begin was a properly legal manner of stating its causes and objectives.

Although Columbus' scheme provided a correct legal context for the conquest of the Western Lands, another event in 1492 underscored the practicality of his plan. This was the publication of the first grammar ever written of a Modern language, Antonio de Nebrija's Spanish *Gramática*. When he presented his new book to Her Majesty Isabella, she quite pointedly asked him: "What is it for?" Answering for Nebrija, the Bishop of Avila responded, "Your Majesty, language is the perfect instrument of empire[10]."

---

[10]

Quoted in Lewis Hanke, *Aristotle and the American Indians: A Study in Race Prejudice in the Modern World* (Bloomington: Indiana University Press, 1959), p. 8.

The Bishop, however, was merely paraphrasing a remark in the introduction of Nebrija's *Gramática*. What Nebrija had written there was: *"Siempre la lengua ha sido compañera del imperio."*[11] In his use of the word "always (siempre)," Nebrija had updated the familiar incantation from the introduction of Donatus' classic Latin grammar, and he had also invented what was to become the typically Modern phrase of mindless pessimism and human hopelessness. How many times have we all heard--or even uttered ourselves--those Reason-stunting words so popular in our own time: "Man has *always* been a greedy creature?" or: "Humans will *always* exploit those who are weaker?" Nebrija, with his use of the one word "always," had moved a quantum leap beyond merely putting misused language at the service of empire, he had created an insoluble union between empire and language abused. Thus, the present-day Sioux historian Vine Deloria, Jr., made ignorant (as we *all* are) by the flow of rhetoric which constantly surrounds all of us, writes in the introduction to a recent book, words to the effect that: 'nations have always destroyed one another'.

Christopher Columbus' contribution to Modernity, to the worldwide destruction of Ancient societies, was the most dreadful of things ever done to destroy the human mind. It was a contribution which is the source of the worst woes of Modern times.

It should be perfectly clear by now that because of all of his research, as well as from his own personal experience, Columbus knew exactly where the *Epeiros*, the "land promised to the Saints," *Atlantis*--as it was known in very Ancient times--lay. Columbus knew exactly what the Americas were, and he knew with utter certainty that the people living there were not

---

[11]

Ibid., p. 127. In English, the phrase is: "Language has always been the companion of empire."

"Indians."   Columbus, the inventor of the concept of "discovering" lands which are already known to exist, was also the inventor of the "race" idea, and the inventor of "Indians," the first "race" ever conceived of in the human mind.

Conventional scholarship has for a long time supposed that the earliest origin of a "race"-like idea lay in the distinction made by every nation between "*we*-who-are-of-the-same-one-nation," and "*they*-who-are-not-of-our-nation." It has been common to point to the Ancient Greek word, known in English as "barbarian," as an illustration of this point. However, the word in its proper original sense simply means "a person who does not speak the Greek language." Scholars have stressed that the word was used derisively by the Greeks. But there is no source of "race" thinking here. No nation could exist for long if its citizens did not believe that they lived in the best of all places, and that all others who did not belong to their collective "we" were missing out on a good thing. Citizens who do not believe that their own nation is superior, become immigrants to another nation which they do believe is superior. There is no origin of the "race" idea to be found in the "we"--"they" concept of self-identity by which nations have eternally understood their own primary grounds of existence. Furthermore, in the Ancient world, within any given nation, there was a much, much wider range of variation in the color of human complexion than our Modern minds are prepared to realize.

The origin of a "race"-like idea is, however, to be found in a very significant perversion of the "we"--"they" concept which occurs in the earliest Middle Ages. This is the invention, by Christian Romans, of the "they" known as *heretics*. Like every other "they" group before them, heretics were actually a multitude of diverse groups, not at all like one another. Unlike previous "theys" however, heretics were not made into a single entity simply for the sake of self-identification and sense of communal superiority of a "we" group. Heretics were artificially made into a single entity, just as every "race" subsequently has been, solely for the purpose of extermination. If, at this time the word extermination seems to be too strong to associate with the purpose of "race"-creation, let us then for the moment say that "races" are created for exploitation *or* extermination.

There is also an important second theme associated with the origins of the "race" idea which begins in the Middle Ages, and is given birth in Roman culture. Commencing with Clovis' conversion to Catholicism, the new western Eurasian nobility was instructed by its Roman tutors in the manner of tracing its family genealogy directly back to the Biblical first man, Adam. A genealogical connection with the local gods or with a founding culture-hero had been important to rulers here and there upon the world for perhaps as far back as the time when Sargon of Akaad overthrew the dynasty of a God-King. For quite a long time, genealogical lines of descent were connected to arguments issued in support of political ambitions.

Ancient Rabbinical scholars had, for example, traced the descent of the Phoenician Canaanites--the people whose deed to their own country was, according to the Old Testament, revoked by God "Himself," and then transferred to the Israelites--through Ham, the least favored son of Noah. Those who were descended from Ham were to be eternally bound to servitude. The Rabbinical scholars found the Jews to be descended from Noah's son Shem, who sired a more favorable lineage, and other neighboring peoples in the region were said to be descended from Noah's son Japheth--which was not so bad as being one of Ham's descendants.

Present-day scholars--projecting the Modern "race" idea backward in time to the Ancient world--have assumed that Canaan was a "black" nation, and that the Ancient Jewish custom of tracing descent to Adam principally through Noah's three sons was an early attempt at a global system of "racial" classification. But the Jews, whose Ancient merchants traveled the world as extensively as any other trading people, knew better than to do that. The Phoenician nations (which included the Carthaginians), like Ancient Israel, Egypt, Libya, the Greeks and Celtiberians' nations, contained citizens of many different-colored complexions. The degree of a person's citizenship within any of these nations was in no way associated with the color of their skin.

When Romans, who had become Christian, adopted this tradition of tracing Biblical genealogies, they infused it with their usual 'energy'. In its earliest Catholic form, Adam's genealogy was traced through Noah thusly: the Jews were descended from Shem, Romans from Japheth, and the lowliest, most subject peoples of the Empire, from Ham. Descent from Japheth was extended to include the Franks upon their conversion to Catholicism. In the sixth or seventh century, descent from Ham was shifted from the westernmost Eurasian peasantry, and placed hundreds of miles eastward, upon the Slavs (whose name--and it should be noted, originally this was not their own name for themselves--means "slaves"). Hence, through this modifiable line of descent, Medieval Spaniards came to consider slaves from Africa and elsewhere to be the descendants of Ham.

But, although the importance of genealogies had by this time been firmly established, the introduction of African slaves to Spain by its Islamic conquerors was by no means the beginning of a "racial" concept. This is because in Ancient times, "black" Africa was not as unambiguously "black" as it is now. The reason behind this is thousands of years of trade between Africa's coastal and northern desert cities and Phoenicians, Egyptians, Libyans, Arabs, Indians, and Chinese. And of course the interior of the African continent was just as subject to the establishment of trade routes and to the migration of peoples as were Eurasia, the Americas, and Australia. Illustrative of the variation in the color of African complexions was:

The Portuguese raid for slaves on the Guinea coast in 1444, [which] for example, records that when African captives in the mid-fifteenth century were exposed for sale in Lagos, Portugal..."it was truly a thing astonishing to behold; for among them were some well-nigh white...others were as black as Ethiopians."[12]

It was *after* Columbus' sanctioned invention of the "Indian" "race" that the Catholic genealogy was adjusted once again, in order to show that light-skinned people were descended from Japheth, dark-skinned people were descended from Ham, and people of a medium-colored complexion were descended from Shem.

This brings us directly to the subject of exactly how and why Columbus invented "Indians," the first "race" in history. The *why* is the simplest part. Fifteenth- and sixteenth-century Spain was a nation which--like Ancient Rome, and all Modern nations as well--was deeply impressed by the Roman concept of law, and by the legal profession. It was a nation which felt the special need to justify all official state actions with the proper legal pretext. In order for Spain to launch a Crusade upon the *Epeiros*, or lawfully do War thereon, something unique was in order. No provocation had issued forth to western Eurasia from those lands for over *seventeen hundred years.*[13] Columbus' proposal was the following: the pretended "discovery" of the Americas would present the powers of western Eurasia with a strange new 'moral' dilemma, capable of only one solution.

---

[12]

Ivan Van Sertima, *They Came Before Columbus* (New York: Random House, 1976), p. 241.

[13]

Specifically, the Americans had not intervened directly in the affairs of Eurasia or Africa since the end of Rome's first War with Carthage, which had been heavily financed, on the Carthaginian side, by Central American gold. See Barry Fell, *Saga America, op. cit.*, pp. 74-87.

The supposedly heretofore unknown lands would be found to be heavily populated with human beings. Hence, the fictional "discovery" of new lands implied the "discovery" of "new men" whose existence could be assumed to have been previously entirely unknown on the continents of Africa and Eurasia. The false premise that the peoples of the Americas were a "variety" of human completely unknown in the eastern hemisphere allowed the conclusion that the Americans were completely ignorant of Eurasia and Africa. Thus, in the all-important political realm of religious affairs, the "new men" could be neither Jew, nor Christian, nor Moslem, and no Modern nation would be obliged to interact with the nations of the Americas as if they were of, or even knew of, these three faiths. Of course, the "new men" would have to be "classified;" their descent from Adam would have to be properly traced. But most important of all was the inescapable 'moral' and legal conclusion: they must be evangelized. No Christian nation, upon "discovering" "new men" who had existed entirely without the benefit of knowledge of Adam and Eve, the Prophets, or Jesus Christ, could be expected to shirk its responsibility of bringing Catholicism to such a people[14]. And beneath the veneer of evangelization lay the true objective of the invention of "Indians:" plunder and mayhem in the American nations. For the word *india*, the root from which *Indio*, the Spanish word for "Indian" is derived, quite literally means, we must note here, nothing else than "wealth," or "riches."

---

[14]

The Church of Rome has never denied its sanction of Columbus' "enterprise," or the vast increase in political power which Columbus' "discovery" brought to Catholicism. Of course the Church would prefer to phrase all of this in other terms. For instance, in October, 1984, Pope John Paul II journeyed to Puerto Rico and the Dominican Republic, specifically in order "to launch eight years of 'spiritual preparations' to commemorate the Christianization of the Americas that began with Columbus' first voyage." Reported in *Time* (New York: Time Inc., October 22, 1984), p.66.

This was the hardest point for Columbus to sell to potential clients, principally because of the enormous commission he was demanding for his services. With the fall of Constantinople to Turkish armies in 1453, Genoa, a leading colonial power in the Mediterranean, had lost control of all of its eastern colonies. Furthermore, at the time when Columbus approached this city with his proposal, the most wealthy and powerful among the Genoese families were involved in what amounted to a civil war over control of the city. Their bloody conflict extended into the early sixteenth century, and so depleted the city's resources as to rule out new colonization endeavors. Similarly, England had seen its resources seriously drained by the Hundred Years' War with France, which had ended only a few decades before, in 1453. Also, the power struggle for supremacy between England's royal families had not yet ended when Columbus approached the English throne with his proposals. And furthermore, English privateers had already been profiting from the North American trade of the Greenlanders for at least a century.

This latter sort of difficulty is what stymied Columbus' plan when he brought it to Portugal. The Portuguese had already been conducting trade with South America for probably at least one hundred years.[15]

---

[15] Columbus had a number of conferences with King Juan of Portugal; notably, one before his first official (or recorded) voyage, and one before his third. On the first occasion King Juan told him of the long-standing trade between Africa and South America in goods such as tobacco, cotton, shell money, and bread root. On the occasion of their second conference, King Juan gave him the directions to reach the South American mainland, which, on this third voyage, Columbus did indeed come within sight of. For the record, however, Columbus documented the sighting of that mainland as that of "another island." Yet he did record in his log that upon reaching Haiti (on the first voyage) the natives there told him of the six latest voyages to reach that place from Eurasia, just prior to his own. Finally, at least three charter grants of land were made by the Portuguese king, John II, between

But Spain had been energized by its War with Grenada, and it had been filled with Christian self-righteousness by the banishment of all Jews from the country. Finally, on April 30, 1492, after a series of inconclusive meetings, the two Catholic Kings agreed to grant Columbus the following terms: he was to search for and take possession of "certain islands and mainland in the Western Ocean," and if he succeeded, he was to be granted, among other things, a peerage, the title of "Admiral of all the Ocean Seas," viceroyship and governor generalship of all islands or mainlands which he might acquire for Spain, and *one tenth of all profits* resulting from his "discoveries," to be bestowed *in perpetuity*.

Now, how exactly did Columbus propose to invent a "race" of "new men" ripe for Christian evangelization? Or, more properly, how did he plan to "discover" lands whose existence was already well known? To begin with, his proposed "discovery" would meet with no objections from the uneducated common people of western Eurasia, for among them, the Church of Rome was still propagating the old dogma[16] of Imperial Rome: "the world is flat." Among the devout and faithful commoners of the region there would be no objection to Spain's unprovoked War upon the Americas. Among them, Columbus' "discovery" would be hailed as a glorious fact, a momentous new act of audacious courage which had linked Spain and the other Modern nations with heretofore unknown lands in a world now known to be spherical.

1484 and 1486, specifically for the purpose of establishing colonies in the lands across the Atlantic. See Dr. Samuel D. Marble, *Before Columbus: The New History of Celtic, Egyptian, Phoenician, Viking, Black African, and Asian Contacts and impacts in the Americas Before 1492* (New York: A.S. Barnes and Company, 1980), pp. 23-27.

[16]

Yet *another* word for rhetoric.

To meet with the objections of learned Africans and Eurasians, and of nations in rivalry with Spain, a complex new rhetorical formulation was in order. Something was needed which would be of use to *any* prospective colonial power. Of course no such plan could have been executed without the approval of Rome. But still, Columbus could not merely sail to the Americas and claim to have "discovered" them; such a claim would have been hotly contested by Portugal, in spite of its Catholicism. Indeed, as it turned out, Spain's claim to the Americas *was* very seriously challenged by the Portuguese after Columbus' voyages.

What Columbus therefore proposed was that he would sail to the Western Lands, but rather than acknowledging that he had landed there, he would insist that he had made his landfall somewhere else. He would claim that he had landed in the islands off the coast of China, known in the Spanish usage of his day as the "Indies." (In Columbus' time, Spaniards called everyone living east of the Indus River "Indians.") Thus Columbus, who only wrote in the properly grammatical languages of Spanish and Latin, was, by pretending that his American landfall was in the Indies, perfectly justified in labeling the "new men" he had "discovered" there as "Indians."

However, in order for Columbus' rhetorical formulation of "discovered new men" to be fully mentally mystifying, and hence, effective, he could never claim his own "discovery." It was necessary that *others* must recognize Columbus' "mistake" in reporting that he had arrived in the Indies, and that *they* then go on to deduce that he had "discovered" something "new." This did indeed occur quite soon after Columbus' voyage of 1492. In fact it happened a bit too soon, considering Columbus, outspoken public insistence that his landfall had been in the Indies. After all, the new Admiral was the person who had actually visited those faraway lands, he should be expected to be the expert on where he had gone. True to his part of the bargain, Columbus insisted to his dying day (*in public*, at least) that his four voyages had taken him to the Indies.

Columbus' fabrication was supported by his excellent knowledge of geography, the extent of which has not been suspected since his own time, when history was so broadly rewritten. In order to claim that he had landed in the Indies when he had actually reached the Americas, Columbus needed mathematical support for the proposition that his Caribbean landfall could be considered an arrival in Cipango (the islands of Japan, among which he probably included Taiwan). For this purpose he selected Alfraganus' very accurate calculation of the earth's circumference as the basis for his own figures. But Alfraganus' calculation was in Arabic miles, and Columbus, the expert mathematician and geographer, Columbus the seasoned mariner and navigator, Columbus the traveler and map maker, claimed not to know the difference between Arabic miles and the Italian miles which he used in his own calculations. He translated Alfraganus' Arabic miles into Italian miles in a one-to-one ratio. Since Arabic miles were longer than Italian ones, Columbus was able, through this purposeful 'mistake' to reduce the earth's size by about one quarter.

It is amazing that scholars to this day have believed that Columbus' mistranslation of Arabic miles was a mistake. In Medieval Spain, Christian and Islamic societies had been having mercantile as well as warlike interactions for over seven hundred years. For the sake of commercial interests as well as those of military intelligence, the accurate translation of weights and measures had become commonplace in Spain by Columbus' time. The same can be said for Italy and the Vatican, as well, in fact, as for all of western Eurasia. After all, the translation of Arabic scholarship, *via* the Saracen Connection, formed the basis for the Modern scientific movement, the beginnings of which occurred over three hundred years before Columbus was born. And science, we must remember, is so often a matter of weights and measurements.

A thoughtful look at a world map shows what Columbus' fabricated 'error' accomplished. He had rhetorically erased about 90 degrees of western latitude. Depending upon where one chooses to place this gap in the world, almost all of North and South America can be made to disappear. Of course the distance between the Canary Islands and Guanahani could still not be made equal to the distance between the Canaries and Cipango (which remained much farther away than Guanahani), but Columbus had altered the earth well enough (as legend has it, he had altered the egg) to suit his purpose.

On August 3, 1492, Columbus embarked upon his world-shaking voyage. On October 12, he made his landfall on exactly the latitude and day he had predicted he would. Upon his return to Spain he was received by the Spanish Monarchs in Barcelona, in April of 1493. So grateful were the Catholic Sovereigns to Columbus for what he had done in their service, that when he entered the throne room, they made the unprecedented gesture of rising to greet him, and they had a chair placed for him alongside of the royal thrones.

The propagation of the "racial" name "Indians" commenced from that time, beginning with Columbus' often reprinted letter of 1493.[17]

There were, however, moments when Columbus was remarkably forthright about the true nature of his enterprise as well as the monumental difficulties he faced in making it work. On his first voyage he recorded in his log--the one he kept for his

---

[17]

Robert F. Berkhofer, Jr., *The White Man's Indian: Images of the American Indian from Columbus to the Present* (New York: Vintage Books, 1979), p. 5.

own records, which is to be distinguished from the altered one which he kept in order to deceive his crew--that among the "Indians" he observed ladies who in complexion and features looked like the ladies in Spain.[18] Those natives, he observed, were "the color of the Canary Islanders, neither black nor white."[19] This was a telling remark indeed, as the Guanches--the Ancient population of the Canary Islands--were of very mixed complexion tone. Some were very dark-skinned, some were of a very light complexion with blond hair, and there were a variety of medium-colored complexions.[20] There was no social ranking according to skin color among the Guanches.

Columbus returned from his first voyage with metal spearheads which some of the Caribbean Islanders were using. The islanders had told him that traders from Guinea had brought them there, and Ferdinand's royal mineralogist confirmed: "The very alloy is of African origin."[21] On Columbus' second voyage he recorded how deeply impressed he had been by both the Christian and African influences in the Caribbean.[22]

A letter which Columbus wrote to the governess of Prince don Juan late in 1500, on his return--in chains--from his third

---

[18]

James Bailey, *The God-Kings & The Titans: The New World Ascendancy in Ancient Times* (London: Hodder & Stoughton, 1973), pp. 234-235.

[19]

John Schofield, "Christopher Columbus and the New World He Found," in *National Geographic* (Washington, D.C.: National Geographic Society, November, 1975), p. 595.

[20]

Heyerdahl, *op. cit.*, pp. 123,374, and 375-376.

[21]

Marble, *op. cit.*, pp. 23-24.

[22]

Ibid., p. 24.

voyage, is most revealing in yet another light: "I should be judged," he wrote,

> as a captain who left Spain for the Indies to conquer a warlike nation, whose customs and religious rites are very different from ours, where by divine will I have placed under the sovereignty of the King and Queen, our lords, another world whereby Spain, which was reputed to be poor, is now the richest nation in the world....

> I have opened the doors to great quantities of gold, pearls, precious stones, spices and a thousand other things.[23]

Toward the end of Columbus' life, his distorted figure for the earth's circumference came to be disputed and ridiculed by a number of learned geographers in western Eurasia. And so he concocted a new rhetorical formulation in defence of his "discovery" of "Indians." This has never received the attention which it deserves. The earth, he now claimed, was not really spherical at all. Rather, it should be thought of as pear-shaped; or even better, as a ball with a protrusion resembling a woman's nipple on top of it, pointing upward toward the heavens. And Columbus--who everyone knew had taken a tropical heading toward the Caribbean--now claimed to have taken the shorter, northern route, across the top of the "ball."[24]

After Columbus had "opened the doors" to the "racial" division of humanity, the "race" idea was quickly propagated in legal, ecclesiastical and scholarly circles. In the very beginning, "Indians" were to be found nearly *everywhere* on earth. Not only were all peoples between the Indus River and Japan "Indians,"

---

[23] André M. Collard, ed., Bartholomé de las Casas, *History of the Indies* (New York: Harper Torchbooks, 1971), p. 75.

[24] Heyerdahl, *op. cit.*, p. 147.

but so too were Guanches of the Canary Islands, the Americans, and the Pacific Islanders. This means that all of the human beings living within 270 degrees of earthly longitude were "racially" "Indians." At as late a period as the eighteenth century, during the Pacific voyages of Captain Cook, Englishmen were calling the Pacific Islanders "Indians." To this day, Spaniards still call the people of the Philippine Islands "Indians." Perhaps the popularity of the "Indian" "racial" classification was due to the confluence of people who were so labeled and who were also ruthlessly conquered. Surely the intent of calling people "Indians" was made clear by the ease with which Spaniards in the Americas interchanged the words "Indian" and "dog."

In fact, all of the key words of the "race" idea originated in the Iberian peninsula in the late fifteenth and early sixteenth centuries.[25] These words, so familiar to all of us today, are: "mestizo," "mulatto," "negro," "Indian," "caste," and "race," the latter word being introduced into the dictionaries of five Modern languages (Spanish, Italian, Portuguese, English, and French) in 1513.[26] The word "mulatto," which is derived from the Spanish word for mule[27] gives a clear indication of the dehumanizing intent behind placing a "racial" classification upon people. Up until the nineteenth century, "half-breeds" were popularly

---

[25]

Léon Poliakov, Edmund Howard, translator, *The Aryan Myth: A History of Racist and Nationalist Ideas in Europe* (New York: Basic Books, Inc., Publishers, 1976), pp. 135-136.

[26]

The Oxford English Dictionary (Compact Edition), p. 2400, dates this introduction at 1512, but omits mention of the word's inclusion in the English lexicon at that time. Other equally accessible sources date the word's introduction at 1513.

[27]

Poliakov, *op. cit.*, p. 135.

considered to be reproductively sterile, as are mules.[28] This division of "races" from the human species shows one of the major purposes for the rhetorical instrument known as the "race" idea: the destruction of humanity's Ancient sibling relationship.

The word "race" is itself most likely derived from two sources. One of these, the late Latin *generatio*, indicates the relation of species within a single genus. Different species, of course, cannot produce fertile offspring, and in most cases cannot produce offspring at all. This derivation underscores the dehumanizing imperative which the "race" idea embodies--at the time of its origin the "race" idea was a classification of "others" by a "we-who-are-human." The second probable derivation of "race" is from the Arabic word *ras*, which means a "breed of cattle."[29] This word origin has a great bearing on the uncanny ability of "race" identification to create--in the manner of a self-fulfilling prophecy--a "racial" group *after* the group has been labeled. This is a topic to which I shall return in the fifth chapter below.

Rome was quick to respond to the question of the 'moral' obligation of Spaniards who had "discovered" a new "race," and Rome was also quick to mediate between the conflicting claims of Spain and Portugal. In 1493, Pope Alexander VI issued his bulls of donation which specifically gave the task of Christianizing the "West Indies" to the Crown of Castile. He drew a 'line of demarcation' from the north to south pole, and decreed that all "new world" lands west of the line belonged to Spain, while all those to the east of it belonged to the Portuguese. This 'donation' gave the Portuguese dominion over only around six hundred miles of South American coastline where they had been

---

[28]

Ibid.

[29]

Eric Voegelin, "The Growth of the Race Idea," in *The Review of Politics* (Notre Dame, Indiana: The University of Notre Dame, July, 1940), p. 296.

engaged with well-established trading partners for so long. Portugal was most unhappy with the arrangement. So the next year, in 1494, by the Treaty of Tordesillas, the line was moved about five hundred miles further west, greatly increasing the Portuguese foothold in South America. This heated quarrel between Spain and Portugal must have been a source of great confusion to dedicated believers of Columbus' rhetoric, for conventional history records that Portugal's first expedition to South America was that of Cabral, in 1500. In 1501, Alexander VI issued yet another papal bull, this time authorizing Spain to take over the tithes (the Church taxes) imposed on the "Indians." This license had very broad implications to Castilian conquerors in the Americas.

Meanwhile, the Spanish concern for the Christian purity of Spain--and with it a concern over the purity of bloodlines of descent--continued along with the flow of the "race" idea's development. In 1502, a decree was enacted in Spain banishing all Moors from the country, just as Jews had been 'lawfully' expelled ten years earlier. At about the same time, the Dominican Order of Rome--customarily in charge of such matters--once again stoked up the fires of the Pontifical Inquisition in Spain. This time the problem to be "inquired" into was that of the *conversos*, recent Jewish and Islamic converts to Catholicism, who were also known as "Marranos" (Spanish for "vile," "dirty," or "swine") and "Moriscos." The difficulty with these *New Christians* was that since they definitely were not descended from Japheth, their blood was corrupted by their descent from persons whose ancestors had "denied" Christ. (Notice here, that with the application of the new "race" idea, the Ancient tradition of adopting converts and immigrants into the 'bloodline'--as, for example, *the Franks* had been--was abandoned entirely.) As the flames of the *Auto de fé* raged, and the secrets of the torture chamber multiplied, Spain--ever mindful of the profession of lawyers--enacted the first "blood quantum" law in human history. The new Decrees of Purity of Blood relegated *conversos* to the bottom of Spain's social scale.[30]

The legal clarification of the "race" idea proceeded further in 1512, with Spain's promulgation of the Laws of Burgos, which were designed for application in Spain's American colonies. Law 24 of this code declared that: "no one may beat or whip or call an Indian dog or any other name unless it is his proper name."[31] In grammatical usage, a proper name--in the only senses which could be applied to Law 24--is either the name of a specific person, or the name of a "race" of people. It would be absurd to assume that the intent of Law 24 was to compel Spaniards in the Americas--ruthless conquerors who destroyed millions of human beings--to call each of their victims by a proper personal name. Clearly, Law 24 was the first "racial" classification legislation in human experience. From the day it was enacted, all Spaniards in the Americas were commanded to call the native human population thereof by the "racial" name "Indians."

"Racial" classification was then, and still is, a very useful rhetorical device. It legally and administratively reduces many national, vastly differing population units into a single entity, a "racial" one. The single "racial" entity may then be interacted with, or "dealt with," with one single set of laws or procedures. This avoids the inconvenience of having to devise a new set of procedures by which to interact with each one of many differing nations. This is precisely the manner in which "race" has been and is the most potent force of ethnocide ever in the world. And this is only the psychological side of ethnocide, leaving the bloodshed, or physical aspect out of it. The "race" idea has

---

[30]

Poliakov, *op. cit.*, pp. 136-137.

[31]

Hanke, *op. cit.*, p. 15.

allowed countless nations to be literally written out of existence. Over the generations during which such rhetoric was devised and perfected by the Spanish in the Americas, the basis was laid for the interactions between all Modern nations and the victims of their conquests, in what has come to be known as the European "Age of Discovery."

Spanish jurists concocted the legal declaration known as the Requirement in 1513. This document was to be read aloud to "Indians" prior to the invasion of their lands by the Castilian conquerors, and it was designed to ensure that the rights of "Indians" would be protected, and to guarantee that their submission would proceed according to 'just and Christian principles'.[32] The Requirement, to be read in Spanish, in the presence of an "Indian" king, noble, headman, or council, reviewed Pope Alexander VI's donation of the Americas to Spain, explained that the peoples of the Americas were now under the sovereignty of the King of Spain, and ended with a *demand* that the people being addressed acknowledge the new sovereignty being placed upon them, and more importantly, that they immediately adopt the Catholic faith. Should the natives refuse any of these conditions read to them in an unintelligible foreign language, or should they even fail to respond, the Spanish soldiers were legally free to do their work.

The question of whether "Indians" were capable of doing their work formed the basis of the first 'social experiments' in America, beginning in 1508. The answer to the question, more or less obtained by 1518, contributed mightily to the body of Spanish opinion about the aptitudes of the new "race," and outlined a most effective means of dealing with it. The second experiment commenced in 1516, when the Spanish regent, Cardinal Ximénez--besieged by a flurry of contradictory opinion about the condition

---

[32]
Op. cit., pp. 15-16.

of the "Indians," and the proper manner of dealing with them, dispatched a commission of three Jeronymite friars to the island of Española to discover the truth.[33]

The stated objective of this Jeronymite interrogatory was to determine if the "Indians" were "capable of living by themselves." Put otherwise, the Jeronymites were to find out if the "Indians," captive in lands which had once been their own, would be able to support themselves using the implements of, and living in the lifestyle of the Spanish peasantry. An earlier, though unofficial, experiment along these lines, from 1508 through 1514, had already failed.[34] To conduct their experiment, the three friars had all of the natives of Española rounded up and concentrated into a small number of "test villages." By the time the Jeronymites were released from their investigative obligation by the King, in 1518, they had amassed an enormous amount of testimony from Spanish colonists which would be drawn upon quite heavily in future disputations on the same subject. In the year following the Jeronymites' departure, the highly demoralized natives of Española (still concentrated into the "test villages") were nearly exterminated by a smallpox epidemic which swept through their new communities.[35]

---

[33]

Lewis Hanke, *The First Social Experiments in Indian Pi\ America: A Study in the Development of Spanish Indian Policy in the Sixteenth Century* (Cambridge: Harvard University Press, 1935), p.25.

[34]

Ibid., pp. 36-37.

[35]

Ibid., pp. 38-39.

Oh! How the loss of those innocent lives was lamented! But here the Spanish had learned a most useful lesson in biological warfare.[36] Concentrating a conquered enemy under mentally tormenting and physically unhealthy conditions was a most efficient means of destroying that enemy. And such a form of destruction could be conducted under the auspices of Christian charity! This lesson diffused very quickly among colonial powers. Less than ten years later, England, in its war to conquer Ireland, concentrated captive Irish people into "Prayer Towns." A hundred years later "Prayer Towns" came to the North American colonies of the English, and established a tradition leading directly to the "Indian Reservations" of the present-day United States.

The next formidable development in rhetorical mentality-- and it is a development which is not at all unrelated to the progress of the "race" idea--came on Assumption Day in 1534. On that day, Ignatius Loyola, a Spanish soldier turned mystic, founded the Society of Jesus--the "Militia of Christ"--or as it is more commonly known today, the Catholic order of Jesuits. Only the best and the brightest were permitted to join the Jesuits. The order's new recruits were conditioned with the Spiritual Exercises. These Exercises consisted of four weeks of intensive and highly sophisticated psychological training--in our own time such conditioning is called "brainwashing"--during which the recruit was completely isolated from all persons except a director. The training was designed to utterly break the will of any person, and to "imbue into him spiritual forces which he would find very

---

[36]

By far the greatest proportion of the Spanish depopulation of the Americas was accomplished by the spread of diseases. It would be a serious mistake to think that the dissemination of new plagues in the Americas was always an accidental event.

difficult to eliminate later."[37]   The ultimate objective of this training was to render the initiate totally obedient to the General of the Society, as its leader was called.[38]   If the goal of utter obedience seems scarcely credible, Loyola's letter to the Portuguese Jesuits leaves little room for doubt. "We must see black as white, if the Church says so," he wrote.[39]

If this consideration of the technique for 'mental discipline' invented by Loyola seems irrelevant here, it would be wise to consider the enormous amount of such 'discipline' exhibited in Spain, on a *national* scale, during the period in which first the "Indian," and then very shortly thereafter, the "Negro" "races" were invented. Making uniform "races" out of people some of whom were "well-nigh white," while others were "as black as Ethiopians;" and of yet others who were "neither black nor white," was not an easy task. It literally *was* a case of seeing "black as white," and *vice versa*.   The process entailed extraordinary mental conditioning, intense fanaticism, and a profuse amount of bloodshed. But that this terrible sort of 'discipline' has succeeded, no one may deny today. For in our own time, so many of our sisters and brothers look upon a "race" other than "their own," and see but one single face. And what is worse, an even greater number--a much greater number--look upon "races" and see a distinctive mental attitude and set of behavior for each.

---

[37]

Edmond Paris, *The Secret History of the Jesuits* (Chino, California: Chick Publications, 1975), p. 21.

[38]

Ibid., pp. 20-22.

[39]

Quoted in *Ibid.*, p. 26.

"Race" hypothesis was further advanced through the efforts of Spanish jurists, ecclesiastics and scholars in 1550. In that year the Spanish Crown sponsored a most unique sort of foreign policy debate, a disputation of a kind never before and never since engaged in. The University at Valladolid hosted this oratorical contest between the Dominican, las Casas, and the academic, Sepulveda. The purpose of the great debate at Valladolid was to determine, once and for all time, under what just and Christian principles, if any, Spain could lawfully make War upon the Americas. Father de las Casas, known as the benefactor of the "Indian," promoted the image of the "Indian" as a noble savage--the same sort of rhetorical image which had been most useful to Roman conquerors fifteen hundred years earlier. Las Casas insisted that the "Indians" were genuine descendants of Adam, and that their rights therefore must be respected and could not lawfully be infringed, unless after extensive and thoroughgoing catechism, they persisted in rejecting the true Catholic faith.

Sepulveda, giving the Ancient Greek philosopher Aristotle a somewhat imaginative interpretation, argued that the "Indians" had no rights whatsoever, for they were "slaves by nature." The most notable feature of the great debate, however, was the way in which both disputants studiously avoided making serious reference to the Americans as constituting the many and various nations which in reality they were. Both sides insisted that the numerous American nations comprised but a single "racial" entity: the "Indian." This occurred in spite of las Casas' many years of living in the Caribbean, and his first hand knowledge of the great variation in skin color among the "Indians."

The official judges of the debate took a full twenty years to reach and publish their conclusions. Their findings were sufficiently ambiguous so as to render it most difficult to proclaim which side had won the debate. But that would be of little importance; henceforth there would never be any doubt in the world that there was a "race" of "Indians."[40]

Three years later, in 1573, a new body of law was proclaimed by the Spanish Crown to govern the conduct of Spanish colonists in the Americas. Among its provisions, the new Basic Law stipulated that in all records of Spanish activity in the Americas, the word "pacification" should be used in place of the word conquest.[41]

But I have said that classifying human beings "racially" is a fifth and most terrible form of cannibalism, and I have implied that there is ultimately but a single purpose for "racial" classification. In the manner of an illustration of this, there is the example of the confrontation, in 1532, between Atahualpa, king of the Ancient Inca dynasty, and Francisco Pizarro, military representative of the Modern Spanish conquest state.

Not long after Pizarro's marauding army had arrived in Peru a meeting was held--under a truce--between Atahualpa and Pizarro. There, a second meeting was arranged between the two, to be held, at Pizarro's suggestion, in the square at Caxamalca.

At that time the Spanish were holding the town of Caxamalca, and on the appointed day of the meeting they waited concealed, crowded into the alleyways leading from the main square, waiting for the Inca to appear. Eight restless hours passed for them that day in the Caxamalca Square. And then, in the words of historian Maurice Rowdon, Atahualpa

---

[40]

For a detailed discussion of the debate at Valladolid, see Hanke, *Aristotle and the American Indians, op. cit.*

[41]

Ibid., p. 88.

...and his unarmed attendants (many hundreds of them) entered the town, singing what the Spaniards afterwards called 'songs of hell'....First came hundreds of servants, then noblemen with their maces of copper and silver, some of them dressed in pure white, others in chequered red-and-white cloaks. The guards had rich blue liveries, full of ornaments....Atahualpa's litter...was seen not to be coated with gold but to be one solid piece....And the noblemen had massive pendants hanging from their ears, the lobes of which from childhood had been stretched by weights, so that they hung almost to their shoulders....Hence [the Spaniards'] name for Indian noblemen: '*orejones*' or 'big ears'. The royal litter was lined with the vivid plumes of tropical birds. Round Atahualpa's neck was a collar of immense emeralds. He had golden ornaments in his hair, and on his brow was the crimson *borla* or fringe down to his eyebrows. It was the Inca crown.

When he and his five or six thousand men had filled the square they waited. Not a Spaniard was to be seen. He turned to one of his attendants and was just about to ask him where the foreigners had got to when...out came Friar Vicnete de Valverde, a Dominican (afterwards bishop of Cuzco), with a Bible in one hand and a crucifix in another. He approached Atahualpa, and began to explain through the interpreter Felipillo the doctrine of the Trinity....He started at the Creation and worked his way...to the redemption of mankind by Jesus Christ at Calvary. He then told the spellbound Atahualpa that Christ had left a St. Peter to rule the earth for him. That was a long time ago, and even St. Peter could not be expected to live for ever, despite the divine mandate. He had passed his office on to successors and these...were called popes. They were the absolute spiritual rulers of the whole earth. Friar Vicente finished by saying that the present pope had authorized the Spaniards to subjugate Atahualpa's part of the world...and bring the people into the same religious system, mostly for their own good. Pizarro, the military commander, would now step forward and--if the Inca would be so kind as to accept his rule from now on--would do the job of subjugation. All Atahualpa had to do was to treat the commander nicely, apart from confessing the error of his religion, and declare himself the vassal of the emperor Charles V.

Atahualpa had probably never heard anything so confusing in all his life. This foreigner's God was One, and then He was Three. 'That makes four'. he said to little Philip the interpreter, and little Philip agreed.

Then the Inca exploded with rage. He told the friar that he would be no man's vassal, and that while he did not doubt that this other emperor was a great man--he must be, he added, if he had sent his soldiers so far across the seas--no one could make Atahualpa serve him. He would, however, become his 'brother'. As for the man the good friar called a pope, he must be mad to talk of giving away countries that did not belong to him! In any case, this God he had just heard about had apparently been put to death by the very people he had created! What sort of a religion was that? And what sort of people were they who had committed the murder? After all the Inca God was still there--Atahualpa pointed to the last rays of the sun--'and looks down upon all his children'. He then asked the friar on whose authority he said all those things about the Creation and the Trinity. The friar's answer was to hand him the Bible. Atahualpa took a long look at it, turning over the pages[42], and then suddenly threw it to the ground

---

[42]

In spite of the fable that the people of the Inca were completely illiterate, knowing only the *quipu* (knotted rope) system of notation, Atahualpa, in

and asked the friar to tell him what his comrades were doing in his land. He added that he would not move from the spot until they had accounted for all the wrongs they had been doing to his people, stealing and making war.

The friar picked up the Bible and hurried off to the hidden Pizarro....He could now [according to the provisions of the Requirement] hand over to the secular arm. He went in to Pizarro and told him not to waste any more time talking to 'this dog' but to attack. 'I absolve you', he added.

Pizarro went out and waved a white scarf, his signal for the gun [the cannon hidden on a rooftop above the square] to fire. It fired. And from every corner Spanish soldiers dashed out to their war-cry of 'St. Jago and at 'em'! They poured into the square on foot and on horseback. They fired their muskets, drove their horses into the terrified crowd, trampled them down and put them to the sword while smoke from the guns obscured everything. The Indians offered no resistance, except for those close to the Inca's litter. These massed together and tried to tear at the Spaniards with their fingers. They clung to the horses' legs. The rest were trying frantically to get away. But every escape route was closed. Their bodies piled up in the narrow exits of the square as they were cut down. The pressure of the fleeing crowd was so great that part of the [massive] town wall crashed down, and hundreds got away. They were pursued by horsemen, and most of them died in the fields outside. None of the army surrounding the town came forward to help. There had been no plan on the Inca side for such an emergency....Meanwhile the battle round

---

fact, knew perfectly well what a book was, although he surely did not read Latin. Two samples of writing from Inca Peru are shown in Garrick Mallery, *Picture-Writing of the American Indians* (New York: Dover Publications, Inc., 1972), Volume Two, p. 672.

the litter went on. Atahualpa was still held high above his attendants' shoulders, swinging about perilously and almost toppling down on them. A soldier dashed forward to finish the job off his way by running a sword through the emperor but Pizarro screamed out at the top of his voice, '*Nadie hiera al Indio so pena de la vida*'![43] The litter was overturned at last and Atahualpa fell--straight into Pizarro's arms. The imperial band was snatched off his brow by a soldier,....It was suddenly all over. Not an Indian apart from Atahualpa was left alive in Caxamalca. It had taken no more than half an hour.

The army outside the city simply drifted away. A people that had been taught to depend on those above them--and essentially on one man, the Child of the Sun--had no resources in the face of the Child's disappearance. They scattered to their homes and the story of the massacre began traveling all over the empire.

Pizarro's secretary recorded afterwards that 2,000[44] natives had been murdered that day. That was almost certainly an underestimate: no doubt it was designed to soften the wrath of Charles V when he heard about it. The figure may have been as high as 10,000, though no one can be sure about it.

---

[43]

"No harm to the Indian on pain of death!"

[44]

Ethnocidal activity and population underestimation are customarily concomitant in the Modern epoch. The wide variation in the death toll figures for the fire bombing of Dresden, Germany, or Pol Pot's reign of terror in Cambodia, are but two examples out of hundreds.

That evening Pizarro kept his promise [made at their first meeting] and entertained the king at a splendid banquet. They sat side by side and looked out on to the square, which was still littered with piles of the dead. Atahualpa had little appetite, and sat gazing in silent gloom across the town while Pizarro tried to jolly him out of his mood by telling him that he had lost the battle because Christ had

not protected him. He had been 'punished' by God also for throwing down that Bible. So he should not take it too badly. The Spaniards, he added, were forgiving people, so long as you were careful not to make war on them.[45]

Atahualpa was then held prisoner, for a ransom. Altogether, the Inca's ransom totaled over *thirty three hundred cubic feet* of gold.[46] During the course of his captivity, Atahualpa began to suspect the very worst of his captors' intentions toward him. And so he told Pizarro that if the Spaniard was going to kill him after all, he must not strangle him, for that would send his spirit into a realm of torment. History records that when Pizarro did revoke the ransom and have Atahualpa put to death, the king was garrotted.

Everywhere the conquering armies of Modern nations went, they disseminated the "race" idea thusly, sometimes with a bit more finesse, sometimes more brutally. Although the "white" "race" is generally considered to be the last major "race" to be 'identified'--originating in the eighteenth-century scientific

---

[45]

Maurice Rowdon, *The Spanish Terror: Spanish Imperialism in the Sixteenth Century* (New York: St. Martin's Press, 1974), pp. 135-138. This fine study is principally a discussion of Spanish imperialism in western Eurasia.

[46]

Op. cit., p. 140.

'natural histories' of first Buffon and then Blumenbach[47]--the idea of the "white man" quickly became firmly fixed in the minds of the conquered. For while the conquering armies sometimes contained persons of varied complexion to a degree which matched the conquered (slaves, for example, and also servants and *conversos Moriscos*), the social ranking according to skin color in the Modern forces was always readily apparent.[48] And almost without exception, the leaders of Modern expeditionary forces were of a lighter complexion. Thus, the essential trinity of every official and semi-official Spanish expedition of conquest-- the priest, the military commander, and the lawyer[49]--created the "white" "race" nearly simultaneously with the "Indian" and "negro" "races."

As conquerors, the Spanish were in the Roman mold, and thereby were very Modern. Their conquests were always accompanied by an enormous loss of life on the opposing side. Sometimes, as in the case of the Aztec city of Tenochtitlan, a captured city was leveled entirely, and the rubble used as the foundation for a new Spanish town. Always, as a matter of policy, the priests rushed in after a conquest, sacking the temples and libraries, and destroyed every manuscript, codex, inscription and note they could find.[50] Thereby they eliminated people, places,

---

[47]

Voegelin, "The Growth of the Race Idea," *op. cit.*, pp. 295-297.

[48]

One notable exception to this was Esteban, the "Black Kachina," who led the Spanish quest for the Seven Cities of Cibola in the North American southwest.

[49]

No Spanish expedition could be organized or lawfully conducted without these three key personnel on board.

[50]

The Roman Church decreed that all "Indian" works be banned, as "works of the devil."

and ideas--they wiped the slate clean, so to speak. The height of Spain's "pacification" program in the Americas was from 1492 to 1650, and the degree to which the pre-Spanish nations of those continents were depopulated shows just how clean a wipe of the slate it was. Over that one hundred and fifty eight year period the drop in the population of the Americas is estimated to have been eighty million.[51]   On such a slate, history could easily be rewritten.

When, in the eighteenth century, Buffon and Blumenbach first turned the attention of the scientific movement toward the political concept, "race," it was determined that five "races" were in existence: the "black," "red," "white," "yellow," and "brown." By the early twentieth century, scientific inquiry into "racial" hypotheses had so 'progressed' that a minor luminary such as psychologist Stanley Porteus of Hawaii, could boldly assert that:

> ...whether apparent or not there is going on a ceaseless racial struggle for dominance that no number of platitudes about brotherly love will obviate; and...this struggle for dominance is by no means waged on equal terms.

> ...the differences between races that are of importance are not merely differences in mentality, but differences in mental energy to which emotional, volitional and tempermental traits contribute.[52]

---

[51]

Henry F. Dobyns, "Estimating Aboriginal American Population, an Appraisal of Techniques with a New Hemispheric Estimate," in *Current Anthropology*, Volume VII, Number 4 (October, 1966), pp. 395-416. See also: Virgil J. Vogel, *This Country Was Ours: A Documentary History of the American Indian* (New York: Harper & Row, Publishers, 1972), pp. 251-253.

[52]

Stanley D. Porteus and Marjorie E. Babcock, *Temperment and Race* (Boston: Richard G. Badger, Publisher, 1926), p. 327. Doctor Porteus had his racism enshrined when, in 1975, the social sciences building at the

Thus science came to offer testimony similar to some of that given to the three Jeronymites on Española in 1518. Indeed, this sort of slander has always accompanied the "race" idea, and is useful, furthermore, in keeping 'groups', once defined, apart from one another. And, as every competent cattle-breeder knows, keeping the groups, once defined, apart from one another is the essence of purifying the line. This brings us, really, to the Modern terror, the mass psychological distortion--the "race" system--of our own present time.

But before we look at the world about us, let us first examine a bit more closely the Ancient order which began to crumble and fall with the Modern onslaught of "discovery" and "race."

University of Hawai'i at Mānoa was named in honor of him.

Gotta take a little time
A little time to think things over
I better read between the lines
In case I need it when I'm older
This mountain I must climb
Feels like a world upon my shoulders
Through the clouds I see love shine
It keeps me warm as life grows colder...
I want to know what love is
I want you to show me
I want to feel what love is
I know you can show me
                              --M. Jones

CHAPTER IV
The World Before "Race"

During the process of opening the great tumulus at Grave creek, in Western Virginia, in the year 1838, and the extension of a gallery to its centre, a small inscribed stone was discovered, in connection with the remains of a human skeleton and its accompanying momentoes, which appears to possess an alphabetical value. This curious relic, a drawing of which is given, appears to reveal, in the unknown past, evidences of European intrusion into the continent, of which no other vestiges have, thus far, been discovered. Copies of the inscription have been transmitted to London, Paris, Copenhagen, and Lisbon. Mr. Rafn, with considerable confidence, pronounces it to be Celiberic; but no interpretation has, however, been attempted[1].

---

[1]

Henry Rowe Schoolcraft, LL.D., *History of the Indian Tribes of the United States: Their Present Condition and Prospects, and a Sketch of Their Ancient Status* (Philadelphia: J.B. Lippincott & Co., 1857), Volume VI [Summary Volume], p. 610, and Plate 38.

So wrote Henry R. Schoolcraft, the founder of Modern American anthropology, in his 1857 *History of the Indian Tribes of the United States*. Schoolcraft, a Doctor of Laws and member of both the American Philosophical and American Ethnological Societies, had been requested by the United States' Congress to undertake and publish a comprehensive study of the American "Indian."

Over a century later, Mr. Rafn's identification of the tablet's language was proven to be quite correct. The alphabet of the tablet was identified and published in 1968, and the inscription was translated by Professor Barry Fell. The language is Punic (Iberian Phoenician), and the tablet is the gravestone of the king who was laid to rest in the mound. The inscription reads:

> The mound raised-on-high for Tasach
> This tile
> (His) queen caused to be made[2]

Schoolcraft's paragraph on the Grave Creek tablet, quoted in its entirety above, is the only mention he makes of Bronze Age America in the summary volume of his *History*.... However, although Schoolcraft asserts that "no other vestiges" of "European intrusion" had at the time been discovered, on Plate 39 of the summary volume a view of Monhegan Island, Maine, is shown, and Inscription Rock thereon, with a closeup viewpoint of its Hinge Ogam[3] inscription is pictured. Plate 39 is the illustration on the page immediately following Plate 38, which pictures Tasach's gravestone and skull.

---

[2]

Barry Fell, *America B.C.: Ancient Settlers in the New World* (New York: Quadrangle/The New York Times Book Co., 1976), p. 21. *Cf. Ibid.*, p. 158, the Adena tombstone of Teth.

[3]

Ibid., p. 58.

Modern American archaeologists have placed Tasach's burial mound within what they call the Woodland tradition of eastern North American culture. The specific culture group to which Tasach belonged has been correctly identified as being native to North America, and has been arbitrarily named Adena culture. The central North American homeland of Adena culture was along the river systems of the Ohio Valley. Adena was a very long-lived culture, beginning, according to conventional scholarship, about three thousand years ago, and lasting for almost one thousand years. Actually, Adena culture did not even come to a well-defined close, but rather, it merged into the succeeding culture, known as Hopewell. And in fact, as the contemporary archaeologist Gordon R. Willey has noted, the Woodland tradition continued to exist up until 1700.[4]

Three problems have troubled some contemporary American archaeologists (but not all of them) in their study of Adena culture and the Woodland tradition: the source from which ceramics were introduced into the region, the origin of the burial mound tradition, and why Woodlands burials contain human skulls of two shapes.

In the words of Professor Willey:

The problem of pottery origins in the Woodland tradition can be summarized only by saying that although the prevailing features of Woodland pottery were more reminiscent of northern Asia and Europe than they are of *any other* world areas, other features hint at Mesoamerican affiliations.

---

[4]

Gordon R. Willey, *An Introduction to American Archaeology, Volume One: North and Middle America* (Englewood Cliffs, New Jersey: Prentice-Hall, Inc., 1966), p. 267.

Burial mounds have been found throughout most of the
Eastern Woodlands area, with the exception of parts of the
Northeast....To be sure, mound burial, including the
building of special tomb chambers, was an Asiatic and Old
World trait complex; but as Chard has pointed out, no
geographical continuity of the complex across Asia and into
the New World can be established. A vast gap exists in
eastern Asia and northern Canada[5].

The extent of the burial mound tradition in Asia and the
"Old World" was from roughly midway across the Eurasian land
mass, westward to the Iberian peninsula, including what is now
Spain and Portugal. Much more than three thousand years ago
this burial custom was well-established in those lands. The
Iberian mounds average about sixty feet tall. Tasach's tomb, the
largest in North America, is somewhat over twenty meters high.
The Punic language with which Tasach's gravestone is engraved
was commonly spoken on the Iberian peninsula three thousand
years ago. But here, I am getting ahead of myself a bit.

The third problem confronting non-somnambulant
archaeologists is skull shapes. Among human beings there are
roughly two shapes of skulls, these are "round-headed" and "long-
headed." Both shapes of skulls have been distributed around the
earth for tens of thousands of years. Their distribution is uneven
but general. Thus, round-headed people are to be found from
western France to the northern Alps, and from there to the
Balkans and the mountains of Asia Minor. Round-headed people
are found predominantly throughout Asia, they are found in the
nations of the Pygmys, the Bushmen and the Hottentots; they are
found in Polynesia, and somewhat in Africa and Australia among
the general population of the oldest nations there, and they are
found in the northern polar region. Round-headed people are

---

[5]

Willey, *op. cit.*, pp. 267-268, *emphasis mine*.

found in North, Central and South America among Ancient and Modern populations. Long-headed people are found predominantly in Europe and Africa, but also in Polynesia, Australia, in the Ancient and Modern populations of the Americas, and in parts of Asia.[6]

Adena burials show a significant and sudden increase in the number of round-headed people living in the North American Woodlands, and although Professor Willey notes that some round-headed people were present there in the preceding Middle and Late Archaic periods, he is somewhat puzzled by the cause of the quick increase in their numbers in Adena times.[7] He reports that: "...some archaeologists have suggested that the brachycephalic [round-headed] Adenans represented a new and intrusive population element in the Ohio Valley..."[8] Willey finds that in spite of the above, the effect of present evidence about Adena culture is to "lessen the possibility that Adena brachycephals were new immigrants from Mesoamerica"[9] So where did these Adenans come from? Willey does not speculate about it.

One would suppose that the traditional Adena gravestones, with Punic inscriptions upon them, would provide a clue to the Adena origins. However, at the present time Ancient America's written languages are given scant recognition, for American archaeology currently does not admit the alphabetic nature of North America's plentiful inscriptions. Hence, of Tasach's and

---

[6]

Alfred S. Romer, *The Vertebrate Story* (Chicago: The University of Chicago Press, 1959), pp. 387-411.

[7]

Willey, *op. cit.*, pp. 267 and 272-273.

[8]

Ibid., p. 272.

[9]

Ibid., pp. 272-273.

others' Adena gravestones Willey says: "Adena decorative carving was expressed in small stone tablets. These were small, flat, a little over 1 centimeter thick, and measured about 10 by 8 centimeters on the other dimensions[10]." In a similar fashion of mis-perception, Ancient Arabic inscriptions in the southwestern portion of North America are known by other anthropologists as "Great Basin Curvilinear" designs, coin design carvings in western North America are called "circular shield designs," Ogam inscriptions (of a kind like those at Monhegan Island) in eastern North America have been the "marks of plowshares," or the "marks of colonial masons' stone-cutting drills[11]," and Dakota hieroglyphs are known as "picture writing."

It is truly unfortunate that such an informative link with Ancient America as its own written records should be entirely overlooked. Had that not been the case, anthropologists would have readily grasped the fact that the Adena-Punic people, the Celts, and others were *trans oceanic* cultures, just as Eskimos or Polynesians have long been recognized to be. (Indeed, the vast open ocean distances routinely crossed by Ancient Polynesians traveling from one end of their realm to the other, make the much shorter trans Atlantic crossing seem like child's play. It is the *Atlantic Ocean* which provides the "geographical continuity" for the mound burial culture trait complex to move into the "New World.")

But in this case, we may see the very moment in which Ancient America's history was destroyed, and we may know exactly by whom it was done. Thirty-two years after Doctor Schoolcraft had entered into the founding document of American

---

[10]

Ibid., p. 271.

[11]

Fell, *America B.C., op. cit.*, pp. 13 and 61, and *Saga America, op. cit.*, pp 248 and 354.

anthropology that Mr. Rafn had identified the Grave Creek inscription as Celiberic (Celtiberic), and that it pointed to "in the unknown past, evidences of European intrusion into the continent...," the record was altered. This was the rhetorical accomplishment of Colonel Garrick Mallery. In 1893, his *Picture-Writing of the American Indians* comprised the entire issue of the *Tenth Annual Report of the Bureau of Ethnology to the Secretary of the Smithsonian Institution, 1888-'89*, and was published by the United States Government Printing Office. In this volume Colonel Mallery displayed his prodigious ideological[12] acumen in dismissing the tombstone of Tasach. Mallery began his effort with detailed descriptions of three copies of the tombstone: Captain Seth Eastman's accurate reproduction for Schoolcraft's volume, and two rather imaginative spurious copies. Next, he quoted three inventive 'translations' of the inscription. Then he asserted that in addition to Celtiberic, scholars had identified elements from eight other languages in the tablet's alphabet. On the weight of this 'evidence', Mallery concluded, regarding the Grave Creek tablet that:

> A mere collection of letters from various alphabets is not an alphabet. Words can not be formed or ideas communicated by that artifice. When a people adopts the alphabetical signs of another it adopts the general style of the characters and more often the characters in detail. Such signs had already an arrangement into syllables and words which had a vocalic validity as well as known significance. A jumble of letters from a variety of alphabets bears internal evidence that the manipulator did not comprehend the languages from which the letters were selected. In the case

---

[12]

Yet *another* word for rhetorical.

of the Grave creek inscription the futile attempts to extract a meaning from it on the theory that it belongs to an intelligent alphabetic system shows that it holds no such place[13]

Using Mallery's rhetorical system, an English language inscription on a Modern tombstone could as easily be dismissed as being nonsensical. The first step would be to make copies of the inscription. One accurate copy would be permissible, but several inaccurate copies would be crucial. The inaccuracy of the latter copies could be sufficiently accomplished by changing some letters, and omitting others (after Mallery's technique). Next, 'translations' of the inscription (based on the accurate and inaccurate copies of it) would have to be obtained from 'scholars' who had absolutely no understanding whatsoever of the English language (again, following Mallery's technique). These 'translations' would, of course, conflict wildly with one another, and they would be quite senseless, as well. This would be 'proof' that any and all attempts at translation were doomed to futility. Finally, knowledgeable scholars could be called upon to point out quite truthfully (also a technique used by Mallery) that the inscription contained alphabetic elements of the Phoenician, Hebrew, Greek, Celtiberic, Latin, and Old English languages. Thus, the tombstone's inscription could easily be discounted as "a jumble of letters from a variety of alphabets" which "bears internal evidence that the manipulator did not comprehend the languages from which the letters were selected." But as we know, such a sharing of language/alphabet elements is in actuality very common among written languages, and it is, in fact, yet another indication of the great amount of communication which existed between nations in Ancient times.

---

[13] Garrick Mallery, *Picture-Writing of the American Indians* (New York: Dover Publications, Inc., 1972), p. 762.

Colonel Mallery expended far less of his energy on the Hinge Ogam inscription on Monhegan Island. He simply wrote it out of existence by quoting as authoritative an article in Science magazine which had classed the boldly-carved strokes of the inscription as "freaks of surface erosion."[14] However, the inscription on Monhegan Island has also been deciphered recently by the epigrapher Barry Fell. This decipherment was made possible through the use of the Irish Book of Ballymote, a volume which was assembled about eight hundred years ago from a number of much older manuscripts. The older manuscripts were the products of the Irish monks of the early Middle Ages, and the last manuscript in the volume is called the Ogam Tract. This manuscript is the key to the decipherment of Ogam, the Ancient written language of the Celtic nations, and it preserves about seventy varieties of this written language.[15]

Ogam is very rarely found in continental Eurasia, thanks to the efficiency of Roman conquest, but it is quite commonly found at Ancient sites in Ireland. It is in North America though, that Ancient Ogam inscriptions are most abundant. For in North America, Modern conquerors simply did not know what these inscriptions were, and hence, they did not grasp the importance of destroying them. It is because of this fortunate oversight of North America's Modern conquerors that we may gain further insight into the nature of the Ancient world by knowing that the inscription on Monhegan Island reads: "Ships from Phoenicia,

---

[14]

Mallery, *op. cit.*, p.759.

[15]

Fell, *America B.C., op. cit.*, pp. 26-26.

Cargo platform[16]." It is noteworthy that the word "ships" is rendered in the Norse, or Teutonic, as *long-bata* (longboat)[17]. Thus on Monhegan Island--which topographically is an ideal location for a trading station--we find a record of this Phoenician activity written in a Celtic script and employing in its text a Germanic word.

There are a number of forms of writing which were in active use in North America when Modern conquerors arrived, and Colonel Mallery dedicated his efforts toward devaluing the historical significance of these as well. He classed the hieroglyphic system principally used by the Siouan language-culture group of nations (but also used by some Algonquian language nations) as "picture-writing." Thereby, he inventively bestowed upon this ancient form of written language--a form which, incidentally, bears an uncanny resemblance to the as-yet inadequately-deciphered writing of the Ancient seagoing civilization of the Mediterranean Minoans--a "childish," or "immature" character. At the time when Mallery was writing, no scholar across the Atlantic would have dared to characterize Egyptian or Minoan hieroglyphs as "childish picture-writing," for the cultural development of those civilizations was well-known.

Mallery's dismissal of the various forms of Algonquian culture writing, which he lumps together under his discussion of Micmac hieroglyphics, is simply astounding. While he acknowledges that the first Modern missionaries to contact Algonquian nations in 1652 recorded that those people knew how to read and write in their own languages, he asserts that this writing was a "spontaneous use" of characters. He quotes an early Jesuit source as an authority that such writing was

---

[16]

Ibid., pp. 58, and 100-102.

[17]

Ibid.

personally idiosyncratic--or in other words, that each individual made up their own symbols as they went along--and that one person could not read another person's writing! He concludes by suggesting that the major body of the Micmac form of writing was the invention of Father Christian Kauder in 1866.[18] Unknown to Mallery, or rather, *apparently* unknown to him--as we must observe in the case of an ideologist such as the Colonel--the French priest Abbé Pierre Maillard had made a similar claim of having invented Micmac writing more than one hundred years earlier, around 1738.[19]

This is most significant, for the hieroglyphic and hieratic writing of the Micmacs contains an extraordinarily high number of symbols which are very similar to, and sometimes exactly the same in form and meaning, as the symbols used in Ancient Egyptian hieroglyphic and hieratic writing. What is significant about this is the fact that Father Maillard died sixty one years *before* the first Modern translation of Ancient Egyptian writing was accomplished by Champollion--yet he claimed to have been the inventor of a system of writing which, as it turns out, is nearly the same in structure, form and content as the Ancient Egyptian system.[20]

But if Colonel Garrick Mallery was a major actor in the movement spearheaded by the Smithsonian Institution to destroy the Ancient past of North America, he still was not the leader of that movement. That honor was later to fall upon Dr. Ales

---

[18]

Mallery, *op. cit.*, pp. 666-672.

[19]

Fell, *America B.C. , op. cit.*, pp. 253-260.

[20]

Ibid., p. 257. Prior to Champollion's accomplishment, people in Eurasia and Africa had not known how to read or write in the Ancient Egyptian style for about 1500 years.

Hrdlicka, curator of the Smithsonian from 1910 to 1943, and
principal propagandist[21] of the idea that the American continents
had been settled, prior to Modern conquest, by two relatively
recent migrations of the "Mongolian race" across the Bering
Strait, coming from Siberia. Hrdlicka's rhetorical advocacy
should come as no surprise, for after all, the Smithsonian, the
institution which employed him, is the United States' National
Museum, and is, therefore, the repository and guardian of the
treasured national ideology. Since its founding, with regard to
that national ideology, the United States has consistently
followed certain points of Spanish "race" rhetoric. The most
important of these are: first, the sizes of the continents' Ancient
nations populations have been consistently and radically
underestimated[22], and second, the citizens of those nations have
not been allowed to possess their own national identities, but
instead have had the single, uniform "racial" identity "Indians"
imposed upon them by the conquerors.

The idea that "Indians" were derived from a few recent
migrations of nomadic "Mongoloids" was not, however, an
Hrdlickian original. The first version of this rhetorical
instrument was advanced by the Jesuit José de Acosta in his
Natural and Moral History of the Indies, published in 1590, during
the very age when "race" rhetoric was invented[23]. Subsequently,
this rhetorical theme reappeared in 1648, in the Englishman
Thomas Gage's "English-American, A New Survey of the West

---

[21]

Yet *another* word for rhetorician.

[22]

See Francis Jennings, *The Invasion of America: Indians,
Colonialism, and the Cant of Conquest* (Chapel Hill: The University
of North Carolina Press, 1975), pp. 15-31.

[23]

Poliakov, *op. cit.*, pp. 137-139.

Indies."[24] From then on, it was a consistently recurring rhetorical theme among the Modern conquerors of North America, reaching the pinnacle of its perfection during the reign of Ales Hrdlicka as curator of the Smithsonian. In his zeal to propagate his rhetoric of the recent "Mongoloid" derivation of the American "Indian," Hrdlicka was ruthless and intellectually tyrannical, and he destroyed the careers of a number of archaeologists who had dared to find early man sites in North America.

To defend the stern dictates of their ideology, Hrdlicka and predecessors such as Mallery often relied upon the rhetorical device of "forged antiquities."

During the nineteenth century there was an enormous market in North American antiquities. To be sure, antiques and artifacts have been popular collectibles among affluent people for thousands of years, a fact which is testified to by the robbery of some of the tombs of the Egyptian pharaohs thousands of years ago, not long after they had first been sealed. In the nineteenth century, the enormous demands of the east coast American and the western Eurasian collectors took an incalculable toll upon the monuments of Ancient North America. The destruction of the large earthen mound at Spiro, Oklahoma, which was 'excavated' by treasure hunters using dynamite, is perhaps the best example of this.[25] Quite naturally, such brisk market conditions stimulated the manufacture and sale of forgeries as well. In fact forged treasures had been a problem in Ancient times, and they continue to be so at the present time, as there is still an ongoing trade in forged Middle Eastern, Mexican, Central and South

---

24

Louis A. Brennan, *American Dawn: A New Model of American Prehistory* (New York: The Macmillan Company, 1970), p. 2.

25

C.W. Ceram, *The First American: A Story of North American Archaeology* (New York: Mentor Books, 1972), pp. 244-245.

American and other Ancient societies' artifacts. However, from Ancient times to the present day, experts have had reasonably good success at detecting bogus treasures. Only in the Modern field of North American archaeology has the existence of occasional proven forgeries been consistently drawn upon as a convenient excuse to dismiss entire areas of research.

The favorite forgery of reference for turn of the century American anthropologists was the Cardiff Giant. The Giant was a roughly-carved gypsum statue of a man, weighing 2,990 pounds, and ten feet, four and one half inches long. In 1869 its promoters billed it as a fossil of the prehistoric "American Goliath." It was evident from the start that the experts were not taken in by this con job[26]. But although they asserted that a human fossil of such size and conformation, and composed of solid gypsum, to boot, was a *most* impossible phenomenon, the gist of their arguments centered on the assertion that *no prehistoric humans*--of the sort such as the remains of which had been discovered in the Neander Valley of Prussia, in 1857--*could have ever existed in the Americas.* The original American population, they insisted, was solely derived from a few relatively recent migrations of "Mongoloid-type" nomads who were culturally rude, and without the civilized arts.

The reason for this refusal to look accurately upon the Ancient American past by Mallery, Hrdlicka and their colleagues is the basic premise of the United States' national ideology: the United States of America is self-conceived as being the first new nation in the history of the world, a unique and successful experiment in liberty and democratic equality which was brought forth upon a *wilderness continent.* The great American experiment was, and *is*--so the ideology goes--a success, and therefore, America is *Just.* The *handful* of humans who had

---

[26]

Ibid., pp. 282-285.

'occupied' the continent previously were *nomadic hunters*, who *with justice* simply had to make way for a much, much better thing. Couched in the terms of Manifest Destiny, such ideas moved the conquering settlers from the thirteen original United States across the North American continent, from one coast to the other. Couched in the terms of the English rhetorician John Locke, such ideas gave support to the birth of the "first new nation."

After all, what if the true complexity of Ancient North America were to be forthrightly acknowledged? What if the continent was recognized to have been occupied by humans for the longest of times, to, in other words, be a land *with a great deal* of history? What if the nations of Ancient America were admitted to have been literate, to have been agricultural, to have been political, to have been abundantly populous, to have been remarkably non-aggressive, to have been deeply and positively spiritual, and to have been very much in touch with the rest of the world? What if the *pioneers* (quite literally derived from a French root meaning "foot soldiers") who led the United States' invasion of North America were to know that they and the citizens of the Ancient nations they were trampling down even shared, in the Ancient past, some of the same ancestors? Would the conquest of North America have then proceeded along the same course? Would it have proceeded as smoothly as it did? And, after the conquest was over, there was the matter of the survivors of the continent's Ancient nations; the conquered in-house prisoners of war, rounded up and isolated in rural concentrations. According to the national ideology, their treatment was demanded by their "savage condition." How would a truer view of things have affected that?

It is too bad that contemporary American anthropology (especially the sub-discipline archaeology) does not seem to understand this ideological origin of the field's present-day view of Ancient America and its living survivors. For, as things now stand, American anthropologists and archaeologists--encumbered with intellectual prejudices often not even perceived by themselves--have been most useful among the agents who have reconditioned the thinking of those survivors of Ancient America regarding their own origins. Now nearly everyone believes the old story which began with Acosta, and, of course, with Columbus. But we should not be surprised to find that the finest advocates of the United States of America's "Indian" ideology were not burdened with the need to believe their own rhetoric. Hrdlicka, for example, was a medical doctor. He pursued and published his "racial" hypotheses with vigor, and, attempting to find support for them, he assembled what may have been the world's largest collection of human skeletons. His collection of human skulls unearthed in Ancient American tombs was extensive. However, this evidence has shown, as contemporary scholars have confirmed, the complex composition of the original American population, and pointed to *numerous migrations* of peoples as its source.

This brings us back to the matter of the two principal shapes of human heads. The generous distribution of both shapes throughout the earth rather upsets the neat scheme of conventional, or 'popular' "race" classification. Of the five "races" popularly, or we might say *politically* conceived of--the "red," "brown," "yellow," "black," and "white"--only one, the "yellow" possesses a single head shape--round-headedness--exclusively. Given the United States ideology's position that "Indians" are rather recently derived from "Mongoloids," an insoluble problem emerges. The oldest human skulls found so far in the Americas are long-headed.

This indeed presents the ideology with a paradox, for zoologists agree that of the two head shapes, round-headedness is by far the newest development.[27] It would be a biological and temporal impossibility for the long-headed people of Ancient America to be descended from round-headed "Mongoloids." However, the worldwide distribution of round-headedness does show the ongoing and long standing migration of human populations. Zoologist Alfred S. Romer, in the fourth edition of his *The Vertebrate Story*, discusses the same problem of differing skull shapes in Ancient America which is mentioned by the archaeologist Gordon Willey.

Professor Romer--also a Harvard scholar like Professors Willey and Fell--remains somewhat mystified by the "race" idea, but he is obviously not encumbered by the prejudices of American anthropology regarding the peopling of Ancient America. He observes in his concluding chapter, "Human Races," that:

> We have every reason to believe that long-headed brunets, essentially Mediterranean, passed still farther to the northeast to become early, perhaps the earliest, inhabitants of the Americas. The Indians are usually classified as a subdivision of the Mongoloids, and rightly so, *it seems*, as regards the majority of the population. But there are Indians and Indians. *In many regions* there are groups which show few if any of the characteristics of typical Mongoloids and tend to have long heads, cheek bones less prominent than in typical Mongols, and other features suggesting the basic Mediterranean type. The earliest known Indians of the Southwest, the basket-makers who preceded the present tribes of that region, are known to have been markedly dolichocephalic [long-headed]; long-heads are abundant among the Indians of the Amazon

---

[27]

Romer, *op. cit.*, p. 384.

basin, and the Yahgans of far Tierra del Fuego are apparently of this type. Even in North America the eastern Indians, now nearly extinct, lacked a full Mongoloid development.

Presumably the peopling of the Americas did not consist of a single migration but of a series of successive waves of invasion. The last immigrants were definitely Mongoloid; the earlier ones, however, appear to have been essentially Mediterranean (and there may even have been some still earlier comers representing Australoid types).[28]

The historian James Bailey agrees with Romer that the Ancient people of Australia were among the earlier migrants to the Americas, but he adds that at the time they came, about 27,000 years ago, the people now known as Pygmies also began to migrate to the Americas.[29]

Barry Fell, who draws most of the evidence in his investigation of Ancient America from *epigraphy*--the decipherment of Ancient inscriptions in stone--has come to the same conclusion (although much less ambiguously) as that to which the skeletal evidence led Professor Romer: the settlers of Ancient America came from all over the world, in many different migrations.

Before moving on to discuss the Ancient Americas in some greater detail, I must, however, point out a few minor inaccuracies in Romer's account. First, the peopling of the Americas cannot justly be referred to as "waves of invasion" until *after* the Modern epoch commenced, in 1492. Second, the Ancient nations of eastern North America are far from being "now nearly extinct." During the period of the Modern conquest of the

---

28

Romer, *op. cit.*, p. 397. The *emphases* are mine.

29

Bailey, *op. cit.*, p. 273.

Woodlands region, some nations remained in place, and others departed westward to the plains, across the Mississippi River. Of those nations remaining in the east, many descendants remain today, principally from the Iroquoian, Algonquian and Muskogean language-culture groups; but there are also some from the Siouan group as well. Those nations moving across the Mississippi were principally from the Siouan and Algonquian groups but also included some from the Muskogean group too. The living descendants of these nations today number in the hundreds of thousands.

This is known because archaeologists have succeeded in associating the North American language-culture families with their Ancient heritage with some precision. For example, the mainly long-headed people of the Archaic phase of the Woodland tradition are known to have been of the Algonquian group, and the mostly long-headed Hopewell who merged with and succeeded the Adena culture--as well as the round-headed Adenans themselves--were of the Siouan group.[30] These Ancient nations of America remain well-represented in both the American west and east. In the plains west, the more well-known migrant Algonquian groups include the Cheyenne and Arapahoe of today. The Lakota-Dakota nations (commonly known as the "Sioux") of the Dakotas, Montana and Nebraska are the descendants of trans Mississippi migrant Siouan-speaking peoples who remain very much alive today.

Finally, as we have seen in the third chapter above, the "race" idea is a false concept, a rhetorical invention, useful only for the political purpose of the mass-destruction of human beings. In Romer's chapter on "race" he appears, at first, to be determined to follow the four- or five-fold division of humanity

---

[30] George E. Hyde, *Indians of the Woodlands, From Prehistoric Times to 1725* (Norman: University of Oklahoma Press, 1962), pp. 3-50.

into "races" established by Columbus and his colleagues, and
given "scientific" basis by Blumenbach and Buffon centuries
later, but by the end of the chapter he has presented his reader
with about twenty distinct "racial" groups.[31] This sort of system
of "racial" division is often followed by those among present-day
zoological scientists who still continue to even bother with
recognizing "race" at all. Some of these scientists have defined
upwards of a hundred "races." Such classification amounts to
little more than the recognition of real human variation, of this
variation's approximate--or statistical (but never perfect, or exact)-
-geographical concentrations, and the *arbitrary* division of this
variation into classifying groups. In this scientific sense the
political concept "race" is rendered utterly meaningless, and
indeed, the use of the word "race" in such a scientific context is
quite unnecessary. If Romer seems to be quite certain of the
existence of "races" in the passage from The Vertebrate Story
which I have quoted above (and in my discussion of his chapter
on human "races"), I must in all fairness include here his remarks
at the beginning of his chapter, "Human Races." He observes
that:

> ...crossing between races must obviously have been *a
> common occurrence* throughout human history....Probably
> there is not, and *never has been*, a really pure race....A pure
> racial type is a man-made ideal...[32]

We have now come to the point of discussing the Ancient
Americas--a world before "race" in the fullest sense of the
meaning--if only we suspend our conditioning[33] long enough to

---

[31]

Romer, *op. cit.*, pp. 387-411.

[32]

Ibid., pp. 378-379. The *emphases* are mine.

[33]

The rigid mental training resulting from indoctrination with rhetoric,
dogma, cant, or ideology.

consider it with an honest gaze. The difficulty of achieving such reality recognition in a conditioned mind was observed over three hundred years ago by Francis Bacon (a rare example of a Modern devotee of *philosophia*) when he wrote the following in his *New Atlantis:*

> You shall understand (that which perhaps you *will scarce think credible*) that about three thousand years ago, or somewhat more, the navigation of the world (especially for remote voyages) was greater than at this day....The Phoenicians, and specially the Tyrians, had great fleets; so had the Carthaginians their colony, which is yet further west. Toward the east the shipping of Egypt, and of Palestine, was likewise great. China also, and the great Atlantis (that you call America)...abounded then in tall ships.[34]

So that we may understand all of this, it is necessary to first return to the original peopling of the earth, for the story of humankind's seafaring and of trading between nations is vastly more Ancient than Columbus and the supporters of his rhetoric would allow us to know.

Paleoanthropologists uniformly agree that the first humans came into being a debatable number of millions of years ago in the tropical grassland region of, in all probability, Africa. These humans were not yet of our own species, but it is generally assumed that they led directly to it. They are therefore our earliest ancestors. Their habitat was tropical, they were omnivorous scavenger/hunters, and their complexion color was what we today would call "black." Although travel was difficult and slow in those times (when travel was exclusively pedestrian), by half a million years ago, the succeeding species of humans (still not our own, but still in the line of our 'family tree') had

---

[34]

Francis Bacon, *The Advancement of Learning, and New Atlantis* (London: Oxford University Press, 1974), p. 271. The *emphasis* is mine.

clearly come to inhabit much of the African and Eurasian land masses--this much is agreed upon by conventional paleoanthropologists.

This Ancient epoch may also very well be the moment when the Americas were *first* peopled--at a time commensurate with *the rest* of the world's continents. (This is, of course, excluding the island continents Australia and Antarctica, which had to be sailed to on watercraft.) Such, at any rate, was the conviction of geographer George F. Carter in 1956, when he was certain he had discovered man-made fireplaces which at the time were estimated to be five hundred thousand years old. Carter's fireplaces at the Texas Street site in San Diego, California, included the remains of burned animal bones, and crushed marine shells.[35]

By the time our well-known and closely-related 'cousin' species had arrived--*Homo sapiens neanderthalensis*--some 200,000 years ago, human populations were much larger and very well-established the world over (still with the exception of Australia and Antarctica). That human ancestors had by then arrived in the Americas is evidenced by archaeological discoveries made over the past few decades. Lewis Leakey, patriarch of the noted family of archaeologists which has discovered the fossil remains of some of the earliest-known human progenitors, discovered a very Ancient human tool industry at his Calico, California site.[36] The oldest deposits in which Leaky found tools were estimated to be nearly 120,000 years old.[37] In 1970, while he was visiting Brazil, Dr. Alan L. Bryan of the University of Alberta photographed a locally-

---

[35]

Brennan, *op. cit.*, pp. 133-134, and 146.

[36]

Brennan, *op. cit.*, pp. 147-148.

[37]

Ibid.

unearthed skull which he believed belongs to the human species *erectus*.[38] And near Taber, Alberta, Canada, a child's skeleton has been unearthed and initially estimated to be 60,000 years old.[39]

But during this most Ancient of times, world-wide contacts between human groups did not swiftly or easily occur, and great migrations must have been rare. Travel was still by foot, and climate was often very harsh. (It is eminently possible that it was during this long period when human groups were truly living in relative isolation from one another, that the range of variation in human appearances may have had its origin.) During the great Ice Ages, much of North America, for example, was under a sheet of glacial ice which at some places was two miles thick. In those times topography and coastline were considerably altered the world over. The sea level had dropped by sometimes as much as 600 feet as significant amounts of the earth's water became locked into enormous continental glaciers, and at mid-continent locations, the land sagged beneath its heavy burden of ice. During milder periods between the coldest extremes of glaciation, Eurasia and North America were one single enormous continent, as the lowered sea level had vanquished the shallow sea between Siberia and Alaska. At such times, human populations *could* relatively easily have moved either from or to the Americas.

At some time during the last 25,000 years of the great Ice Ages our own species, *Homo sapiens sapiens*, became predominant the world over. It is generally presumed that this

---

38

Thomas Y. Canby, "The Search For The First Americans," in *National Geographic* (Washington, D.C.: National Geographic Society, September, 1979), p. 351.

39

Richard S. MacNeish, "Introduction," in *Early Man in America* (San Francisco: W. H. Freeman and Company, 1973), p. 9.

emergence began to have some global impact starting at some time between 40,000 and 35,000 years ago. Our species, however, is considerably older than that.

Although the farther back in time we look, the less clearly we may see the shape of Ancient human cultures, a surprising amount *is* known about human life, going back about half a million years. For example, that long ago the species of humans-- *Homo erectus*--preceding our own, knew the use of fire. Those people lived in extended family groups, sometimes sought shelter in caves and rock overhangs, and made tools of wood, bone, and stone. Although their lifestyle most probably was "usufructian," that is to say, hunter-gather/scavenger, they were skilled big-game hunters as well. Their prehistoric fireplaces have yielded evidence that their diet included elephant, rhinoceros, ox, stag, horse, pig, hippopotami, sheep, baboon, and possibly even some of their own kind.[40]

Neanderthalensis, now considered to be a species closely-related to our own, but not on our direct line of descent, co-existed with the earliest members of our own *sapiens sapiens* species.[41] *Neanderthalensis* was prodigiously skillful at the usufructian and big game hunting lifestyles. These people lived in larger communities than *Homo erectus*. *Neanderthalensis* is known to have extended the permanent frontier of human settlement further northward at the very time when glacial ice sheets were bearing southward on the Eurasian and North American continents, and this advance was made possible by

[40]

Grahame Clark, *The Stone Age Hunters* (New York: McGraw-Hill Book Company, 1967), p. 37.

[41]

Laura Tangley, "Not so close, after all," in *U.S. News & World Report* (Washington, D.C.: U.S. News & World Report Inc., July 21, 1997), p. 29, and Philip Elmer-DeWitt, "No Sex, Please," in *Time* (New York: Time Inc., July 21, 1997), p. 58.

their possession of skin clothing in addition to fire.[42] The most well-known tool making tradition of *neanderthalensis'* culture, known as Mousterian, lasted from roughly 70,000 to 32,000 years ago. Mousterian and "Mousteroid" culture elements have been found across Eurasia and the length of Africa, in Australia and to date most likely do exist, but go unrecognized, in the Americas. Archaeologist Jacques Bordaz describes the culture of neanderthalensis in some detail:

> Neanderthals often lived in caves or rock shelters which protected them from the elements. In some instances, remains of stone paving and post holes indicate that they sometimes built rough constructions, probably of skins or branches, held up by rows of posts set near the entrance to a cave. But open-air sites are quite common; the summers must have been relatively warm in the middle northern latitudes. The open-air sites sometimes show rings of debris pushed into rough circles probably serving as walls to support roofs made of skins or branches.

> One of the most interesting of these Mousterian sites is Moldova, in Soviet Moldavia, where a hut was found with a wall made of skulls, shoulder blades, tusks, and bones of mammoths. It enclosed an area of approximately 20 by 26 feet containing the remains of fifteen small hearths.

> It is also from Neanderthals that we have the first evidence of aesthetic considerations divorced from functional ones.

> At arch-sur-Cure, 100 miles southeast of Paris, Professor Leroi-Gourhan found a few objects in Mousterian layers that had apparently been collected by Neanderthals as

---

[42]

Clark, *op. cit.*, p. 41.

curiosities: the fossil cast of a gastropod shell, a spherical polypide, and a few nodules of iron pyrite stuck together.

Tata, a Mousterian site in Hungary, yielded incised pebbles and an oval piece of mammoth ivory covered with ochre pigments.

Pieces of ochre and lumps of black manganese dioxide, probably used for skin decoration, are actually quite common in Mousterian sites. Of particular interest have also been the cave burials of flexed bodies, sometimes covered with stones, the first available evidence for funerary practices.[43]

The existence of funerary practices strongly suggests that *neanderthalensis* held spiritual beliefs. These funerary practices also contributed to the preservation of *neanderthalensis* remains, and hence, have made possible a more detailed knowledge of their material life. For example, many of the *neanderthalensis* individuals whose fossilized remains have been unearthed were discovered to have been individuals who had lived to between 40 and 60 years of age--a considerably advanced age for the time. Also, rare among these people was an individual who had not sustained, at one time or another in their life, at least one major traumatic injury. An interpretation of this has been forwarded by anthropologist Erik Trinkaus. He suggests that:

> ...The presence of so many injuries in a prehistoric human group, many of which were debilitating and sustained years before death, shows that individuals were taken care of long after their economic usefulness to the social group had ceased. It is perhaps no accident that among Neanderthals, for the first time in history, people lived to a comparatively

---

[43]

Jacques Bordaz, *Tools of the Old and New Stone Age* (Garden City, New York: The Natural History Press, 1970), pp. 48-49.

old age. We also find among the Neanderthals the first intentional burials of the dead, some of which involved offerings. Despite the hardships of their life style, the Neanderthals apparently had a deep-seated respect and concern for each other.[44]

Not all that much unlike ourselves--even to their lifespan-- were our 'cousins', these *neanderthalensis* people. Their posture was fully erect, as is our own, and their brains were as large as, if not a bit larger than, our own. Although their bones were more robust than ours are, and they were considerably more heavily-muscled than we are, a *neanderthalensis* individual dressed in a contemporary business suit would go unnoticed in any Modern city today. Yet as close to our species as *neanderthalensis* was, the archaeological evidence strongly suggests that they had not developed certain cultural abilities common to our own species. They apparently did not know of written language, the use of domesticated plants and animals, the use of metals, and they probably had no water craft. All of these cultural developments (or at least their perfection) fall within the life span of our own species, *Homo sapiens sapiens*.

It was at the *dawn* of this age, the age of *our* humanity, much longer ago than we--thanks in part to Columbus and his rhetoric-- are able to believe, that the great and continuous age of human discovery commenced, and for the first time ever in human existence, cultures mingled over the vastest of distances. This we may know by virtue of the settlement of Australia, well over 30,000 years ago.[45] For although the earth's sea level dropped by

---

44

Erik Trinkaus, "Hard Times among the Neanderthals," in *Natural History* (New York: American Museum of Natural History, December, 1978), p. 63.

45

As noted in Geoffrey Blainey, *Triumph of the Nomads: A History of Ancient Australia* (Melbourne: Sun Books, 1976), p. 6, fossil human remains have been found in Australia which have been dated at 25,000 and 38,000 years

around one third of a mile during the Ice Ages, the Lombok Strait between southeastern Eurasia and Australia was still at that time several miles deep. In fact, throughout the life span of *the entire human genus*, Australia has always been surrounded by very deep-water seas, and the only way for people to get there was on water craft. Since New Guinea and Australia were a single land mass during most periods of glaciation, people could have taken sea routes to it going either above or below the equator, but whichever route they took, it was still necessary for them to sail a considerable distance into the open sea, *out of sight of land*, before reaching their destination there. The voyages of these early seagoing people were no simple matter.

They traveled from the Indian Ocean to the South Pacific, and then to the North Pacific and North America. At the earliest stage of their voyaging it has been surmised that they followed coastal and island-hopping routes. Yet such coastal sea-voyaging, as experienced mariners know, is--due to treacherous shoals, reefs, sudden storms and shifting, unpredictable currents--the most dangerous form of all ocean travel. Much, much safer and more dependable is transoceanic travel on the great 'conveyor' currents of the earth's oceans, such as the Canary Current, the Gulfstream, or the Japan Current. It is reasonable to presume that it was the settlers of Australia who were the first--and not Christopher Columbus--to discover the use of such transoceanic 'conveyors'.[46] Recent history has for example recorded the

---

old; early man sites there have yielded dates of 31,500 and 38,000 years old. However, it has recently been asserted that two migrations, one northern, and one southern, first settled the Island Continent, *perhaps as long ago as 50,000 years*. See Louise E. Levathes, "The Land Where the Murray Flows," in *National Geographic* (Washington, D.C.: National Geographic Society, August, 1985), p. 269.

[46]

Although coastlines were subject to considerable fluctuation during the various phases of the Ice Ages, the force which sets the flow of the ocean

predictable regularity with which the Japan Current has conveyed shipwrecked Japanese fishermen alive and well on their survival rafts to the northwest coast of North America. The discovery of sufficient fossil remains of the first Australians in American soil to be unprejudicially recognized by such eminent zoologists as Romer, constitutes evidence of a significantly large migration. It is certainly logical to conclude that such a migration was conducted by these seagoing people in their water craft, rather than on foot. This is especially so, since their travels had brought them to the embarkation point of the Japan Current's journey to North America. The first settlers of Australia then were the first immigrants--the first among many--to the Americas, but as we have seen, they were far from being the first people of the Americas.

There can be no doubt that in part, trade was a great motivator of the movements of the first Australians. The earliest evidence of human trade--and of mining as well (the mining of precious stones, ores and metals being among the greatest stimuli for trading)--may be inferred by the plentiful presence of ochers and metallic oxides in *neanderthalensis* burial sites, even in areas where these could not have been easily obtained by those people. That human cultures were in some contact, even that long ago, and that they shared technical knowledge with one another, is demonstrated by the global spread of Mousterian culture elements in the epoch of *neanderthalensis*.

It is from the era when seafaring emerged, however, that we begin to have the clearest view of early human mining and trading activity. The Lion Cave site at the Ngwenya Iron Mine in Swaziland has yielded, through radiocarbon dating, an age of

---

currents in motion--the very rotation of the earth--has ever remained constant. So, although the starting and ending points of these currents have changed slightly with changes in coastal configurations, nothing has ever stopped their steady flow.

around 40,000 years for the earliest mining which took place there.[47] At that time, people were mining for hematite, or red ochre, the very substance which, by about 30,000 years ago, had become a major commodity on a worldwide basis. Dating of the site showed the Ngwenya Mine to have been in continuous use up until well into the Christian era. Similar evidence of early mining--for flints, cherts, and whetstones--has been found throughout Eurasia, Africa, and the Americas.[48] The presence of these kinds of Stone Age commodities great distances away from where they naturally occurred testifies to the existence of the far-flung trade routes of Ancient Stone Age humanity.

The global spread of Mousteroid culture, and specifically of the ceremonial use of red ochre, are facts which, I have said, support the notion that ideas are, and have been, shared by cultures on a worldwide basis for a long, long time. This, a phenomenon which is still going on in our present-day Modern world, is known as cultural diffusion. If our capacity to effectively use our minds had not been crippled by Christopher Columbus' mendacious rhetoric, we would be able to grasp in an instant the fact that the use of water craft for local and long-distance voyaging was an idea which literally had the means of its own cultural diffusion built into itself. The use of water craft was an idea which virtually sailed around the world more than three hundred centuries before Columbus was born.

As if to underscore the diffusion of water craft technology, there emerges the globally-widespread colonization of a second, somewhat younger group of seagoing people, the short-statured people known as the Pygmies. That these people learned and used marine technology is attested to by their presence on the

---

[47]

Raymond A. Dart, "About the Earliest Mining," in Bailey *op. cit.*, p. 14.

[48]

Ibid., pp. 13 and 15.

Andaman Islands in the Indian Ocean, in Australia, and in the archaeological record of North America. In addition, they are also found in three distinct groups in the equatorial Congo region of Africa,[49] in Sri Lanka, in southern India, in Sumatra, in the Malay Peninsula, in Southeast Asia, and in the Philippine Islands. Excluding Africa, the migrations of the Pygmies indeed seem to be quite parallel to those of the first Australians. Undoubtedly these seagoing people were engaged in trade also, but, like the Australians, no evidence exists to date to tell us when they quit the business or why.

In the case of the Pygmies, however, there is evidence that they continued to engage in commerce for some tens of millennia. Such, at least, would seem to be the testimony of a large jade pendant (pectoral) of Ancient Maya manufacture. This five and three quarters inches wide plaque, made around the year 750 C.E., shows two seated figures, carved in excellent detail.[50] One is a Maya nobleman sitting cross-legged on a throne. He is leaning over to his right, and is clearly addressing his attention to the other figure, who is also seated cross-legged right next to the throne, and on the same level with it. The other person, much smaller than the Maya, sitting straight-backed with his arms folded on his chest is unmistakably a Pygmy. Furthermore, he is clearly dressed as a foreigner, and not as a Maya: he is wearing a turban, a short-sleeved pullover-type shirt, and knee-length

---

[49]

Some anthropologists have argued that because they possess differing blood type groupings than do other Pygmies, the African groups do not share a common origin with them. The question, however, essentially remains unsettled.

[50]

S. K. Lothrop, *Treasures of Ancient America: Pre-Columbian Art from Mexico to Peru* (New York: Rizzoli International Publications, Inc., 1979), pp. xiii, and 116-117.

trousers. Nothing in the demeanor of either figure indicates that the shorter person is a servant or a captive; in fact, the pendant clearly indicates a meeting between two free persons.

Yet the exact nature of this, and other similar encounters in Ancient America must ultimately remain a mystery. For the book-burning Roman priests who accompanied the Spanish conquerors of Mexico and Central America eight hundred years after the pendant was made, did their job of destroying previous existing records all too well. However, since the Maya, like the Pygmies, were very interested in the business of trade, it is most reasonable to assume that trade was the business of the meeting depicted on that jade plaque.

It is out of this great epoch of free trade, lasting in some parts of the world perhaps longer than 30,000 years, that one of the oldest myths shared by many Ancient nations the world over had its origin. This is the myth of the Golden Age, the time when all of humanity met in friendship and tranquility. This, and other myths of the Ancient world were, as we shall find, in actuality poetic condensations of great and complex past events committed in this manner to eternal memory.

So it was that over the tens of millennia, following the lead of the settlers of Australia, and then of the Pygmies, other peoples joined into the flow of international trans oceanic trade. This age of human discovery did not begin to become obstructed until the Roman Empire invented "the law of the seas." And the waters were not finally stilled until Rome's Modern successor, Spain, invented the "Age of Discovery." For the "Age of Discovery" was in actuality an age of conquest, an age of unselfconscious and unrestrained ethnocide, and the beginning of the end of worldwide free trade.

As the last Ice Age gradually came to an end, humanity turned to the seas not only for trade, but for food as well, for the world's altered climate had rather adversely affected the availability of the herds of big game animals which had been an important source of protein for many human societies at the time. As anthropologist Raymond Dart sees it:

> The basic need of Mesolithic and Neolithic mankind during the last 10,000 years B.C. in his Neolithic and Mesolithic phases was better axes for making improved water-vehicles, such as canoes and sailing ships out of bark and wood furnished by the biggest and lightest trees available. Dependence upon fishing rather than the diminishing hunting available during the last Ice Age had been facing all the people inhabiting Europe, the Near East and North Africa through the preceding 30,000 years. The love of shells and fish vertebrae for personal decoration, the invention of the harpoon and of the harpoon (or spear) thrower--known in America as the atlatl--are manifestations of Aurignacian i.e. early Paleolithic existence. Both of them are meaningless without aquatic attachments such as floats and aquatic vehicles of some type, such as are also world-wide in their distribution.[51]

Also early Paleolithic in its origin and world-wide in distribution are the beginnings of the human symbolization of abstract ideas and verbal expressions in visual form--the beginnings, in other words, of writing. Although such *neanderthalensis* artifacts as the inscribed pebbles of Tata, and even much older finds (for example, an over 235,000 year-old intricately-engraved bone, recently discovered in a cave in France) undoubtedly held great significance for their Stone Age owners, present-day scientists, recognizing the impossibility of correctly interpreting the meaning of such objects, have refrained from assigning them a place in the development of written language. However, it is a different matter entirely in the case of engraved bones and stones, and carved figurines and paintings

---

[51]

Raymond Dart in Bailey, *op. cit.*, pp. 15-16.

made by the people who lived between 35,000 and 10,000 years ago. These human artifacts are most abundantly known from western Eurasia (principally because the search for them has been the most intensive there); but they also have been found to the east, and to the south, in Africa, and in Australia, and quite recently an example has come to light in North America.[52]

Years of careful study of artifacts such as these by Harvard researcher Alexander Marshack has illustrated what may be the most productive means of interpreting them. In his investigation, Marshack subjected the objects he studied to microscopic examination and infrared and ultraviolet light photography. These techniques revealed details of workmanship which had never before been seen by previous researchers, and the results of Marshack's work are rather astounding. Paleolithic humanity appears to have been extremely interested in, among other things, the passage of lunar time, and the repetition of seasonal cycles as reflected in plant growth and animal migration and behavior patterns. Furthermore, Paleolithic people made symbolic notations of such things in a somewhat conventionalized manner. Although these archaic visual representations of ideas such as the passage of time, which otherwise would have been subjects of speech, are not writing in the 'proper' sense, they clearly represent the origins of that human ability which had fully-developed by around 5,000 years ago. As Marshack puts it:

> Apparently as far back as 30,000 B.C. the Ice Age hunter of western Europe was using a system of notation that was already evolved, complex, and sophisticated, a tradition

---

[52]

The American example of this class of objects of archaic human manufacture, discovered at a site in Mexico, was determined to be 22,000 years old. It is an engraved mastodon bone bearing the superimposed images of a mastodon and a great cat. The bone bears abundant additional line engraving. See Canby, *op. cit.*, p. 350.

that would seem to have been thousands of years old by this point. Apparently it was also in use by other types of modern man, such as Combe Capelle man of the East Gravettian culture in Czechoslovakia and Russia and by other peoples and subcultures in Italy and Spain, as we shall see. The tradition seems so widespread that the question arises as to whether its beginnings may not go back to the period of Neanderthal man.

What is significant...is that this notation was a cognitive, time-factored, and time-factoring technique.

These facts are so new and important they require the widest possible interpretation and evaluation. They raise profound questions concerning the evolved intelligence and cognitive abilities of the human species. We cannot, for instance, assume that Ice Age man was an "astronomer" or a "scientist" in the modern sense, or even that he used a modern system of arithmetic. It is clear, too, that the notations we have analyzed are not yet writing as we know it. Nevertheless, the roots of science and of writing seem to be here. Apparently we have archaeological evidence for the use of the same basic *cognitive processes* that appear later in science and writing.[53]

With the discovery of a sample of such symbolization in America, we must recognize the global manifestation of this human activity, and the parallel, intertwined, and contemporaneous development of all human cultures. Such recognition will enable us to dispel the hold upon our minds of

---

[53]

Alexander Marshack, *The Roots of Civilization: The Cognitive Beginnings of Man's First Art, Symbol and Notation* (New York: McGraw-Hill Book Company, 1972), pp. 57-58.

yet another rhetorical device--the concept of "pre-" and "non-literate" societies--which was invented first by the Romans, and then perfected by their heirs, the Spanish book-burning priests.[54]

So it was, some 10,000 years ago then, that the last Ice Age came to a gradual end. And as the warmer climate of the earth released water which had been locked in the great glaciers into the world's oceans, the sea level rose very appreciably. Australia, for example, may have lost as much as one seventh of its land mass to the rising ocean.[55] Coastlines everywhere were altered tremendously. It was from this period of human existence that another myth shared by many nations the world over had its origin. This is the tale of a founding culture hero who escapes the ravages of a Great Flood on a water craft. Noah is but one name for this hero.

One crucial piece of the puzzle about humanity's maritime past came to light in the mid-1950[s]. The process of rediscovery really began in 1929, when in the old Imperial Palace in Constantinople, Turkish scholars discovered an early Modern map, dated 1513, whose authorship was attributed to the Admiral Piri Re'is. The chart contained margin notations indicating that it had been supplemented by information about "new lands discovered by the infidel Colon," and it was titled "Map of the Seven Seas." In 1956 a Turkish naval officer presented a copy of this map to the U.S. Navy Hydrographic Office. Although the map had been known for over a quarter of a century, and a copy of it already was in the Library of Congress, its reappearance created a new flurry of interest.

----

[54]

To be sure, on every continent there are--and from time immemorial have been--"backwoods" cultures, simpler folk knowing no system of writing *of their own.* But as a *widespread* phenomenon in human societies, "pre-" and "non-literacy" is a fantasy invented by rhetoricians.

[55]

Blainey, *op. cit.*, p. 10.

Intrigued by the notion that a map could so accurately show newly-known lands this quickly after their 'discovery', Charles Hapgood and his history of science class at Keene State College began a detailed study of it. The map of Piri Re'is was remarkable on several accounts. It showed a lengthy portion of the South American coastline at a time when that region had not yet been 'discovered'. Even more startling was the fact that the Piri Re'is chart showed the eastern coastline of South America and the western coastline of Africa not only in their correct latitudinal relationship, but also in their correct *longitudinal* relationship. This discovery was quite unanticipated, because when the map apparently was made, mariners and cartographers were not yet able to calculate longitude with *any* degree of accuracy. By the time Hapgood and his students began their study of the map, its authenticity and dating had been absolutely verified. But historians, not knowing what to do with such an anomalous bit of information largely left it alone.

Hapgood and his students' study of the map led to further intriguing disclosures. One portion of the Caribbean section of the map had been rotated, a lengthy portion of the eastern coast of South America was duplicated, the map was torn--indicating that a significant portion of "The Seven Seas" was missing, but might indeed have been a part of the original document--and extending from the southern tip of South America there were what appeared to be features of the Antarctic coastline. The Piri Re'is chart had every indication of having been pieced together from even older maps, and appeared to have been compiled by an individual or individuals not entirely familiar with the geographic features contained in the older, original charts from which the Piri Re'is copy was made.

At this point in the investigation, Hapgood sought further research expertise. He submitted facsimile copies of the map and some of his group's preliminary calculations to the M.I.T. Mathematics Department to see if the mathematical basis on which the map's projections were drawn could be determined. He also submitted copies of the map to the Cartographic Section of the U.S. Air Force's Strategic Air Command to see if the geographic features indicated on the map could be verified. The results he obtained were most surprising.

The map was drawn on a plane trigonometric projection (plane trigonometry was not 'invented' until long after the original charts from which the map was compiled were drawn), and the land forms shown on the map were *very* accurate, including a section of the Antarctic coastline. The section of Antarctic coastline was shown as if it was *ice free*.

These preliminary results led Hapgood's study group into the investigation of other early maps. They next turned their attention to the early Renaissance maps of the Atlantic Ocean drawn by Gerhard Mercator, Oronteus Finaeus, and Hadji Ahmed. Both the map drawn by Finaeus in 1531, and one made by Mercator in 1538, indicate an Antarctic continent. The location of this land mass on Mercator's map is near the equator, and hence, is quite incorrect. However, both Finnaeus' and Ahmed's maps give the Antarctic continent a polar location. Indeed, Ahmed's 1559 chart (which, like Finnaeus', is actually a world map), although showing Ptolemaic conventions in its representation of the eastern hemisphere, has a "surprisingly modern look" in its depiction of the Americas and Antarctica. The maps also indicate geographic features in Antarctica such as mountain ranges, river valleys, and coastline, including the Ross Sea (rather than the Ross Ice Shelf).

Hapgood's research group next investigated a series of maps of western Eurasia, North Africa, and the Mediterranean Sea known as the Portolano maps. The Portolano maps were used by mariners in the Mediterranean region during the Medieval period of Eurasian history. As is the case with the Piri Re'is Map, the Portolano charts are very accurate in their representation of geographic land forms. Indeed, the quality of the Portolano maps surpasses the work of Ptolemy and that of the Renaissance map makers alike. These maps too are drawn on trigonometric projections, and very precisely represent latitudinal and *longitudinal* relationships between geographic points. Both trigonometry and the accurate finding of longitude were unknown during the Eurasian Middle Ages. Most of the Portolano charts show a number of islands in the Aegean Sea where none exist today.

Hapgood was beginning to *very* strongly suspect that the Piri Re'is and Portolano charts were derived from originals of great Antiquity which had been reworked and compiled in the library at Alexandria in perhaps the fourth century B.P. Both the Portolanos and the Piri Re'is had zero meridians running through Alexandria. Hapgood and his students were, however, no closer to determining who the authors of the original charts had been. Trigonometry had not yet been reinvented by the Greeks during the fourth century B.P., yet these charts were clearly based on *spherical* and plane trigonometric projections.

The final major focus of Hapgood and his students was an 11th Century C.E. map of China's river system. This map comes from a time when China's interest was fixed exclusively on internal matters, and does not even represent any of the Chinese coastline. However, this map too turned out to have been based on a much older chart. Once again, it was drawn on a trigonometric projection, had geographic points in accurate latitudinal and longitudinal relationships, and accurately represented the courses of China's major rivers.

When Hapgood's research group submitted facsimiles of the maps and their research conclusions to the Cartographic Section of the U.S. Strategic Air Command to be cross-checked, they were surprised to learn that the geographic features represented in these maps were indeed accurate and true, and that some of them, namely mountain ranges and river valleys in Antarctica had recently been 'discovered' during the scientific activities of the International Geophysical Year of 1958. This compelled them to conclude that Antarctica had been mapped a very long time ago, during a period when it was relatively ice-free. The research group, however, did not know if there had ever been such a time on the Antarctic continent during the lifetime of the human species. To their surprise, they learned that in 1949, during one of the Byrd Antarctic Expeditions, seabed sediment core samplings drilled through the Ross Ice Shelf had shown that there had been at least two such ice-free periods within recent geologic history. One ended six thousand years ago, and the other ended thirty thousand years ago.

The conclusions which Hapgood and his study group were drawn to were unavoidable:

> As our studies extended from map to map we accumulated more and more evidence of the ancient existence, in an era long before Greece, of spherical trigonometry and its application to mapmaking.[56]

> In Greek times mathematics was in advance of mechanical instrumentation: There was no instrument for easily and correctly determining the longitude of places. However the Piri Re'is and the other maps we went on to study, seemed to suggest that such an instrument or instruments has once existed, and had been used by people who knew very closely the correct size of the earth. Moreover, it looks as if this people had visited most of the earth. They seem to have been quite well acquainted with the Americas, and to have mapped the coasts of Antarctica.[57]

---

[56]

Charles H. Hapgood, *Maps of the Ancient Sea Kings: Evidence of Advanced Civilization in the Ice Age*, (Philadelphia: Chilton Company, 1966), p. 183.

[57]

Ibid., p. 182.

During this age when the earth grew warmer, humanity turned not only to the seas, but to the land as well. For somewhere on this planet (we may never know exactly where) people at that time began to learn the arts of domesticating plants and animals. Scholars had for some time believed that the Middle East was the cradle of this agricultural revolution. However, the recent discovery by Professor Wilhelm Solheim of the University of Hawaiʻi of a 10,000 year-old farming village site in Thailand has reopened the debate. Yet, wherever it may have first occurred, the concept of settled village life based upon domesticated crops and animals spread around the world in less than three thousand years. Farming was established at Jarmo in the Middle East around 9,000 years ago. And the first use of hand-sown maize appears in Middle America at least about 7,200 years ago.

During roughly the same period human cultures--the world over--began to discover the use of metals. At the Çayönü village site in southeastern Turkey, copper objects have been unearthed and dated at 9,000 years old. In North America, the earliest date obtained so far for the Algonquian Old Copper Culture of the Lake Superior, Michigan and Huron basins is around 7,550 years old.

Gradually, the world round, the traditions of agriculture and metalworking diffused northward and southward, becoming fully global, as had the traditions of mining, seafaring, trade, and incipient writing (it must be surmised that the most Ancient of cartographers who mapped the ice-free coastline of Antarctica, and used plane and spherical trigonometry did of course have a system of writing, but that system, unlike their sea charts, is apparently lost to us). Within a few thousand more years writing proper had been developed on a widespread basis, and so too had the alloying of tin and copper. The Bronze Age and the Ancient epoch had commenced.

At this time, the peoples of the Ancient world tell us directly, abundantly, and in a variety of different ways the numerous details of the last three or so thousand years of the golden age of world commerce, before the advent of Rome and the new tradition of ethnocide which Rome established.

A converging body of scholarship provides a firm basis for our knowledge of Bronze Age Antiquity, and in particular, Bronze Age Antiquity in the Americas. James Bailey discusses science, technology, politics, and seafaring during pre-, early, and middle Bronze Age times. Thor Heyerdahl describes water craft technology, culture-sharing (especially in terms of botanical items, and ocean travel routes from early to post-Bronze Age times. Barry Fell studies the original first-hand accounts of the many Ancient North American nations. He deciphers the records which over the past four thousand years have been chiseled by them onto rocks, cliffs, cave walls, and stone tablets across the continent. And Alexander von Wuthenau presents the 'photographic', or visual first-hand accounts of the Ancient Central and South Americans--the pre- through post-Bronze Age self portraits which those very people made of themselves.

The global spread of domesticated plants, known to have been first cultivated by certain people at a certain place and time, tells much about the past movements of peoples and cultures. Consider for example, the case of weaving (long-linted) cotton. Wild cotton existed in the Americas a long, long time before the human genus, Homo, ever came into being. The genetic structure of this wild cotton--which does not produce the long lint fibers necessary for cloth weaving--is unique; it possesses thirteen small chromosomes. Similarly, the genetic structure of both the wild and domesticated long-linted cottons of Africa and Eurasia is also unique; they all possess thirteen large chromosomes. About 5,000 years ago, domesticated cotton suddenly appeared in Peru, along with the art of weaving, the loom, and other tools associated with weaving. The domesticated American cotton which appeared at that time also has a distinctive and unique genetic structure; it has thirteen large, and thirteen small chromosomes, for a total of twenty six chromosomes all together. There is only one way for this to have occurred: five thousand years ago, or longer, people from the Middle East or Africa shared the secret of cotton weaving with the people of Peru. They brought cotton seeds, or plants, across the Atlantic Ocean to South America, and then across the continent to Peru. There, they or the Ancient Peruvians crossed the imported plant with the local variety, and produced the unique domesticated American cotton plant--a hybrid with twenty six chromosomes.

But the story does not end there. There is no native cotton to be found in Australia, New Guinea, or in most of Melanesia--or in other words, in the intervening territory between Polynesia and eastern Eurasia. However, domesticated American cotton was found growing wild on all of the Polynesian islands, eastward to the Fiji Islands, by the first Modern conquerors to arrive there.[58] The Ancient Americans, it appears, brought cotton to the Polynesian islands at a very early date. In fact, in the centuries and even millennia preceding Columbus' voyages, numerous crops changed hands across the Atlantic and Pacific Oceans; and they crossed in all directions.

American maize arrived in West Africa at around 1100 C.E., and then was introduced to East Africa, South Africa, India and China, and finally to Greece, Russia, and the nations to the west.[59] The common garden bean, of Mediterranean origin, was introduced to Peru in Ancient times.[60] Conversely, cultivation of

---

[58]

Heyerdahl, *op. cit.*, pp. 77-78, and 237-239.

[59]

Van Sertima, *op. cit.*, pp. 240-251.

[60]

Heyerdahl, *op. cit.*, pp. 74-75.

the sword bean, or jack bean, a Peruvian domesticate, spread eastward across the Atlantic to Mediterranean lands.[61] The African bottle gourd was introduced to the Americas at a very early date, and then spread to Polynesia; and the banana diffused along a similar route as well.[62] Numerous plants of American origin were passed on to Polynesia, and beyond, to Southeast Asia. The coconut and yam traveled the greatest distance, to Southeast Asia and Indonesia.[63] The sweet potato and hibiscus were widely cultivated from the Atlantic shores of America, to Polynesia in the Pacific.[64] A few centuries before the opening of the Modern Era, the tropical Eurasian plants breadfruit, wet-land taro, and sugar cane were introduced to Polynesia.[65]

A number of other native American crops were planted on various Polynesian islands in Ancient times: on Easter Island there were chili pepper, tomato, pineapple, manioc, tobacco, arrowroot, dry-land taro, totora reed, and the medicinal *Polygonum acuminatum*.[66] In the Marquesas Islands there were pineapple, papaya, and dry-land taro.[67] Dry-land taro was also

---

[61]

Ibid., p. 75.

[62]

Ibid., pp. 75-76, 78-80, 235-236, and 237.

[63]

Ibid., pp. 234 and 252.

[64]

Ibid., pp. 233 and 239-241.

[65]

Ibid., p. 241.

[66]

Ibid., pp. 243-245, and 251.

[67]

Ibid., pp. 246-247, and 251.

cultivated in Tahiti.[68]   There were pineapple, husk tomato, and Mexican poppy in Hawaii.[69]   And in the region bordering Melanesia, *Heliconia bihai* and yam bean were grown.[70]

Certain species of domestic animals also traveled the sea lanes from continent to continent in Ancient times. An Egyptian-Mesopotamian breed of dog came to Polynesia *via* Mexico and Peru.[71] The pig and chicken entered Polynesia from the opposite direction, via Southeast Asia.[72] The American parrot was present at the Polynesian atoll of Takaroa in Ancient times.[73]   And the gerfalcon of the North American arctic was to be seen in Medieval royal courts from the Middle East, westward to Norway.[74]

Besides plants and animals, other culture items tell us a great deal about the busy pathways of the seas in Ancient times, thousands of years ago.   About 4,500 years ago, a tradition of ceramics-making suddenly appeared at the fishing village of Valdivia, Ecuador.   There was no pre-ceramic developmental period preceding the Valdivian pottery complex, and the earliest pottery discovered there showed an interesting peculiarity of construction.   Early Valdivia ware exhibits advanced decoration

---

[68]

Ibid., p. 251.

[69]

Ibid., pp. 248-249.

[70]

Ibid., pp. 251-252.

[71]

Ibid., pp. 73-74, and 230.

[72]

Ibid., p. 230.

[73]

Ibid., pp. 229-230.

[74]

Ibid., p. 138.

techniques overlaid on a beginner's (clumsy, that is) style of pot construction. Clearly, at Valdivia, pottery-building and a set of fully-developed ceramics decoration motifs were introduced from somewhere else. But where? The answer comes from across the Pacific Ocean, on the Japanese islands of Honshu and Kyushu, where the fishing village culture of Jomon flourished for more than five thousand years. Beginning around 9,000 years ago, the Jomon ceramics tradition is among the oldest in the world (just as the Valdivian ceramics tradition is among the oldest in the Americas). At the time when ceramics were introduced to Valdivia, however, Jomon and Valdivia ceramics were an excellent match "in vessel shape and decorative techniques and in construction methods.[75] The Jomon people, in other words, brought the art of ceramics across the Pacific Ocean to the people of Valdivia.[76]

In the Americas, as in all the rest of the Ancient world, such sharing of cultural knowledge and technique was quite common. Illustrative of this is a list of 53 culture traits compiled by Thor Heyerdahl. Taken as a complex interrelated whole, these traits are considered to typify the Ancient Mesopotamian culture of the Middle East--and they also, so taken, are considered to typify the Ancient cultures of Mexico and Peru. Some items on the list include:

A fully developed system of script...; Paper manufacture...and the production of books filled with polychrome hieroglyphic inscriptions...; The...practice of mummifying deceased persons of high rank by evisceration through the anus and use of certain resins, cotton padding, and wrappings; Great skill in the difficult magico-surgical

---

[75]

Brennan, *op. cit.*, p. 344.

[76]

Ibid., pp. 342-348.

trepanning of the skull bone of living persons, with a high percentage of survival among patients; Identical types of leather and rope sandals; The importance of the first century of the third millennium B.C. as an ancestral beginning;

and not the least important,

The appearance on both sides of the Atlantic of the same favorite kind of watercraft: ocean-going reed ships with sickle-shaped, maritime lines, a composite bundle body ingeniously lashed together with a continuous spiral cord, and a canvas sail hoisted on a double-legged mast straddling the two main reed bundles.[77]

Indeed, water craft of a variety of similar types were in universal use perhaps even well over 10,000 years ago. Such vessels are based upon one of the oldest mainstays of maritime design: a wash-through cargo platform built of a bundle of self-buoyant materials lashed together with a binding cord. Among this class of vessels are canoes, outriggers and rafts made of rolls of buoyant tree bark. Such vessels were used until the last century in Australia and parts of Polynesia. Of similar principle are large oceangoing rafts built of balsa wood logs, or of other wood of high buoyancy. Water craft such as these were a mainstay of shipping in Pacific coast South, Central, and North America. They were also used in Polynesia. And they were favored by Ancient fishermen of Peru and Ecuador for oceanic fishing expeditions which sometimes lasted several weeks. Most popular, however, were the reed bundle water craft. In fact, these kinds of water craft are still being used in Polynesia, in America, in Africa, in the Middle East, and as far east on the southern coast of Eurasia as the Bay of Bengal.

---

[77]

Heyerdahl, *op. cit.*, 84-91.

The cargo and crew carrying capacities of Ancient shipping were very impressive. Nearly 3,500 years ago an Egyptian river barge was built to carry a load (the two stone obelisks of Queen Hatsheput) weighing 1,500 *tons*. At around the same time the vessels of Ugarit had reached 500 tons displacement.[78] The seagoing reed ships of Ancient Uruk commonly carried loads of around 100 tons.[79] At the close of the third Egyptian dynasty, Pharaoh Dseferu over the course of two years commissioned the construction of sixty ships 100 feet long, and four ships 170 feet long.[80] The larger vessels of China's Sung Dynasty, circa 999 C.E., were divided into watertight compartments, and could carry six hundred people, plus "a year's supply of grain."[81] In 1405, the flagship of the Chinese admiral Cheng Ho measured 444 by 180 feet.[82]

In Ancient times long oceanic voyages out of sight of land did not hold the terrifying prospects which rhetoricians have asserted. One reason for this was because Bronze Age and later mariners (and no doubt earlier ones too) preferred to travel in flotillas of a dozen or more ships when undertaking lengthy voyages on unknown seas.[83] Some of these seamen had at their disposal--in addition to vast amounts of sea and sky lore--that

---

[78]

Bailey, *op. cit.*, p. 91.

[79]

Heyerdahl, *op. cit.*, p. 24.

[80]

Bailey , *op. cit.*, p. 87.

[81]

Steiner, *op. cit.*, p. 60.

[82]

Ibid., p. 62.

[83]

Bailey, *op. cit.*, pp 92 and 94.

formidable navigational aide, the compass. The compass is referred to in the Ancient Sumerian Epic of Gilgamesh, and also in a Chinese tradition dating to 2634 B.P.[84] The compass was in early use in the Mediterranean by the people of Sumer and the Indus River, it was used by the Phoenicians, and by the predecessors of the Maya, as well as by the Maya themselves.[85] Although water craft built of wood planks--a style of ship which has been in use for as long as five thousand years--float by displacing water and are therefore subject to sinking when their hulls are broken, reed and log vessels are virtually unsinkable. The most violent of storms and greatest of waves *can* severely damage the superstructure of such water craft, but since they are built on the principle of wash-through buoyancy, the vessels themselves (unless torn completely apart, which is unlikely) will always bob to the surface like a cork, no matter what happens to them, for the materials which they are built of simply cannot sink.

In Ancient and even in more recent, Modern times, lengthy ocean voyages such as Columbus claimed to have been the first human being ever to dare to undertake, have proven to be easily survivable on the meagerest of rations. In the year 399 C.E., a Chinese traveler, Fa Hsien, described his journey to India. On the return voyage to China by way of Java, the captain of the ship on which he sailed lost his way, and they sailed aimlessly on the China Sea for *seventy days* before land was sighted again.[86] In 1952, Dr. Alain Bombard set out "to prove by his example that a

---

[84]

Ibid., p. 93.

[85]

Ibid., pp. 93-94.

[86]

Steiner, *op. cit.*, p. 59. This captain's search for his bearings *lasted more than twice as long* as Columbus' first voyage.

shipwrecked sailor could live off plankton and the fish he caught for food, and off rainwater, sea-water and water squeezed out of fish for drink. This he accomplished..."[87]   He set out from Morocco in a small rubber raft without provisions of food or water, and in sixty-five days made landfall in the Caribbean at Barbados. To put it quite simply, the dangers of Ancient maritime activity have been grossly overrated, and that fact has been more than adequately proven over and over again, both in Ancient records, and in our own time.

The messages written by the Ancient mariners, immigrants and traders upon American rock; left buried beneath the soil by the Ancient nations of the Americas, are informative and fascinating in their variety.

Around 2,500 years ago, a traveler named Gwynn left his autograph, written in two languages--Ogam and North Iberian script--upon a rock on Turkey Mountain, near the site of present-day Tulsa, Oklahoma.[88]   Ancient Iberian script in a cave in Paraguay announces the passage of explorers from the city of Cadiz.[89]   An inscription in Celtiberian Ogam on a rock at Barouallie, Saint Vincent Island, in the West Indies, carved around 2,800 years ago, states that "Mabo discovered this remote western isle."[90]   In Texas, on a rock overhang along the Rio Grande, an inscription in Ancient Libyan records that "A crew of

---

[87]

Bailey, *op. cit.*, p. 94.

[88]

Fell, *America B.C., op. cit.*, p. 49.

[89]

Ibid., p. 98.

[90]

Ibid., p. 114.

Sishonq the King took shelter in this place of concealment."[91] Along the Cimarron River in Oklahoma, a chief named Ras left bilingual autographs at two sites about 2,500 years ago--one is in Libyan and Egyptian, and the other is in Libyan and North Iberian letters.[92] A Libyan inscription carved on a rock on a Southern California mountainside bordering the Mojave Desert some 2,200 years ago warns: "All Men, Take care. Great Desert."[93] Bilingual Arabic and Greek inscriptions at a Nevada site command passersby to "Crush scorpions underfoot," and to "Look out for snakes."[94] A Libyan inscription in Leflore County, Oklahoma, records a great battle. The text reads: "Inscription for the victory by the river. (Chiefs) Kaya, Yana, and Yaha were killed. The enemy commander, Pepe ('butterfly') hid and took flight, (then) they retreated and gave up."[95]

The passage of many Ancient travelers and the limitation of Ancient borders and boundaries is amply recorded in American monuments. At Peterborough, near Toronto, Canada, a gigantic petroglyph site records the visit, nearly 3,700 years ago of a Scandinavian king named Woden-lithi. His activities there, including the establishment of a trading colony to barter for raw American copper, are thoroughly chronicled in the Ancient

---

[91]
Ibid., p. 185.

[92]
Ibid., pp. 182-183.

[93]
Ibid., p. 182.

[94]
Fell, *Saga America, op. cit.*, p. 95.

[95]
Fell, *America B.C., op. cit.*, p. 181.

Tifinag script engravings he had left behind.[96] A Nordic Tifinag script message carved into a rock at Crow Island in Penobscot Bay, near Deer Isle, Maine, declares: "A sheltered island, where ships may lie in a harbor. Haakon brought his cog here."[97] Petroglyphs carved in Colorado stone at a much later date depict Vikings and their weapons.[98] Kufi letters at a Nevada site announce the arrival of "Newcomers from Libya."[99] A bilingual Egypto-Libyan inscription carved on a tablet and left near the present-day site of Eagle Neck, Orient, Long Island, New York, over 2,700 years ago, records the passage of an expedition from Egypt.[100] An Arabic text, executed between the tenth and twelfth centuries of the current era in a cave at La Gruta de Corinto, El Salvador, is a "record of a visit by voyagers from Malaya."[101] A stone tablet unearthed in Massachusetts in the last century records--in the Punic language--the Ancient annexation of the area now encompassed by most of that state by a Carthaginian suffete named Hanno.[102] In Oklahoma, an Ancient Libyan inscription on a boundary stone proclaims "Land belonging to

---

[96]

Fell, *Bronze Age America, op. cit.*, pp. 46-48, 106, and *passim*.

[97]

Ibid., pp. 116-118.

[98]

Fell, *Saga America, op. cit.*, p. 354.

[99]

Ibid., p. 189.

[100]

Fell, *America B.C., op. cit.*, p. 270.

[101]

Fell, *Saga America, op. cit.*, p. 276.

[102]

Fell, *America B.C., op. cit.*, pp 95 and 160-161.

Rata."[103]   Elsewhere in Oklahoma, a marker executed in alphabetic Celtic writing near Ardmore, states that there is "Tribal land as far as this Boundary Stone."[104]

The spiritual life of the Ancient Americans--and indeed of the Ancient world as a whole--is bountifully recorded in the messages left behind by Ancient Americans. Discovered in 1874, the Davenport, Iowa, calendar stele marks the time for the celebration of the Ancient Festival of the Djed. Engraved about 2,600 years ago, the tablet is a trilingual text in Egyptian hieroglyphs, Iberian-Punic, and Libyan.[105] A gold lamina zodiac tablet was written about 2,200 years ago in the Paphian script of Cypress, and buried at Cuenca, Ecuador.[106] (One contemporary racist author, disparaging the possibility that the great monuments of the Ancient Americas were actually the products of the hands and minds of Ancient Americans themselves, suggested that "space-men" were their true source. As part of his 'evidence', he offered the Cuenca zodiac as a sample of "space-man" writing!)   A Kufi Arabic zodiac near Little Lake, Inyo County, California, notes the arrival of the new year at the time of the spring equinox (before the advent of the Modern Christian calendar, the new year commonly began for *many* cultures at springtime).[107] On the cliffs of the Cimarron River in Oklahoma,

---

[103]

Ibid., p. 168.

[104]

Fell, *Saga America, op. cit.*, p. 38.

[105]

Fell, *America B.C., op. cit.*, pp.261-276.

[106]

Fell, *Saga America, op. cit.*, pp. 68-69.

[107]

Ibid., pp. 108-109.

a Greek inscription identifies a petroglyph as Taurus, the Bull.[108] The name of Bel, the sun god, is plentiful at a number of Ancient American sites. It appears in Ogam script temple dedications at Mystery Hill, New Hampshire; at South Royalton, Vermont; and South Woodstock, Vermont.[109] At Mystery Hill it is also rendered in Iberian characters as a dedication to Baal of the Phoenicians.[110] Between the eighth and ninth centuries of the current era, numerous Kufi Arabic inscriptions were made at sites in Nevada and California in reference to the Islamic faith. "Mohamed is the prophet of God," and "In the name of Allah," appear at two Nevada sites.[111] An Inyo County, California, inscription reads: "Jesus was the Son of Mary."[112] On Boundary Peak, on the California-Nevada border, it was written that: "Satan is the fount of lies."[113] The name of the prophet Mohamed, as well as a variety of Berber 'autographs', appears at numerous California and Nevada sites.[114] Old Irish Ogam inscriptions in West Virginia dating to around 600 C.E., make reference to Christmastime and the birth of Jesus. At one of these sites, in Wyoming county, the text is trilingual, appearing also in Libyan and Algonquian

---

108

Ibid., p. 110.

109

Fell, *America B.C., op. cit.*, pp. 54-55.

110

Ibid., p. 91.

111

Ibid., pp. xiv and 188.

112

Ibid., p. 173.

113

Ibid., p. 182.

114

Ibid., pp. 184-185.

script.[115] In a rock crevice in Big Bend National Park, Texas, a clay tablet bearing a Mithraic text was discovered in 1962. The text is principally in Libyan alphabetic script, but also employs Lycian and Lydian letters in two lines.[116] At Massacre Lake, Nevada, a prayer for rain was inscribed in Carthaginian Punic.[117] An abbreviated version of the Ten Commandments was carved into stone at Las Lunas, near Albuquerque, New Mexico. Its language is Greek-Phoenician, or Greek-Hebrew.[118] A Hebrew inscription of the Decalogue Tablet was unearthed in a burial mound near Newark, Ohio, in 1860, and at Bat Creek, Tennessee, an inscription in Hebrew dating from the time of the First Revolt in Jerusalem has been discovered.[119] An epigraph located at Hickison Summit Pass, Nevada, warns in Numidian script that: "It is sacrilege to scrape off an inscription; do not offend Baal."[120]

The Tombstone of Tasach is by no means the only monument of its kind left behind by Ancient Americans. The tombstone of Palladis, discovered near Cripple Creek, Colorado,

---

[115]

Barry Fell, "Christian Messages in Old Irish Script Deciphered from Rock Carvings in W. Va.," in *Wonderful West Virginia* (Charleston: State of West Virginia Department of Natural Resources, March, 1983), pp. 12-19.

[116]

Fell, *Saga America, op. cit.*, p. 165.

[117]

Ibid., p. 65.

[118]

Ibid., p. 167.

[119]

Robert L. Pyle, "A Message from the Past," in *Wonderful West Virginia, op. cit.*, p. 4, and Fell, *Saga America, op. cit.*, p. 168.

[120]

Fell, *Saga America, op. cit.*, p. 242.

was written in Byzantine North African Greek.[121]   Teth's tombstone from West Virginia, like Tasach's is Adena-Punic. Its inscription reads:

        The memorial of Teth

        This tile

        (His) brother caused to be made[122]

Iberian letters at a site near Boston, Massachusetts, caution passersby not ot loiter, for the place is a cemetery.[123] At Bache, Oklahoma, Haga's tombstone was executed bilingually, in both Ogam and Southern Iberian script.[124]   In Vermont, the tombstones of Yoghan and Lugh were written in Ogam characters.[125] In the Susquehanna Valley of Pennsylvania, 500 grave markers dating from 2,600 to 2,700 years-old were collected by Dr. William Strong. They are inscribed in the Celtiberian, Phoenician, and Basque languages.[126]

A number of sites, particularly in Nevada, but also in California, Oregon, Washington, and British Columbia, show evidence of having been outdoor classrooms. In Ancient Nevada, lessons seemed to center around the problems of ocean navigation. The effect of leeway and how to counter it were illustrated, as was the technique for conversion in mapmaking;

---

[121]

Ibid., p. 175.

[122]

Fell, *America B.C., op. cit.*, p. 158.

[123]

Ibid., p. 89.

[124]

Ibid., p. 160.

[125]

Ibid., p.59.

[126]

Ibid., p.170.

especially for the achievement of conical and rectilineal projections from spherical surfaces.[127] Maps dating to the third century C.E. have been discovered in Nevada as well. Written first in Libyan, and later on updated in Kufi Arabic, two of these maps show the Hawaiian Islands in their correct geographical relationship with the North American continent. One map places the international dateline just east of Hawaii, or in other words, 180° away from Alexandria, Egypt, where the zero meridian of the times did in fact lay.[128] Other sites include alphabet lessons, such as the Libyan example at Allen Springs, Nevada (and similar examples at other California and Nevada sites), and spelling lessons, as in the Gaelic Ogam examples from British Columbia, Washington, Oregon, and parts of Nevada.[129] That math lessons formed a portion of the Ancient American curriculum is also apparent. This is evidenced by the appearance at numerous California and Nevada sites of multiplication grids of the very sort still in use to this day in parts of North Africa for giving instruction in arithmetic.[130] And at the Lagomarsino, Nevada site, a basic demonstration of Euclid's theorem for calculating the area of a triangle has been found.[131]

Often the artifacts unearthed at Ancient American sites clearly demonstrate the widespread contact between cultures that occurred in the Ancient world. A potter's tool from a grave at

---

[127]

Fell, *Saga America, op. cit.*, pp 262-295.

[128]

Ibid., pp 270, 284-285, and 290-292.

[129]

Ibid., pp. 301, 305, and 296-310.

[130]

Ibid., pp. 314-320.

[131]

Ibid., p. 327.

Snapp's Bridge, east Tennessee, is marked in letters conforming to the early Greek style (from the eighth to the fifth centuries B.P.) which spell out "Imprint-stamp for pottery."[132] A metal urn manufactured in the style of the Cypriot Phoenicians of about 2,600 years ago was unearthed at the junction of the Susquehanna and Chenango Rivers in New York.[133] Several Roman lamps and a perfume vial of Roman manufacture came to light at a site on the Coosa River in Alabama. A goblet of the Pompeiian style was found at Clarksville, Virginia, and a Roman blue glass bead was discovered near Rumney, New Hampshire.[134]

The money of the Ancient world has turned up abundantly at American sites. The discovery of Roman coins in burial mounds was frequently reported in the last century.[135] There have been well documented finds of Roman coins in Venezuela, Massachusetts, Tennessee, Georgia, North Carolina, and Oklahoma.[136] Carthaginian coins have been found in the mid-Atlantic Azores, and also in Connecticut and Alabama.[137] Hebrew coins from the second century C.E. have been discovered in Arkansas and Kentucky.[138] A North African Medieval Islamic

---

[132]

Fell, *Bronze Age America, op. cit.*, pp. 266-269.

[133]

Fell, *Saga America, op. cit.*, p. 79.

[134]

Ibid., pp. 124-125.

[135]

Ibid., p. 127.

[136]

Ibid., pp. 55, 124-125, 127, 132, and 143.

[137]

Ibid., pp. 54,56, and 59.

[138]

Ibid., p. 168.

coin has been unearthed in Massachusetts.[139] Ancient Greek and Celtic coins have been dug up in Illinois.[140] One of the oldest and most common forms of money in the Ancient world, however, was the pure copper ingot, cast or hammered into the shape of a stretched ox hide. Such ingots had a wide distribution the world over. Because of their more or less standardized shape, they could easily be packed for shipment to the distant foundries-- always located near the rare accessible sources of tin--where they were alloyed into bronze, the principal metal of Ancient times.[141] American archaeologists have long recognized the appearance of such ingots as typifying North America's Adena and Hopewell cultures, for they regularly appear at such sites.[142] Yet another form of currency, Iberian wheel money--stone disk token coinage sometimes bearing west Libyan inscriptions--is found in Tennessee and Ohio at a number of sites.[143]

At some North American sites coins are not found, but depictions of them are. On the upper Rio Grande in Colorado, there are engravings of four denominations of sixth and seventh century Byzantine copper coins.[144] Depictions of Han and Sung

---

[139]

Ibid., p. 31.

[140]

Ibid., p. 153.

[141]

Ibid., pp. 142-143.

[142]

Willey, *op. cit.*, pp. 270 and 276. Willey refers to these ingots (as most American archaeologists do) as "reel-shaped gorgets."

[143]

Fell, *Saga America, op. cit.*, pp. 123-133.

[144]

Ibid., p. 147.

Dynasty Chinese coins occur in Nevada.[145] Byzantine and Islamic coin drawings occur at sites in California, Nevada, Colorado, Texas, and Oklahoma.[146]   A site near Moneta, Wyoming, apparently was a 'bank'. A prominent bilingual inscription there declares: "Moneychanger. The first to come here. No Usury."[147] This inscription is rendered in old Gaelic, written in Iberic letters, and in Greek, in the form of a rebus in which coins are being discharged onto a dish from a money bag. At the Moneta site engravings of Roman coins, Roman Celtic coins and Italian coins also appear.[148]

The association between Micmac writing and Ancient Egyptian is not the only such case of a similarity between an American language and a language of Africa or Eurasia. The Pima confederation of the Southwest (in its Ancient manifestation it is known as the Hohokam culture) "speaks a Semitic tongue evidently derived from that of the Iberian Punic colonists who settled America 2,500 years ago."[149]   The Zuni nation speaks "a tongue directly derived from the Libyan speech of North Africa, in which the Coptic, Middle Egyptian, and Nubian vocabulary is overwhelming."[150]   The language of the

---

[145]

Ibid., p. 323.

[146]

Ibid., pp. 180-181.

[147]

Ibid., p. 149.

[148]

Ibid., pp. 148-152.

[149]

Ibid., pp. 300-314. Also, Fell, *America B.C., op. cit.*, pp. 171, and 169-173.

[150]

Fell, *America B.C., op. cit.*, pp. 171, and 174-191.

Takhelne of the Northwest, is Celtic, related to Gaelic.[151] And in 1979, the Ancient Basque syllabary of Spain and Portugal was deciphered for the first time in the Modern Age, using as a guide the Algonquian syllabary which is currently in widespread use in Canada, principally among the Cree.[152]

The worldwide sharing of the Golden Age and Flood myths are far from being the only cases in which myths and tales of the Ancient world inform us about Ancient culture contacts. Many of the Hohokam-Punic chants preserved by the Pima have proven to be renditions of Aesop's Fables, apparently passed from Cyrenian Greeks to the Ancient Libyans.[153] James Bailey, through exhaustive linguistic, historical, geographic, archaeological, and epigraphic research has become convinced that Ancient mythologies about the god-kings and the Titans contain much more accurate information about the Ancient past than we have hitherto suspected.

> Dominating everything, setting their civilized stamp upon the world,

he asserts

> are the god-kings. According to Homer, they were born out of Ocean, sea-people, dependent upon sea-power. They were the brilliant forerunners of the Titans. They commanded the sea in the second half of the fifth millennium and the first half of the fourth [millennium B.P.]. The world has never been able to escape their influence. Who were they? The Indians claim they were Aryans and India was certainly in on the deal. We shall probably find when the excavating has been done that

---

[151]

Fell, *Saga America, op. cit.*, pp. 197-199.

[152]

Fell, *Bronze Age America, op. cit.*, pp. 149 and 141-152.

[153]

Fell, *Saga America, op. cit.*, pp. 311-314.

Persia, nominally the home of the Aryans, was involved
also. Egyptian records suggest some of them were certainly
Semites. I believe both statements are true, the two were
variously intermingled in the professions of merchants and
seamen. Both taught the Sumerians who carried on much
of their tradition...[154]

The story of the Titans... is an actual historical record of the
struggle for power in the Mediterranean and the Atlantic
and, above all, in the American colonies; with

reverberations in all the ports of the entire world. It is a
highly important legend because it gives the sequence of
the sea-dynasties, expressed in homely language.[155]

Bailey considers the case of the Titan, Atlas, in some depth.
Atlas was the son of Uranus, who was the brother of Chronos. The
name Atlas was, Bailey suggests, the title of office of the king of
a dynasty, such as was the title *Pharaoh*, or the title *Inca*.[156] He
finds that the capital city of Atlas was Tiahuanaco, on Lake
Titicaca in Peru,[157] and he asserts "...that Atlas traded from Peru
and Mexico, eastward across the Atlantic, which bears his name,
[and] westwards across the Pacific..."[158] The name Atlas, Bailey
points out, belongs to both the Americas and to the
Mediterranean world, where Atlas figures prominently in all the

---

[154]

Bailey, *op. cit.*, pp. 150 and 290.

[155]

Ibid., p. 287.

[156]

Ibid., p. 160.

[157]

Ibid., p. 159.

[158]

Ibid., p. 92.

Greek tales of the remote west.[159] In the Americas, the word root *atl*, meaning water or sea, appears repeatedly in the Nahua language of Ancient Mexico, including its appearance in the name of *Quetzalcoatl*, the heroic culture-bringing sea-god.[160]

(Atlas' uncle, Chronos, was also in the business of seagoing trade, and his dominion stretched from the Pacific, across North America, to England. The realm of Chronos, in short, was everywhere that the stone and wood time-measuring circles known as stonehenges, woodhenges, and medicine wheels are to be found.)[161]

Atlas' name, however, was not only given to an ocean, it was also given to an ancient place in the Americas--and that place was known as Atlantis. The myth of Atlantis has perplexed investigators ever since the Greek philosopher Plato wrote of it in his dialogues *Timaeus* and *Critias*.[162] The tale, he informs us through the persona of an Athenian named Critias, was first told to the Athenian Solon (a poet, sage, and lawgiver--and tyrant, according to Socrates) by Egyptian priests while Solon traveled in that country over one hundred years before Plato's own time. The story was then handed down as oral history to Critias' own grandfather, who was also named Critias. It is a tale of a great naval war between Atlantis of America, joined with its western

---

159

Ibid., pp. 160-161.

160

Ibid.

161

Ibid., pp. 168-175, and 287. See also: John A. Eddy, "Probing the Mystery of the Medicine Wheels," in *National Geographic* (Washington, D.C.: National Geographic Society, January, 1977), pp. 140-146.

162

Edith Hamilton and Huntington Cairns, editors, *The Collected Dialogues of Plato Including the Letters* (Princeton: Princeton University Press, 1971), *Timaeus* and *Critias*, pp. 1151-1224.

Mediterranean allies, and the eastern Mediterranean sea powers--
including Egypt and the Greek nations--which was fought over
supremacy of the seas and control of ocean-going trade. The
Greeks themselves, the Egyptian priests told Solon, had
completely forgotten this part of their history, for shortly after the
great conflict had ended, the civilizations of the Greeks and of
other eastern Mediterranean peoples were utterly destroyed by a
terrible natural disaster consisting of earthquakes and tidal
waves. Atlantis, the priests told Solon, had suffered the same
fate, sinking beneath the ocean in the space of a single day, and
leaving behind nothing but muddy shoals. All of this occurred,
according to the dating given by the Egyptian priests,
approximately 3,300 years ago. However, the tale which Plato
begins in his *Timaeus*, he leaves uncompleted in the *Critias*.

Perhaps because it was left incomplete, perhaps because it
dealt with events of enormous magnitude which occurred on both
sides of the Atlantic Ocean, or most of all, perhaps because of the
Reason-stifling rhetoric brought into the world by Columbus and
his supporters, no other bit of Ancient history has been subject to
more willful and fanciful misinterpretation than has the Atlantis
myth. Interpreters of the myth have placed Atlantis in the mid-
Atlantic, the eastern Atlantic, and even in the Mediterranean Sea-
-in short, everywhere but in the western Atlantic, where it
actually lies. However, relatively recent archaeological
discoveries have borne out the accuracy of Plato's account. The
decipherment of Ancient Egyptian hieroglyphs and hieratic
writing has corroborated through various Egyptian records that
around 3,200 years ago, an alliance of western sea peoples did
indeed attack Ugarit, the Hittite Empire, Crete and the
Mycenaean cities, and that they attempted, but failed to conquer
Egypt[163]. Excavations on the eastern Mediterranean island of

---

[163]

Bailey, *op. cit.*, p. 251.

Thera have shown that about 3,400 or 3,500 years ago--or perhaps even a few centuries more recently--that once-circular volcanic island suffered an enormous explosive caldera eruption which was preceded by terrible earthquakes.[164] Thirty two square miles of the island's surface were blown away into the atmosphere. What was left then collapsed into a 1,300 foot deep crater which filled immediately with sea water. Three hundred foot high tidal waves raced outward from the site of the explosion in all directions at speeds of over 200 miles an hour.[165] Within the nearby Aegean Sea and eastern Mediterranean region, coastal cities lying in the path of the waves were truly and totally destroyed. After the explosive eruption, considerably less than half of the island of Thera remained, and that, like Crete and other neighboring downwind islands, was covered over by a layer of volcanic ash up to 200 feet thick.[166] As the recent archaeological work at Thera has proceeded, a number of structures and elements of the Ancient harbor's and town's design have emerged which archaeologists have noted bear a most striking resemblance to Plato's description of the capital city of Atlantis.[167]

---

[164]

The more recent date is from *Ibid.*, p. 129, and Heyerdahl, *op. cit.*, p. 257. The older date is from Spyridon Marinatos, "Thera, Key to the Riddle of Minos," in *National Geographic* (Washington, D.C.: National Geographic Society, May, 1972), p. 718.

[165]

Ibid.

[166]

Ibid., pp. 708-709, and 718.

[167]

Heyerdahl, *op. cit.*, p. 359. For a thoroughgoing discussion of the work on Thera, see also: *Unearthing Atlantis: An Archaeological* Odyssey (New York: Vintage Books, 1993).

But Atlantis, Plato tells us, was much, much larger than any island in the Mediterranean, and he is unequivocal about its location on the western shore of Atlas' Ocean. Furthermore, Atlantis, by Plato's account, sunk entirely beneath the sea. It is noteworthy that "...oceanography assures us that no continents have sunk beneath the sea at any period remotely like the one we are considering except for important subsidences in the Caribbean."[168] This is noteworthy because in the early 1970s, marine archaeologists began to make some very interesting discoveries on the Caribbean sea bed off the islands of Bimini, Andros, and Puerto Rico. There, following leads provided by sightings of peculiar underwater shapes by aircraft pilots, they found a pyramid, a great stone causeway, a circle of pillars, walls, and buildings.[169] The sites off of Bimini and Andros are in shallow water; the one off of Puerto Rico is five miles underwater.[170] To date, the work at the shallow water sites has gone uncompleted, so no precise estimate of their antiquity can be attempted. The style of architecture found there however, is megalithic, reminiscent of middle and late Bronze Age structures. The distance between Bimini and Puerto Rico, as a glance at a map will confirm, is over nine hundred miles, and the indication of such a possibly large arc of submarine archaeological sites at the western edge of the Atlantic, where it meets the Caribbean, fits Plato's description of the size, location, and fate of Atlantis

---

[168] Bailey, *op. cit.*, p. 249.

[169] *Ibid.*, p. 252.

[170] *Ibid.* For further discussion of some of the sites mentioned above, see Henriette Mertz, *Atlantis: Dwelling Place of the Gods* (Chicago: Henriette Mertz, 1976). Mertz also discusses the draining of Lake Theoni above the Blue Ridge, another cataclysmic event which occurred contemporaneously with the other flood and earthquake disasters described in the Atlantis myth.

quite finely. Prior to this subsidence of the western rim of Atlantis, there had been other Caribbean-Atlantic subsidences of land. The area, it appears, is very active. There had for example been major submersions of land in and around Florida, *circa* 10,000 years ago. The latest such incident occurred quite recently, on June 7, 1694, when Port Royal, the capital of British Jamaica, was seized by a violent earth temblor. Within two minutes, two-thirds of the city had sunk beneath the Caribbean sea. Two thousand persons perished in the disaster.[171]

In the trans-Polynesian mythology centered about the heroic demigod Maui the navigator, a more recent tale than that of Atlantis, younger by over a thousand years, is told. It is a tale of travel eastward from Africa to the Pacific, and then eastward across the Pacific to North America. I have already mentioned above that at two sites in Nevada, inscribed maps have been discovered, and that these maps show the Hawaiian Islands in their correct geographical relationship with the American mainland. These charts bear the Libyan name Mawi, which means "navigator," or "guide" in the Egyptian language.[172] Its appearance on the Nevada maps is equivalent to the use of terms such as "Mercator's Projection" in modern chart making.[173] The historical reality behind the legend of Mawi began to first be revealed, however, with a discovery on the opposite side of the Pacific Ocean. There, in a cave on northwestern Irian (New Guinea), Libyan inscriptions were recognized in 1974. These

---

[171]

Marion Clayton Link, "Exploring the Drowned City of Port Royal," in *National Geographic* (Washington, D.C.: National Geographic Society, February, 1960), pp. 151-158.

[172]

Fell, *Saga America, op. cit.*, pp. 262 and 265.

[173]

Ibid., p. 283.

inscriptions included a notation that they had been executed "in the fifteenth year of Pharaoh's reign," and that an eclipse of the sun, visible from that location, had just occurred.[174] Now, it just so happens that the only eclipse of the sun visible from New Guinea at that Ancient time occurred in November of 232 B.P., and that year was also the fifteenth year of the reign of the Pharaoh Ptolemy III. The Irian inscriptions--like the Nevada charts--are accompanied by the signature Mawi, and they include "star maps, navigation diagrams, and even calculations attributed to Eratosthenes."[175]

According to Polynesian legend, Maui the navigator fished up new lands from the sea--that is to say, he discovered new lands--and he made the sun slow--*double*--its time of passage through the daytime sky. The place, according to Hawaiian legend, where the latter feat was accomplished, was on the island bearing Maui's name, on the great mountain known, in the Ancient language of the Islands, as *Hare a ta Ra*; the House of the Sun.[176]

---

[174]

Ibid., p. 263.

[175]   *Ibid.*, p. 262.

[176]

In the Modern Hawaiian language R[s] and T[s] have been transposed into L[s] and K[s]. This was accomplished by Boston missionaries who arrived in the Hawaiian Islands early in the nineteenth century, and were the first to compose Modern Hawaiian dictionaries. These missionaries noted that when they taught the Islanders to read and write in the English language, although they learned it readily, they persisted in writing alternating lines from right to left, and then from left to right, or in other words, *boustrophedon*, a technique of writing commonly used in Ancient times. For further discussion of the prospects of Ancient Hawaiian literacy, see: W.A. Kinney, *Hawaii's Capacity for Self-Government All But Destroyed* (Salt Lake City, Utah: Frank L. Jensen, Publisher, 1927), pp. 13-86, 88, 98, 105, 174, and 201.

The Nevada maps confirm that these accomplishments were in fact actual deeds done by an Ancient Libyan explorer named Mawi. These charts are labeled "Land Across the Sea," and "Announcement of new discoveries in the Ocean."[177] The northeast Pacific chart labels the following of the Hawaiian Islands thusly: Kauai as *Gawi*, Oahu as *Uwahu*, Maui as *Mawi Zara* (Mawi's Plantation or Estate), and Hawaii as the "Great Volcanic Island."[178] The island chain is marked *Hawa*, which is Libyan for "windy isles."[179] About ten degrees to the east of Hawaii on Mawi's map of North America, a meridian is indicated, and labeled "The Curve-of-Ra;" or in other words, the Meridian-of-the-Day, or international dateline. This meridian is in fact 180° of longitude (or twelve hours of time) away from Alexandria, the city which bore the primary meridian from Eratosthenes' time, until five hundred years later.[180] Here we must note that then as now, when crossing the international dateline from west to east, one must observe the same day twice over, otherwise one will arrive on the American mainland one calendar day ahead of the date being observed by the Americans.[181] Hence, by observing the same day twice on his way to North America, Maui/Mawi had truly slowed the sun in its course.

---

[177]

Fell, *Saga America, op. cit.*, p. 291.

[178]

Ibid., pp. 290-292.

[179]

Ibid., p. 292.

[180]

Ibid., pp. 283-284

[181]

Ibid., pp. 284-294.

Elsewhere in Polynesia, the legends of Mangareva record the visit made to that island by the Inca Tupac Yupanqui (Tupa) and his entourage of some 20,000 retainers. The duration of Tupac's voyage is given as nine months in the Inca (Quechua) tradition which also records his journey in very great detail.[182]

A number of trans Atlantic voyages are recorded in Mediterranean mythology. The *Voyage of the Argo* details the route from the Mediterranean to the Caribbean, down the South American coast, and eventually to Tiahuanaco.[183]   Homer's *Odyssey* follows the orbit of America's Gulf Stream current.[184] Such were the findings of Americanist Henriette Mertz, also an oceanographer, who diligently retraced the geographical clues provided by Apollonius Rhodius and Homer in their tales.[185] Such a literal interpretation of mythological geography is the same technique which, when applied to Homer's Iliad, led Heinrich Schliemann directly to the discovery, in 1868, of the ruins of the historic city of Troy.[186]

---

[182]

Heyerdahl, *op. cit.*, pp. 190-192, and 198-200.

[183]

Bailey, *op. cit.*, pp. 287, and 299-307.

[184]

Ibid., pp. 135, 287, and 299.

[185]

Ibid., pp. 299-307. Professor Mertz holds that Apollonius erroneously placed Jason's voyage in the Black Sea out of his ignorance of the Greeks' early seagoing prowess, a past which had been lost to their collective memory through the Thera disaster and the centuries of dark ages which followed it.

[186]

C. W. Ceram, *Gods, Graves, and Scholars: The Story of Archaeology* (New York: Bantam Books, 1972), pp. 36, 38, 39, and 42.

The tale of the eleventh labor of Hercules, detailing his acquisition of the Apples of the Hesperides, is a Greek story of very Ancient origin. The entire body of mythology dealing with Hercules is the equivalent of older stories told about the Phoenician god Melkharth; and the Phoenician story-cycle was based upon the Gilgamesh epic of Babylon, which itself had an earlier Indus Valley-Sumerian predecessor.[187] Hercules' eleventh labor consisted specifically of traveling to Atlas' distant western realm, and there acquiring three golden apples from the Garden of the Hesperides, the fabled garden of the golden fruit. What is remarkable about this tale is not that it takes place in the Americas, but that the tradition which is its centerpiece--the garden of the golden fruit--continued to be maintained in Peru right up until the commencement of the Modern Age. For the Modern Spanish conquistadores who destroyed Ancient Peru reported that they "found beside the Inca's palace an orchard with golden fruit tied to the trees, [and with] flowers, birds and deer in gold and silver."[188]

Even more remarkable was the discovery by the Spaniard Orellana--leader of the first Modern expedition to descend the entire length of the Amazon River--of the nation of warrior women after whom he named the river: the Amazons of *Greek* mythology. According to Fray Carvajal, the expedition's priest, of all the foes which this Spanish force met, these women and the bands of male soldiers which they captained were the most formidable. On cross questioning a prisoner about the Amazons, Orellana was told "that they lived by themselves under the command of a woman, that they had excellent stone houses and much gold and silver, their eating utensils were of gold, they had

---

[187]

Bailey, *op. cit.*, p. 154.

[188]

Ibid., p. 155.

much land and they worshiped women idols and also had temples dedicated to the sun."[189] Carvajal described the Amazons in the following manner: "These women are very white and tall, and have hair very long and braided and wound about the head."[190] These women appear not only in the Ancient writings of Herodotus and Diodorus Siculus and in the Modern observations of Fray Carvajal and Orellana, but also in the legends of the survivors of Brazil's Ancient nations.   Hence, W. Jesco von Puttkamer reports that:

> Brazilian Indians of today have a legend that a large tribe of women, who held in subjugation what few men they allowed to live, once ruled the Amazon jungles....
>
> The Indians say the tribe of women was called Iamuricumá. Some Amazon tribes still hold ceremonies and dances that they call Iamuricumá for the mysterious women warriors of old.[191]

For each of the hundreds of Ancient nations which once possessed the Americas there is at least one myth of origin, and sometimes there are more.   These tales explain the origin of nations from mother-countries across the eastern or western oceans; they speak of continental migrations going north, south, east or west; or they detail the creation of nations out of the very earth herself, at the hands of the gods. They are all undoubtedly--after the manner of all mythology--the truth. For example, three such tales from the Dakotas of eastern North America (a complex,

---

189

Quoted in *ibid.*, p. 240.

190

Ibid.

191

W. Jesco von Puttkamer, "Man in the Amazon: Stone Age Present Meets Stone Age Past," in *National Geographic* (Washington, D.C.: National Geographic Society, January, 1979), pp. 79-82.

'composite' nation) find the origins of that nation in: a trans Atlantic migration, a migration from South America, and the wedding of a mortal survivor of the Great Flood with a spiritual being.

The Dakotas of Minnesota, in fact, recorded in their legends the arrival of *other* people in America before the age of Columbus. As reported by anthropologist Ruth Landes:

> One early spring, the old people used to tell, they sighted a sailboat on the lake. It had mastheads of carved snakes and a great figurehead with a scaly body, horns, and wings, topped by a horse's head. Aft was carved a monster with a beak. The boat had three sails and was rowed with long oars; on each side were strung ten shields, and there were cabins above and below. Thirty-eight sailors or warriors manned the boat; their clothes had scales painted on them; and they wore horned headpieces. They carried spears, knives, and axes on poles....[A Santee] on shore hailed the moving boat with signs, so the men landed and remained all summer....
>
> But they never came back [again]. They had stayed over the winter and in early spring sailed eastward across the lake.[192]

As we become increasingly aware that such bodies of oral and written tradition constitute compact and highly symbolic means of conveying actual historical information, we become more capable of understanding them appropriately, and hence, of being guided toward understanding the immense background of interaction and interrelation with others which underlies each and every human culture. Indeed, given the enormous amount of data which has accumulated over the past few decades from a

---

[192]

Ruth Landes, *The Mystic Lake Sioux: Sociology of the Mdewakantonwan Santee* (Madison: The University of Wisconsin Press, 1968), pp. 21-23.

variety of sources such as those considered above, it should come as no surprise that the more open-minded among investigators of the Ancient past have concluded that "Asians and western Europeans and Africans traveled across the oceans," and that "civilization has been a one-world proposition since the Ice Age."[193] We should have no difficulty in reaching the same conclusion as Professor Barry Fell, that in the Americas, as in all the rest of the world, most Ancient communities were "of mixed derivation."[194]

But we have yet to consider what the 'photographic' or *visual* evidence has to tell us about the Americas in Ancient times. This body of evidence is comprised, among other things, of the small terracotta (fired clay) portrait figurines which were manufactured by the Ancient Americans themselves. The production of such figurines is, in fact, a trait which was common throughout most of the Ancient world. They are usually found among the grave goods which were interred with a dead person at the time of their burial. In Mesoamerica, millions of such works of portraiture were made over a roughly 3,200 year-long period, their manufacture ceasing at the time of Modern conquest.

For fifteen years art historian Alexander von Wuthenau made an exhaustive study of these little terracottas, examining several hundred thousand of them in the course of his investigation. He observes of them that:

> ...The strange thing is that up to now almost no one has bothered to look really closely and reflectively at these extraordinarily real human representations....

---

[193]

Bob Diddlebock, "Archaeological team theorizes early Celts left mark in Colorado," in the *Rocky Mountain News* (Denver: Rocky Mountain News, June 2, 1985).

[194]

Fell, *Saga America, op. cit.*, p. 386.

Viewed only from the physical side, we see bodies represented which are small, medium-sized, tall, fat, thin, muscular, flabby or daintily limbed; heads which are long, short, or deformed, faces which are round, angular, broad or narrow; hair which is straight, kinky, shaved, or even blond (not to mention the great variety of fantastic coiffures). There are eyes which are big, small, round, oval, almond-shaped, slanted or slit, rising toward the temple or slanted downwards....There are noses which are long and even exaggeratedly long, short, pointed, straight, curved, broad and coarse, as well as very delicate ones; there are lips that are thick, puffy, thin, straight, curved, drawn up and down at the corners, and mouths which are depicted open or closed, talking, singing, whistling, and even blowing vigorously. In short, everything is represented that humanity has produced, including ugly and ordinary as well as very beautiful people.[195]

Professor von Wuthenau (who, as he wrote was unaware of the post-Columbian invention of the "race" concept, and of the spurious nature of "racial" classification, and could not, therfore, avoid the use of "race" terminology in his descriptions) continues with his findings:

Fifteen years ago, when I began an intensified study of pre-Columbian terracotta heads, I had no intention of making a study of the artistic representation of various races simply because I did not suspect that this aspect existed. On the contrary, what I was looking for were typical 'Indian' heads. It was not long, however, before I discovered that in the early, lower levels these 'genuine Indians' were not to be found. The earliest figures encountered were those with Mongoloid characteristics and also real Chinese and very

---

195

Alexander von Wuthenau, *The Art of Terracotta Pottery in Pre-Columbian Central and South America* (New York: Crown Publishers, Inc., 1969), pp. 43-44.

Japanese wrestlers, Tartars, all kinds of white people, especially Semitic types with and without beards, and a surprising number of Negroes and those with Negroid elements. What is considered to be genuine Indian only developed, so far as I am able to judge on the strength of these terracotta representations, in early and middle Classic times [*circa* 300 to 600 C.E.], and probably derived from earlier types....

It is clear to me that these unlooked-for results might lead to new perspectives concerning our knowledge of certain ethno-historical events and population migrations.[196]

In the end, von Wuthenau finds his conclusion inescapable (and, we must note, he has arrived--quite independently--at the same conclusion as Professor Fell):

I believe that a real artist is capable of producing a truthful image in accordance with the essential facts of life....

The creative hands of artists from those ancient days have stretched out to guide us to a new and clearer understanding of the history of the Americas, where apparently not only East and West but in fact the whole world met, a long, long time ago.[197]

These very same Americans, so superbly described in their manifest diversity and beauty by von Wuthenau, are precisely the people who met Columbus, and--although they truly were "neither black nor white"--were converted by him into "Indians," the first "race" ever, on the face of this earth.

---

[196]

Ibid., pp. 49-50.

[197]

Ibid., pp. 187-188.

But what sort of place *was* the world before "race," the world where commerce flowed freely across the world's oceans, the world where full citizenship in any nation on earth did not ever depend upon the prerequisite of a particular "racial" identity? While an exhaustive description is not within the scope of this essay, we are justified in taking a look at some of the primary features of Ancient societies in the Americas and elsewhere. From South America to North America, there were hundreds of diverse nations in Ancient times. Some of these were large, and some were small--some of them were even very small; some were aggressive or warlike, and some were not, living in equilibrium in their surroundings. There were principally Monarchies and Aristocratic forms of government among these nations.

In South America, the conquest state of the Inca was most renowned. This dynastic monarchy began its campaign of political expansion about 900 years ago, in a portion of America which had known such forms of government since the time of Atlas. Within three hundred and fifty years, an enormous realm had been consolidated by the dynasty of the Inca, embracing one thousand miles of the Andes mountains and the west coast of South America from present-day Ecuador to Chile. Yet here was a state which engaged in a form of conquest the likes of which we might scarcely comprehend. From the beginning, the Inca upheld the ideals of clemency, generosity, gentleness, good (and very rigid) social order, and the usefulness of applied technical skills. Within the Inca realm there was no cannibalism, there was no rampant human sacrifice, there was no concept of a slave or of slavery.

Garcilasco de la Vega, a Quechua person who was born just after the Modern conquest of Peru, authored *The Royal Commentaries of the Incas*, a history of the dynasties of the Inca. In it he vividly described the Inca mode of warfare:

The first Inca Manco Capac had expressly ordered all the kings who descended from him never to permit bloodshed in any conquest they might make unless it was absolutely necessary and always to attract the Indians with benefits and blandishments, so that they should be loved by the subjects they had conquered with love, and not perpetually hated by those reduced by force of arms....

During the course of the war the Incas did all the good that was possible to their enemies so as to conquer them by kindness. Those captured in battle were released with kind words which they were to convey to their chiefs with offers of peace and friendship. The wounded were dressed, and on their recovery sent away with similar messages; they were told they could return to fight, and as often as they were wounded and captured they would be healed and set free, since the Incas intended to prevail like Incas and not as cruel and tyrannical enemies. Women and children found in the fields and caves were tended and then returned to their parents or husbands with entreaties not to persist in their obstinancy, since it was impossible for them to defeat the children of the Sun.[198]

The Inca armies did not destroy, but rather, preserved the cultures they conquered, and incorporated them as already functioning parts into the complex of the whole empire. It was a system in which the Incas "strove *successfully* to make all their subjects prosperous and happy within the framework of their separate cultures."[199] To this end the empire was connected

---

[198]

Quoted in Bailey, *op. cit.*, pp. 268-269.

[199]

Philip Ainsworth Means, "The Incas, Empire Builders of the Andes," in *National Geographic on Indians of the Americas; a Color-illustrated Record* (Washington, D.C.: National Geographic Society, 1955), p. 282.   The emphasis is mine.

together by thousands of miles of paved roads, with suspension bridges hung across the deep canyon gorges of the Andes. Post houses were established along these roads at minimum eight mile intervals where *any* traveler might stop and, without payment, rest for a night. Elaborate irrigation systems watered the upland mountain and lowland desert fields; the fresh water delivery and plumbing systems of the Inca towns were--like those of Ancient Sumeria--most superb, and they were not equaled by Modern technology until the late nineteenth century. There was no unemployment, the work day was six hours long, the system was designed to encourage individuals to achieve their greatest potential--any commoner displaying uncommon ability might be admitted into the ranks of the nobility. There was no starvation; the public granaries were always kept full of fresh stores as a hedge against crop failure. There was no poverty--there was no money. There was practically no crime, even so, in Inca law motivation was extremely important: in the case of theft, for example, a distinction was drawn between a crime originating in greed and one caused by a genuine pressing need. In the former class of crime, the thief was liable to face execution. However, if a person had stolen out of true neediness, then the public official who had allowed such need to go unnoticed would be the person to be punished. What few prisons that existed within the realm scarcely ever had any inhabitants; often convicted criminals were sentenced to labor in the slaughterhouses where llama and guinea pig meat was processed. Labor in public works such as roads, irrigation canals, and mining, was performed by all citizens in short shifts once a year, as a tax paid to the state (there were no other taxes). Medical practices were very advanced: coca provided local anesthetic (tincture of coca was used), surgery was performed with bronze and obsidian-tipped scalpels, as in the rest of the Americas there was an extensive list of effective pharmacological plants, and decayed teeth were drilled and filled with gold.

The magnificence and benevolence of the Inca Empire was corroborated by Mancio Serra de Leguicamo, one of the Spanish conquerors of Peru, who confessed to the King of Spain:

...that we found these lands in such a state that there was not even a robber or a vicious or idle man, or adulterous or immoral woman: all such conduct was forbidden. Immoral persons could not exist and everyone had honest and profitable occupations....Everything from the most important to the least was ordered and harmonized with great wisdom. The Incas were feared, obeyed, respected, and venerated by their subjects, who considered them to be most capable lords....We have transformed the Indians who had such wisdom and committed so few crimes, excesses, or extravagances that the owner of 100,000 pesos of gold or silver would leave his door open placing a broom fixed to a bit of wood across the entrance to show that he was absent: this sign was enough to prevent anyone from entering or taking anything. Thus they scorned us when they saw among us thieves and men who incited their wives and daughters to sin....This kingdom has fallen into such disorder...it has passed from one extreme to another. There was no evil: now there is almost no good.[200]

Since it underscores the distinction between Ancient and Modern societies, we must note that de Leguicamo was so utterly fearful of the Spanish nation of which he was a citizen, that he only dared to make this confession posthumously, in a codicil to his will.[201]

Of the nations of Central America, those of the Maya are the most well-known. The Maya were prodigious traders, farmers, astronomers, mathematicians, and architects. Spanish

---

[200]

Quoted in Bailey, *op. cit.*, pp. 267-268.

[201]

Ibid.

conquerors attributed a modest amount of human sacrifice to them, and recent archaeological work bears this out. It is still difficult to discern, however, whether the heyday of human sacrifice among the Maya occurred while they were under the suzerainty of the Aztecs, or whether it was an artifice of their own design. The Well of Sacrifice at Chichén Itzá, in Yucatan, appears however to bear indications of Mexica origin, and to derive from the period during which the city was under Aztec vassalage.[202] The Maya have often been characterized by Modern detractors as being a very warlike people. But such was not exactly the case. The various Maya nations *were* energetic participants in warfare, reveling in the glories of warriors and warrior-kings, as well as taking delight in the tormented misfortune of enemy captives. Yet they knew *nothing* of Total War until it was brought to them by sixteenth century Spanish soldiers.

Little is known of the nations of the Caribbean, other than that the Spaniards liberally accused some of them of cannibalism. Whether the accusation was based on any truth or not may never be known with certainty, for a mere eighty years after Columbus' arrival, the Spanish had depopulated the Caribbean islands by nearly half a million persons.[203] The handful of Caribbean islanders who did survive were quickly assimilated into the flood of West African slaves who were imported to the region to replace its original population.

Most notorious of the nations of Mexico were the cities of the Aztecs. Migrants to the Valley of Mexico from an unknown location to the north in the early fourteenth century, the Aztecs, in the brief two hundred year life-span of their cultural

---

[202]

Sylvanus Griswold Morley, "The Maya of Yucatan," in *National Geographic on Indians of the Americas...*, *op. cit.*, pp. 203-206.

[203]

Vogel, *op. cit.*, p. 255.

supremacy, created the last of a long series of great Mexican civilizations. As did the Incas, the Mayas, and the numerous city states and confederated nations of South, Central and North America, the Aztecs truly did possess all of the traits of what we call civilization.   They were agricultural, literate, had the technology of metalworking, used the wheel (principally on children's toys), and were intensely involved in international trade.   Unlike their predecessors and neighbors, however, the Aztecs were obsessed by human sacrifice in the particular form demanded by their gods.   They appear--and not just on the testimony of Spanish witnesses--to have taken the blood lust of their gods to excess.   In the two hundred year life-span of the Aztec culture, perhaps a hundred thousand or more persons were sacrificed to the appetites of their gods.

There is no doubt that the Spaniards were impressed by the religious practices of the Aztecs.   But that is not all that impressed them.   Bernal Díaz, one of the *conquistadores* who accompanied Cortez during the conquest of Mexico, recorded the Spanish reaction to the city of Mexico and the surrounding towns:

...when we saw all those cities and villages built in the water, and other great towns on dry land, and that straight and level causeway leading to Mexico, we were astounded. These great towns and cues [pyramids] and buildings rising from the water, all made of stone, seemed like an enchanted vision from the tale of Amadis. Indeed, some of our soldiers asked whether it was not all a dream.

...Everything was shining with lime and decorated with different kinds of stonework and paintings which were a marvel to gaze on....we turned...to the great market and the swarm of people buying and selling....Some of our soldiers who had been in many parts of the world, in

Constantinople, in Rome, and all over Italy, said that they had never seen a market so well laid out, so large, so orderly, and so full of people.[204]

Yet the Aztecs did not exterminate the nations which surrounded them, either physically or culturally. Instead, the extracted tribute from them, and from time to time they warred against them in order to acquire live captives to send to their altars of sacrifice. Whether the Aztecs (who in this respect were so unlike every other American nation) ever would have become less excessive in their blood lust over the run of time--had they not suffered the Spanish intervention--shall never be known. One hundred and forty years after Cortez had arrived in Mexico, the region's population had been reduced by thirty million persons, and there were scarcely any Aztecs or anyone else left alive there--with the exception, of course, of the Spaniards, and the slaves who they married and who were allowed, for the purposes and necessities of labor, to survive.[205] In the words of Bernal Díaz: "...today all that I then saw is overthrown and destroyed; nothing is left standing."[206]

In the earlier portion of this chapter we have seen something of the Ancient civilizations of North America. In those times, so long ago, North Americans were absorbed in far-flung trading relations, they were intensely agricultural, they were very literate, they were concerned with astronomy and mathematics, and they built massive architectural monuments, such as the huge truncated pyramid Cahokia, Illinois, which is one of the largest in

---

[204]

Bernal Díaz, J. M. Cohen, translator, *The Conquest of New Spain* (Baltimore, Maryland: Penguin Books Inc., 1972), pp. 214, 215, and 235.

[205]

Vogel, *op. cit.*

[206]

Díaz, *op. cit.*, p. 215.

the entire world. One notable feature about North American archaeology is the absence of sites which show evidence of having been ravaged by warfare. Such sites as do show evidence of violent destruction mostly fall above a time horizon between 1000 and 1200 C.E.[207] This is consistent with Barry Fell's estimation of the time of arrival of 'barbarian' invasions on the continent, and the commencement of an North American dark ages.[208] (The phenomenon of 'barbarism' which we find here is, it should be noted, the same which first began when Rome's ethnocidal conquests displaced, exterminated, or otherwise drove millions from their homelands in Africa and Eurasia. It is the very 'barbarism' which eventually swept back upon the Roman Empire and drove Roman culture into transforming itself into the form of a "universal church." And it is the very same 'barbarism' which was kept alive on the fringes of the Medieval European world by the universal church's lust to become--as the old empire had desired to be--the universal world government.) Of North American governments in Ancient times, it may justly be said that by far the majority were Monarchical and Aristocratic.[209] In Ancient North America it was common for small nations to combine into large and powerful confederations, as in the Siouan Adena-Hopewell sequence which was the model for the much

---

207

Typical of such sites is Crow Creek, South Dakota, where a farming village along the Missouri River was destroyed in 1325 by a band of roving foreign warriors.

208

Fell, *Saga America, op. cit.*, pp. 385-386.

209

My use of these political terms is to be understood in their classical, not vulgar, or *Modern*, sense. Hence, Aristocracy is the rule by those who in the eyes of their peers were best suited to rule. It is *not* rule by the wealthy, the landed, or by a certain hereditary class.

later League of the Iroquois; which itself was the model for the first constitution of the United States of America, the Articles of Confederation.

It is clear from the various sources of information which we have reviewed in this chapter that as Francis Bacon suspected, and as he suggested in his posthumously-published New Atlantis, the world was far more cosmopolitan in Ancient times than the various Modern ideologies will allow us to realize. We have also been seriously misled about the accomplishments of Ancient science and technology. Looking at the record we find, for example, that in Ancient times during two separate eras, there were 'Suez canals' linking the Mediterranean world and the Red Sea. We find that in the Middle East, some 2,500 years ago, batteries were being used to electroplate metals; that in Egypt, temple doors were opened and closed with steam power. We find the very widespread and relatively successful practice of the form of brain surgery known as trepanning; we find the superb dentistry of the Incas and other Ancients. We find that there are many surprises revealed in the reality of human achievement in the Ancient past. The arch proves not to be a Roman invention, but a much older Assyrian development. The scope of Ancient irrigation works the world over is truly impressive. So too are the use of highly accurate relief maps by the Incas, and the mapping of the "hidden side of the world" by western North Americans. It is dumbfounding to contemplate the mystery of the paleolithic charts of the Ancient sea-kings, based upon plane and spherical trigonometric calculations, which show land form features of an ice-free Antarctic continent, and which show *glacial masses* in the north of the western Eurasian land mass. When objectively viewing the scope of Ancient medical practices, it is not really surprising at all to find that now, Modern ethnobotanists are searching furiously--the whole world round--attempting to regain the pharmacological knowledge of Ancient societies which were crushed, or nearly so, upon the arrival of Modern conquerors in their realms. Looking at the record, we see that the arts and sciences of long distance ocean navigation--the roots of world commerce--have originated in the remote Ice Age past, and not in the minor voyages (and major rhetoric) of Columbus.

As we review the statistics showing the numbers of human beings destroyed by the arrival of Modern societies the world over, we are shocked by the enormity of those numbers. And then as the shock passes, and we compare those figures with present-day world population statistics, something else begins to dawn on us. In Ancient times, the human living-space problem we sometimes describe as "over-population," or "the population bomb," did not exist at all; human populations were deliberately held stable, at much lower levels back then.   This was accomplished in Ancient American and other Ancient societies by a number of means including: effective birth control devices, forms of marriage other than monogamy, a post parietal (after childbirth) ban on sexual intercourse between a married couple for as much as four years, and the absence of anything even remotely equivalent to the Modern version of poverty. In the Ancient world, where human beings did not feel as if they were running out of living space, we do indeed find rich people and poor people, commoners and nobles; but we can find nothing to compare with the spiritual and physical filth and degradation which human beings are compelled to live in, in for example, the vast outlying slums of today's Mexico City, or the shattered rubble in the Bronx, in New York City, or in a Modern camp for refugees from famine or War. The Ancient world by virtue of its lesser human numbers was a cleaner, healthier place.   The Ancient Biblical life span of "three score and ten" years was not, it seems, so far off the mark for those surviving childbirth and infancy.   In Ancient times, unlike the Modern Epoch, the causative link between poverty and overpopulation had not yet come to be exploited.[210]

Yet before we move on to ponder the terrors of "race" in our own portion of the Modern Age, let me make one final point. I am not so foolish as to assert that the Ancient world was "the best of all possible worlds." There is no such thing as "the best of all possible worlds." (At least there is no such perfection for human beings to experience so long as they are in the phase of existence which is characterized by the encasement of the spirit within an animal body on a material, physical planet.) As I trust I have mentioned abundantly enough, the Ancient world knew the madness, the cannibalism, known as warfare. Also in those times, individuals and families knew the experiences of homicide, rape, and robbery, just as we do today, although back then those trials may have been much more uncommon (and in Ancient times there was scarcely such a thing--Caesar and his legionaries excepted--as a "serial murderer").

In Ancient times the law of humanity's sibling relation held sway--all humans were sisters and brothers. This law of life was known and respected everywhere. There was no concept of "race;" there was, therefore, no licence to hate or to murder a neighbor or stranger because their skin color differed from one's own.   There was no licence to hate, be suspicious of, or exterminate this or that quarter of the planet's population because their looks or their 'background' might *be said* to differ from what one *is told* to be one's own. As I have pointed out, because Rome was in, but not truly *of* the Ancient world, Ancient societies did not practice ethnocide. Something else was also impossible in Ancient times; something which Modern societies have recently acquired the means to accomplish. In Ancient

---

[210]

More of this topic later, in the following chapter.

times, humanity would--could--never have conceived of confronting itself with the possibility of something which can only be labeled "genocide."

For these reasons, if I were to be asked, I should not hesitate to answer that in *my own opinion*, the Ancient world was a better, a much, much better place than the Modern world.

Finally, it is now to our own present surroundings that we shall turn our attention, as we contemplate the state-sponsored terrorism called "race" as it operates in "the greatest democracy the world has ever known."

PART II

THE MODERN WORLD--THE WORLD TODAY

Whose lot is caste,
he is to wait,
endure his tract of time.
The smell is now,
and half of yesterday;
the lies have lain for ages on
ten thousand tongues.
Tomorrow does not wait,
but taunts instead,
as carrots hung before
the asses nose.
Trudging
shades and color vary,
soldiers come and pass,
tomorrow is aloof.
--A.A.H.

Born down in a dead man's town
The first kick I took was when I hit the
ground
You end up like a dog that's been beat too
much
Till you spend half your life just covering
up
Born in the U.S.A.
I was born in the U.S.A.
I was born in the U.S.A.
Born in the U.S.A.

--B. Springsteen

CHAPTER V
The World Today--The United States of America

There is no such thing as "race." From time immemorial--that is to say, since the last great Ice Age--the various colors of human complexion have been dispersed, in differing proportions, throughout the entire earth. The reason for this, as we have seen, is that most archaic human activity, trade, and its corollary, the long-distance navigation of the world's oceans.

Because of this worldwide mingling of human beings over tens of millennia, the conclusion is inevitable: no human culture has developed in isolation. This has long been recognized with regard to the eastern hemisphere world of Africa and Eurasia where, for example, the influence of the Ancient Indus, Chinese, and Egyptian civilizations upon many cultures is well-known. None have ever felt diminished by acknowledging this complexity of historical origin--at least not in the eastern hemisphere--and it is evident that throughout human existence the peaceful contact between any two nations has always enriched both parties. (Sometimes this has even been the case with warlike contact, as we have seen in the example of the Ancient Inca empire.) It is also evident, therefore, that contact and even lengthy interrelation between two differing nations is not in and of itself destructive of the distinctive culture of either nation. It may seem very trite to have to go over this subject so carefully, but the case of present-day Japan may serve as a fine example. In our Modern world, nations are not only aware of each other and in contact with one another, but they are, thanks to electronic satellite communications, and the global spread of the Internet, instantly in touch. So it is with Japan and the United States of America. Let us for a moment consider this Post-War contact to see how cultures learn from one another, yet maintain their unique culture-identities.

After the end of the First Atomic War in 1945,[1] the United States imposed a democratic constitution upon defeated Japan. In the years which followed, foreign aid from the United States assisted Japan in rebuilding its nation and establishing a most up-to-date Modern industrial base. Now, fifty years later, Japan is preeminent among the world's powerful industrial nations. But has Japanese culture been destroyed? Has Japanese identity been demeaned? Has the intensive contact with and influence by the United States turned Japan into a carbon copy of the United States? The answer to these questions is, of course, a resounding *no*. For although the culture of Japan has undergone many transformations over the past fifty years (just as it has undergone

---

[1]

Symptomatic of the loss of reasoning ability which has been caused by Modern rhetorical mentality is the abundance of contemporary doomsayers who warn that some day in the future a Nuclear War--a War in which nuclear weapons are deployed by one or more of the belligerent parties--might be fought with disastrous consequences for the human species. This is indeed a sad--and *serious*--oversight with dangerous implications for all of us. For although the Great War of the 1930s and 40s is commonly known as the Second World War, it was in fact *the first War which saw the hostile use of nuclear weapons*; it was in fact the *First Atomic War*. Thus, not only has our species *already* engaged in Atomic War, but we also appear to be determined to ignore, *to talk away*, the fact.

transformations throughout the entire course of its roughly 2,000 year existence), Japanese culture is no less Japanese today than it was before the commencement of the First Atomic War. Nor was Japanese culture destroyed by the introduction of beer to Japan by Japanese military observers who attended the Franco-Prussian War (by invitation of the Prussians) during the preceding century. Nor was Japanese culture destroyed by the much earlier introduction of firearms from the 'outside world'. The list of examples of this sort of learning from outsiders in the case of Japan--or *any other nation*, for that matter--could go on quite tediously. For although no culture has ever developed in complete isolation, and no culture has ever remained perfectly static or unchanging, we find that throughout the entire earth, even in our present age of instantaneous communication and contact, of the hundreds of national cultures which yet survive on this planet, each retains its own distinctive character. This can only mean that contact and information-sharing are no destroyers of culture.

There really is only one way to destroy a culture. This was the secret discovered by Ancient Rome, preserved by the Church of Rome, and built into the foundations of all Modern societies. The secret is ethnocide--the mass-extermination of the people of a national culture. But as the Romans and those following them have also understood, simple extermination is not enough, for there will always be *some* survivors (such as slaves, concubines, or peasants). So the language, the spiritual way, all other cultural practices, and the history of the national culture in question must also be utterly destroyed as well.

This brings us rather directly to the consideration of a question asked of the Massachusetts missionary John Eliot by an unidentified citizen of an Ancient North American nation. It was a question which was asked over and over by various citizens of many of the Ancient nations of the Americas--North, Central, and South. The wording of the question, inevitably, was always the same. In 1646, that unknown person asked the Puritan missionary: "Why do you call us Indians?"[2] Although an honest reply from Eliot was not forthcoming, the question has been repeatedly answered, throughout the course of recent history. But because no essay dealing with the subject of "race" would be respectably complete without making mention of the notorious Third Reich regime of the mid-twentieth century, and because I cannot stress often enough that those who have encumbered our minds with "racial" thinking have never been so burdened themselves, let us now turn to that source for an answer to the anonymous tribesman. "I know perfectly well," observed Adolph Hitler,

> just as well as all those tremendously clever intellectuals, that in the scientific sense there is no such thing as race. But...I as a politician need a conception which enables the order which has hitherto existed on historical bases to be abolished and an entirely new and anti-historic order enforced and given an intellectual basis....[3]

Unfortunately, it appears as if any answer comes too late, for now the descendants of America's Ancient nations are nearly unanimous in proclaiming with pride: "I am Indian." For most of these people, their supposed "racial" identity supercedes in importance their actual *ethnic*, that is to say, their *national* (nowadays often called "tribal") identity, even though most are aware of the latter. Almost all of them believe the ideology "Columbus discovered America." (This, however, they believe in a 'schizophrenic' manner, proclaiming: "We were here first, so of

---

[2]

Quoted in Berkhofer, *op. cit.*, p. 4.

[3]

Quoted in Ashley Montagu, *Man's Most Dangerous Myth; The Fallacy of Race* (New York: Oxford University Press, 1974), p. 50. As is common for people living in Modern times, Montagu completely misunderstands the proper usage of the word *myth*.

course *we* discovered America," yet at the same time they paradoxically believe that "Columbus discovered America for the *rest* of the world.") Most, if they were to learn the truth, would be highly offended by that truth; would feel as if their cultures were demeaned by that truth; would believe that the truth has tainted the "purity" of their "race." --"I am Indian." What is the origin of this propaganda,[4] what is the source of this disinformation?[5] How has this "new and anti-historic order" come to be enforced? From what source has it drawn its life? And perhaps the most frightening question of all: Why is it so easy for people today to make 'instantaneous' on-sight identifications of the "racial" identities of other persons?

We have already seen how Columbus was instrumental in the concoction of the concept of "race," and for what purpose it was devised. *This is* the baseline, *the origin of all racism-- institutional, personal, or whatever kind--for the mere belief that "races" are real categories of human beings, is the foundation of, the* source *of racism.* However, in order to more fully understand the operation of the Modern world in which we live, let us now consider the creation and enforcement of "race" concepts in a 'sample' Modern nation, the United States of America, from its self-identified beginnings to the present day.

From the outset of their arrival in North America, English (and also Swedish, Dutch, and French) colonists, following the baseline, heavy-handedly employed the rhetoric of "race," as had the Spanish in their colonies to the south. That was the psychological aspect of conquest. The physical side of their

---

[4]

Another word for rhetoric--*the Ancient Roman* one.

[5]

The *newest* term for rhetoric, this one is a *Soviet* contribution.

colony-making entailed the enactment of a process which historian Francis Jennings had described as "chartered conquest."

The stages of that process were as follows: (1) a head of state laid claim to distant territories in jurisdictions other than his own; (2) he chartered a person or organized groups to conquer the claimed territory in his name but at private expense; (3) if the conquest was successful, the conquering lord (whether personal or collective) was recognized by the chartering suzerain as the possessor and governor of the territory, and the lord in turn acknowledged the charterer's suzerainty or sovereignty. The charter itself served as the new jurisdiction's legal constitution. More often than not, the conquest was launched ostensibly to reduce heretics or infidels to subjection to a protector or champion of an only true religion, this reason being mentioned prominently in the conquest charter, and clerics of the appropriate orthodoxy preceded, accompanied, or followed the troops....

Chartered conquest accompanied by colonization in America did not repeat by mere coincidence the pattern set in Europe; so far as the British colonies were concerned, there was a specific historical link connecting the empire of the Plantagenet kings with the empire begun by Elizabeth Tudor and expanded by the Stuarts. That link was Ireland[6]

In North America as in Ireland, the psychological and physical aspects of conquest were closely intertwined. In both places, ethnocidal War was accompanied by vigorous reality-denial. (In North America, War upon women and children was introduced and ardently promoted by the colonists from England,

---

[6]

Jennings, *op. cit.*, pp. 333-334.

France, the Netherlands and Sweden.)[7] The native inhabitants--
the citizens of the nations of the land--were characterized as
"savages;" they were depicted as being incapable of supporting
themselves by agricultural pursuits, they were called illiterate,
their cultural institutions were viewed as being inadequate, and
their spiritual beliefs--if not denied existence entirely--were
portrayed as being positively evil. (Remember, all of the above
accusations were patently false.)   By the 1640, Puritan
missionaries in New England had established segregated towns
for "praying Indians" just as prayer towns had been created for
the survivors of English ethnocide in Ireland a century earlier.
Unlike the Irish however, the citizens of Ancient North America's
original nations were far enough away from the mother country
to be accused of possessing the unique "racial" identity, "Indian."
     After two centuries of specific Spanish usage, and general
employment by other countries of western Eurasia, the term
"Indian" had come to be an invaluable rhetorical tool. "Indian"
at once meant "savage," or culturally inferior, and "infidel," or
spiritually inferior.   The entire series of assumptions and
arguments about "Indian savages" was incredibly circular. The
purposively gross underestimation of original populations was a
part of this circular cycle which actually persisted up until the
present century. The "savagery" of North America's first nations
was "proven" by the doctored figures which asserted their sparse
population; at the same time, their "savagery" was "proof" that
their nations had been sparsely populated.[8] Similarly, "Indian
savagery" was "proof" of religious inferiority, and participation in
native, non-Christian spirituality was most definitely "proof" of
"savagery." "Savage" meant illiterate (or in the anthropological

---

[7]

Ibid., p. 212.

[8]

Ibid., pp. 15-31.

usage, "preliterate"), and hence was "proof" that native systems of writing were not writing at all. "Savage" meant without history, "savage" meant without politics or nation, and most importantly, "savage" meant not only uncivilized, but antithetical to civilization, and thus, a severe, deadly threat to civilization.

The interrelated concepts of "Indian," and "savage," were of inestimable use in England and the other colonial mother countries where they functioned as effective rhetorical defenses of the most unashamedly unrestrained ethnocidal practices in the colonies. Because of the great distance between the mother country and its colonies, the reality-denial entailed in the concept of "savagery" was not as prodigious a mental feat in the mother country as it was in the colonies. In the mother country farming villagers could *easily* become verbally transformed into "roving hunters." Native systems of literacy could simply vanish from sight in the mother country. In the mother country, citizens of the colonies' original nations--who in actuality possessed virtually every skin color known--could easily be made over into "redskins." Colonists, describing their own means of making Total War upon the nations they were contending with, portraying the slaughter of infants, women, children, and surrendering persons, could easily attribute those practices exclusively to the "Indians." (Yet in truth, the first American nations knew nothing of such practices, and initially they most actively resisted participating in them.) But in the mother countries nearly everyone knew of the terrors of Total War, for it was often a very real part of their personal experience or past national history; it was something of *their own*. Seeing it so vividly described, and identified with "the Indian," they recognized their own practice, Total (or Modern) War, as the menace to human existence which it really was, and they readily agreed that its practitioners should be stamped out. The rhetorical devices "savage," "Indian," and "race," allowed them to make a remarkable transposition, however--*they identified* the victims *of Total War as its perpetrators*.

The compilation of literary tracts filled with such propaganda was not a haphazard process, or one which was simply left to chance. As early as 1646, the Commissioners of the United Colonies of New England--a colonial governing body which was top heavy with Puritan members of the legal profession--took the necessity of propaganda into account as a matter of public record. In that year they passed a resolution expressing their desire that:

> ...all the Colonies (as they may) would collect and gather up the many speciall providences of God towards them,...how his hand hath bene with them in laying their foundations in church and common wealth, how he hath cast the dread of his people (weak in themselves) upon the Indians...that history may be compiled according to *truth with due weight* by some able and fitt man appointed thereunto.[9]

The propagandistic interplay between colony and mother country reached its peak in the work of John Locke, the English rhetorician. Locke, who had never visited the Americas and knew nothing save hearsay about the American nations which the colonies were eliminating, wrote in *The Second Treatise of Government*, in 1690:

> There cannot be a clearer demonstration of any thing, than several Nations of the *Americans* are of this, who are rich in land, and poor in all the Comforts of Life; whom Nature having furnished as liberally as any other people, with materials of Plenty, *i.e.* a fruitful Soil, apt to produce in abundance, what might serve for food, rayment, and delight; yet for want of improving it by labor, have not one

---

[9]

Quoted in *Ibid.*, p. 182. The *emphasis* is *mine*.

hundredth part of the Convenience we enjoy: And a King of a large fruitful Territory there feeds, lodges, and is clad worse than a day Labourer in England....

Thus Labour...gave a Right of Property, where-ever any one was pleased to imploy it, upon what was common [unimproved],...[10]

Thus from Locke was drawn the doctrine of the preeminence of the claim to land title of the "tiller of the soil" over the "roving hunter." Thus from Locke, who did not even set foot in America, was drawn "proof" that the first nations of the Americas have never known agriculture. History has honored Locke's dogma with the label *philosophy*, thereby confronting us with the paradox that propagandizing the extermination of scores of nations should be considered a "love of wisdom." Locke was a favorite 'philosopher' of the Founding Fathers of the American Revolution, especially of Thomas Jefferson. But we shall consider the ideology of Mr. Jefferson in more detail a bit further on.

We must first consider the great domestic challenge which faced the colonial propagandists: convincing the citizens of North America's Ancient nations that they *really were* "Indians." In part, this process was managed by the simple technique of insistent repetition of the term "Indian" whenever any colonial agency or any colonist interacted with a prior American nation or citizen thereof. (Naturally, most colonists, already well-conditioned themselves, probably did this labeling quite unselfconsciously. For others, however--the intelligentsia, the political elite, and those truly open to the data gathered by their own senses--"Indian" labeling remained a strenuous act of sheer will. Of this we may be sure, for like the Modern conquerors of

---

[10]

John Locke, *Two Treatises of Government* (New York: Mentor Books, 1960), pp. 338-339, and 431.

Central and South America, Modern colonists in North America recorded a great deal of variation in appearance among "Red Indians," including [but not limited to] very fair skin color, and grey and blue eyes.) Although national names were also employed by the new colonists, such national names were almost always conjoined with the "racial" name "Indians," forming combinations such as Pequot "Indian," or Narragansett "Indians." More often than not, however, the "racial" name "Indian" was simply used by itself, and any trace of national identity was omitted entirely. The terms "half-breed" and "full-blood" were likewise introduced by the colonists and carefully applied to a few specific *phenotypes* (external appearances) which from time immemorial had been present among the variety of North American human appearances. Eventually, persistent enough casual repetition and official use of all of these terms by the irresistible new conquerors was sufficient, over the long run, to also habituate the native citizens of the older North American nations to their usage. But this simple behavioral technique did not exist in a vacuum.

The prayer towns--direct forerunners of today's reservations, reserves, and homelands--"proved" the "Indian" "racial" identity of their inmates by "proving" their "savagery" or cultural and spiritual inferiority in much the same manner as the "savagery" concept was "proven" in mother countries across the Atlantic Ocean. The inmates of these cruel institutions were to be psychologically tormented by the paradoxical cause of their internment: they were there simply because they were "Indians;" that is to say, they were "savages," and because they were such, they were completely bereft of the common sense necessary to know how to pray to God, how to grow crops to feed themselves, or how to live in villages and towns. Simply because they were "Indians," the English missionaries would have to go to great lengths to instruct them in all of these arts. Internment, concentration of the citizens of the continent's prior political bodies in these Prayer Towns also served the interests of the colonists by segregating docile populations of Ancient North Americans from more troublesome ones. And it also segregated the colonists themselves from the "Indians," beginning a Yankee custom of "racial" separation which by itself has gone a long way toward creating present-day North America's distinctive "racial" appearances. Along with this segregation came the selection and installation by the Puritan missionaries of new, non-traditional civil leaders ('chiefs') among the concentrated North Americans; the enactment of laws prohibiting the practice of their old spiritual ways on pain of death; the passage of laws demanding that they observe the Christian Sabbath and adopt the custom of English-style haircuts; and the promotion by the Puritans of the adoption of the English language by the "savages."

Although concentration in Prayer Camps did teach "Indians" their radical, or "racial" inferiority, and did, hence, greatly assist in instilling in them the idea that they really were "Indians," the "social experiment" aimed at Christianizing and Anglicizing them was doomed to failure from the outset. The reasons for this were precisely the same as those for the failures of the sixteenth-century Spanish "social experiments" on the island of Española. In terms of population reduction, however, the Prayer Towns were nearly as successful as the Spanish efforts on Española.

Straightforward ethnocide, nevertheless, remained the English colonists' favorite interaction with the North American nations, and it was also an effective means of "race" education as well. So when thousands were carried off by plagues, colonists could only celebrate, as in 1616, when much of New England was voided of its original Ancient populace.[11] Here, as I suggested in a note in Chapter III above, we must not make the mistake of presuming that each case of the spread of such a catastrophic

---

[11]

Jennings, *op. cit.*, p. 178.

pestilence was purely accidental. Given what we now know about the abundance of transoceanic trade and migration in Ancient times, it may be rewarding to question our old assumptions about the accidental spread of diseases during the period when Ancient societies were forced to give way to Modern ones. Even at the commencement of the Modern Age, world population was relatively sparse compared with the present time, and such conditions did not make the spread of contagions particularly easy. We might even speculate that the quarantine of diseased persons was perhaps known of and practiced in Ancient times, and that such prosthetic measures were reasonably (but not perfectly) effective because of the lighter world population of the time. It is known with fair certainty that plague, cholera, typhus, smallpox, measles, syphilis, and leprosy never took hold in the Americas in Ancient times. A number of organic and some infectious diseases did exist there, however, and these included intestinal worms, varieties of dysentery, the common cold, influenza, and pneumonia. Scarlet fever was present in some parts of North America, and malaria may have been present in some parts of the tropical Americas; tuberculosis may also have been present here and there, but if so, was very rare.[12] Well into Modern times, though, there is no question that diseases were spread throughout the Americas with malicious intent, for this is well documented.

When, in 1763, following the French and Indian War, Pontiac led a confederation of North American nations against the British forts in the old northwest territories, "General Jeffrey Amherst proposed to spread smallpox among the Indians via disease-laden

---

[12]

Virgil J. Vogel, *American Indian Medicine* (New York: Ballantine Books, 1973), pp.139-151.

blankets."[13] In 1837, disease-laden blankets distributed by fur
traders from St. Louis, Missouri, nearly exterminated the villages
of the Mandan nation along the Missouri River, to the very last
person.   The   ensuing   plague   destroyed,   estimating
conservatively, some 50,000 persons as it swept westward across
the northern plains.

The destruction of approximately 2,000 Mandans is a
particularly interesting event in United States' history. It follows
closely after a visit made to the principal Mandan villages by the
artist George Catlin, in 1833. Catlin had greatly publicized the
Mandan nation in the eastern United States, drawing an
enormous amount of attention to them. Of them he wrote:

> A stranger in the Mandan village is first struck with the
> different shades of complexion, and various colours of hair
> which he sees in a crowd about him;...

> There are a great many of these people whose complexions
> appear as light as half breeds; and amongst the women
> particularly, there are many whose skins are almost white,
> with the most pleasing symmetry and proportion of
> features; with hazel, with grey, and with blue eyes....

> The diversity in the color of hair is also equally as great as
> that in the complexion; for in a numerous group of these
> people (and more particularly amongst the females, who
> never take pains to change its natural colour, as the men
> often do), there may be seen every shade and colour of hair
> that can be seen in our country, with the exception of red or
> auburn, which is not to be found.[14]

---

[13]

Vogel, *This Country Was Ours, op. cit.*, p. 55.

[14]

George Catlin, *Letters and Notes on the Manners, Customs, and Conditions
of the North American Indians Written during Eight Years' Travel (1832-*

In this diversity the Mandan people differed little from some of the other Siouan people and some of the Algonquians, for example, the Lakota-Dakota nation (who *did* have red-haired persons), and the Cheyenne (among whom very fair-skinned persons were common). In reporting such diversity, Catlin was no different than Columbus, or Cortez, or Pizarro, or Orellana, or the early North American colonists. But unlike the others, Catlin's description came not at the beginning of the conquest process, but hundreds of years after that process had commenced. The widely-publicized sudden appearance of such a nation as the Mandan must surely have been an embarrassment to the United States of America. For the United States was a Modern nation in which (like all Modern nations) certain political and social interactions had been based upon an already two hundred year-long custom of "racial" segregation. The great misfortune of the Mandan people was that they had been just as well segregated from "the white man" as every other nation of "Indians" had been. Since they could not possibly be explained in terms congenial with the national ideology, the only other possible response to their 'incongruous' existence was to terminate that existence.

But, I must now return to the colonial period of North America. The ethnocidal segregation of North America's first nations from life proceeded not only through the conventional practices of Total War, biological warfare, and psychological warfare, but by chemical warfare as well. Perhaps the earliest incidence of this was in 1623, when Virginia colonists concluded a peace negotiation with a North American confederation led by Opechancanough with a toast of poisoned wine. In the words of Virginia colonist Robert Bennett:

1839) amongst the Wildest Tribes of Indians in North America (New York: Dover Publications, Inc., 1973), *Volume I*, pp. 93-94.

After a manye fayned speches the pease was to be concluded in a helthe or tooe in sacke which was sente of purpose in the butte with Capten Tucker to poysen them. Soe Capten Tucker begane and our interpreter tasted before the kinge would tacke yt, but not of the same. Soe thene the kinge with the kinge of Cheskacke, sonnes and all the great men weare drun howe manye we canot wryte of but yt is thought some tooe hundred weare poysned and thaye comying backe killed som 50 more and brought hom parte of ther heades[15]

In a short time, distilled alcohol by itself, unadulterated by *other* poisons, would come to be recognized as a sufficient enough toxin to be spread among the Ancient nations of the North Americans. Protests against its dissemination among the "savages" by U.S. presidents such as Jefferson and Jackson, foremost post-colonial proponents of the "racial" necessity of segregating "Indians," had a decidedly phoney ring. (After all, the United States government rigidly controlled the fur trade in the western Louisiana Purchase lands for the first quarter of the nineteenth century, and in that region it was fur traders who most ardently promoted the use of *distilled spirits* by the people of the original North American nations. Protests by fur company tycoons such as Manuel Lisa and John Jacob Astor--men who had direct, personal access to U.S. presidents--that the suppliers of illegal spirits were "bad men, not under our control," are at variance with the facts of the matter. The fur company monopolies had divided up the entire western territory among themselves during the course of often bloody struggles. There was no room left for unlicenced and uncontrolled independent

---

15

David R. Wrone, and Russell S. Nelson, Jr., editors. *Who's the Savage? A Documentary History of the Mistreatment of the Native North Americans* (Greenwich, Connecticut: Fawcett Publications, Inc., 1973), quoted on p. 55.

operators in the western lands. (The business life of attempted independent operators was always very short, and in many cases the lives of independent operators themselves were cut short.) But, again, I must return to the colonial period.

In nearly parallel and almost simultaneous development with "Indian"-"white" segregation was the appearance of "Negro"-"white" segregation. As historian Winthrop D. Jordan has most accurately noted:

> The first Negroes landed in Virginia in 1619, though very, very little is known about their precise status during the next twenty years. Between 1640 and 1660 there is evidence of enslavement, and after 1660 slavery crystallized on the statute books of Maryland, Virginia, and other colonies. By 1700 when African Negroes began flooding into English America they were treated as somehow deserving a life and status radically different from English and other European settlers.[16]

The first "Negroes" 'imported' to New England, "were brought by Captain William Peirce of the Salem ship *Desire* in 1638 from Providence Island colony..."[17] This 'importation' was--consciously or unconsciously--a highly symbolic enactment of the burgeoning North American technique of "race"-making through segregation, for the slaves had been received by Captain Pierce in exchange for a load of Pequots (among the few survivors of the Puritan's ethnocidal War upon that nation) he had brought with him to Providence aboard his *Desire*.[18]

---

[16]

Winthrop D. Jordan, *White Over Black: American Attitudes Toward the Negro, 1550-1812* (Baltimore, Maryland: Penguin Books Inc., 1969), p. 44.

[17]

Ibid., pp. 66-67.

[18]

Ibid., p.68.

The slave trade was accompanied by ethnocide on the African continent which was as brutal as that which accompanied the conquest of the Americas. Conservative estimates for its nearly four hundred year course set the depopulation of Africa at nearly twenty million persons.[19] Liberal estimates have run as high as sixty million. While the truth undoubtedly lies somewhere between these extremes, it should not be surprising--given what we now know about the magnitude of the depopulation of the Americas--to find a higher figure to be more accurate. I have not yet, however, mentioned the figures for the destruction of North America's original population in any depth. Although North America was not as densely-populated as Middle and South America, the statistics reflect equally severe devastation. Over the more than three hundred year-long process of the conquest of North America, the continent's original population dropped from a high level of around ten million, to a low point--by 1930--of under half a million.[20] This statistic represents a much greater loss of life than one might suspect at first glance (which would indicate just over 9.5 million persons 'depopulated'). The reason is that this statistic reflects the result of an *extended* 'depopulation' process occurring amongst a population which over the course of more than three centuries *was attempting to replenish itself.* Perhaps in recognizing this, we may begin to perceive another mechanism of Modern "race"-making.

19

Gary B. Nash, *Red, White, and Black: The Peoples of Early America* (Englewood Cliffs, New Jersey: Prentice-Hall, Inc., 1974), on pp. 172 and 187, Nash gives an indication of such dimensions of lost human life, but shies away from committing himself to a concrete figure.

20

Vogel, *This Country Was Ours, op. cit.*, p. 253.

Imagine if you will, the entire, complex, multi-national population of a whole continent being reduced by well over nine tenths. Imagine such a massive depopulation occurring during the course of three hundred or more years of no-holds-barred Total War; during a time when many of the continent's nations disappeared entirely; during a time when nearly every surviving nation, perpetually engaged in guerrilla warfare, was compelled to move from its Ancient ancestral homeland, and often forced to move again and again. Consider the cultural damage which was done, think of the dark ages which at that time fell upon those nations; think of what portions of themselves they could have forgotten, must have lost, merely in order to survive. Then contemplate the conqueror--endlessly denying to them the very existence of the nationalities of its victims--ruthlessly infiltrating the very minds of its adversaries, repeating to them over and over the conditioning words "Indian," "full-blood," "half-breed," and "white man." Given such circumstances, such terror, shall we be surprised to find a marked declension in numbers of native citizens of those nations with "white" complexion? Should we not suppose, as well, that the same destructive process also afflicted the "white" "Blacks" of the West African nations, and, indeed, of all Ancient African nations, south and east, during the carnage of the slave trade? And then there was, added to all of this, the rigidly enforced policy of "racial" segregation.

But still this was not enough to overcome the natural flow of human species nature. From the earliest colonial period, some English people got along too easily and too well with the North Americans, as in the case of the Anglican colonists at Wessagusset, on the south side of Massachusetts Bay. In 1622, Captain Miles Standish marched a troop of Plymouth soldiers to Wessagusset to "save" the colony from an "Indian conspiracy" which the Puritans of Plymouth had 'discovered'. On his arrival at Wessagusset, Captain Standish was informed to the contrary by

one of the colonists there that: "We fear not the Indians, but live
with them and suffer them to lodge with us, not having sword or
gun, or needing the same."[21] But, as Francis Jennings reports:

> Standish promptly created a need for the same. Pretending
> to the Indians that he had come to Wessagusset to trade, he
> enticed a few of them into his hands and then massacred
> them without warning. After this no Englishman could be
> safe at Wessagusset. Indian avengers, not grasping the
> difference between the Englishmen of the two colonies,
> took a toll of three Wessagusset men, and the rest of that
> unhappy community chose to abandon the site. They
> showed their confidence in Plymouth by refusing
> Standish's invitation to return there with him, and they set
> sail eastward in a small boat to make contact with the
> Maine fishing fleet....[22]

For certain periods, the dissenting Rhode Island and the
Pennsylvania Quaker colonies had provided, each in their own
turn, fine models of honest and good-hearted interaction with the
original North American nations, but these departures from the
'true way' were brief, and in the long run ineffective. On the
whole, relations between the Ancient North American nations and
the Modern colonists remained purposely strained and based
upon deceit. Historian Virgil J. Vogel has characterized it in this
way:

> The pattern of white relations with the Indians that was
> established in Virginia was, with few exceptions,
> characteristic of the relations that were to prevail
> everywhere for three centuries. In the stage of weakness,
> friendly relations were to be maintained in the interest of
> self-preservation: a crown for Powhatan in Virginia; a

---

[21]

Quoted in Jennings, *op. cit.*, p. 186.

[22]

Ibid.

hundred Indians invited to the first Thanksgiving feast at Plymouth; recognition of the prior right of Indians to the soil, and negotiations between supposed equals. When settlements appeared to be permanent, the numbers of whites had grown, and their stock of arms was adequate, the attitude shifted to one of overbearing arrogance. The English then took the position that they were not guests in the country, but masters, and that the Indians were subjects bound to obey their laws, and submit to whatever demands the English might make of them. If an accommodation was occasionally necessary, it would only last so long as required to accumulate strength for another blow.[23]

In 1867, following the negotiation of the Treaty of Medicine Lodge, Senator Edmund G. Ross of Kansas restated this position on behalf of the United States. Historian Douglas C. Jones reports that:

Ross said feeding the Indians was cheaper than fighting them. But he went on to say that he did not feel the cheapest course was the best one. He wrote, "The forts on the frontier must be permanently and amply garrisoned and additional posts established." He frankly opposed any system of treaty-making with the wild tribes. When Indians on the frontier had been the stronger of the two parties, treaties had been necessary to pacify the tribes while the country filled up with white settlers, Ross said. But the situation was now reversed, he added gleefully, and it was foolish to dignify the Indians by negotiating with them. In short, when the enemy was stronger, connive to have him talk peace instead of make war; when the tables were turned, refuse him the chance to do the same.[24]

23

Vogel, *This Country Was Ours, op. cit.*, p. 31.

24

Douglas C. Jones, *The Treaty of Medicine Lodge: The Story of the Great*

Ross, however, was merely echoing the sentiments of Andrew Jackson, who, in 1817, had written to President Monroe, "...I have long viewed treaties with the Indians an absurdity not to be reconciled to the principles of our government...."[25] Jackson's view was itself an outgrowth of Thomas Jefferson's opinions regarding the necessity of segregating "Indian" and "white." And views such as Jackson's and Ross' led directly to the U.S. Congressional declaration "That hereafter no Indian nation or tribe within the territory of the United States shall be acknowledged or recognized as an independent nation, tribe, or power with whom the United States may contract by treaty."[26] This legislative enactment passed through Congress on March 3, 1871, without even so much as a debate. It was simply attached by the House of Representatives as a legislative rider to the appropriations act which supplied funds for the Department of Interior during the coming fiscal year.

On the level of individual Modern persons--the colonists, and later on, United States' citizens--the developing custom of segregation was enforced through legislation and propaganda. By 1754, laws prohibiting marriage between "whites" and "Indians" or "Negroes" had been passed in Maryland, Virginia, Massachusetts, North Carolina, South Carolina, Delaware,

---

Treaty Council As Told by Eyewitnesses (Norman: University of Oklahoma Press, 1966), p. 152.

[25]

Quoted in Harold E. Fey, and D'Arcy McNickle, *Indians and Other Americans: Two Ways of Life Meet* (New York: Harper & Row, Publishers, 1970), p. 62. The *emphasis* is mine.

[26]

Quoted in Charles J. Kappler, editor, *Indian Treaties: 1778-1883* (New York: Interland Publishing Inc., 1973), Brantley Blue, "Forward," second page (no page number given). Also in Fey and McNickle, *op. cit.*, p.63.

Pennsylvania, and Georgia.[27] These laws remained on the books for long after the United States achieved independence from Great Britain, and in many states, legislation like this was still in effect well into the present century. It must be observed, however, that such sex laws were principally applied to the middle and lower classes, or that--as in the "Indian" case--certain groups were exempt from them.

Throughout the period when slavery was legal in the United States, male slave owners very often took unofficial (and usually secret) second and sometimes even third wives from among the residents of their slave quarters, and fathered children by them. The membership of this upper class company who practiced a most corrupt form of polygamy included Founding Fathers of the American Republic whose status was fully equal of that of a Thomas Jefferson or George Washington. Among the results of their willful and wanton misuse of captive human beings was to discredit--in the eyes of both Ancient and Modern societies' persons alike--some of the traditional family-building customs practiced in Ancient societies, where forms of marriage other than monogamy were common.

During the first half of the nineteenth century, similar license was bestowed upon the field agents employed by businesses such as John Jacob Astor's American Fur Company. These 'mountain men' often maintained families in St. Louis, Missouri, and cities east of the Mississippi, and also among one of the "Indian" nations with which they plied their trade in the west. As a rule, they rarely upheld a deep, abiding allegiance to the tribal nation which they had married into, but, on the whole, they *were* most useful agents in furthering the cultural disintegration of North America's original nations. They introduced, among other things, the previously-unknown practices of wife- and child-

---

[27]

Vogel, *This Country Was Ours, op. cit.*, p. 29.

beating to the nations into which they had married.   They advanced the cause of drunkenness, and promoted greed and indebtedness through the inauguration of Modern money economy and credit purchase. Among their company numbered the exterminators of the Mandan, and such 'colorful' figures as Liver Eating Johnson, who obtained his nickname because of his appetite for the fresh raw livers of Crow people he killed.

Although both slave owners and mountain men were foremost among the promoters of the inhumanity of their victims, bestowing upon them "racial" nicknames such as "niggers," and "red niggers," they obviously also found them to be intensely attractive 'objects' of sexual desire. Similar trouble sometimes vexed even the most ruthless of military commanders. George Armstrong Custer for example (the ever-faithful and doting husband of Libby Custer), fathered a Cheyenne son--Yellow Swallow--by one of the captive victims of the Washita massacre of Cheyennes in 1868.[28]

But on the frontiers of colonial and later United States' expansion, liaisons of even (or is it *especially*) an honest sort were never to be tolerated between "red" and "white" commoners. The threat implicit in such congress was the immigration of U.S. citizens to North America's Ancient nations, which at that time-- although they had already become rather fully-inculcated in racism, and had gotten an occasional taste for certain aspects of Total War--were still very willing to admit new citizens. In order to forestall such forbidden unions, a uniquely American genre of propagandistic literature was developed: the captivity narrative.

Such narratives were usually presented in a feminine first person. The formula for captivity narratives--from the colonial period through the nineteenth century--was to depict, in the most

---

[28]

Mari Sandoz, *Cheyenne Autumn* (New York: Avon Books, 1964), pp. 16, 25, and 41.

vivid manner possible, the details of Modern, or Total War. The images invoked invariably included the slaughter of entire innocent (non-combatant) families, helpless infants having their brains dashed out against a tree trunk or boulder, surrendering persons being slaughtered pell-mell, others preferring suicide to capture, yet others being captured merely so that they might provide entertainment for their captors by being systematically tortured (skinned alive, perhaps); the mutilation and dismemberment of the dead victims of the "savages" would be graphically described; and lastly, the surviving captive--often a pre-pubescent girl--would be beaten mercilessly by her captors, compelled to submit to gang rape, and other "acts too vile to be mentioned." In the end, she would be delivered by her captors into a bleak existence as a chattel slave, a condition which the "Indians" would make sure she understood was being forced upon her because of the "difference" in their "races."

As terrorizing as these accurate descriptions of Modern War and Modern slavery were, as convincing as their misapplication to North America's Ancient nations was, the United States' retention of "white" citizens on its frontiers still was not perfect. In the nineteenth century, notable immigrants to North America's original nations included: John Dunn Hunter, the Osage founder of Freedonia, the short-lived "Red and White" Republic in eastern Texas; Cynthia Ann Parker, the Comanche mother of Quanah Parker, that nation's most notable nobleman and military commander; and Robert North, the Arapaho leader and military commander. There were many more "black" and "white" "redskins" than this, and some among the multitude were the Arapaho known as Kansas who was an ex-Seventh Cavalryman; the Arapaho *Nibsi*, whose English name was Black Jack; the *Lakota* Frank Huston, a self-described "Unreconstructed Rebel;" and Sitting Bull's turncoat *Lakota* brother Frank Grouard, who claimed Hawaiian ancestry.

The case of John Dunn Hunter is particularly interesting. Hunter was born about twenty five years after the founding of the United States. As a young Osage, his travels paralleled those of Lewis and Clark. At an older age he journeyed to England where he captivated the western Eurasian imagination with his pleas for justice for the original North American nations, and where he became friends with the industrialist Robert Owen, the man who first coined the term "socialism." As the tragic end of his life approached in 1827, he became involved with Thomas Jefferson (who Hunter initially believed held views similar to his own regarding the future of the surviving Ancient nations of North America), a portion of the Cherokee nation, Peter Ellis Bean (an agent of Jefferson's, as well as a friend of both the pirate Jean Lafitte and Andrew Jackson), and Stephen F. Austin of Texas.

Hunter's experience of life in North America's tribal nations commenced when, at the age of two or three years he was taken as a captive by the Kickapoo nation. After a few years with them, he and some other Kickapoos were captured by the Pawnees. In a later encounter, Hunter and some Pawnees were captured by the Kansas nation. Some time after that, when Hunter was about thirteen years old, the Kansas and Osage nations were engaged in warfare, and the band Hunter was with found itself cut off from the main Kansas forces by an overwhelming number of Osages. So they claimed "the rights of hospitality," and were peaceably taken in by the Osages. Not long afterward, Hunter was adopted by a prominent family of that nation. He remained with the Osages until he reached the age of nineteen, at which time an incident provoked by a whiskey-bearing trader piqued his interest in the Modern world.[29] He spent the next three or four years easing himself from the Ancient into the Modern world,

---

[29]

Richard Drinnon, *White Savage: The Case of John Dunn Hunter* (New York: Schocken Books, 1972), pp. 7-10.

working occasionally for trading companies, meeting both wealthy and common citizens of the United States, and also spending a great deal of time alone in the 'wilderness'. Toward the end of this transition period, Hunter devoted a monumental effort toward learning the English language, first studying briefly at a school in Cape Girardeau, Missouri, and later on engaging in extensive studies at a seminary at Pearl River, Mississippi. In the autumn of 1821, Hunter crossed the Allegheny Mountains and headed to the eastern United States where he hoped to further his education, and to publish the autobiography of his life with the western Ancient nations of North America. His story, entitled *Memoirs of a Captivity Among the Indians of North America, from Childhood to the Age of Nineteen...* was published in 1823, the same year he embarked upon a journey to England.

Hunter's narrative quickly became a success, and from the outset its distinction from other captivity narratives was readily apparent.[30] Hunter had no qualms about declaring that he felt that his "captivity" had been an entirely good experience, and that, furthermore, the community-based social ideals of Ancient life had much more to offer to the Modern world. Like others who made the journey from Ancient to Modern, and there have been others,[31] Hunter immediately recognized the enormous threat which the raw mechanical power possessed by Modern societies

---

[30]

Early in 1824, the *Cincinnati Literary Gazette* carried the first of many favorable reviews of Hunter's book. See *Ibid.*, p. 103.

[31]

Another such individual was *Ohiyesa*, who left the *Dakota* nation in 1874, at the age of sixteen, and sixteen years later, at the age of thirty two, attained a degree of Doctor of Medicine from Boston University. *Ohiyesa* practiced medicine for a time on the Pine Ridge *Lakota* reservation, worked tirelessly for the preservation of North America's Ancient nations, and published, among other books, two autobiographical works: *Indian Boyhood*, and *From the Deep Woods to Civilization*.

posed toward the remnant nations of the Ancient world. Once he had arrived in England, Hunter found a warm reception for his notions about both the potential contributions of, and threat to the continued existence of Ancient North America's nations. Having been provided with letters of reference by leading citizens of the United States, possibly including Thomas Jefferson and James Madison, Hunter set about meeting with the upper crust of English society, beginning with the noted agriculturalist Thomas William Coke.[32]

As he toured England, Hunter elaborated upon his ideas concerning the conflict between Ancient and Modern on the North American continent. He reasoned that if the promised contribution of North America's Ancient nations was to be realized, those nations must first be preserved from that which threatened them. To that end, he began to propose the establishment of an independent "Indian" nation beyond the borders of the United States, which would be composed of rural agricultural communities. Soon this advocacy brought him into contact with, and friendship with Robert Owen, a wealthy English industrialist. Owen had dreamed of bringing community back into fragmented industrial society by establishing small industrial-agricultural settlements of workers which would be based upon the principle of self-sufficiency. He called these settlements "villages of cooperation." It is probable that both men exerted a considerable influence upon one another. In 1824, they both traveled to the United States in order to embark upon their individual experiments in human community, Owen's at New Harmony, Indiana, and Hunter's at Nacogdoches, Texas.

While he had been in Britain, Hunter had been surprised to learn that his idea of an independent "Indian" nation, which he had conceived of as a protection for some of North America's

---

[32]

Drinnon, *op. cit.*, p. 22.

Ancient nations, had been paralleled by British diplomacy. The British, he discovered, had sought to establish an independent "Indian" buffer state between first, United States' expansion and Canada (this, he found, had been one English goal during the War of 1812), and later on, between the U.S. and Mexico.

Back in the United States, Hunter traveled with Owen's party for several months in late 1824. Along with Owen and his son William, Hunter had occasion to be informally introduced to Andrew Jackson on December 1, shortly after the November presidential election which had almost brought Jackson into office. The meeting took place in Pennsylvania, outside of the Smithfield Village Inn. In the late summer or early autumn of 1824, Hunter had paid a visit to his 'friend' Thomas Jefferson, in Virginia. There, in the course of the usual amiable conversation, Hunter had been strongly dissuaded from pursuing his dream of an independent "Indian" nation beyond the borders of the United States. Before moving on to join his friend Robert Owen's party in Philadelphia that November, Hunter had written a final letter to James Madison in order to inquire whether a copy of his narrative had arrived properly, and to forward some turnip seeds to him from Thomas Coke's farm.

Hunter's travels and association with Robert Owen had instilled in him the expectation that a great advancement for humanity lay just beyond the horizon. Both men, moreover, shared the conviction that humanity's new age would see the old "individual selfishness system" replaced by a rediscovery of human community bonds and ethical standards, and that "Red" and "Black" would be included as equal partners along with "whites" as beneficiaries of the new social order.[33] And so, filled with such hopes, in early 1825, Hunter commenced a year of travel among some of the western nations of Ancient North

---

[33]

Ibid., p. 168.

America in what are now the states of Arkansas, Louisiana, Missouri, and Texas. All the while he sought to further organize his plans for an independent "Indian" nation outside of the borders of the United States. During the course of the year he observed the westward removal of the Quapaw nation from Arkansas, and the removal of his own Osage nation from Missouri, as an expression of the Jefferson-Monroe-Jackson policy of removing *all* eastern "Indian" nations from United States' lands east of the Mississippi River. In November, 1825, Hunter arrived in east Texas, in the territory of "The Cherokee and Their Associated Bands."

This portion of Texas, north of the town of Nacogdoches, and bordered by the Trinity, Red, and Sabine rivers, was actually home to a loose confederation of a number of nations besides the Cherokee, and embraced a population of some 30,000 persons. Among the twenty-three nations represented there were the Shawnee, Quapaw, Delaware, Kickapoo, Choctaw, Biloxi, and Caddoe. These confederated nations supported themselves primarily by farming and cattle raising. They were so successful at this that when the Mexican governor visited their territory in 1822, he was greatly impressed by their industry. Yet ever since the Mexican revolution had severed Mexico's connection with Spain, the confederated nations of east Texas had vainly sought after a grant from the Mexican government to the lands on which they were living. On several occasions Richard Fields, the principal Cherokee chief, had led delegations to the Mexican authorities seeking to legitimize the confederated nations' title to their east Texas lands. Then, in 1825, the Mexican government gave large grants of land to emigrants from the United States, entitling them to settle on or near the confederated nations' claim.

Hunter arrived on the scene just as the council of the confederated nations was deliberating what course of action to take in response to this new challenge. Joining the council as a representative of the Quapaws, Osages, and other nations across the border in United States' territory, Hunter persuasively counseled against war, an option favored by a number of the council's other representatives. In the end, "...it was resolved to abandon for ever their Ancient Homes and seek beyond the Rocky Mountains or even beyond the shores of the Pacific a refuge from persecution."[34] Before abandoning their lands, however, the confederated nations decided that they would make one final application for a grant of land. As their representative in this petition, Hunter undertook a journey to the City of Mexico.

On March 19, 1826, Hunter arrived at the federal capital. One of his first contacts there was Henry George Ward, the British chargé d´affaires. As Britain at that time was still seeking to limit the United States' (and all other nations') expansionism in the western hemisphere, Ward agreed to indirectly sponsor Hunter's petition on behalf of the confederated nations. Unfortunately, Ward and Hunter's efforts immediately ran into opposition from Joel R. Poinsett, the United States' Minister to Mexico. Poinsett's involvement in Mexican politics had begun the year before when he had engineered a purge of the leading British sympathizers from the Mexican cabinet. Poinsett saw Hunter's request for a land grant as a British-inspired plot to frustrate U.S. objectives in Mexico. Those objectives, he once unofficially acknowledged, included the U.S. acquisition not only of Texas, but also of California, New Mexico, and parts of Lower California, Sonora, Coahuila, and Nuevo León.[35] Throughout that spring, Poinsett succeeded in blocking Hunter's petition. (The move was a precursor of Poinsett's position on "Indian" affairs. As U.S. Secretary of War from 1837 to 1841, he oversaw the

---

[34]

Ibid., p. 182.

[35]

Ibid., pp. 186-187.

deportation of 40,000 "Indians" to lands west of the Mississippi, he ordered General Winfield Scott to march the Cherokee nation down the Trail of Tears to Oklahoma, and he energetically pursued the Seminole War.)[36] Discouraged, Hunter returned to the principal Cherokee village with the bad news just in time for another major council in the early summer.

This time, the council's sentiments were clearly in favor of a war with Mexico. The first objective of that war, it was decided, would be to attack the Haden Edwards grant--bestowed the year before--which had conflicted with the confederated nations' claim. But before the military campaign began, there was time, in early autumn, for Hunter to travel to Nacogdoches and investigate the conditions in the nearby Edwards land grant. There he learned that Edwards and his band of settlers from the United States had experienced a year of very rough times at the hands of earlier squatters and holders of old Spanish land grants. Just prior to Hunter's arrival in Nacogdoches, the Edwards faction of settlers had in fact run out of patience with the situation they were in, and verging on open rebellion had arrested and jailed the mayor of Nacogdoches and a number of leaders of the old settlers' group. It occurred to Hunter that a change in the confederated nations' plans might be in order. One hindrance to their War strategy had been the enormous disparity between the size of their forces and those of the Mexican military. An alliance with Edwards' group of settlers might improve the odds. So an alliance was indeed proposed and eventually agreed upon. On December 16, 1826, the Republic of Freedonia was proclaimed, and a new flag bearing the words "Independence, Freedom and Justice" over two vertical

---

[36]

Ibid., p. 189.

stripes, one red and one white, was hoisted above Nacogdoches.[37] Hunter, Richard Fields, Herman Mayo, and Edwards' brother Benjamin were the first representatives of the new government.

Meanwhile, on his land grant further to the west, Stephen F. Austin had been protesting to the Mexican government about the growing "Indian" population north of Nacogdoches for over a year. When he heard about the proclamation of the Fredonian Republic by way of an invitation to join forces with it, he became enraged. He viewed Freedonia as a direct threat to the prospects of importing the institution of slavery into Texas, and he fulminated that Edwards' settlers "by their unnatural and bloody alliance with Indians" were "no longer Americans."[38] Austin prepared to move on several fronts. He wrote a long letter to Hunter, attempting to split him from the alliance with Edwards. At the same time José Saucedo, the Mexican government's political chief in Texas, and Colonel Ahumada of the Mexican Army wrote to Fields with similar intent. Austin then quickly raised a militia of several hundred of his settlers to augment Ahumada's force of cavalry and infantry, and jointly they prepared to move against Nacogdoches.

Austin also enlisted the services of Colonel Peter Ellis Bean. Bean, who had been employed as a spy during the Jefferson administration, may have met Hunter as early as 1818. Bean and Austin worked closely together to secure a division among the Cherokee. This they did indeed accomplish as Bean and his agents played upon the desire for land security of two of the lesser Cherokee chiefs, Big Mush and The Bowl. With promises of amnesty, and most importantly, of guaranteed land title, Austin and Bean discovered the price of Hunter's life. At the end

---

[37]

Ibid., p. 205.

[38]

Ibid., pp. 212, and 216.

of January, 1827, while traveling between the principal Cherokee village and Nacogdoches, Hunter and Fields were murdered by Big Mush and The Bowl acting under the orders of Austin and Bean.[39]   On January 28, Edwards' settlers abandoned Nacogdoches, fleeing before the advancing Mexican army and Austin's militia.   On February 1, a dispatch from those forces declared Freedonia to be "totally exploded."[40] Big Mush and The Bowl's Cherokee bands never obtained the lands that they had been promised.

Almost *exactly* one year before Hunter's murder, his character had been assassinated in an anonymous article which appeared in the January 1826 issue of the *North American Review*.   Given the United States' self-understanding, and especially in light of Hunter's popularity in Britain as well as his association with Owen, such an attack was inevitable. In terms of the United States' ideology, Hunter was an impossibility, and a dangerously subversive one at that.   As a captive who had enjoyed captivity, as a 'genuine' "white man" who at the same time was truly and completely "Indian," Hunter stood as a living testimonial against the "race" idea; he brought to life the very humanity of those people who the United States' ideology had denied were human, and who had been marked for "extinction." The unnamed author of the article, "Indians of North America," supported his attack upon Hunter's character with letters from such luminaries as lawyer and "Indian" agent Henry R. Schoolcraft, and General William P. Clark. Twenty two years later that author, no longer seeing a need to conceal his identity, bragged that he had unmasked Hunter's entire existence as a

---

[39]

Ibid., pp. 212, and 216.

[40]

Ibid.

"palpable forgery."[41]   The occasion for that boast was the Democratic U.S. presidential candidacy of Lewis Cass, former governor of the Michigan Territory, and Secretary of War under the presidential administration of Andrew Jackson. By the turn of the century, Hunter's life had become reduced to an obscure footnote in the history of Texas.

Throughout all of Hunter's literary and political tribulations his 'friends' Jefferson and Madison never once lifted a finger to defend or help him. But then they never attacked him either, and that, perhaps, was statement enough. One thing is certain though; Hunter was an inestimably valuable source of information about North America's first nations (although he was unknowingly one) for Thomas Jefferson. Throughout his lifetime, Jefferson soaked up information about Ancient North America like an eternally dry sponge, yet he shed scarcely a drop of it. Although he was one of the first Modern investigators to undertake the scientific excavation of an Ancient North American burial mound, Jefferson reported nothing about the artifacts he discovered there, but instead concentrated his attention upon the location, number and kind of skeletal remains contained within the mound.[42] Being a brilliant lawyer, Mr. Jefferson knew how to argue his case most effectively. Discussing the possible places of origin of the people of North America's first nations, for example, Jefferson commences with the observation that: "Discoveries, long ago made, were sufficient to show that the passage from Europe to America was *always* practicable, even to the imperfect

---

[41]

Ibid., p. XV.

[42]

Thomas Jefferson, *Notes on the State of Virginia* (New York: Harper & Row, Publishers, Incorporated, 1964), pp. 93-96.

navigation of ancient times."[43] Yet he ends his speculation on origins with a strong assertion that these could be deduced from "the resemblance between the Indians of America and the eastern inhabitants of Asia."[44] This he asserts in spite of the fact that the forced segregation of "Indians" and "whites" had not yet 'perfected' that resemblance, and in spite of his own previously-stated opinion about "Indians" that: "we shall probably find that they are formed in mind as well as in body, on the same module with the 'Homo sapiens Europaeus'."[45]

Concerning the languages of the Americas, Jefferson was equally double-minded. In one paragraph of his *Notes on the State of Virginia*, he declares that: "Were vocabularies formed of all the languages spoken in North and South America...it would furnish opportunities to those skilled in the languages of the old world to compare them with these...and hence to construct the best evidence of the derivation of this part of the human race."[46] But in the succeeding paragraph he appears to strongly preclude the need for such a study by insisting that the languages of the "red men" of Asia and the "red men" of America "have lost all vestiges of their common origin."[47] This latter statement may indeed be Jefferson's contribution to the present-day anthropological fable that "the languages of the Americas are totally unrelated to all other languages in the world." However,

----

[43]

Ibid., p. 96, *my* emphasis.

[44]

Ibid.

[45]

Ibid., p. 59.

[46]

Ibid., p. 97.

[47]

Ibid.

the evidence shows that Jefferson himself had an extremely powerful interest in conducting such comparative linguistic research, especially regarding the relationship between Ancient Mediterranean and North American languages. During his presidency, Jefferson "instructed Lewis and Clark to make careful lists of words used in the languages of the various tribes through whose territory the explorers were to pass."[48] After the conclusion of the Barbary Wars--which occurred during Jefferson's presidency--the selection of consular officials to staff the new United States' diplomatic offices in North Africa seems to have been dictated by the linguistic ability of the candidates. Through 1823, United States' consuls at Algiers, Tunis, Morocco and Tripoli were compiling word lists of exactly the kind requested by Jefferson of Lewis and Clark.[49] Yet no results from Jefferson's 'personal' linguistic research ever came to light, even though he had ample time to consider the data which had been gathered at his request. This, it seems, was the result of a most unfortunate 'accident'. According to Jefferson's biographer Thomas Fleming:

> What Jefferson hoped to make the great intellectual work of his retirement was destroyed by a scoundrel. In a trunk shipped from the White House to Monticello were notes and observations he had accumulated over fifty years, on Indian languages and dialects. He planned to write a definitive book on the Indian languages, which would help trace their origins, by comparing their basic linguistic patterns to those of other cultures. With his knowledge of Anglo-Saxon, Greek and half a dozen other languages, Jefferson was superbly qualified for the task. But a thief broke into the ship while it was en route to Monticello, and stole this

---

48

Fell, *Saga America, op. cit.*, p. 218.

49

Ibid., pp. 219-220.

irreplaceable trunk. Finding nothing salable in it, he threw it into the James River. Friends managed to fish out a few of the manuscripts that drifted to shore, and sent them to Jefferson, mud-smeared and illegible. But all hope of doing a comprehensive work was gone.[50]

Curiously, no satisfactory explanation has ever been offered for this thief's extraordinary selectivity. He appears to have singled out the trunkful of manuscripts as if he knew exactly what he was looking for. At any rate, following the loss of all of his data on the subject, Jefferson remained completely mum on the topic of similarities between North American and North African and Eurasian languages. Surely a person as intelligent as he should have remembered some of the conclusions which fifty years of research had led him to.

If all of this seems confusing, Jefferson's policy regarding the United States' relations with the Ancient North American nations appears to be clear enough. "In truth," he wrote in 1803, "the ultimate point of rest and happiness for them is to let our settlements and theirs blend together, to intermix, and become one people."[51] But at the same time, Jefferson sought "the rapid extinguishment of Indian land titles" east of the Mississippi.[52] And in 1808, when a delegation of Cherokee farmers petitioned Jefferson with a request for assignment of land title in severalty, and bestowal of U.S. citizenship, he gave them a cool reception and suggested that they pack up and move across the Mississippi.[53]

---

[50]

Quoted in *Ibid.*, p. 220.

[51]

Quoted in Jordan, *op. cit.*, p. 480.

[52]

Drinnon, *op. cit.*, p. 170.

[53]   *Ibid.*, pp. 170-171.

Jefferson was both condescending and menacing at his first meeting with a delegation from the Dakota-Lakota nation. He told them that:

> The French, the English, the Spaniards have now agreed with us to retire from all the country which you and we hold between Canada and Mexico....Be assured you shall find advantage in this change of your friends....
>
> My children, we are strong, we are numerous as the stars in the heavens, and we are all gunmen. Yet we live in peace with all nations; and all nations esteem and honor us because we are peaceable and just[54]

After that and other nations of the northwest had allied themselves with the British during the War of 1812 (an alliance which, after all, was in the interest of their own survival), Jefferson's tone became more than menacing. In a letter to John Adams, he wrote: "...we shall be obliged to drive them, with the beasts of the forests into the Stony [Rocky] mountains."[55]

So perhaps there were two Thomas Jeffersons: the one who wrote tirelessly about Freedom and human Equality, who rigidly opposed the very concept of slavery; and the one who tediously expounded upon the inferiority of "the Negro," and energetically crusaded for a solution to the "Negro" problem in the United States by advocating 'their' complete removal from the North American continent, and 'their' shipment to Africa. Or at least we might think that there were two Jeffersons were it not for a slip

---

[54]

Quoted in Virginia Irving Armstrong, compiler, *I Have Spoken: American History Through the Voices of the Indians* (Chicago: The Swallow Press, Inc., 1971), pp. 40-41.

[55]

Quoted in Drinnon, *op. cit.*, p. 157.

of the pen which he once made in a letter to a friend in Paris, and which that friend most injudiciously neglected to destroy. Referring to the slaves which he himself held, he wrote:

> ...my debts once cleared off, I shall *try* some plan of making their situation happier, determined to content myself with a small portion of their ~~liberty~~ labor[56]

It would appear that Jefferson *tried* but did not *do* for the rest of his life, and that his economic fortunes did not improve sufficiently for him to relinquish his hold on his slaves' labor--or should we say *liberty*--until after he had died, at which time he did 'emancipate' them.

In light of all this prevarication, perhaps there was only one Thomas Jefferson after all--Thomas Jefferson the consummate ideologist. Surely this is the Jefferson which we may see in the *Declaration of Independence*. It is the ideologist *par excellence* who as a slaveholder makes the unequivocal statement that: "We hold these truths to be self-evident, that all men are created equal..." and who at the same time unequivocally believes in and writes extensively on the subject of the inferiority of--the *inequality* of--"the Negro." It is the ideologist *par excellence* who writes in the *Declaration* of "the merciless Indian Savages, whose known rule of warfare, is an undistinguished destruction of all ages, sexes, and conditions," and who also writes in *Notes on the State of Virginia* while describing the excavation of an Ancient North American burial mound containing the remains of one thousand individuals of all ages, sexes and conditions, that of all of those human remains, "No holes were discovered in any of them, as if made with bullets, arrows, or other weapons."[57]

---

[56]

Quoted in Jordan, *op. cit.*, p. 432, *my* emphasis.

[57]

Jefferson, *op. cit.*, p. 95. Jefferson's observation here is perfectly in tune with the majority of data for the Eastern Woodlands culture area, which shows a remarkable lack of warlike activity in Ancient times.

For all of the talk about liberty which Jefferson and his co-founders of the United States indulged in, mental freedom appears to have been an item which was not high on the agenda. Although James Madison expressed the opinion, in *The Federalist Papers*, Number 10, that "giving to every citizen the same opinions, the same passions, and the same interests" would be "impracticable," he and the other Visitors of the University of Virginia--which was founded by Thomas Jefferson--agreed with Mr. Jefferson that the study of politics should most surely be subject to 'prescription'. In a mood to censor by prescription rather than by proscription, these gentlemen of Virginia sought to regulate the shape of political thinking in the university--and in the developing nation as well--by resolving in 1825, that:

> Whereas it is the duty of this Board...to pay especial attention to the principles of government which shall be inculcated...and to provide that none shall be inculcated which are incompatible with...the Constitution of this State and of the United States...it may be necessary to point out specially where these principles are to be found legitimately developed: Resolved, that it is the opinion of this Board that as to the general principles of liberty and the rights of man, in nature and in society, the doctrines of Locke in his *Essay concerning...Civil Government*, and of Sidney in his *Discourse on Government* may be considered as those generally approved by our fellow citizens of this, and the United States, and that on the distinctive principles of the government of our State and of those of the United States, the best guides are to be found in (1) the *Declaration of Independence*,...(2) the book known by the title of *The Federalist*,...(3) the *Resolutions of the General Assembly of Virginia* in 1799 on the subject of alien and sedition laws,...(4) the valedictory address of President Washington, as conveying lessons of particular value; and that in the

branch of the School of Law, which is to treat on the subject
of Civil Polity, *these shall be used as the text and
documents of the school.*[58]

The purpose of all this very directed reading was in fact to
"inculcate" a strong bias in favor of the form of government called
democracy, for as another prominent Virginian, George
Washington, phrased it in his December 7, 1796, message to
congress:

> The more homogeneous our citizens can be made in these
> particulars, the greater will be our prospect of permanent
> union; and a primary object...should be, the education of
> our youth in the science of government.[59]

In spite of James Madison's reservations, this program of
limited, or limiting education seems, over two centuries later, to
have been a remarkable success. At the present time, Locke's
Essay..., the *Declaration of Independence*, and *The Federalist*
constitute the core not only of high school civics courses, but also
of standard university instruction in political science in the
United States. And as a whole, most citizens of the United States
today are in unanimous agreement that there exist in the world
but two forms of government: tyranny (or dictatorship) and
democracy. The level of agreement is, indeed, quite uncanny--
communists and socialists in the United States complain that the
general government is not democratic enough, populists seek to
improve democracy, liberals of the left wing work for the
inclusion of the unenfranchised into democracy, middle of the
road liberals and conservatives point with pride to the smooth
operation of democratic institutions, conservatives further to the

---

[58]

Bernard Crick, *The American Science of Politics: Its Origins and Conditions*
(Berkeley: University of California Press, 1967), quoted on pp. 14-15, *my*
emphasis.

[59]

Quoted in *Ibid.*, p. 3.

right feel that democracy is being eroded, reactionaries fear that democracy might be tainted by its extension to the unworthy, extremists of both wings refer to the democratic ideal, and the political reference point of anarchists often seems to come closer than anyone else's to the Ancient definition of democracy.

This agreement about democracy is all the more remarkable considering that Jefferson, Madison, and the other Founding Fathers read Latin, and in some cases Greek, and that they were familiar with the Ancient language of politics. The Founding Fathers knew perfectly well that in terms of that Ancient language, there are six basic forms of government; three good, and three corrupt. The elements of the six 'pure' forms may be combined together to create a nearly innumerable array of real governments. The three good forms of government, listed from the most to the least desirable are: Monarchy (as in the rule of the God Kings or Titans), Aristocracy (the rule of those who are ablest, or best qualified), and Timarchy, or Timocracy (the strict constitutional rule according to the laws). The three bad forms of government are corruptions of the three good forms. Listed in corresponding order, they are: Tyranny (the rule of a tyrant or dictator), Oligarchy (the rule of the few rich--today known as Plutocracy), and Democracy (the rule of the mob). All of this, however, is what has been deliberately ruled out of the public discussion about politics in the United States.

The extraordinary unanimity of Yankee opinion does appear to coincide nicely with the opinion (or is it the desire?) of Jefferson and a number of his colleagues that men (let us not forget that when the United States came into being, it was intended by its creators that women should have no share of the business of politics) to match *their* wits should never again enter into the profession of politics. In fact, that curious unanimity of opinion might even be seen as guaranteeing that result, for it has insured that in the U.S., politics is not among the most intellectually-stimulating fields of endeavor.

Perhaps the assertion that Jefferson and some of his colleagues were ideologists *par excellence* seems unwarranted, or not susceptible to documentation. However, for some twenty years, Jefferson conducted a lively correspondence across the Atlantic Ocean with Antoine Destutt de Tracy, the Modern French rhetorician (and Revolutionary 'Minister of Grammar') who coined the term "ideology."[60] Indeed, Jefferson was the English translator of Tracy's *A Treatise on Political Economy; to which is prefixed a supplement to a preceding work on the Understanding, or Elements of Ideology; with an Analytical Table, and an Introduction on the Faculty of the Will....* Jefferson's opinion of ideology was summed up most succinctly by Tracy's biographer Emmet Kennedy:

> ...Tracy's educational ideas, with which Jefferson had long been familiar, influenced Jefferson's plans for the University of Virginia. In a letter addressed to the president of the Albemarle Academy, which was to later become the University, Jefferson adopted Tracy's fundamental distinction of 1801 between two classes of citizens, "the laboring and the learned. The laboring will need the first grade of education to qualify them for their pursuits and duties; the learned will need it as a foundation for further acquirements." A technical division would "abridge" subjects taught in greater detail to professional men. The commissioners charged with finding a site for the University omitted Jefferson's and Tracy's class distinctions, but they did include "ideology" of the "doctrine of thought" as one of the University's ten projected departments, as did the legislature's incorporating act of 1819. In the following years, Jefferson,

---

[60]

Emmet Kennedy, *A Philosophe in the Age of Revolution: Destutt de Tracy, and the Origins of "Ideology"* (Philadelphia: The American Philosophical Society, 1978), pp. 208-250.

as rector of the University, promised Tracy that his translated works would "be the elementary books of the political department in our new University," a promise which Lafayette found fulfilled in 1825.[61]

In light of such rhetorical acumen as was possessed by the United States' Founding Lawyers, we should not be surprised to find the origin of institutional (as well as personal, or 'practical') racism written into the primary legal document of the nation, namely the *Constitution*. Since, as we have already seen, the mere contention that "racial" categories are real categories is the very source of racism, we find that legally-sanctioned racism in the United States begins in the Constitutional discernment of "Indians not taxed" (Article I, Section 2), and in the determination that: "Congress shall have Power...To regulate Commerce...with the Indian Tribes" (same Article, Section 8). The second reference to "Indians" is, in fact, a very direct declaration of the United States' intention to use the 'politics' of the "race" idea in pursuit of its national objectives. This is so because the Founding Fathers knew perfectly well that the other nations--the older nations--of the continent were just that--*other nations*--and not a uniform "race." There is no mention made of "whites" or "Negroes" in the *Constitution*, but "Negroes" are *implied* in Article I, Section 2, as "three fifths of all other persons."

(If, however, the *Articles of Confederation* had remained the legal basis of "perpetual union" in the United States, racism would have been no less firmly established in United States' law. In Article IX, we find: "...Congress...regulating the trade and managing all affairs with the Indians," and we also find Congress making "...requisitions from each State..." [for the purpose of building and equipping an army and navy] "...in proportion to the number of white inhabitants." Oddly, the authors of the *Articles*

61

Ibid., pp. 231-232.

did, in Article VI, refer to "some *nation* of Indians (*my* emphasis)." Yet this 'slip'--referring to North America's Ancient nations *as* nations was, however, 'corrected' in the writing of the *Constitution*.)

From that founding moment to the present, the semi-permeable hereditary social class system--the "race" system--of the United States has kept the lower and middle classes of the nation fragmented into separate, hostile, mutually-suspicious color ghettoes, incapable of uniting over the issues which are of genuinely common interest to all of them.

This separation of the lower classes in the United States into hostile camps incapable of uniting into a politically-effective majority is a fulfillment of an important objective of the Constitution: the establishment of a potentially extended republic (stretching from the Atlantic to the Pacific coast) as a defense against the threat posed by "factions" to the conduct of business as usual.   In the words of James Madison in *The Federalist Papers*, Number 10:

> Extend the sphere and you take in a greater variety of parties and interests; you make it less probable that a majority of the whole will have a common motive to invade the rights of other [that is to say, the *wealthy*] citizens; or if such a common motive exists, *it will be more difficult for all who feel it to discover their own strength and to act in unison with each other.*[62]

Although the power of an extended republic to diffuse the formation of 'undesirable' majorities may be a debatable topic, the desire to create an extended republic was an established reality in the United States.   As Jefferson put it in his first inaugural address, in 1801, the United States would be: "A rising

---

[62]

Alexander Hamilton, James Madison, and John Jay, *The Federalist Papers* (New York: The New American Library, Inc., 1961), p. 83, *my* emphasis. My comment in brackets.

nation, spread over a wide and fruitful land,...advancing rapidly to destinies beyond the reach of mortal eye..."[63]   One thing is certain; the inclusion of racism in the basic founding law of the nation was a great help to the continental expansion of the United States. With the stroke of a pen, the use of the word "Indian" in the U.S. *Constitution* psychologically--*rhetorically*--invalidated scores of very old and politically-viable nations holding prior claim to the North American continent.   This simplified the United States' expansion across North America, because the need for entering into *serious* negotiations with those scores of nations had been removed by the refusal to 'formally' recognize their existence.

The practice of interest group (lobbyist) politics intrinsic to the extended republic which the *Constitution* encourages, works very well with the constitutional promotion of racism. Originally, this combination of ideas insured that the lower classes of "whites" (which included the 'middle' class) would never see the need or the logic of joining forces with "Negro" slaves, or "Indians."   As things have turned out in the United States, however, 'freedom' has ultimately been granted to persons of all colors of complexions. "Negroes" scheduled for deportation by no lesser figures than Jefferson, Jackson, and Lincoln; "Indians" 'destined' for 'removal'; "Asians" never included in the original 'plan'; "whites;" all are now 'equal'. And now, the constitutional safety valve of interest group politics *continues* to function as an effective protection against the formation of 'undesirable' majorities.   Dovetailing with the constitutional mandate to recognize "races," the barrier to the union of the non-ruling classes of the United States is perpetuated as each well-defined

---

[63]

Quoted in L. Earl Shaw, editor, *Modern Competing Ideologies* (Lexington: D.C. Heath and Company, 1973), p. 190.

'group' of 'equals' pursues its own goals in *competition* with (and to the exclusion of the interests of) the other 'groups'. But more of this a bit later.

The unbridled "destiny" to which Jefferson referred in 1801, had developed, by the late 1840^s into the concept "Manifest Destiny." Specifically, Manifest Destiny meant:

> ...expansion, prearranged by Heaven, over an area not clearly defined. In some minds it meant expansion over the region to the Pacific; in others, over the North American continent; in others, over the hemisphere....It attracted enough persons by the mid-1840^s to constitute a movement. Its theory was more idealistic than [President] Adam's [of 1819] had been....It meant opportunity to gain admission to the American Union. Any neighboring peoples, established in self-government by compact or by a successful revolution, would be permitted to apply. *If properly qualified*, they would be admitted.[64]

The admission of the Republic of Texas, proclaimed in 1836, to become the 28th state of the Union in 1845, was to serve as an example. It was not Hunter's Freedonian Texas where "Indian" and "white" cooperated which was acceptable--it was Stephen Austin's slaveholding Texas that was the perfect example of 'proper qualification'. So in that spirit, the California Republic of 1846 was admitted to the Union in 1850, and the Hawaiian Republic of 1893 was annexed to territorial status in 1898 (immediate statehood for Hawaii was out of the question, because of the Islands' very high population of "non whites").

After the catastrophic U.S. Civil War (which claimed over one million lives), the *Constitution* was amended to reflect the new status of "Negroes," who no longer could be legally enslaved. However, there was nothing in the post-Civil War amendments,

---

[64] Frederick Merk, *Manifest Destiny and Mission in American History: A Reinterpretation* (New York: Vintage Books, 1966), p. 24, *my* emphasis.

specifically numbers XIV and XV, which altered the constitutional condoning of racism in the United States' basic law. Section 2 of the former amendment left the mostly indirect recognition of "racial" categories unchanged by retaining the original wording of Article I, Section 2 of the *Constitution*, which refers to "Indians not taxed." Section 1 of the latter amendment went even further, actually demanding the recognition of "racial" groupings. The wording here is: "The right of citizens of the United States to vote shall not be denied or abridged...on account of race, color, or previous condition of servitude."

In such an environment wherein a heightened consciousness of "racial" classification is commonplace, a remark such as that of U.S. Army General William Tecumseh Sherman in 1868, is not at all out of context. At that time the general observed that:

> The more Indians we can kill this year, the less will have to killed next year. For the more I see of these people, the more I am convinced that they will have to be killed or maintained as a species of paupers.[65]

In the year before Sherman made his observation about the future of the "Indian" "species," the Ku Klux Klan was formally organized at a convention in Nashville, Tennessee. The reason for the Klan's creation was to 'deal with' the 'problem' created by the emancipation of the slaves which had been held in the Southern states. Although the Klan was quickly challenged by the U.S. government, and was considered to be dissolved in 1871, organizations of similar intent continued to exist in the South. At any rate, throughout the 1870s, the Southern states developed a new segregation system in response to the emancipation of slaves: "Black" and "white" were to be educated separately, were to live in separate communities, were to sit in separate sections of

---

65

Quoted in Ray Stebbins, editor, "Custer, He Wanted Glory but Found Death Instead," in *Colorado* (Denver: Colorado Magazine, Inc., July-August, 1972), p. 14.

theaters and restaurants which both "groups" were allowed to enter (almost always, only one "group" would traditionally be allowed into particular restaurants), and marriages between the "races" were strictly forbidden. Even service in the United States' military forces was conducted in rigidly-segregated units up until the late 1940^s. All of these aspects of "racial" segregation were written into the laws of the Southern, and a large number of the Northern states. Such laws were upheld in U.S. federal statutes, and by U.S. Supreme Court rulings. In Northern states in which segregation was not legally enforced, it was often encouraged in a subtle *de facto* manner. Laws and customs of separating "Black" and "white" stayed in force in the United States until the civil rights movement of the mid-1950^s began to erode some of them. The results of this longstanding system of "racial" segregation have been thoroughly studied and well-documented. Facilities which were legally alleged to be "separate but equal" were not at all so. Lower class citizens of the United States unfortunate enough to be "racially" classifiable as "Black" suffered from systematic miseducation, acute *and* chronic poverty, severely dislocated family life, chronically poor health, and a markedly reduced life expectancy.

The Ku Klux Klan was reborn twice after its 1871 demise. Once in the vicinity of Atlanta, Georgia, in 1915, and again in 1944. Although the Klan is considered to be a "white" supremacist organization, over the years it has pursued a very limited form of "white" supremacy. At various times victims of Klan attacks have included (in addition to "Blacks"): Roman Catholics, Jews, Northern European immigrants, Southern European immigrants, Eastern European immigrants, and liberals from the Northern states, to name just some. Since the end of the First Atomic War, the Klan has been paralleled and supplemented by the development of an American Nazi Party.

However, because the enforcement of "racial" classification and subsequent segregation of human beings along "racial" lines engenders hatred among all people, the Klan has also been paralleled by hate groups focused outside of the "white" group. Among the oldest of such groups in the United States is the Black Muslims--the Lost-Found Nation of Islam--founded by the 'Prophet' Elijah Muhammad. Recent additions include the American Indian Movement, and the Jewish Defense League.

Meanwhile, although certain rights of United States' citizens were allegedly not to be denied or abridged "on account of race," the United States sought to take into account the "race" which might be right among those who sought to become citizens--the potential immigrants to the nation. Beginning in 1882, the United States Congress passed a series of "racial" exclusionary immigration laws. The first, in 1882, banned all Chinese immigration. In 1908, Japanese immigration was banned. The Immigration Acts of 1917 and 1924 banned all "Oriental" immigration to the United States. Finally, in 1943, the Chinese ban was relaxed and replaced with a quota, and three years later quotas for immigration from India and the Philippine Islands were fixed. Although the United States ended all "racial" immigration bans in 1952, the quota system remains intact, enforcing subtle "racial" restrictions on immigration to the present day.

Meanwhile, the United States Congress diligently discharged its "Power" to regulate "Commerce" with the "Indian Tribes." At first, lasting from Washington's Presidency until 1822, that Power was discharged under the auspices of the United States Indian Trade Bureau. Two years later, the exact nature of United States "Commerce" with "Indian Tribes" was more precisely defined when the Bureau of Indian Affairs was created as a division of the War Department. In 1849, with the conquest of North America's first nations finally in view, the Bureau of Indian Affairs was appropriately transferred from the War Department to the

Interior Department. In the 1870^s the resistance of the Sioux Nation--the last great nation of Ancient North America to fall to United States' conquest--was broken once and for all. Although military problems persisted for the United States in the form of the Ghost Dance "craze," or as small guerrilla bands of Apache hold-outs up until the 1890^s, and although there were even massacres of very small "Indian" bands as late as the early years of the twentieth century, the present-day period of concentration of "Indians" on "reservation" camps began in earnest in the 1870^s.

This period saw the most intensive "race" idea conditioning of the remnants of Ancient North America's nations which had ever occurred up to that point. This was the period during which the United States began to successfully breed an eternal "species of paupers." From the moment that the present-day reservations were established, the United States' authorities sought to keep track of every "Indian" concentrated thereon. In order to do this, tribal enrollment codes were imposed upon the various incarcerated nations via the U.S. Bureau of Indian Affairs. Enrollment--membership--in the various nations was redefined for them by the B.I.A. in accordance with the "blood quantum" laws. The "blood quantum" system was the method by which the B.I.A. determined the "degree of Indian blood" of each individual member of the captive nation in question. Persons determined to possess an 'insufficient quantity' of "Indian blood" were liable to be ineligible for tribal membership. Initially the desirable "quantum of Indian blood" was set by the government. But that eventually changed.

Unfortunately, history remains mute on the identity of the clever government official who rediscovered the old sixteenth century Spanish legal device of the "Degrees of Purity of Blood" which had served the Spaniards so effectively in their oppression of persons of Moorish and Jewish ancestry. Nevertheless, the device has been an effective one. And the form of oppression and culture destruction known as the "blood quantum" laws did not work alone.

As the various nations came to be "civilized," or "pacified" (that is to say, conquered), and concentrated on reservations, one of the first 'requests' made of them by their captors was that they hand over to the authorities all "captives" (the "Black" and especially "white" persons who had been naturalized as citizens of those nations according to the Ancient law of adoption) who still remained among their numbers. (When Cynthia Ann Parker was 'rescued' in this manner she sank into a terminal case of severe depression, for she had no desire to think of herself as anything other than a Comanche.) This surrender of "captives," along with the introduction of the "blood quantum" laws, began the systematic erosion of North America's Ancient nations' functions as real nations, eliminating for them the regulation of immigration. Much more subversion of their cultures was to follow.

As every individual member of the captive reservation nations came to be enrolled, the custom of bestowing English-style names--consisting of a surname and a given name--was established for them. In most cases, individuals were simply assigned a name by the B.I.A. official in charge. (After all, every internee had to be listed, had to be accounted for.) Early in the 1880^s the religious practices of the various nations--with especial attention paid to the Sioux--were by United States' law declared to be illegal. Enrolled persons could not travel off of their reservation without a pass to do so. In the same decade, boarding school education away from home was established for enrolled children. Carlisle and Haskell were the first model institutions for such education, but soon mission schools sponsored by various competing Christian sects were found to provide sufficient separation from family and community for enrolled children. Once so separated, the children were allegedly to be instructed in the same manner as any other Modern citizens of the United States. In fact, in those days (and even up to the present day) the great majority of victims of boarding school education graduated scarcely able to read and write in plain English, unable to perform most simple mathematical operations, and ignorant of much of their own culture as well as the culture of the United States. There were things which *were* learned, however. Upon arrival at a boarding school, young males were forced to submit to a Modern short-style haircut (the type of haircut first made popular by soldiers in the Roman army, and later on reintroduced by the Roman Church). All new arrivals were forbidden to use the native language of their own nation. Those who insisted on doing so had the desire quite literally beaten out of them. Such punishment remained a common practice up until the 1920ˢ. Indeed, abusive physical punishment was easily resorted to for *any* reason in the boarding schools. On the still darker side of things, the amount of pederasty--the companion of battery--practiced upon boarding school children may never be known, but a great deal did occur.

From as early as the 1870ˢ, there had been non-tribal ranchers and farmers living adjacent to reservations who were getting along on very friendly terms with the inmates of the camps. Some married persons from the reservations. But during the 1880ˢ and 90ˢ, nearly all of those friendly "whites" (the males were labeled "squaw men," a usage which originated in the 'mountain man' era) who had married into reservation communities were hounded off of the reservations at the insistence of B.I.A. officials.

From the outset of the present reservation system, the traditional national governments of North America's Ancient nations were quite deliberately undermined by the United States. This was immediately demonstrated by the political supremacy of the agency superintendents of the reservations. Superintendents freely overruled and displaced the decisions of

Ancient traditional governing councils, and usually appointed new puppet political "chiefs" often against the wishes of the citizens of reservation communities. National customs of timeless antiquity were continually undermined on all fronts. Land use patterns were deliberately destroyed by the Dawes Act of 1887, which allotted all reservation lands in fee simple lots of 160 acres to each individually-enrolled tribal member. Ancient systems of national jurisprudence were displaced by tribal courts and tribal judges appointed by the B.I.A. Ancient customs and laws were replaced by Modern codes of tribal laws. Families and communities were further sundered by the illegalization of polygynous marriage. At every step of the way, institutions of education and authority never relented in spreading the message that the Ancient laws and customs being destroyed by the conqueror were inadequate, stupid, backward, and disgraceful.

By 1924, the United States was so confident that the national identities of North America's Ancient nations had been utterly destroyed and replaced with the bogus "racial" identity "Indian," that once again Congress acted by fiat (as in the cessation of treaty-making) and bestowed United States citizenship upon all "Indians." However, this "citizenship" is of an exceptional nature and possesses a unique "racial" qualification such as might only be found elsewhere under the old apartheid regime of the Union of South Africa. Persons living in the United States ordinarily tend to think of U.S. citizenship as a uniform phenomenon, the rights and privileges of which apply equally to all who are eligible to partake of it (excluding, of course, persons found guilty of committing felonies). But this is not so. Off of a reservation, an "Indian" person is a fully-equal citizen of the United States, subject to the basic federal law of the *Constitution*, and due the protection of the Bill of Rights, the first ten amendments of the *Constitution*. But should the same "Indian" person stray onto a reservation--*any* "Indian" reservation--*none* of the above will automatically apply.

That duplicity is largely due to the major focus of the United States' twentieth century psychic attack upon the remaining vestiges of the first North American nations. One would think that the program of systematic national and cultural destruction undertaken by the United States between the 1870ˢ and 1930ˢ would have been enough, but it apparently was not. In 1934, the Indian Reorganization Act guided the B.I.A. toward a new "mission:" the "protection" of "Indian" "sovereignty." The I.R.A., as the act was known, stipulated that those tribes deciding to comply with its provisions (and nearly all did, as was also the case with the bestowal of U.S. citizenship) were to establish new *written* constitutions. These new constitutions would be modeled after the U.S. Constitution, and would form new tribal council governments. Such governments were to be considered "sovereign" entities, and by this Act, the "Indians"--who were in fact the descendants of nations which had governed themselves with perfect competency for hundreds, and in many cases *thousands* of years--were to be taught the arts of self-government. At any rate, this new establishment of tribal governments and the new federal position on "sovereignty" compounded an already confused question of legal jurisdiction on reservations. Federal laws applied on reservations, but the Bill of Rights did not (and so, the ineffective Indian Civil Rights Act was passed in the 1960s), tribal governments had no jurisdiction over "non-Indians" on reservations, state laws did not apply on reservations, and there was still the unsettled question of the jurisdiction of tribal governments over "foreign Indians." All of this made legal 'no man's lands' of the reservations--all of them--in the post-I.R.A. period. Reservations literally became legal 'free fire zones' in which almost anything goes. That condition persists to this day.

The new tribal governments (as well as the governments of tribes which refused to adopt the I.R.A.) have learned to artfully mimic the style of their conqueror. Almost without exception, present-day tribal councils are business oligarchies staffed by the men and women who are the most successful ranchers, farmers, or businesspeople on their respective reservations. On the whole, they rule with an eye toward the protection of their own specific personal business interests. This tends to leave the majority of the other enrolled reservation members (excluding favored family members, friends and cronies of the council members) out in the cold, without government in a lawless land. Many of these unenfranchised people are convinced, however, that they are being properly governed, because they know that the members of their tribal councils possess a sufficient "degree of Indian blood" to qualify under U.S. and tribal laws as genuine "Indians." For them it is enough to simply know that they are being governed by honest-to-God (pedigreed) "Indians."

In a small number of cases, tribal business enterprises such as logging, oil wells, oil leases, or gambling casinos turn a handsome profit, and in these cases a monthly *per capita* payment is issued to each individual enrolled tribal member. Here, it is common for tribal board members to face easy re-election simply by associating themselves with the distribution of *per capita* payments. In *per capita* tribes, common greed often gets the upper hand, and enrollment laws are the toughest of all, working against even those persons who possess the requisite "quantum of Indian blood." The objective in these situations is a desire by enrolled members to make the tribal rolls get even smaller and smaller, for the fewer the number of enrolled members, the larger the payments to those who do qualify for tribal membership. Over the long run, this results in a sort of voluntary tribal self-destruction. However, that trend toward suicidal population declension is slightly offset by those families which opt to take advantage of the fact that the more legitimate children a family has, the more *per capita* payments it gets. On these affluent reservations when marriages go bad, as they very often do in the psychologically-tormented reservation environment, child custody battles in tribal court are usually *per capita* custody battles in actuality. It is in the majority of cases on affluent reservations that children reach the age of eighteen years with absolutely no *per capita* money left in their B.I.A.-held Individual Indian Money (I.I.M.) accounts, for it has already been bled off and spent by their parents.

On some of the poorer reservations, *per capita* payments may be made only once or twice a year. The occasion for such payments is sometimes the settlement of an old treaty dispute. On one Montana reservation a payment is usually made at Christmas time--sometimes at the risk of bankrupting tribal finances. The reason for such risk-taking is clear: a grateful reservation community--made up of people who easily rank among the poorest in the United States--can be expected to keep the tribal chairman and council members responsible for such a gift in office for as much as--and sometimes more than--a decade.

Thus, over the period of one hundred years, the United States has subverted traditional forms of government some of which were thousands of years old. Their inversion was nearly perfect. In Ancient North America most constitutions were firm and unwritten (a constitution does not need to be written down in order to exist), now most are written down, and are very weak. In Ancient North America, government was basically monarchical or aristocratic (that is, it was conducted by true monarchs--persons who genuinely took the best interests of the people of the state as their own--or by the *aristoi*--those who were really best suited to *serve* as governors), now tribal governments--which fulfill every criterion of colonial puppet governments--are tyrannical and oligarchical, led by dictatorial strong men, and councils of self-interested rich persons. Corruption, which was once an unimaginable vice, has become a positive *value*.

After one hundred years of U.S. government imposition *via* the "blood quantum" laws and other supplemental strategies, the "race" idea has firmly taken hold on reservations, successfully destroying Ancient national identities. Reservation inmates now think of "what kind of Indian" they are, rather than of what their nation is. To throw this form of mental derangement into its proper perspective, imagine people in western Eurasia identifying themselves as English "white men," or Italian "white men," or Bosnian "white men." Or imagine people in eastern Eurasia describing themselves as a particular 'kind' of "Yellow man," rather than as Chinese, or Korean, or Okinawan.

By now, most tribes have completely forgotten the very-widespread Ancient customs of exogamy (whereby persons married outside of their own tribe or community), and adoption, two methods--which in addition to the national birth rate--had allowed North America's oldest nations to increase in size, and had also enabled them to diversify their populations. The "blood quantum law"--which most tribes now think they themselves invented--has eroded the Ancient nations in two further ways: 1.) some persons, not wanting to "dilute" the "bloodlines" have come dangerously near to marrying very close relatives--this is a problem on most reservations because of their relatively small sizes; and 2.) the children of "fullblood" parents from two different reservations may only be legally-enrolled on *one* reservation, and with only a 50% "blood quantum." (In the succeeding generation such "half breed" children, if they marry persons from other reservations with similarly 'diluted' "blood quantum," will produce children with only 25% of legally-defined "Indian blood quantum." Eventually, [*as the authors of United States' law and policy understood perfectly well*] such healthy exogamy will result in the development of "full-blooded" "Indians" who have absolutely *no* legally-recognizable "quantum of Indian blood.")

Then there is another result of the "blood quantum" laws: the obsessive and compulsive dialogue about the "degree of purity of blood" on reservations has, beyond creating a "species of paupers," created people who are unselfconsciously and spontaneously very racist. Of course "Indians" hate "the white man," and this hatred is even encouraged and indulged by such governmental agencies as the B.I.A., but the most unrestrained flow of "racial" hatred evinced by "Indians" is, after the grand Yankee manner, reserved for the 'group' they know as "Niggers." Along with such hatreds comes a "racial" paranoia. If an "Indian" is arrested off of the reservation, caught, for example, in the act of committing some crime, the on-reservation response is likely to be that the arrest was a frame-up, or that the trial will be unfair, because "they hate Indians." This form of mass-paranoia is compounded by the reality of and dynamic workings of "racial" segregation. In almost all cases, rural reservations are surrounded by rural communities of self-described "whites." Although some of these persons are actually very direct relatives of some of the people on the reservations, as a rule, the "white" residents of off-reservation communities may be found to simultaneously loathe and romanticize "the Indian." Both of these attitudes are unrealistic and destructive. At the same time, both 'sides' promote the fable of "racial" non-communication: no "white" will *ever* be able to fathom the working of the "Indian" mind, and *vice-versa*.

This is the manner in which the oldest nations on the North American continent have been subverted by the "race" idea. This is the manner in which they have been turned inside out and stood on their heads. And here, although some of what I am saying now is nothing new, some of what follows is a closely-guarded secret on the reservations. In the early twentieth century, tuberculosis and severe childhood ear infections were epidemic on reservations. The situation is somewhat better now, but these problems still persist to a degree much higher than anywhere else in the U.S. Life expectancies are considerably shorter on reservations than elsewhere in the United States as well. But there are other serious epidemics on the reservations which endanger psychic as well as physiological health.

Fermented alcoholic beverages were by no means unknown in the Ancient Americas, but alcoholism was a rare condition; now there is scarcely a reservation family which has not been touched at some time or other, to a greater or lesser degree, by the disease of alcoholism. As recently as the nineteenth century, people of the Ancient North American nations complained abundantly about and earnestly questioned Modern patterns of battery in the United States. Often they asked: "Why do you beat your women?" or, "Why do you beat up little children?" Now, thanks in large measure to generations of abuse in the boarding and mission schools, as well as to alcoholism, child abuse--including incest and other sexual abuse--is epidemic on reservations. The battery of a spouse, a rare experience in Ancient North America, was once sufficient cause for an easy divorce (divorce itself being not that common an experience was, nevertheless, non-stigmatizing). Now divorce is a common and very uneasy experience on reservations, and spouse and sweetheart abuse has become so widespread that "Indian love" is jokingly referred to as "a hickey and a black eye." The violence is not limited to either sex. A woman, or for that matter a man, not able to beat up their mate, may resort to the use of a deadly weapon to vent their rage, or very commonly, they might take a hammer to the windshield of the mate's automobile. Perhaps a mate so aggravated will get a gang of friends or family together and attack their partner or that person's ubiquitous lover. And in the lawless reservation environment such gang violence, often resulting in uninvestigated--and hence unsolved--homicides is not at all rare. In the nations of Ancient North America human sexuality provided for the creation of children, the pleasure of adults, and the lifetime bonding of marriage partners (whether monogamous or polygynous). Now, although sex still results in children on reservations, the conception of a child is often regarded as an 'accident' by at least one of the persons involved. Permanent bonding by adults of the opposite sex is becoming an increasingly-rare experience on reservations, and whether or not sexual pleasure still exists there is a matter which is completely open to question. This is so for several reasons. To begin with, it has become customary that the almost universal introduction to sexuality for prepubescent girls in certain reservation settings consists of being taken to a drinking party by someone they trust, then being administered alcohol until they become unconscious, then being gang-raped ("trained," in the language of the 'rez') by every male present. Curiously, few reservation residents seem outraged by such behavior. Most persons, from ordinary citizens to police personnel and even Special Investigators (the latter being the people charged with investigating such incidents) hold the attitude that any female who passes out from drinking at a party *deserves* such treatment. It is questionable whether women receiving such "training" will thereafter be able to link sexuality and pleasure in a healthy manner. Some victims of this mistreatment escalate (as childhood victims of incest or sexual abuse often do) to a lifetime of excessive, unfocused 'loose' sexual behavior. The men are also damaged by the gang rape phenomenon, for although they do not realize it, they are being "trained" as well. They are being *conditioned* to be unable to form a healthy relationship with women; they are being trained to be unable to think of women as anything other than things, or objects of exploitation. On reservations, human sexuality is at once desperate and compulsive. Given the firm connection between alcoholism and sex on reservations, the possibility of pleasure in human sexuality is all the more questionable, because drunken persons often "don't know" what they are doing, or afterward "don't remember" what they have done. On top of all this, sexuality is likely to be regarded on reservations with a point of view resembling the antique New England Puritan attitude; and that decidedly anti-traditional perspective is usually defended as being 'traditional'.

On reservations poverty is of course epidemic. Miseducation, a phenomenon common to "racial" ghettoes across the United States is also epidemic. After all, what better means is there to keep people out of the cultural mainstream than to deny them the tools, the knowledge, with which to operate competently within that mainstream? And recently, the United States federal government has found a most clever method of reinforcing "race" idea consciousness among the people on reservations, and also of easing any reservations or misgivings they may have had about being the victims of miseducation, all in a single stroke. The new device is called "Indian preference." This is a job-hiring system in which federal law mandates the hiring, wherever possible, of "Indian" persons for federal jobs on reservations over "non-Indians," usually regardless of the qualifications of any of the parties involved. That is to say, according to U.S. federal law, the qualification of "Indian genetics" often overrides all other job qualifications found within an applicant pool. The system has spilled over into the hiring practices of most tribal governments as well. The result of this has been the filling of tribal and B.I.A. positions with underqualified and incompetent employees far in excess of levels which could be explained by the normal operation of the 'Peter Principle". Another result is that important positions on reservations sometimes go unfilled for periods in excess of a year, due to a lack of "preferenced" applicants. This is exactly the opposite of what one would expect if the federal government *honestly* did believe that the various tribes really *were* like "developing nations." *If* that were true, the federal government as trustee for and tutor of the tribes would guide them toward the acquisition of the most highly-qualified employees and public servants at all times. The argument on the other side, advanced by liberal supporters of "Indian" preference is the 'genetic gap in mentality'. Only an "Indian," they argue, is equipped to grasp the unique conditions existing on a reservation. Only an "Indian" is equipped to apperceive the unique qualities of "Indian" culture. Now, inasmuch as the U.S. federal government is the sole creator of the "Indians" and of the "Indian culture" of the United States, it is, after all, appropriate that the U.S. government should dictate how and by whom "Indians" are best served.

Perhaps the most extreme example of this sort of reasoning is a recent decision by a Federal Appeals Court judge in San Francisco. An "Indian" woman in Alaska had taken a fancy to a social services position being advertised by her local B.I.A. office. But a "non-Indian" person with some education in the field of Social Work and with some field experience too, also applied for the position and was hired instead of her. The "Indian" woman decided to fight the hiring decision and took her case to court. Finally, in the federal court it was ruled that the "Indian" woman was indeed most supremely qualified to help manage her local B.I.A. Social Service Division's overburdened caseload of general assistance, emergency assistance, and most importantly, child protection cases. Although she had never received any education above the high school level, nor had she received the education which travel affords, nor had she ever had the experience of holding a social services job previously; the federal judge found that by virtue of living in the community in which she was going to be employed, she must have somehow 'absorbed' a grasp of the complex field of Social Work--it somehow must have been 'in her blood'.

Of course there is no substitute for experience for a great deal of what we do in this life. This is why *recovering* alcoholics form the successful core of Alcoholics Anonymous. This is why recovering alcoholics who have had *extensive training* in the fields of psychotherapy and counseling make such good alcoholism counselors at the various alcoholism treatment centers. This is why women who have successfully *broken out of the cycle* of an abusive marital relationship make such good counselors and administrators at spouse abuse shelters.

However, this was not the essence of the federal court judge's reasoning. The "Indian" woman in question had lived the reservation experience, to be sure, but lacking education or former on-the-job training, she had *nothing to indicate* that she had made *any effort toward understanding* what that reservation experience was about; that is to say, her experience was truly internalized, but not externalized--there was no evidence of an effort on her part toward self-understanding. To argue that experience without understanding constitutes qualification is akin to saying that the pedophile is the most highly-qualified expert on child abuse.

In rendering such a decision, the Federal Appeals Court judge in San Francisco in effect reaffirmed the federal position that "Indian preference" is a legitimate means of continuing with the oppression of the first nations of North America. Unfortunately, the memories of the remaining descendants of those nations have recently become very short. Otherwise, they would recall that Andrew Jackson, an under-the-table promoter of alcohol for "Indians," an above-board promoter of money and 'education' for "Indians," an "Indian" fighter *par excellence*, and the Great Remover, was the *first person* to propose an "Indian preference" law. The wording of Jackson's proposal, made in 1835, was nearly identical to that of the current "Indian preference" law. In it he said that: "in all cases of appointment of...persons employed for the benefit of the Indians a preference shall be given to persons of Indian descent...."[66] Considering that there was little, if anything, which Jackson did in relation to North America's original nations out of a love for them (or out of respect for them), there is left but a single meaning for the policy of "Indian preference" in his own day. After over one hundred years of concentration camps for "Indians" in the United States

---

[66]

Quoted in Vogel, *This Country Was Ours, op. cit.*, p. 135.

it is extremely unlikely that the meaning of federal policies such as "Indian preference" which periodically reappear, could ever have changed. In addition to the other problems caused by "Indian preference" which I have mentioned above, there is also, on almost every reservation, a general resentment felt by local persons toward B.I.A. employees who are "foreign Indians."

I have not yet, however, completed my survey of epidemic conditions on the reservations of the United States. Political corruption has become so rampantly epidemic among the various tribal councils, that in reservation country the words politics and corruption have become synonyms. Nepotism in the job marketplace is so epidemic that it is not merely a saying, but a fact that one gets a job because of who one knows, rather than because of what one knows (unless, that is, one is an accomplished blackmailer). The situation of favoritism and nepotism has become so extreme, in fact, that a very hard-edged class system has arisen on reservations. It is a two class system composed of the in-group and the out-group; the haves and the have-nots. It is a system which stands radically opposed to the Ancient virtue of generosity which was upheld by almost all of the nations before their incarceration on reservations. It is a system which is not discussed with outsiders, and hence, it has not yet been 'discovered' by anthropologists and others who 'study' "Indians." So have nations which throughout Antiquity were accustomed to the best of governments become conditioned to accept the worst, in the form of a grotesque caricature of the government of their conquerors.

But I must continue with my survey of epidemics on reservations. Denial--a symptom common in a number of mental disorders (as well as in alcoholism and the abuse of other drugs)--is epidemic on reservations. Hence, when a few years ago, then Secretary of the Interior James Watt accurately described some of the serious conditions existing on reservations, the response from "Indian" country was an angry wave of denial. The refrain heard issuing from all quarters was: "Nothing is wrong here. People always only say negative things about us. Our troubles are no different than anyone else's. *We're* in charge here. What we have here is an accurate reflection of our own unique culture, which is something which outsiders are simply incapable of comprehending, and so they should keep their mouths shut."

Above all, delusional thinking prevails on reservations, its greatest symptoms manifesting themselves around the U.S. government-inculcated notion of "sovereignty." Since its inception, the United States, as we have seen, did everything possible (short of complete extermination) to erode and displace the sovereignty of the prior nations of the North American continent. Yet since the Indian Reorganization Act of 1934, the 'mission' of the B.I.A. has been to "prevent the erosion of Indian sovereignty." The practical result of this purposively self-contradictory policy on behalf of the United States is that people on reservations fanatically believe that they are members of "sovereign nations" and at the same time, no one on any reservation has the slightest idea of what the rights, duties, and obligations of a sovereign are. This may be taken as a matter of fact, because on no reservation are a complex of sovereign governmental functions performed.

With but one exception, no reservations issue passports for foreign travel to their citizens. Reservation borders are by no means sovereign; they are violated thousands of times daily by unregistered airborne, vehicular, equestrian, or pedestrian traffic. There are no border crossing stations on U.S. highways entering and leaving reservations, as there are between the U.S. and Canada, or the U.S. and Mexico. No reservation has a customs department, or customs agents. Reservation governments do not tax their own citizens. Reservation governments do not issue their own currency, they establish no rate of exchange with foreign currencies, they have no postal departments. Not a single reservation possesses an army or military establishment of its own; not even one of a ceremonial nature. With few notable exceptions, the business of most tribal councils is conducted in English--a foreign language. And indeed, in far too many instances, native national languages are nearly extinct. Without exception, all tribal governments are patterned after models imposed by the United States--a nation foreign to them. None bear any resemblance to the Ancient governments of North America which preceded them. Tribal Courts and Courts of Indian Offences reflect the Modern United States system of jurisprudence, and not indigenous cultural systems. Tribal constitutions and codes of law are based upon the model provided by the United States. In some cases, tribal codes have even been written by a particular large Washington, D.C. law firm. No reservation has immigration statutes or admits any immigration whatsoever. This of course is a result of the "blood quantum" laws initially imposed by the United States, and by now assimilated by every tribe.

Let us consider this last point a bit further. Consider the consequences if the United States had restricted its own citizenship by such a suicidal measure as a "blood quantum" requirement. In this century alone the results would have been disastrous. Had Albert Einstein and his colleagues in the field of nuclear physics been denied U.S. citizenship because of "race"-- because they could not measure up to some standard of required "blood quantum"--the United States would in all probability not have been the first nation to develop the atomic bomb. The outcome of the First Atomic War would surely have been different because of that. Atomic diplomacy would have been a tool at the disposal of some other nation. If Wernher von Braun and *his* colleagues had not been admitted to U.S. citizenship because they in effect lacked the qualification of "prior genetic citizenship," the space program in the U.S. could have never proceeded along the same lines that it has. There would never have been U.S. moon landings or a space shuttle. Throughout its history, the United

States has been made what it is because of the immigration it has actively encouraged and admitted. There have in fact been no viable nations in the entirety of history which have completely barred immigration. The regulation of immigration is indeed one of the foremost functions of a sovereign government. It is also a function which is, as I have said, totally unknown on every reservation in the United States.

And yet, if measured by the standard of the "blood quantum" laws, many of the founders, leading citizens, and heroes of the Ancient North American nations would today be ineligible for tribal citizenship. Washakie, the Shoshone leader who was born a Flathead would, by today's standards, be unqualified to be a member of, and hence, to serve the Shoshone nation. The very large number of Crow people who were made Cheyenne by adoption and marriage after the Battle of Prior Creek in the early nineteenth century, would now be ineligible for Cheyenne citizenship. And Robert North, who gave his life for that nation, could not now legally be an Arapaho.

Now, I must say a little bit about the background of this section immediately preceding, regarding the conditions on reservations today, for almost none of what I have written here is accompanied by documenting sources. There is a very good reason for this. Even though for the past twenty-five years I have made an exhaustive study (in the academic sense) of the relationship between the United States and "Indians," what I have written in the section above comes not only from research, but also directly from my personal experience. I am the member of a large extended family. The smaller portions of my family live in California and Oregon, and are of middle class background. The larger portion of my family is very poor and lives mostly on the Pine Ridge Reservation in South Dakota. For the past twenty years, I have lived on the reservations of the *Lakota* ("Sioux," in English) nation and its old allies. During that time I have viewed the flow of daily events from various 'stations' including 'in-group' and 'out-group'. In discussing the events, situations and circumstances which characterize the darker aspect of reservation life right now, it has been my preference to rely exclusively on direct sources and personal experience. All of the people whom I know are my *primary resources* for the section above; they have been involved as bystanders, or perpetrators, or victims of every malady I have mentioned.

To be sure, there is a brighter side of reservation life. There is normality to be found; there is faith, there is trust, there is great love. At times it seems as if nothing has been lost culturally at all (for example during the sun dance time of the year). But it also remains a fact that there is great pain on the reservations. That there, there is a great, unending scream. Indeed, so clever, so invidious is the tormented psychological environment of "Indian" reservations that now, over a century after their reestablishment, they resemble prisons in which each and every inmate has a key to the cell door, and yet still, and quite willingly, chooses to lock her or himself inside. It is strange that such multi-national humanitarian organizations as Amnesty International do not make a serious inquiry into the psychological and physical condition of the "Indian" reservations. Reservation psychology is curiously similar to that of the victims of systematic torture. According to Richard Reoch of Amnesty International's London office, one encounters among torture victims a sort of "a moral inversion where every human being you encounter has as his purpose to be cruel, to inflict pain, to lie or *make you feel worthless.*"[67] One does not have to travel far in reservation country to encounter a similar inversion. Coupled with this, there is an excessive distrust of outsiders, manifested by an unwavering unwillingness to discuss with them, or even *admit*

---

[67]

John Leo, "Salvaging Victims of Torture," in *Time* (New York: Time Inc., February 18, 1985), p. 86, the *emphasis* is mine.

the existence of problems. There is a hatred of and distrust of bureaucratic authority, there is depression, there is guilt, and there is "a form of weary aimlessness born of disorientation."[68] Complicating all of this, as I have already mentioned, is the psychological defense mechanism known as denial. The observation made by the Canadian founder of Survivors International about torture victims applies equally well to the inmates of reservations: "Some people live in an environment of such general brutality that they don't realize they've been tortured."[69] Finally, as a recurrent, persistent theme, there is the everpresent process of delusional thinking based upon hypotheses of "race."

There are countless examples of this, but a few of my own personal encounters with such thinking include the following: A young Dakota man in Montana--a very average person in all respects--explained to me on one occasion in great detail how "when the white man destroys himself with environmental pollution, we need not worry, for Indians possess a secret internal organ which is capable of digesting and neutralizing such things." In Poplar, a beloved and respected Dakota elder explained to me at great length the mental deficiencies of "half breeds." "They are crazy," he phrased his thesis in summary. I was left to wonder at his adoption as son that very summer of a "very white-looking" nephew of his, and his long-term--apparently very happy--marriage to a woman who is "a breed." On Pine Ridge, someone very close to me once observed regarding his life work as a healer: "I love everybody--even a Nigger." A more

---

68

Ibid.

69

Genevieve A. Cowgill quoted in Christopher S. Wren, "Salvaging Lives After Torture," in *The New York Times Magazine* (New York: The New York Times, August 17, 1986), p. 19.

impersonal example is drawn from a Denver newspaper. An article discussing the housing and jobs shortage faced by persons who leave the reservation to move to urban areas, quoted the belief of a young *Lakota*: "Indian people adjust more easily to being outdoors than any other race."[70]   On the reservation, "racial" convictions such as these are the rule, not the exception.

Elsewhere in the United States--off of the reservation--the terrors of "race" continued to multiply, from the nineteenth century through the twentieth. Beginning with a conversation which President McKinley had with God in 1898, we shall consider but a few instances of this, as an exhaustive accounting would fill much more than the present volume. The subject of McKinley's conversation was the best possible future for the Filipino "race." Addressing a group of Methodist clergymen who were visiting the White House, McKinley revealed his moment of divine inspiration:

When...I realized that the Philippines had dropped into our laps I confess I did not know what to do with them. I sought counsel from all sides...I went down on my knees and prayed Almighty God for light and guidance more than one night. And one night late it came to me this way--I don't know how it was, but it came:

1. That we could not give them back to Spain...;
2. That we could not turn them over to France or Germany...;
3. That we could not leave them to themselves-- they were unfit for self-government--and they would soon have anarchy and misrule worse than Spain's war [the Spanish-American War];

---

[70]

Quoted in William Gallo, "Tall teepees illustrate housing shortage," in *Rocky Mountain News* (Denver: Rocky Mountain News, July 16, 1985), p. 7.

4. That there was nothing left for us to do but to
take them all, and to educate the Filipinos,
and uplift and civilize and Christianize them
as our fellow-men for whom Christ also died.

And then I went to bed and slept soundly, and the next morning I sent for the chief engineer of the War Department (our map-maker), and I told him to put the Philippines on the map of the United States (pointing to a large map on the wall of his office), and there they are, and there they will stay while I am President![71]

The Filipinos, however, did not agree with President McKinley and God about their unfitness for self-government, and so they declared War upon the United States. The ensuing struggle exacted an unrecorded toll of thousands of Filipino lives, and dragged on in some parts of the Philippine Islands until the second decade of the twentieth century.

Meanwhile, on the home front, the lynching of "Blacks"--for crimes entirely imagined--was a common occurrence in the southern states of the U.S. throughout the first half of the twentieth century. The high point of such violence was reached in January of 1923, when a man from the "Black" town of Rosewood, Florida, was accused of raping a "white" woman. In response, a mob of 1,500 "whites" from the surrounding area assembled and sacked Rosewood. The entire town was burned, and at least 40 "Black" people were murdered. No member of the "white" *demos* was ever brought to justice for the murders.

With the United States' entry into the First Atomic War in 1941, a group of enterprising west coast businessmen saw a seductive "racial" opportunity for a quick and enormous profit.

---

[71] Quoted in Morton Borden, editor, *Voices of the American Past: Readings in American History* (Lexington, Massachusetts: D.C. Heath and Company, 1972), p. 224. The emphasis is *mine*.

They immediately began to foment a hysterical fear and hatred of persons who were immigrants from Japan, or whose parents or grandparents had immigrated from Japan. Such persons, they asserted, posed an enormous security risk to the United States. Because of "racial" loyalties, the argument ran, they might all indeed be spies for Japan. In a quick response to this west coast hysteria, Executive Order 9066 was promulgated: it ordered the removal of all Americans of Japanese ancestry to concentration camps, the most well-known of which were Manzanar in the California desert, and Heart Mountain in the Wyoming desert. The government maintained that this 'relocation' had been "largely for the protection of the internees." In a quick response to their relocation, all real, business, and personal property of the incarcerated persons was confiscated by the fomenters of the hysteria. Many of the sons of these families, seeking to demonstrate their loyalty to the United States, joined the 442nd battalion, an "all Japanese" army unit fighting for the United States in the European theater of operations. As things turned out, the 442nd was *the most highly-decorated of all U.S. military units* which fought in the First Atomic War. But the surviving Americans of Japanese ancestry who were sent to those concentration camps during the First Atomic War had to wait over forty years to receive a *fractional* compensation for the property they and their families had unjustly lost at that time.

In its vigorous persecution of the War effort, the United States differed little from its adversaries. In the course of the struggle three powers, Germany, Japan, and the United States actively pursued the development of a nuclear weapon. The Germans, who had lost many of their most brilliant nuclear physicists to the United States, were unable to overcome the problems inherent in the development of an atomic bomb, but they did perfect a missle-delivery system. After the War, German developments in rocketry formed the basis of both the United States' and the Soviet's space programs. In Japan, the physicists working on the bomb project were inadequately funded, and they were also quite distrustful of the military regime's potential for responsibly dealing with such an awesome weapon. And so, they proceeded with deliberate sloth. The United States' effort under the code name Manhattan Project, however, moved full-speed ahead, and on July 16, 1945, the first atomic bomb was exploded in the New Mexico desert. Although in years to come, a number of the people who had worked on the project would have second thoughts about their creation, on the morning of the first explosion, only one of the scientists present, Bob Wilson, morosely intoned the words: "What a thing we've made!"[72]

By the time of the first nuclear explosion, Italy and Germany had already surrendered, and deployment of that weapon in the European theater of operations was out of the question. Throughout the course of the War, "racial" stereotyping had played a key role in the War propaganda of all nations involved: the Nazi concept of an "Aryan" German "master race" and the 'evil' Jewish counter-"race" is well-known , as is Hitler's characterization of the United States as a nation of "mongrels." In his speeches, Winston Churchill countered the Hitlerian rhetoric with his notion of the British "race." The United States, for its part, proclaimed the inborn evil of the "Jap" and "Kraut" (Germans had been bestial "Huns" during the First World War-- there were no concentration camps for Americans of German ancestry, however, not even for the open Nazi sympathizers of the German-American Bund), and abhorred the racist excesses of the Nazi regime (at the same time, the U.S. was fielding military units which were almost perfectly segregated--the officers were always "white"--into "Black," "white," and "yellow" divisions). But in

---

[72]

Quoted in Stephane Groueff, *Manhattan Project: The Untold Story of the Making of the Atomic Bomb* (New York: Bantam Books, Inc., 1968), p. 408.

spite of all the racism which the war nurtured, it was probably not just antagonism toward the "Jap" which prompted the United States to drop the first wartime nuclear bombs on the cities of Hiroshima and Nagasaki. The real target of the first use of nuclear weapons was much more likely the Soviet Union.

Although the official and popular versions of the first deployment of nuclear weapons in human history insist that "if the bomb had not been used, Japan would have never surrendered without a costly invasion of the Japanese homeland which would have resulted in the loss of over two million American lives," the reality behind the events is a bit more complex. In February of 1945, the three major Allied Powers-- Britain, the Soviet Union, and the United States--had met in conference at Yalta, in the Soviet Union, to discuss the terms of the approaching end of the war. There, Churchill, Stalin, and Roosevelt began to iron out an agreement between themselves about the post-war partition of Germany, the treatment of Axis war criminals, and the payment of reparations by the losers of the war to the winners. Also at the Yalta conference, Stalin agreed that the Soviets would declare War upon Japan, and join in the War on the Asian front after the surrender of Germany.

From its outset, the alliance between the Soviet Union and the United States had been an uneasy affair at the upper levels of government. Now, as the sequel to Yalta, the conference at Potsdam, Germany, in July of 1945 took place, President Harry Truman had the ultimate bargaining chip: "atomic diplomacy," and the Soviets would not be able to bully the democratic nations about any longer. Much had changed since the meeting at Yalta earlier that year.

President Roosevelt had died and had been succeeded by Truman. Prime Minister Churchill's tenure in office was coming to an end--he was replaced midway through the Potsdam talks by Clement Atlee. The War with Germany was over--Hitler was dead, the Soviet Army had advanced into Berlin, and was in possession of Eastern Europe; the process of prosecuting War criminals had commenced. De Gaulle was in France, Mussolini was dead, the United Nations had been founded, and there was immanent unrest in the colonial world. Russia had not yet joined the War against Japan, but was preparing to do so. However, United States military operations were achieving impressive successes against Japan in the Pacific island campaign, and the U.S. was not so sure that the Soviet Union should now join the War in that theater--Japan had now already suggested its willingness to surrender (albeit conditionally).

But most importantly, the very day before the conference at Potsdam began, the United States had exploded the first test nuclear device ever. Secretary of War Stimson--with Truman at Potsdam--had been sent a coded message from the New Mexico test site on the day of the explosion. The message said: "Operated this morning. Diagnosis not yet complete but results seem satisfactory and already exceed expectations. Dr. Groves pleased. He returns tomorrow. I will keep you posted."[73] The next day another message followed: "Doctor has just returned most enthusiastic and confident that the little boy [the bomb scheduled for Hiroshima] is as husky as his big brother. The light in his eyes discernable from here [Washington, D.C.] to Highhold [Stimson's house on Long Island, New York] and I could hear his screams from here to my farm."[74]

Churchill and Truman were jubilant. From Potsdam, Truman dispatched to Washington the following message regarding the first military use of the bomb: "Suggestion

---

[73]

Quoted in *ibid.*, p. 410.

[74]

Ibid.

approved. Release when ready but no sooner than August 2."[75] Now, although the Soviet Union's dominion over Eastern Europe would be agreed upon at the conference, the United States and Britain would be intractable in their insistence that the Soviet Union have no share in the victory in Asia. Stalin as yet had no idea of exactly what was going on.

Four days after the Potsdam conference was ended, the Hiroshima bomb was dropped, and Stalin *did* find out what was going on. When Harry Truman got word of the nuclear bombing of Hiroshima as he was *en route* back to Washington aboard the cruiser *Augusta*, he proclaimed: "This is the greatest thing in history!"[76] In appreciation of that day's 'greatness', the Soviets, two days later, declared War on Japan. The following day Soviet forces moved into Manchuria, proceeding irresistibly and with great speed. But that same day a *second* bomb was dropped by the United States, this time on Nagasaki. Stalin balked. It was apparent that the U.S. not only had developed the most destructive weapon ever, but that it possessed several of them. It was also apparent that the United States was prepared to deploy that weapon against an enemy. Truman's demonstration had been an effective one. Five days later Japan cabled its unconditional surrender to the United States.

Now, when the U.S. suggested to Stalin that he hand over the territory the Red Army had acquired in Manchuria to the Chinese Nationalist forces of Chiang Kai-shek, Stalin agreed. When the United States insisted that the Soviet Union take a

---

[75]

Quoted in United Press International release, "Note authorizing the first atomic bomb is uncovered," in *Honolulu Advertiser*, (Honolulu: Honolulu Advertiser, Inc., May 18, 1979), p. C-5.

[76]

Quoted in Gar Alperovitz, *Atomic Diplomacy: Hiroshima and Potsdam: The Use of the Atomic Bomb and the American Confrontation With Soviet Power* (New York: Simon and Schuster, 1965), p. 189.

stand against the Chinese Communist forces, Stalin agreed. When the United States insisted that General Douglas MacArthur would be the chief and sole administrator of occupied Japan, Stalin agreed. When Stalin requested that the Red Army be allowed to take a token surrender in the Japanese homeland, Truman simply and flatly refused. Eight days after the surrender of Japan, Stalin issued a declaration in support of the United States' traditional "Open Door" policy in China.

The question of whether the bombings of Hiroshima and Nagasaki were necessary in order to end the war--in order to save millions of lives--is a debatable one. Dwight D. Eisenhower described his own misgivings during a discussion he had with Secretary of War Stimson shortly after the two events. He reported that:

> During [Stimson's] recitation of the relevant facts, I had been conscious of a feeling of depression and so I voiced to him my grave misgivings, first on the basis of my belief that Japan was already defeated and that dropping the bomb was completely unnecessary, and secondly because I thought that our country should avoid shocking world opinion by the use of a weapon whose employment was, I thought, *no longer mandatory as a measure to save American lives.* It was my belief that Japan was, at that very moment, seeking some way to surrender with a minimum loss of "face." The Secretary was deeply disturbed by my attitude, almost angrily refuting the reasons I gave for my quick conclusions.[77]

Whether or not millions of lives were saved, it remains a fact that a large fraction of a million lives were sacrificed in the two

---

[77]

Quoted in Borden, *op. cit.*, p. 326.

Japanese cities. In the two bomb blasts--each one lasting but a millisecond--two hundred thousand human beings (by former U.S. President Richard M. Nixon's account) were destroyed.[78]

The War ended with the United States in a mood of effervescent elation. In spite of the Soviet gains in Eastern Europe, all of Asia was under the influence (at least temporarily) of the United States' "Open Door" policy. The United States proudly joined in with the rest of the world in the United Nations assembled, and denounced the atrocity of the Nazi extermination of six million Jews, and denounced the "race" hypotheses of the Nazis. Yet, what is extermination? What is a "racial" hypothesis? In persecuting a War against "Krauts" and "Japs," the United States exacted a terrible toll in human life which is simply left undiscussed. Before its nuclear experimentation, the United States experimented in non-nuclear holocaust bombing techniques on two cities of its enemies. The incendiary bombing raids on Tokyo and Dresden which were intended to--and which did indeed--generate enormous uncontrollable fire-storms, were each executed on only one night. (The day after the bombing of Dresden, U.S. fighter planes followed up by strafing refugees fleeing from the ruined city with machine gun fire.) And between them, these two bomber attacks killed two hundred eighteen thousand people.[79] If the toll of Hiroshima, Nagasaki, Tokyo, and Dresden is added up, it may be seen that the United States--in four separate attacks occurring in less than twenty four hours time--took over four hundred thousand lives. There was no other

---

[78]

Roger Rosenblatt, "A Nation Coming Into Its Own," in *Time* (New York: Time Inc., July 29, 1985), p. 48.

[79]

The figure for Tokyo--83,000--is from Nixon, in Rosenblatt, *ibid.* The Dresden figure of 135,000 is from Kurt Vonnegut, who *was there* at the time of the bombing, in a prisoner of War camp for captured British and American personnel.

nation at that time which actually did, or was even *able* to kill so many people in so short a space of time--even in concentration camps. This figure of over 400,000 is larger than the total United States Armed Forces personnel death toll for the entire War.[80]

With the War over, and with the bomb squarely in place, the United States settled into a new position as a nation of genuine world preeminence. On the home front there was movement toward the normalization of life, and then toward prosperity. Numerous intellectuals who had immigrated to the United States in the early years of the war, fleeing political and "racial" persecution in Europe, had fulminated against the Nazi state and the "race" idea, and contributed toward the creation of an environment--in academic and civil circles--which was favorable to "race" toleration. Attitudes such as Stanley Porteus' of twenty years earlier were becoming 'unfashionable'. The U.S. Army was "integrated" soon after the end of the War. Then baseball was "integrated." By the middle of the 1950[s], *schools* were "integrated." Soon there was a Voting Rights Act.

(Although the desegregation of the U.S. Army started earlier than that of any other sector of U.S. society, and although it has progressed further, this movement has been halting, and grudging. As an example of this, I have a most vivid personal recollection of one moment in June, 1965, well after the first intense flurry of civil rights legislation in the U.S., and almost 20 years after the "integration" of the army. My new friend Robert Felix--who came from the Los Angeles, California, community of Watts--and I, along with hundreds of other draftees and recruits sat assembled on a large lawn between the barracks, and overlooking the mess hall at Fort Polk, Louisiana. We had been

---

[80]

The U.S. casualty figure, 396,637, is from Erwin Christian Lessner, "World War II," in *The Encyclopedia Americana* (New York: Americana Corporation, 1962), Volume 29, p. 548.

gathered there to hear special lecture by First Sergeant Paterson. The subject was to be: official U.S. Army policy regarding the 'etiquette' we new soldiers were to observe while on leave in the nearby town of Leesville. Sergeant Paterson rambled on for a while, and then got down to the point: "I know," he observed,

> that some of you white boys and some of you nigra boys get along just fine with each other out here, 'specially you boys from the big cities up north, and that's just fine--here. But we want you to know that the townfolks in Leesville have certain traditions that we want you to respect. They get along just fine with us, and we want to keep things that way. So, while some of you nigra and white boys might be friends here--and that's just fine--we don't want you to be going into town together. Don't you try going into the moviehouse or bars together [I later discovered that at that time, Leesville had a segregated theater]. And you white boys, you make damn sure that you stay out of the wrong end of town. You aren't wanted there....)

Overseas, the United States had a host of new responsibilities to attend to after the end of the First Atomic War. Occupied Japan was to be administered. And so were occupied Germany and west Berlin, too. And there were other new territories acquired in the War to be looked after. And the Philippines were to be freed.

Included in the United States' new territories was the Trust Territory of the Pacific Islands, which was granted to the U.S. by the United Nations in 1945. The territory included all of Micronesia save Guam, Nauru, and the Gilbert Islands. In granting the trust, the U.N. mandated the United States to: "promote the political, economic, social and educational advancement of the people and to move them as directly as practical towards self-government."[81] The United States was also

---

[81]

Quoted in David Nevin, *The American Touch in Micronesia* (New York:

granted a *strategic* trust over the area by the U.N. *That* trust provided the United States with the authority to set aside certain areas for military and security purposes.

In pursuit of its U.N. social mandate in Micronesia, the United States promulgated education after the "Indian" model. At the beginning, education was placed in the hands of government-approved mission schools. Eventually, government schools were established as well. English was promoted as the language and standard of education. Modern U.S. social customs and values were encouraged and inculcated in Micronesian students. The Ancient language and traditions of the Micronesians were intended to be relegated to the past. Administrators from the Bureau of Indian Affairs were transferred over to the Trust Territory to manage the affairs of the Micronesians.

In dispatching its strategic trust privileges the United States was equally energetic, and with good reason. Micronesia is in the western rim of the Pacific, adjacent to the Philippines, midway between Japan and Australia, and midway between Australia and Hawaii. It offered a fine addition to the United States' string of fortifications along the Soviet Union's eastern frontier. And for a variety of reasons, including that island region's relatively sparse population, the Trust Territory of the Pacific offered an ideal site for the continuation of nuclear bomb testing.

So, late in 1945, government authorities decided upon test sites not only in the remote western North American deserts, but also on Bikini Atoll in the Marshall Islands of Micronesia. The armed forces were charged with educating the 166 Bikini Islanders in the exigencies of the nuclear age. They would have to leave their homes, their gardens, their fishing grounds, their

---

1977), p. 211.

cemeteries--their homeland--they were told, so that nuclear explosions could be conducted there "...for the good of all mankind and to end all world wars."[82]

In March, 1946, the Islanders were relocated 177 miles eastward to the uninhabited atoll of Rongerik. Shortly thereafter, the U.S. Navy conducted the first test nuclear bombing of a naval fleet anchored in Bikini Lagoon. By the time the testing had ended in 1958, the United States had exploded 23 nuclear devices--including multi-megaton hydrogen bombs--on Bikini Atoll. The Bikini Islanders did not fare well in the harsh environment on Rongerik. So, in 1948, they were again relocated, this time south of Bikini, to Kili Island. Although Kili, lacking a barrier reef, was isolated by heavy surf and only afforded good fishing about half the year, it was still a more hospitable environment than Rongerik. The Islanders did their best to work out a living.

Meanwhile, in the 1954 test of an enormous fifteen-megaton thermonuclear device code named "Bravo," an ill-consideration of upper atmospheric wind conditions caused the Marshall Islanders of Ailinginae, Rongelap, and Utirik to be dusted by a thick coat of highly-radioactive fallout. On Utirik the fallout was the lightest, precipitating as a fine mist. On Rongelap and Ailinginae it fell as white, fluffy flakes, covering everything to a depth of an inch and a half. The islanders had not been instructed in the precautions to take in case such a rain of fallout should occur. The Islanders had not even been instructed that there *was* such a thing as deadly radioactive fallout. And so, they conducted the normal business of life as usual; gardening in the fallout, fishing in the fallout, and children playing in the fallout, particles of it sticking to their bodies. Some gazed up to the sky,

---

[82]

Quoted in Nancy Terasaki, "Who Gives a Damn?" in *The Asian American Journey* (Los Angeles: Agape Fellowship, February, 1980), p. 8.

flakes falling into their eyes, others tested the substance by tasting it. The fallout rained into their wells and water cachements, and onto their food supplies.

The islands of Rongelap, Ailinginae and Utirik were finally evacuated 51, 55, and 78 hours after the explosion, respectively. The people of Ailinginae were suffering the most acutely from radiation burns, nausea, diarrhea, hair loss, and changes in the blood. The islands were then quarantined for three years. During that time the islanders were temporarily relocated to a village built for them on Majuro Atoll. When they returned to their homes at the end of the quarantine period, radioactivity levels there were still high. In the words of the Brookhaven National Laboratory's three year report on the islands: "...the levels of activity are higher than those found in other inhabited locations in the world." But, the report went on, "The habitation of these people on the island will afford most valuable ecological data on human beings."[83] That body of data, one must infer, would include the medical data showing on Rongelap beginning in 1964, and on Utirik, beginning in 1977, a markedly unusual increase in thyroid disorders, especially tumors. Other data showed that Rongelap was so 'hot' with radioactivity that persons living there since the repatriation of 1957, but who had not been present during the rain of fallout, had, by 1969, been dosed with the same amount of radiation as the victims of the direct fallout.[84]

Also in 1969, President Lyndon B. Johnson announced to the Bikini Islanders that, as nuclear testing there had been over for more than a decade, the atoll was now ready for reoccupation. The Islanders had been petitioning the U.S. government for repatriation almost since the start of the testing, and so, on

---

[83]

Ibid., p. 11.

[84]

Ibid.

hearing the good news they began to return to their home at once. By 1975 almost all of them had returned. But the effects of 23 high-yield nuclear bomb explosions on the atoll were not as transitory as the Bikinians had been told. In 1977, all food and drink produced or stored on Bikini was quarantined because of dangerously high radiation levels. From then on, the U.S. government supplied all food and drink which was consumed on Bikini. By 1978, the home of the Bikini Islanders was officially declared to be absolutely unsafe for human life. The Islanders were once again removed--temporarily--to Kili. And so it was that in the tiny Marshall Islands group, a few hundred Islanders had their lives touched by the awesome nuclear might of the United States.

But the hold of the United States upon the rest of Micronesia was much more insidious--it was education and B.I.A.-style administration. Although a U.N. report in the early 1960[s] had criticized the U.S.'[s] discharge of its Micronesian trust responsibilities, official policy remained unchanged, and Americanization-education proceeded.

At the beginning of the U.S.-Micronesian relationship the first Islanders to become educated were indeed rewarded with good government and government-related jobs. But as was inevitable in the remote, sparsely-populated, scattered Micronesian Islands, the job marketplace soon became saturated. Then an education led only to the inculcation of Yankee desires and no possible way of fulfilling them. By the 1970[s], 'reservation syndrome' had set in in Micronesia: poverty, dependency, joblessness, high drop out rates in school, poor achievement in school, and epidemic alcoholism were to be found everywhere.

But by then the strategic trust of the Pacific Islands was less strategically-important. Much had changed since the end of the War. The Islanders would now grudgingly have to be "maintained as a species of paupers" until the Islands might become 'important' again. The new position of the U.S. toward the Micronesians was summed up by Secretary of State Henry Kissinger (who, ironically, had come to the U.S. as a refugee from "racial" persecution). As Kissinger saw it, after all, "There are only 90,000 people out there. Who gives a damn?"[85]

In the post War years, although the War had finally ended the depression at home, and there was rising prosperity in the United States through the 1950ˢ, the U.S. did not always have its way in foreign affairs. Following the surrender of Japanese forces in Korea to both the Soviet Union and the United States, Korea had been partitioned along the 38th parallel of latitude. The following year the Soviets encouraged the formation of a provisional government in North Korea headed by Kim Il-Sung, a renowned partisan leader. The year after that, the United States petitioned the United Nations to resolve the dilemma of a divided Korea. The General Assembly of the U.N. resolved subsequently, in 1947, that Korea-wide elections must be held under U.N. supervision. In the year following the Soviet refusal to comply with the U.N. resolution, a national assembly was elected entirely in South Korea. On August 15, 1948, the Republic of Korea was formally proclaimed south of the 38th parallel. On September 9, 1948, the Democratic People's Republic of Korea was proclaimed north of the parallel. In 1949, skirmishes between North and South Korean forces began to occur along the parallel. And on June 25, 1950, the North Korean Army moved across the 38th parallel in full-scale invasion of South Korea. The forces of the United Nations struck back quickly, and by November they had advanced north across the parallel to within fifty miles of the Chinese border. On November 24, China entered the War, fielding at once a force of one million three hundred thousand. The U.N. forces were driven well south of the parallel, rallied, and

---

[85]

Quoted in Robert C. Kiste, *The Bikinians: A Study in Forced Migration* (California: 1974), p. 198.

pushed back north again. The War seesawed in this manner until armistice talks commenced on June 21, 1951. From then on the lines remained relatively stable, although fighting did continue up until the final truce on July 27, 1953. The border agreed upon at that time is in roughly the same place as the 38th parallel (it crosses it), but it ceded pre-1950 territory in the west to North Korea, and in the east, to South Korea.

Atomic weapons were not employed during the War in Korea, but their use was briefly considered by the U.S. Incendiary (fire storm) bombing, however, *was* used. In the course of the War 400,000 civilians perished. The United States' losses were 38,382 dead and 103,284 wounded. The North Korean and Chinese--"Gooks" in the lingo of the now-"integrated" U.S. troops--suffered staggering losses, however. The total amounted to 1,420,000 killed and wounded.[86]

Almost as soon as the First Atomic War had ended, the Soviet Union became 'unmanageable' in Europe. In 1948 and '49, the Soviets blockaded West Berlin, which, while entirely surrounded by Soviet-occupied East Germany, was jointly-held by the United States, Britain and France, and was the seat of the Allied Control Council of West Germany. (East Berlin was the site of the Central Administration of the Russian Occupied Zone.) West Berlin survived the blockade largely through a massive Allied airlift.

Atomic diplomacy was proving not to be the ultimate power it had been expected to be. In 1949, in Siberia, the Soviet Union exploded an atomic bomb of its own. Now atomic diplomacy was a shared power; the race was on. In 1951 the United States conducted a highly-secret bomb test on Bikini Atoll which was

---

[86]

These figures are from Vincent J. Esposito, "Korean War," in *The Encyclopedia Americana* (New York: Americana Corporation, 1962), Volume 16, p. 582.

announced as "contributing to thermonuclear research." The following year a "thermonuclear device" was exploded at the Pacific test site. The Soviet Union countered with dazzling speed, detonating a hydrogen bomb in Siberia the following year, in 1953. Then, also in 1953, the United States successfully test fired the 280mm atomic artillery shell at the Nevada test site. Over the decades, in each of over two score of escalations in nuclear armaments which the United States initiated in its weapons race with the Soviet Union, the Soviet Union eventually managed to catch up. In at least a couple of instances--including the introduction of cruise missiles--the Soviet Union initiated the escalation.

In Eastern Europe, the Soviets seemed more determined than ever to tighten their hold. In 1956 Soviet armored units crushed a popular rebellion in Hungary; in 1968, the same thing happened to the rebellious nation of Czechoslovakia.

At length, all of the tensions on earth were exacerbated by a new contest in the very heavens above, the race into outer space. This began in earnest in October of 1957, when the Soviet Union orbited the first artificial earth satellite, Sputnik I. The United States was taken completely by surprise by this, for it had long been expected that the U.S. effort, rapidly reaching its conclusion, would be the first to successfully orbit a satellite. Embarrassed by having been caught napping, the U.S. orbited Explorer I about three months later, in January, 1958. The battle for prestige in space was touch and go for a decade, but then at the end of the 1960[s], the United States leapt forward mightily with the first manned lunar landing. The mostly successful space shuttle program of the early 1980[s] in the opinion of some observers closed the metaphorical "missile gap" opened up by Sputnik I, clinching U.S. dominance in space. But other experts point to the great number of very lengthy Soviet missions in space and the numerical preponderance of manned Soviet space flights, suggesting an indisputable Soviet lead. All in all, the post War years were not easy ones for the United States, as tensions between the great Atomic Powers periodically heightened and lessened, and the temperature of the "Cold War" fluctuated while weapons developments in one nation were matched by weapons developments in the other, and technological developments in one place were duplicated in the other. In the end, however, from 1989 through 1991, the "evil empire" of the Soviet Union broke apart into its originally-constituent nations, crushed by the unwieldy weight of its elitist bureaucratic institutions and military infrastructure, and doomed by the flawed Marxian hypothesis which placed economics in a place of preeminence before politics. The latter point of Soviet weakness is one which should be heeded by the United States' oligarchy.

In the meantime, things were not going quite as the United States had wished in Southeast Asia. Although the U.S. had granted independence to the Philippines on July 4, 1946, and a democratic regime had been established there, a little more than five hundred miles to the west, in French Indochina, the Vietnamese communists had commenced a war of liberation against the French colonial administration. In March, 1946, the French had been forced to recognize the Viet Minh administration in North Vietnam, and in December of that year, War broke out between the two sides. Apparently, the United States' "Open Door" was being swung shut by the desire for national independence on the part of the people of Southeast Asia. It would seem that what appeared to the U.S. to be an "Open Door" often looked like old-fashioned colonialism to the people of Asia.

Then, in October of 1949, the unthinkable occurred. Mao Tse-tung's communist forces seized control of China and proclaimed the People's Republic. In the United States this unauthorized act of self-determination was so mystifying, so terrifying, and so infuriating that the U.S. did not grant official diplomatic recognition to the People's Republic of China, and the quarter of the earth's human population therein, until 1973.

Back in Indochina, the War between the French and the Viet Minh raged on with ever-greater intensity. The United States had supported Viet Minh resistance against Japanese colonialism, beginning in 1941, but now found the Vietnamese to be unqualified for liberation from French colonialism, and so the U.S. backed the French. Following Mao's successful Chinese revolution, China aided North Vietnam. (And as in the case of Korea, China's enemy, the Soviet Union, also provided aid to the Viet Minh.) Once again the United States found itself involved-- indirectly this time--in a proxy War with the Soviet Union and the People's Republic. But in 1954, the French were decisively defeated at Dien Bien Phu, and peace was negotiated in Geneva. The French withdrew completely from Indochina; Cambodia and Laos were granted independence, and Vietnam was temporarily divided, with the Viet Minh retaining control of the north. That year, Ngo Dinh Diem took over control of the government of South Vietnam as premier, and the following year, the Republic of South Vietnam was proclaimed with Diem as its president. In 1958, North Vietnam stepped up its program of insurgency against the U.S.-supported Diem regime in the south, with the objective of reunifying the country and expunging all foreign influence.

Two years later the United States responded by sending 2,000 military advisors into South Vietnam. Now the U.S. was once more directly involved in a War against people who the military commanders would actively encourage their troops to characterize as "Gooks." At the peak of its involvement there, the United States had over 540,000 military personnel in Vietnam. The War dragged on for over a decade until finally a cease fire was signed between the United States and North Vietnam in 1973. The following year the last U.S. troops were withdrawn from the country, and the year after that the Viet Cong guerrillas and North Vietnamese Army toppled the regime in Saigon, completing their effort at liberating and unifying the country which had begun thirty four years earlier.

Although nuclear weapons were not employed directly in the Vietnam War, their use was threatened in Henry Kissinger's "madman scenario" presented at the peace talks in Paris. The gist of Kissinger's threat to the North Vietnamese negotiators there was that President Nixon was an "unstable madman" who was even capable of using the bomb if the North Vietnamese did not join with the U.S. in bringing the War to an end. Incendiary bombing, per se, as in Korea and in the First Atomic War, was not used either. However, the United States made very wide use of napalm bombing. Napalm is a sort of jellied gasoline, which when deployed in a bomb, explodes into flame and spreads with great ease over a very wide area. The burning jelly clings most stubbornly to everything it lands on, including living tissue. The United States also devised a new generation of "anti-personnel" weapons for use in Vietnam, the cluster bombs. These weapons contained hundreds of tiny mines or bomblets which the 'mother' bomb would aerially spread over a large plot of ground. Some were designed to explode on contact, while others were intended to lie unexploded until disturbed by a human being or other animal. Some of these aerial mines exploded into fragments of plastic shrapnel. Such non-metallic fragments would not show up on x-ray photographs of their victims, and were intended to keep the enemy medical personnel overextended. Others of the aerial mines were shaped like little steel butterflies, and seem to have been designed with an appeal to children in mind.

In an attempt to cut the military supply lines between North and South Vietnam, thousands of acres of Vietnamese soil were "defoliated"--stripped of all vegetation and most life--by highly toxic, carcinogenic chemicals sprayed from airplanes. (More than a decade after the close of the War, a number of U.S. servicemen involved in handling the Agent Orange defoliant have developed directly-related cancers, and many of their children have been born with severe birth defects, also caused by the deadly toxin.)

During the course of its War with Vietnam, the United States dropped more tonnage of bombs on that tiny country than the entire total dropped on the Axis powers during the First Atomic War. Throughout the War in Vietnam, the rhetorical proclamation heard over and over on the battlefield, and back in the United States was: "Asians simply don't place any value on human life." The same phrase had been in use during the Korean War, and before, when the United States was fighting in Japan. The death toll of the Vietnam War was truly staggering. The United States lost nearly 60,000 killed (about double an average year's alcohol-related highway fatalities in the U.S.); and over 2,000,000 Vietnamese--mostly civilians--died.

But while the United States made "racial" war abroad, the promise at home was one of "racial" peace. Throughout the 1950^s and 60^s, it appeared as if genuine progress was being made toward obliterating the old custom of segregating "Black" and "white." In the early 1950^s, due largely to the conditions I have mentioned above--increasing prosperity in the U.S., and a propensity, following the atrocities committed by the Nazi regime, to feel uneasy about exploitative "race" relations--a number of U.S. citizens began to push for equal citizenship *for all* in areas beyond soldiering and athletics. They wanted to get out of the United States' class system's "Black" box.

Pressure was applied, and the U.S. Supreme Court was the first governmental institution to give forth results. In 1954 and 1955, beginning with the case of *Brown v. Board of Education*, the court ordered the desegregation of U.S. schools "with all deliberate speed." By 1962, the Southern universities were being "integrated." That year James Meredith entered the University of Mississippi, accompanied by federal troops. The following year two "Blacks" entered the University of Alabama accompanied by federal troops, and over the objections of Alabama Governor George Wallace. Congress took the next step, passing the Civil Rights Acts of 1957, 1960, 1964, and 1968. All four of these Congressional acts were in a sense supports for and enforcement for the 15th Amendment of the *Constitution*. The latter two acts, however, those of 1964 and 1968, delved more deeply into the area of civil rights. Respectively, they provided for the elimination of segregation in public places, gave the U.S. Attorney General the power to bring school desegregation cases before the court, made the Civil Rights Commission a permanent body, forbid segregation by unions or by employees involved in interstate commerce, forbid segregation by public accommodation involved in interstate commerce, provided for the protection of civil rights workers, and guaranteed open housing in about 80% of the nation's housing market.

The Voting Rights Act of 1965 went even further toward putting teeth into the 15th Amendment, and among its provisions, it specifically outlawed poll taxes and voter's literacy tests. This act was renewed, or legislatively extended over the years, in 1970, 1975, and 1982, and it was also strengthened to include Spanish-speaking persons and other 'language minorities'.

In the early 1960[s], Dr. Martin Luther King, Jr. emerged as the dynamic leader of the civil rights movement in the United States. More than anyone else at that time, he captured and conveyed the spirit of human kinship. On August 28, 1963, he led the massive, peaceful Freedom March to Washington, D.C. The following year Dr. King received the Nobel Peace Prize in recognition of his non-violent advocacy and leadership of the civil rights movement. Non-violence, however, was the attribute of only Dr. King's movement, and those who opposed the extension of genuine citizenship to all U.S. citizens indulged themselves quite freely in the tactics of terrorism. Civil rights workers and advocates were on a number of occasions murdered from ambush, four school children in a church were blown up with dynamite, and brutal beatings were common. Threats against civil rights workers were even more common.

Yet, in spite of threats and violence from the opposition, the movement for uniform civil rights for all U.S. citizens continued undaunted. From March 21 to 25, 1965, Dr. King led the Freedom March from Selma, to Montgomery, Alabama. He was accompanied by 3,200 men and women; a mix of all "races" freely associating together for a common purpose. That summer 20,000 human beings of all colors of complexion joined together to attend his protest of *de facto* school segregation in Chicago. Progress seemed to be being made. That same year the U.S. Commissioner of Education announced that any school still segregated in 1967 would cease receiving federal aid. The next year the bussing of school children to achieve "racially"-balanced schools was commenced. But things apparently were not moving quite fast enough, for that summer--the summer of 1966--100 cities erupted in flames, as riots broke out in "Black" ghettoes across the country.

The following year Thurgood Marshall became the first "Black" justice of the Supreme Court. This was also the year when Martin Luther King, grasping the importance of the "racial" misunderstanding inherent in the United States' involvement in Vietnam, threw his support behind the growing anti-War movement in the States. Then, on April 4, 1968, Dr. Martin Luther King, Jr., brother to the entire human species, was murdered. Also in 1968, the National Advisory Commission on Civil Disorders--created by President Johnson in response to the "long hot summer" of 1966--presented its findings to the public. The commission, assessing two decades of efforts toward desegregation, warned with great urgency that there was a disturbing trend in the United States toward the creation of two radically-separated societies--one "white," and one "Black."

Perhaps in response to this grim prediction, the Supreme Court the very next year ordered a halt to all school segregation "at once."

As the decade of the 1970ˢ began, the lower U.S. courts continued to weigh the obligations of school desegregation, public protests against the Vietnam War continued with such mounting passion that they would eventually be a factor contributing to the War's end, and the growing women's movement began to attract ever-wider public attention. Perhaps it was unrealistic to expect a class system based for hundreds of years upon the custom of "racial" segregation to undo itself in a little more than a couple of decades. Or perhaps there was never really any intention at all of dismantling that class system, for its basis--its underpinning, the concept that "races" are real categories--was never challenged, save by those few persons such as Martin Luther King or Malcolm X, who quickly became martyrs for the system. So, braced by the mental blocks conditioned into the minds of oppressor and oppressed alike, the "race" system asserted its own internal equilibrium, seeking a new balance.

The systemic correction began in 1971, when the Supreme Court, ostensibly strengthening the power of lower federal courts to undo the effects of past segregation, confirmed the correctness of bussing school children from one school district to another in order to achieve "racial" balance in schools. In the same decision, the Court also affirmed the notion that "race" may be taken into consideration for the purpose of framing corrective court orders. The latter portion of the decision was of utmost importance, for it amounted to nothing less than the reestablishment of a U.S. federal government policy in favor of "racial" discrimination[87]-- the very thing which civil rights workers had been struggling

---

[87]

The word *discrimination* simply means *distinguishing, differentiating, or discerning* differences.

against for so long. Although various state legislatures had enacted statutes against "racial" discrimination in employment as early as 1962, the Equal Employment Opportunity Act of 1972 gave the Equal Employment Opportunity Commissioner the power to take job discrimination cases to court and brought state and local government jobs under federal equal employment standards. This was the commencement of enforced "racial" hiring quotas in job markets across the nation.

As a support for "racial" thinking and of "racial" segregation, the quota system was nearly as invidious and at the same time as powerful an invention as the entire "Indian" reservation system. As in the case of "Indian" preference hiring and all welfare and health services on reservations, "racial" quota hiring linked "racial" identity--that is to say "racial" discrimination--directly to monetary rewards (or punishments, as, for example, in the case of persons not "racially" qualified--or preferred--to work in certain jobs). At this time, and not purely by chance coinciding with the rise of the women's movement at the end of the Vietnam War, and with the loss of momentum by the civil rights movement, the newest "race" in the United States was invented: the "whitemale." "Whitemales" constituted a high-visibility scapegoat group to which guilt and blame could be attributed for a class system created and propagated by men and women who lived hundreds of years ago. Ranging in age from the 20^s to 40^s, "whitemales" embraced every male of fair complexion with a "white-sounding" surname, who could not adequately 'prove' another "genetic identity." In addition to those few 'sons of the American Revolution' who had not adequately secured their fortunes to be exempt from such classification, "whitemales" included the male children and grandchildren on immigrants who themselves had usually suffered "racial" persecution in the United States. The new "race" "whitemales" also counted among its involuntary membership the male descendants of individuals who, due to the terror of the United States' "race"-class system, and by the birth 'chance' of a light complexion, had 'passed' from the "Brown," "Indian," "Asian," or "Black" groups into the "white" one. The misfortune of these latter victims of continuing racism in the U.S. was that their "passing" ancestors had improperly assessed the future penalties and rewards of "race," and feeling confident that the "group" they had just left would *always* be in the down position, they had been very careful to obliterate all traces of their former "origins." Often the descendants of persons who have "passed" are not even aware that they are such.

Excluded from membership in the group "whitemales" were all of those "non-minority" male persons already well-entrenched in positions of power and influence: judges, politicians, corporate board members and executives, federal employees at the mid- and upper management levels, and military officers. From their invulnerable position on the heights, these "white" men-- especially the judges and politicians--directed a withering hail of negative criticism upon "whitemales." Those most visibly and immediately affected by this attention were low-level civil service employees such as firefighters and police. These persons, being almost archtypically average U.S. citizens, were so thoroughly immersed in the environment of Yankee racism that they scarcely stood a chance of understanding what was happening to them. Frightened, angry and disoriented, they labeled their experience "reverse discrimination," implying, one might only suppose, that prior "racial" discrimination had been 'forward', or 'correct'. But, in truth, they were merely feeling (in a most personal way) the *continuation* of "racial" discrimination in the United States.

Much less visible, but perhaps carrying a greater impact, was the effect of "whitemale" labeling upon the academic community. Since so many colleges and universities receive a variety of forms of federal monetary assistance, the 1975 governmental ruling that all such aid would be withheld from those institutions not complying adequately with the general government's guidelines for affirmative action prompted a stampede of obedience. Quotas were established for entry into special graduate programs, and for the hiring of new faculty. Although a "racial" quota for medical school entry was successfully challenged in 1978, the Supreme Court affirmed the correctness of "racial" hiring quotas in 1979, and again in 1980. At this point, academic personnel offices might as well have posted notices reading: "'Whitemales' need not apply." Not affected by this, of course, were those well-established, tenured, highly-reputed professors, the "white" men of academia who were ever so quick to point out how top heavy with "whitemales" the academic system was.

The academic purge of "whitemales" probably affected no more than a few thousand persons, scarcely a significant statistic in terms of the well-proven destructive potential of racism. But the purge did present certain ironies. Those who were flushed out of the system just as they were entering it, or were barely getting established in it, were highly educated persons, most of whom had Ph.D. degrees. Most of them were persons who had been active in the civil rights and anti-Vietnam War movements. As they entered the broader job marketplace, these "whitemales" found no work in the public school systems, for their doctorates placed them in the upper salary range, and most schools preferred hiring cheaper employees. Approaching the business community, many of them were informed that they were "overqualified." And so, most settled into unskilled jobs at the lower end of the employment market. Some, those whose consciousness was burdened with the ideology known in the U.S. as liberalism, even went so far as to convince themselves that-- because of the color of their skin--they deserved their fate. But such self-blaming is a most common occurrence among all "racially" oppressed groups.

This disappearance of a few thousand of the nation's most highly-qualified teachers coincided with fund-raising pleas by the United Negro College Fund touting the slogan that "A mind is a terrible thing to waste," and also with the appalling discovery that at least 28 million citizens of the United States are classifiable as functionally illiterate.

The invention of the "whitemale" was a great boon to the women's movement. That movement--which originally was the brainchild of affluent, upwardly-mobile "white" women seeking fully-equal opportunity and equal wages in the U.S. business 'achievement' system--needed an image to equal that of the civil rights movement. With the invention of "whitemales," history could be appropriately rewritten. Suddenly, one half of the "majority" population achieved the status of a "minority." No longer would the Daughters of the American Revolution be associated with the racist crimes of the sons of that revolution. The proper imagery would conjure up visions of Martha Washington or Martha Jefferson (and maybe even Scarlett O'Hara, too) spending day after dreary day washing out toilet bowls, tidying up the family mansion, toiling in the kitchen, and suffering the ignominy of a sex slave. The fact that from the very beginning, the women in the United States' upper class were relieved of *all* of the above chores by slaves and servants who were chosen for that station because of their "race," could now be conveniently purged from the system's selective memory. The fact that Martha Washington's dowery included over 100 of her own personal slaves, could now be conveniently forgotten. Now the "race" system and segregation--invented and perpetuated, *enforced*, by men *and women* in the upper class--became the sole responsibility and guilt of "whitemales" of those classes below the uppermost social level.

No doubt I have not adequately researched the matter, but I have yet to come across the feminist ideology's apology for some of the most powerful and brutal historical figures of the Renaissance. For example: how must we *now* understand the lives of Isabella of Castile, Lucretia Borgia, or Elizabeth Tudor? Female persons of power such as these were by no means a rarity at the dawning of the Modern Age. Are we now obliged to conceive of their existences as powerless and void of achievement? For the sake of ideological consistency must we now view them as mere pawns of the men in their lives? Shall we now be forced to imagine *these* creators of present-time society spending day after boring day doing little more than cleaning out toilet bowls?

As an ideology, feminism constitutes a fully-Modern body of rhetoric which very logically follows after communism, the dogma invented by Karl Marx. Marx had anticipated the medical future in his *Communist Manifesto* when he called for "the elimination of women as *mere* instruments of production." Now, with the current technologies of *in vitro* fertilization and abortion, this goal is within the grasp of Modern humanity. So too is the extension of the role of worker to all who now live (save the elites, of course) a real possibility.

The issue of 'abortion on demand' clearly illustrates the fully-Modern nature of feminism. To see this, it is first necessary to realize that the continuing refinement of micro-surgical technology has currently made it possible for the sterilizing procedures of vasectomy and tubal ligation to be reversed in most cases. Yet guided by feminist ideology, Modern men and women of the middle and upper classes who seek to indulge themselves unrestrainedly in the transitory pleasures of sexual congress without facing the lifelong attachments which are often derived therefrom, seem by a vast majority to prefer to define their "freedom to choose" by choosing in favor of abortion--the termination of an incipient human life. Abortion is seen as a reasonable 'back-up' system in cases where one's preferred birth control practice has failed. After the Modern way, it is preferable to inflict death upon another rather than injury or 'inconvenience' upon oneself. After the Modern way, the act of inflicting death is called something else. After the Modern way, an individual human being is granted the right of final and ultimate say in the matter; the existence of a Higher Power is not acknowledged, the intervention of that which is not acknowledged is not to be allowed.

In defense of abortion on demand, pro-choice advocates are adroit rhetoricians. Their ideology characterizes the human foetus--the developing human being--as "a mere collection of cells." The issue of "viability," the inability of a foetus to survive if torn prematurely from the mother's womb, is called upon as a defense of the "right to choose" abortion. ("Viability," of course, thoroughly ignores the fact that a newborn infant's dependence upon others is every bit as intensive as that of a foetus. Just as a prematurely-ejected foetus is not "viable" when left completely alone, so too is a baby not "viable" when left utterly on its own. In both cases the necessary means of support has been withdrawn, and an "unviable" human life will cease. Indeed, the post-natal dependency--the non-"viability"--of human infants lasts for at least as long as the period of prenatal dependency.)

Additional argument in favor of "freedom of choice" is drawn from the relatively rare cases in which the impregnation of a woman has been caused by rape or incest, and from instances in which the mother's life is jeopardized by her pregnancy, or in which the foetus is a 'genetic monstrosity'. These last four kinds of situations do indeed present genuine ethical or medical emergencies; they raise *hard questions* which may often justly be answered by recourse to abortion. However, these kinds of situations present an entirely different issue than the selfish desire which is the essence of the "pro-choice" argument. Ironically, the Modern viewpoint considers the Ancient practice of infanticide--usually resorted to in cases of lethal congenital defects which Ancient societies did not possess the medical technology to correct--as evil, backward and savage. However, in Modern times, when the issue is sex for fun (or perhaps to advance a career) without making any lasting human attachments, the form of prenatal murder known as abortion is perfectly all right.

As a Modern ideology, feminism has a fertile interplay with the "race" idea. Consider here the abortion issue's application to the lower class. Although recent directors of the Planned Parenthood organization have been sensitive to the subject, Margaret Sanger, founder of the birth control movement, was quite outspoken on the following matter: it was her conviction that cheap (or free) and readily-accessible abortions might hold the answer to a rising population of impoverished ghetto "Blacks." As a Modern American ideology, feminism makes excellent use of the Madisonian principle of divide and rule by further fragmenting the social order into mutually-hostile and suspicious camps, in this case male and female.

Very early on in its development, the women's movement acquired the allegiance of like-minded "minority" women who also admired and were seeking equal access to the United States' business system. With the participation of sufficient numbers of these "achievement-oriented" "minority" women--people who in the language of the most impoverished of the ghetto communities are characterized as "white-thinking," or "white-acting"--the women's movement had a still-firmer hold on the status of a full-fledged "minority" movement.

As a movement to end human suffering, feminism is either a failure or a counterfeit. The movement is nowhere to be seen in protest of the torment of the homeless, of the hungry poor, of the residents of the ghettoes, or of the concentration camps known as reservations. To issue forth with such protest would be to shake the foundations of the very system to which feminism seeks entry for its advocates. The human failure of feminism is that it is a movement of sisters with no brothers.

By the middle of the 1980ˢ, the results of the forty-year struggle for civil rights in the United States had settled out. There had been the appearance of great movement, but little substantial change. By that time all of the prominent leaders of the civil rights and women's movements had acquired positions of power and wealth. From time to time they continue to stir up the resentment of the masses which support them, focusing it toward the easily-identified groups of "others" who are taken to be the source of their supporters' continuing misery. The leaders point to their own achievements, their own successes, in order to illustrate to their followers that progress is truly being made. However, during this period, the very conservative statistics compiled by the Reagan administration showed that 40% of "Black" teenagers remained unemployed, that unemployment on the reservations still ran as high as 70 to 80%, and that there were at that time at least two million homeless persons of all ages, sexes, and colors of complexion who lived on the mean streets of the big urban areas of the U.S. In the intervening years since those statistics were culled in the manner most likely to minimize them, the homeless have still not become housed. It must be observed of the homeless that they are not all shell-shocked War veterans, or schizophrenic individuals who were "freed" from the asylums in the legally-induced State Hospital diaspora of the 1970ˢ. Many, perhaps even more than half, are the 'new poor': former working people often accompanied by their families, who have joined the ranks of the unenfranchised, living on the streets. This large group, representing nearly one out of every twenty U.S. citizens, has now become invisible. Just like the dwellers of the tenements. Just like "Indians."

Now it appears that the civil rights protests, so prominent in the 1960ˢ, have petered-out and disappeared entirely. Now miseducation in the ghetto, in the barrio, and in the reservation schools is even more pronounced than ever. The borders of "racial" ghettoes are at least as sharply-defined as ever. As a result of such clear definition, there persists, *de facto*, an unequal enforcement of the laws according to "race." And now, on college campuses across the country a new generation of students has emerged which is by and large thoroughly disinterested in issues of social justice or societal service, but which instead is absorbed in the personal quest for riches in the Modern business system. Now, "racial" identity concepts are more sharply defined for all citizens of the United States than ever before. But in spite of all of this, the potential for individual recognition that something is quite wrong still remains. For example, in March of 1985, James Meredith--"integrator" of the University of Mississippi--publically declared that "integration" is a "con job."[88]

This brings me to a subject which earlier on I had promised to discuss. Why does it appear to be so easy to make a snap, on-sight "racial" identification of other persons in the present day? Here it is appropriate to begin by once again quoting Adolf Hitler's conversation with Hermann Rauschning, this time in some greater detail. Rauschning was a cattle breeder, and what Hitler said to him was:

> I know perfectly well, just as well as all those tremendously clever intellectuals, that in the scientific sense there is no such thing as race. But you, as a farmer and cattle-breeder, *cannot get your breeding successfully achieved without the conception of race*. And I as a politician need a conception which enables the order which has hitherto existed on historic bases to be abolished and an entirely new and anti-historic order enforced and given an intellectual basis....With the conception of race, National Socialism will carry its revolution abroad and recast the world.[89]

---

[88]   Meredith made this statement on the *Today* program of the N.B.C. television network, on March 8, 1985.

[89]   Quoted in Montagu, *Man's Most Dangerous Myth, op. cit.*, p. 50. *My* emphasis.

While this may be a blunt enough statement to suggest the answer to some, let me continue with a brief consideration of the breeding of "purebred" dogs and cats. Although a dog (or a cat) of any "strain" may engage in sexual congress with a dog (or a cat) of the complimentary sex of any other "strain," the efficient animal breeder seeks to rule out such random intercourse. In order to 'bring out' or 'perfect' the physical appearance (the phenotype) of their animals, breeders of "pureblood" stock allow their charges to mate only with other beasts possessing the appropriately-matching physical appearance. Over the passing generations, aberrant animals possessing deviant appearances are systematically excluded from the breeding population. Eventually, the "strain" is perfected, and will "breed true," unless, of course, it is allowed to "mix" with another "breed." In fact the knowledge of this process as applied to plants and animals has been a human possession ever since the agricultural revolution which preceded the Bronze Age of Antiquity. And this is exactly how the "races" of the United States have been made and are being maintained. The key operative word for selective breeding in this case is *segregation*.

The appropriate image for such selective breeding is *the puppy farm*. Within the United States, some human "breeding populations" had to be forcibly-isolated, broken down and then mentally-conditioned into accepting the premises of "race," others were intimidated and coerced into it, and still others were gulled into readily-adopting the "race" idea. Yet the fact remains that "Indian" reservations are the human equivalent of puppy farms, that ghettoes are puppy farms, that barrios are puppy farms, that Chinatowns are puppy farms, and that yes, even the "white" suburbs are puppy farms. Under the influence of the "race" idea, the children of "racially-mixed" marriages are forced to make an unconscious or conscious choice about which "group's" identity they will adopt, in effect "passing" into one "group" or another, and they usually then will choose mating partners accordingly. All of this is the ultimate form of human self-degradation, accomplished in our own age entirely outside of the realm of self-consciousness.

In the early years of the struggle for civil rights in the U.S., those who opposed the movement, or resisted it, often privately bemoaned what they thought to be the unhappy 'fact' that as a result of the extension of true citizenship to all citizens, "all people will some day in the future be 'brown' or 'grey'." However, if that movement *had* succeeded, it appears as if quite the opposite would have been the case. The record of terracotta portraiture from Ancient Mexico, where people from all over the world met and mingled for thousands of years, shows a great abundance of varied human appearances throughout its *entire* duration. The unfortunate legacy of the Modern Age very clearly appears to be a marked reduction in the wonderful, beautiful variation in human appearances. It is a sad thing, because we are *not* cattle, or dogs, or cats, and yet we go (most of us) thoughtlessly, unconsciously into the puppy farm to choose our mates. Over the past several centuries this program of selective human breeding has indeed sharpened the images of the "races" for all of us.

As a tool for political control, the "race" idea has been an inestimably-useful instrument for every Modern nation, for it is the great divider of humanity. Most importantly, the "race" idea divides the poor, disabling them and keeping them from joining together to overthrow the rich or the elites who invariably stand behind the governing apparatus of every Modern nation. It is beyond me to understand *exactly* why Modern systems need to create enormous masses of impoverished persons whose relative level of poverty far exceeds anything ever known in Ancient societies. I might only offer the speculation that perhaps the pool of cheap, disposable laborers provides a partial answer. It may be that--capitalist and communist alike--we have all been 'bred' to be workers. It is also evident that excluding the poorest of the poor--

the street people and hoboes (who *do* enrich merchants in the *drug* [including alcohol] *marketplace*)--poor people *do* offer an enormous pool of product consumers.   On the Pine Ridge reservation, for example, the humblest of homes is usually found to contain a television set, radios, tape recorders, and a variety of consumer goods of all sorts.   Outside one sees junked-out automobiles which were purchased in minimally-running condition from nearby off-reservation used car dealers.   The majority of homes possess at least one automobile or pickup truck in useable condition. Some homes have a midden or two of liquor and beer bottles and containers.   It appears obvious that in Modern times the 'bottom line' simply is the more consumers the better.

One thing is statistically certain, however.   The earth's present population explosion commenced only *after* the first Modern societies exported ethnocide and the "race" idea to other parts of the world.   And the reciprocal relationship between poverty and overpopulation must have been consciously or unconsciously one of the basic operating principles of Modern societies from the beginning.   The operation of that relationship, as described by biologist Barry Commoner, is rather straightforward.[90]   Simply stated, poor people have more children than rich people, it seems, as a sort of 'life insurance', or 'old age insurance'.   The idea behind this proliferation is that in their declining, dependant years, they will have some surviving offspring still dwelling in their home, and willing to look after their needs, and care for them.   (Many generations of severe, unrelenting poverty often lead entire communities into an emotional version of this coping strategy: "babies having babies."

---

[90]

See Barry Commoner, "How Poverty Breeds Overpopulation (and not the other way around)," in *Ramparts* (San Francisco: Ramparts, Inc., August/September 1975), pp. 21-25, and 58-59.

In such situations the poverty environment has become so emotionally-perverse and voided of healthy deep human feelings--the drug abuse problem known as alcoholism is often a contributing factor--that barely-pubescent girls become unwed mothers in order to "get someone of their own to love." This too causes population to soar, and also marks the nearly-hopeless condition of the affected community.) Whether or not these strategies for dealing with poverty actually work for poor people in a Modern setting may be debatable. But the statistical fact remains to gall Dr. Commoner's critics, that as a nation's *per capita* income and standard of living increase, its birthrate declines.

It would not be surprising to find this relationship between poverty and overpopulation at work even in specific "race" groups within the United States today. It would not be surprising either to find this poverty-overpopulation relationship working in *any* other Modern nation in the world today. Nor would it be surprising to find in this Modern world in which we live, in any--that is to say in *every*--nation a small upper class or a small elite (perhaps some political or religious party) standing far above the common masses. And so, with this observation as a point of departure, let us move on to consider the rigors of "race" identity in other portions of the Modern world.

You say you want a revolution, well, you know,
We all want to change the world.
You tell me that it's evolution, well, you know,
We all want to change the world.
But when you talk about destruction,
Don't you know that you can count me out?
                              --Lennon and McCartney

CHAPTER VI
The World Today--A Word of Caution

The question arises as to why I have taken such a harsh, seemingly one-sided view of the history of the United States. There are several reasons of equal importance. The ideological version of the United States' history, the glorious story of the first new nation, a nation founded upon the high principles of freedom and lawful justice; the story of the magnificent democratic republic of North America, is very well-known the world over. As with every other ideology, there is some truth in this story. But a history of rhetoric, a critical study of language abused, of Reason misdirected, must avoid any indulgence in such shallow self-congratulation. What I have indicated in the chapter above is that portion of the past which by virtue of its very nature as an ideology, the United States' official ideology *cannot* include. What I have shown is the depth of human experience which the story, as long as it remains just a story, *will not* tell. The good aspect of the United States' past has long been standing fully in the light, and my purpose in the preceding chapter has been to bring *more* of the past to light. A wise person knows that no nation, no people, is all good or all bad. A wise person knows that out of the possible range of mixtures of goodness and badness, to live with other human beings--every individual must make choices, ethical judgements, about what is preferable in one's life, and in society, and what is not. Decisions must be made about what is tolerable and what is intolerable; decisions must be made about what must be changed and what may be left alone. A wise person knows that without a reasonably clear understanding--that without adequate information--the execution of such judgements is an act of folly.

I was born a citizen of the United States. As a student, a teacher, and a scholar, the history of the United States has been more readily accessible to me than any other body of information about any nation across the oceans. But my selection of the United States for a case study of the operation of the "race" idea in a Modern state was based on more than that. Over fifty years of experience of life in the United States has taught me a great deal. From these two perspectives then, the scholarly and the experiential, I literally have been immersed in my subject matter. Yet without some sort of counterbalance (as a spur to critical reflection), such immersion *per se*, might have been detrimental to accurate perception.

One such counterbalance in my own case has been that I also belong to another nation. Like every other citizen of a reservation community, whether living away or at home, I also hold a sort of dual citizenship. As a *Lakota* (a "Sioux"), I also belong to a small and powerless nation which is completely within the borders of, and at present, thoroughly under the control of the United States of America. As might be expected, the self understandings of the two nations to which I belong are sometimes at great variance. There is still to this day a good deal of tension between these two nations. Over the years my awareness of this tension, and of the variation between the self explanations of the two nations, has forced me on repeated occasions into very carefully evaluating the relationship between the two, as well as the stories presented by each.

This brings me to yet another reason for choosing the United States for a case study of the "race" idea's operation in a Modern context. Every time I critically investigated the conflict, the tension I have outlined above, I ran into highly prejudicial thinking. I began to realize that as a rule, the Modern education of my countrymen (of *both* the large *and* the small nations) has instilled in them sets of conflicting prejudices about the United States and its past, as well as about the nations known as "Indians" and their pasts. Prejudices of any sort, whether perceived as positive or negative, have never encouraged the growth of Reason. Presently, we are living in the midst of a very dangerous age. I shall discuss this in more detail further on, but if ever there was a time for the human species to put Reason to its service, that time is now.

In widening and deepening our view of the past, and in seeking to dispel some of the uglier prejudices which surround all of us, my aim has been to serve the best interests of *both* nations to which I belong. Upon my graduation from the university which I attended, and my induction into the scholarship organization *Phi Beta Kappa*, I learned that *philosophia*, the love of wisdom, has been embodied in the principles of the United States from its very beginning as a nation. As a graduate student I learned that *philosophia* was deeply embedded in the roots of those mother countries from which the United States sprang. I know too that in the nation of the *Ocheti Shakowin*--the Ancient "Sioux" nation--wisdom was held most highly among the virtues. There too did *philosophia* abound. And so, in seeking to bring to light what heretofore has been hidden, my objective has been to do honor to, and to continue with the Ancient tradition of *philosophia* which lies at the core of both nations.

There is another counterbalance to my immersion experience of the United States, and a final reason for my choice of the U.S. for a case study of the inner workings of the "race" idea and racism. Over the years my modest travels have taken me from Canada to Central America, and from Europe to the mid-Pacific. Perhaps because of some kind of 'cross-cultural competency', or perhaps because of something else completely beyond my own understanding, I have always traveled unobtrusively. I have always traveled humbly and moved about in my travels quite freely. Over the years I have met and made friends with many persons of both 'high' and 'low' birth, and I have always been most observant. From all of this, one overbearing lesson has impressed itself upon me with great clarity. The United States is a genuinely open, or free society. It is not my place to claim that it is *the most* open nation in the present world, or *ever* in existence, but it clearly ranks high among the best which exist today. Another thing is also clear: there is a vast difference between the potential for positive human development in open and closed societies. As an open society, the U.S. is truly amenable to the possibility of *Just* social change. It is in light of this *possibility* that I have reviewed some of the more unpleasant aspects of this nation's past. It is my conviction that the rediscovery of Reason which the human species so desperately needs at this time, stands no better chance of commencing than in such a nation as the United States.

It would have been abundantly simple to write the foregoing chapter as a chronicle of the terrors the "race" idea has spawned in other parts of the Modern world. In truth, these terrors are almost everywhere far more severe than in the U.S. So as a balance to what I have written above, a brief sketch of some of that sorrow shall now follow. And what follows may be considered to exceed in brutality what has been described above.

To begin with, reservations, reserves, homelands, "autonomous regions," and "minority" ghettoes are found all over the world. Most people are aware of their existence in the United States and in the old apartheid regime of South Africa, but in fact they abound among the nations of the western hemisphere where the precedent was originally so firmly established. They are to be found from Canada to nearly the southern tip of South America. Outside of South Africa, they are to be found here and there in Africa. They are found in Europe--the seemingly-insoluble turmoil in Northern Ireland is at least in part derived from centuries of such a policy of segregation. Reservations or their equivalent are to be found in Australia, in Russia and the old constituent nations of the former Soviet Union, they are to be found in China, in India, elsewhere on the Asian mainland, and in Japan. For over forty years in Israel, such ghettoes were called "Palestinian refugee camps." The most notorious were the Gaza Strip and the West Bank concentrations.

To briefly consider another well-established example, let us look at how Japan's interaction with its islands' Ancient Ainu population is equivalent to the United States' interaction with the Ancient nations of North America. At first, trade relations flourished between the two parties, then relations turned martial and exploitative, as the Ainu were driven northward to the island of Hokkaidō. Over the past century the Ainu saw some of their cultural and religious practices made illegal by the government of Japan, they came under the influence of Shinto missionaries, and they were subjected to education. They were afflicted by subtle subversions of their culture such as the 1899 Hokkaidō Natives Protection Law which provided them "with land and tools for farming."[1] Until 1937, Ainu students were educated in strict segregation from Japanese students. As culture has gradually slipped away from the Ainu over the years, they have become increasingly aware of "blood quantum" descent.

We should not be at all surprised to find such a relationship between Japan and the prior owners of the land it now holds. Japan is, after all, a perfectly Modern nation. During its involvement in the First Atomic War, for example, Japan showed every bit as much of the Modern perversion as any of the other belligerents. In its occupation of China, Japan killed at least

---

[1]

Sister Mary Inez Hilger, "Japan's 'Sky People', the Vanishing Ainu," in *National Geographic* (Washington, D.C.: National Geographic Society, February, 1967), p. 279.

twenty million Chinese. Throughout the course of the War, Japanese Army Unit 731 conducted cruel chemical and biological medical experiments upon Chinese, Korean, British, and American prisoners of War. (However, upon the conclusion of the War, those crimes were never prosecuted, for the Soviet and American secret services were much more interested in the results of the experiments than in bringing the perpetrators of the crimes to justice.)

Although many people around the world are aware that six million Jews perished as a result of Adolf Hitler's evil intentions during the First Atomic War, and many are familiar with infamous place-names such as Belsen, Treblinka and Buchenwald, few outside of the afflicted nations remember that in addition, some four million Slavs and political dissidents from throughout Europe were also systematically murdered by the Nazi regime. Outside of the Russia, the Ukraine, and Belorussia, much of the world seems to have forgotten that over fifteen million Soviets were slaughtered during the German occupation of that nation. How is it that a large portion of the earth's population can remember the systematic murder of six million Jews, but forget twenty million Chinese, fifteen million Soviets, and four million Slavs and political dissidents? Perhaps a partial answer is to be found in the worldwide Jewish outcry against the terrors of the Nazi Holocaust, the cry of "Never again!" But what was--what is--the meaning of this "never again?" The slogan is incomplete, and only the passage of time could reveal its deepest meaning.

Now more than fifty years have passed since the conclusion of the First Atomic War. Now the nation of Israel is among the foremost suppliers of military armaments in this troubled world. Among the nations which Israel has willingly supplied the weapons of war to in the past, was the old apartheid regime of South Africa, which was a nation which openly followed a policy of "racial" separation, and which aggressively enforced the establishment of "racial" concentration camps and ghettoes. Now, the majority of Israeli citizens look upon fellow citizens of a militantly conservative persuasion such as the late Rabbi Meir Kahane--founder of the militant Jewish Defence League--as an embarrassing nuisance, but a *tolerable* one. Yet when Meir Kahane publically and unashamedly referred to all Arabs living within the borders of Israel as "dogs," how was he to be distinguished from the Friar Vicente de Valverde when *he* called the Emperor Atahualpa a "dog?" What difference was there between Rabbi Kahane and the infamous Dr. Goebbles who referred to Jews as "dogs?" If the outbursts of Rabbi Kahane were not an intolerable disgrace to the state of Israel, then the meaning of "never again" had been made clear enough; its meaning must be: "never again *to us*, and *who cares about anyone else?*"

Since the great Holocaust, there has been *no Jewish protest* against the concentration camps known as reservations, reserves, homelands, and "autonomous regions" which continue to exist on every inhabited continent of this earth to this very day. However, when a student of the American past recently published a work on *The American Holocaust*, there was an outcry by some Jewish scholars against the book's title. There has only been *one* holocaust in the *entire* history of the earth, they asserted. It was a systematic attempt to totally erase the existence of a religious-culture group of human beings, the Jews. This *never* happened anywhere else to anyone else, they said. Look at the "Indians," they said. There *are* still "Indians" left, so therefore, there couldn't have been an American holocaust.

What they said, however, was a self-deluded lie. The entire culture, the religion, and the whole population of the Natchez people of the North American southeast is gone, systematically exterminated, murdered, forever by the French colonists in Louisiana. The Californians killed the Yana people *totally*. The twenty three nations of eastern Texas have vanished completely from that land. Traders acting under the authority of the United States government destroyed the Mandan with a plague of smallpox. Scholars have yet to treat appropriately with accounting for the nations which were exterminated during the African holocaust of the slave trade. The English colonists on Tasmania hunted the Tasmanians like animals until there were none left. Until they were completely gone. Until they were all murdered, *systematically*, *never again* to be found *anywhere* upon the earth. The claim that "this kind of systematic extermination was never attempted at any other time or place" seems to be making the claim that if a nation happens to be small, or maybe if it is *savage*, *then the systematic, total extermination of its population doesn't count.* This is *not* an acceptable proposition.

Forty-eight years ago, the founding of the nation of Israel was the foundation of a possible hope for all of humankind. In the establishment of a nation intolerant of intolerance itself, humankind could have taken an enormous step forward. We might have all begun to appreciate that the mass murder of our own sisters and brothers halfway around the globe deeply affects us and diminishes us all, even if our brothers and sisters there are not exactly of our "own kind." It all depends upon what "Never again!" really does mean.

Since the conquest of the western hemisphere there have been only two genuine revolutions against colonial authority there. One, as we have seen, was quickly overthrown largely through the activity of agents of the U.S. government acting in Mexico City and in east Texas. The other was suppressed even more cruelly, for before being destroyed, the resulting nation was allowed to struggle through roughly fifty years of turbulent existence. This nation was the Maya Nation of the Cruzob, which survived in eastern Yucatan from approximately 1850 until 1900, when it was finally crushed by Mexican federal troops, and the area was shortly thereafter incorporated into the Mexican nation as the territory of Quintana Roo.[2]

As unbelievable as the inhuman brutality of Modern War may be, it is far surpassed by the horror of the internal purge, that violent act designed to 'purify' the citizenry of the Modern state. During Joseph Stalin's purges of the 1930[s], as many as thirty million Soviet peasants, "minority" people, and political dissidents were slaughtered in the Soviet Union. During the brief rule of Pol Pot's Khmer Rouge in Kampuchea, perhaps four million persons out of a total population of seven million were systematically exterminated (the world's accepted 'official' figure for this is 'only' two million). The dead had been found "racially" unfit to survive *as Cambodians* because they had been teachers, professors, college students, public officials in the former regime, women who wore their hair in the "Western" style, persons who wore eyeglasses, or others who had been 'unduly' influenced by "the West." The secrets of the torture chamber and the cannibalistic excesses during Idi Amin Dada's rule in Uganda are unmatched in this century. Amin's excuse was "tribal rivalry," (the same excuse which has been used in Rawanda during the civilian murders in the conflict between Tutsi and Hutu factions), but nothing in the tribal warfare of Ancient times ever came *close* to the viciousness expressed during his regime. The persecutions executed by Idi Amin clearly bear the mark of Modern "racial" thinking. So too do the massacres of civilians executed by Serb militiamen (and to a lesser extent by Croatians and Moslems also) in Bosnia. Our entire human species must bear the shame and disgrace of the fact that Idi Amin Dada, Slobodan Milosevic,

---

[2]

See Nelson Reed, *The Caste War of Yucatan* (Stanford, California: Stanford University Press, 1964).

Radovan Karadzic, and Pol Pot still live among us, the former three still safely 'in hiding', and the latter serving a 'sentence' which hardly matches his crime.

   In our Modern Epoch there survive but three of the forms of government out of the six basic ones which were known in Ancient times.   The survivors are: tyranny, oligarchy, and democracy. The so-called monarchies of our age are in most cases parliamentary democracies.   In some cases they may be oligarchies, and in others they are simply tyrannical regimes. Most democratic regimes are approximately what they claim to be, but in some cases--in those cases where the head of state is a "president for life," or president over the course of two or so decades--are actually tyrannies. Most tyrannical regimes claim to be democracies, and a few claim to be monarchies. Military regimes whether claiming to be benevolent or not, are always tyrannies. But what most people in our age have never meditated upon is the possibility that nearly all Modern regimes might in actuality be blended forms of government.

   Since the inception of the first Modern nation, the acquisition, handling, and disposal of enormous amounts of money--what is now known as *capital* (during Spain's heyday it was *bullion*)--has played a central role in the life of the state. Given the association between capital and the Modern state, and the association of the "race" idea--which impoverishes and separates the mass of people--with the Modern state, it is reasonable to surmise that Modern governments are either all oligarchical democracies, or all oligarchical tyrannies, with the oligarchical element being of supreme importance, yet also being the most hidden aspect of Modern government.

   It is a recognized fact that in Modern nations the national economy is of utmost concern. And when it comes to economics, there is one Modern individual who stands above all others, one person who 'wrote the book', on capital, so to speak. That person is Karl Marx, and the name of the book is simply *Capital* (*Das*

Kapital, in the original German). Marx has with justice been labeled *the* philosopher of Modernity. Communism, Marxianism, and Scientific Socialism are not, however, forms of government, but are instead theories of economic relations within the Modern state, just as is capitalism. Marx drew out the implications of the Modern industrial state to their fullest. The only meaningful form of human existence in his view was *Modern* human existence. In his view, or rather, I should say in the view for which he speaks, the whole world, eventually, must comply with Modern standards: human existence will not be *fulfilled* until this has come about. But while this may be true for some, it may not be true for all.

Native, Ancient, traditional or tribal nations have not fared well under communist (or Socialist) systems. The Mongolians and the Tibetans have been the subjects of systematic, forced culture-removal at the hands of the Soviet and Chinese regimes. After the Sandanista regime came into power in Nicaragua, it halved its 'problem' with the *Miskito* alliance on the Caribbean coast. By the Sandanista government's own census, the combined population of the *Miskito* tribes of the *Rama* and *Sumu* declined from a high of 290,000 in 1972, to 150,000 in 1985. By the mid-1980^s, as the civil war in Ethiopia had raged on, the central government had bombed parts of Eritrea into a wasteland resembling a scene from a doomsday comic book. (The same socialist regime conducted the purge of an entire generation of its citizens in the capital of Adis Ababa, and precipitated a flow of war refugees which further engorged the ranks of North Africa's starving millions during that period in the sub-Sahara region.)

While the attempted Soviet takeover of Afghanistan was underway it truly appeared as if the now-defunct Soviet Union was determined to possess the Afghani territory whether any native persons remained alive there or not. By the middle of the last decade, four million--about one quarter of that nation's population--had depatriated in order to escape the Soviets' War, and were living in refugee camps in Iran and Pakistan. In the brief time (relatively speaking) during which Soviet troops occupied that nation, the casualty toll equaled and exceeded that which the United States' exacted upon Vietnam. During the course of the Soviets' War thousands of grade school children from Afghanistan were transported--after the "Carlisle Indian School" manner--to Moscow for *education*. In the Soviet case, however, the education process was of *extreme* efficiency.

Now that the former Soviet puppet government in Afghanistan has been ousted, it remains to be seen whether the new Islamic fundamentalist rulers will do any better there. But things do not look good. After all, Islamic-based governments are all still fully-Modern states, and they have every tendency to act just as such.

The old Soviet regime also imposed itself heavily upon the Goldi, the Chuckchi, and other Ancient Siberian nations. The Soviet Union had reservations of all sorts--known as "autonomous regions"--within its borders. There were reservations for Mongolians, for Jews, for Germans, for Poles, for Moslems, and for numerous other "minorities."

The Soviet Union seemed to have had a fondness for chemical and biological weapons, and it used them abroad as well as promoted their use by its allies. Indeed, this form of warfare seems to have been dangerous enough to Soviet citizens right at home. In the 1940^s, 30,000 peasants perished when T2 toxin was accidentally released in the Orenburg district of Russia. And at Sverdlovsk in the Ural Mountains, 1,000 died after anthrax-bearing agents were dispersed by an accidental explosion at a biological weapons storage site there.

Although Soviet Communism collapsed under its own weight, there are still an enormous number of people living under socialist regimes, perhaps most importantly in the People's Republic of China. It is poignantly ironic that so many of the people of this world who are suffering directly from the effects of

Modern culture have embraced or come under the sway of a system inspired by the person who sought to invent a *perfect* Modern order. It is also surprising that few have ever dwelled upon the racism which is woven tightly into the fabric of Marxian thought.   When describing communism in its first post-revolutionary form, Marx wrote: "The role of *worker* is not abolished, but is extended to *all men.*"[3] Thus did he call for the abolition of *all* 'deviant' cultures (*i.e.*: Ancient ones). When he recounted the effects of British ethnocide in India, Marx seemed utterly detached, citing population statistics as if he were accounting for stacks of cord wood or bolts of cloth. He wrote:

> In 1824 the export of British muslins to India hardly amounted to 1,000,000 yards, while in 1837 it surpassed 64,000,000 yards. But at the same time the population of Dacca decreased from 150,000 inhabitants to 20,000. This decline of Indian towns celebrated for their fabrics was by no means the worst consequence. British steam and science uprooted, over the whole surface of Hindustan, the union between agriculture and manufacturing industry.[4]

When he considered the "Global Consequences of the Discovery of Gold in California," he wrote that:

> A coast of 30 degrees longitude, one of the most beautiful and fertile in the world, *hitherto practically uninhabited*, is being visibly transformed into a rich and civilized land, thickly populated with people of all races, from Yankees to Chinese, from Negroes to Indians and Malays, from Creoles

---

[3]

Karl Marx, T.B. Bottomore, translator, "Private Property and Communism," in the *Third Economic and Philosophical Manuscript*, in *Early Writings* (New York: McGraw-Hill Book Company, 1964), p. 153.

[4]

Karl Marx, "The British Rule in India," in *Surveys from Exile: Political Writings Volume II* (New York: Vintage Books, 1974), p. 304.

and mestizos to Europeans. California gold is flowing in streams over America and the Asian coast of the Pacific Ocean, drawing *recalcitrant barbaric peoples* into world commerce, into civilization.[5]

The assertion that the California coast had been "hitherto practically uninhabited" is, I suppose, a matter between Marx and the Ancient nations of the North American Pacific coast. Just what "peoples" are "recalcitrant," or "barbaric," however, is a matter best taken up between Marx and all of his readers or potential followers. It would appear as if one could blithely follow Marx into self-annihilation. Some of Marx's racism is indicated by what he did not say. As a foreign correspondent and political commentator he covered the Civil War in the United States through 1862. In that final year of his American assignment, he failed entirely to take any notice of *the largest mass political execution ever in U.S. history*--the simultaneous hanging on December 26, of 39 Dakota persons accused of participating in the Minnesota "Sioux" 'uprising' of that year.[6] Although Marx publicly decried the exploitation of women, he wrote in his description of early, or crude communism that in "the community of women...women become communal and common *property*."[7] The workers, Marx believed, constituted a "race."

---

[5]

Karl Marx, Saul K. Padover, translator, "The Global Consequences of the Discovery of Gold in California," in *On America and the Civil War* (New York: McGraw-Hill Book Company, 1972), p. 14.

[6]

Two of these hanged "Indians" were later found to be completely innocent of the matter--*from the Yankee perspective*. See Dee Brown, *Bury My Heart at Wounded Knee: An Indian History of the American West* (New York: Bantam Books, Inc., 1972), pp. 59-61.

[7]

Marx, "Private Property and Communism," *op. cit.*, p.153. *My* emphasis.

Still, some persons, in defense of Marx's racism, point out that "he was simply a man of his times," that living in the mid-nineteenth century in western Europe made it impossible for him not to be a racist, and besides, they assert, "his views were comparatively moderate." But then, living in racist times and places did not turn Ghandi or Dr. Martin Luther King, Jr. into racists. Nor did such living conditions turn Malcolm X into a racist--in the end. Just like Marx, Malcolm X was indeed a man of his times par excellence--until he rose above them. He was reared and trained on the mean streets of Harlem, New York, to be a hustler and a hood. He took up early on in his life with the Black Muslims, and quickly rose to be second in command in the "white devils"-cursing church of Elijah Muhammed. But then Malcolm went on a pilgrimage to the Holy Land of Islam, to the city of Mecca. There he allowed himself to be open to his senses, to be open to Reason. There he allowed himself to be touched by what most of us call God. He put it this way:

> You may be shocked by these words coming from me. But on this pilgrimage, what I have seen, and experienced, has forced me to *re-arrange* much of my thought-patterns previously held, and to *toss aside* some of my previous conclusions....
>
> During the past eleven days here in the Muslim world, I have eaten from the same plate, drunk from the same glass, and slept in the same bed (on the same rug)--while praying to the *same God*--with fellow Muslims, whose eyes were the bluest of blue, whose hair was the blondest of blond, and whose skin was the whitest of white. And in the *words* and in the *actions* and in the *deeds* of the 'white' Muslims, I felt the same sincerity that I felt among the black African Muslims of Nigeria, Sudan, and Ghana.

We were truly all the same (brothers)--because their belief in one God had removed the 'white' from their *minds*, the 'white' from their *behavior*, and the 'white' from their *attitude*.

I could see from this, that perhaps if white Americans could accept the Oneness of God, then perhaps, too, they could accept *in reality* the Oneness of Man--and cease to measure, and hinder, and harm others in terms of their 'differences' in color.[8]

No doubt Malcolm would have eventually realized that some of the "white" problem was also in part due to his own (and other persons') projection of "whiteness" in to the minds, behavior, and attitude of "whites." For he had truly begun to cut through the great mystification of the Modern mind. But he did not live that long. Shortly after his return from the pilgrimage to Mecca, and his inevitable split from the racist church of Elijah Muhammed (at this point in our investigation of the "race" idea, we are, of course, not surprised or shocked to find *a church* propagating racist ideas), Malcolm X was gunned down, killed by assassins in a bloody ambush.

So, given the number of other persons who have risen out of the mentality of their own racism--risen out of it against overpowering temptations and iron-clad 'excuses' (as, for example, the oft quoted: "*it is impossible for a 'person of color' to be a racist*")--risen out of it at the cost of their very lives--it looks as Karl Marx will have to own his own racism; it really is his own personal 'property'.

---

[8]

Malcolm X, *The Autobiography of Malcolm X* (New York: Grove Press, Inc., 1966), pp. 340-341.

That elitist oligarchies arise in socialist economies is no secret. In 1961, Frantz Fanon, the physician philosopher to the Algerian struggle for independence against French colonialism, characterized it this way:

> That famous dictatorship, whose supporters believe that it is called for by the historical process and consider it an indispensable prelude to the dawn of independence, in fact symbolizes the decision of the bourgeois caste to govern the underdeveloped country first with the help of the people, but soon against them.[9]

More recently, when Arkady Shevchenko became, in 1978, the highest-ranking Soviet diplomat to defect to the United States since the end of the First Atomic War, he described the operation of Soviet elitism. At "the pinnacle" of his career, Shevchenko realized:

> I had become part of the stratum that tried to portray itself as fighting what it coveted. While criticizing the bourgeois way of life, its only passion was to possess it; while condemning consumerism, the privileged valued above all else the consumer goods and comforts of the West. The cocoon of privilege in which we lived was warm, comfortable--and crippling.
>
> After years spent among the elite, I had finally got my fill of its venality and coarseness. That life is unbelievably ugly.[10]

---

[9]

Frantz Fanon, *The Wretched of the Earth* (New York: Grove Press, Inc., 1968), p. 182.

[10]

Arkady Shevchenko, "Breaking With Moscow: Part II, The Reluctant Spy," in *Time* (New York: Time Inc., February 18, 1985), p. 58.

According to Schevchenko, while they were on assignment there:
> The U.S. was a candy store for our diplomats. During their short tours of duty they amassed an unbelievable amount of goods unavailable or too expensive in the U.S.S.R. In the late 1970^s, the average wage of mid-level diplomats in Moscow was 200 to 250 rubles ($270 to $280) a month. But with a $700 to $800 monthly salary in New York it was possible to purchase many things far beyond their reach at home. One could buy a Soviet car for about $2,000 if it was paid for in U.S. dollars, and receive it on returning to Moscow. In the Soviet Union the waiting list for an auto is three to ten years, and it costs more than 10,000 rubles ($13,000 to $14,000). Automatic washing machines (almost nonexistent and only semi-automatic), dishwashers, cameras, stereo systems, records, cassettes, crates of baby food and disposable diapers, irons, china, tissues and toilet paper, clothes, shoes and fabrics were all transported to the U.S.S.R. And everyone bought extra items that could be resold on Moscow's black market. From ambassadors to the lowliest clerks, all regularly sent thousands of pounds of goods home.
>
> To do that, those paid a low rates severely economized on everything from daily diets to entertainment. Saving money was their permanent and often obsessive preoccupation. But diplomatic personnel could make their money go farther than Americans because they paid no taxes and were skillful, relentless bargain hunters. Besides, their housing and medical care were inexpensive or free.[11]

So it appears most unlikely, given the record upon which Marxism--in fact *socialism*--now stands, that any relief for the suffering derived from Modern society shall be found at that

---

[11]

Ibid., p. 67.

source. Indeed, a final point must be noted. In envisioning and outlining a scheme for total world order, Marx was merely presenting a left-wing reformulation of an idea which was centuries older than himself--an idea which, nonetheless, is classically Modern. The original (and right-wing) version of it was Roman Catholicism's grab for control of all the world's souls. The parallel version of this (also completely right-wing) was Islam's grab for control of all the world's souls. These kinds of ultra-conservative (in fact, neo-fascist) attempts to impose a single-system ordering upon a very diverse world continue to resurface in the present-day in the form of movements to gain political control in the United States by conservative Christians, in Israel by ultra-orthodox Jews, and in Islamic countries by Islamic fundamentalist movements.

Following the inventions of Christopher Columbus, Roman Catholicism claimed, just as does Marxianism, that once the entire world was consolidated under its control, the 'millennial age' of human freedom could--*would* commence. Ironically, the Roman Catholic program, presented in the terms of spiritual rhetoric, cloaked a hidden economic objective: the easy acquisition of enormous volumes of pearls, and gold and silver bullion. Marx's rhetoric, conversely, presents its program in the terms of economics, and yet it hides a spiritual objective, which is to supplant all forms of religious experience with a 'cult of the state'. But as we have seen in our review of proto-Modern Roman, and of Spanish and some other Modern histories, right-wing attempts to create a political or religious order on a grand scale in the Modern Age are always attached to the destruction of human life on a grand scale. The record in this matter still belongs to the 16th-century Church of Rome, which suddenly saw its ranks swollen by the potential addition of over one hundred million souls, thanks to the clever prevarications of Columbus, and then which, over the relatively brief span of a century and a half, actively helped preside over the depletion of that flock to the tune of some eighty-five million human beings. In the case of left-wing attempts at world-consolidation, it is just as obvious that the outcomes are equally lethal. This is indicated well enough by the direction already taken by the Chinese bureaucrats at Tienanmin Square, or by Joseph Stalin and Pol Pot.

This is why--if there is any chance for our human species to survive the seriously self-destructive tendencies which are built into the Modern social form--it is the open, or 'free' societies of this earth which offer our best hope.

We're free to worship, free to speak.
We're free to kill, its guaranteed.
We've got a problem, that's for sure.
Clean up the back yard, go lock the door.
Must be Hell, livin' in the world, sufferin' in the world
like you.
Must be Hell, livin' in the world, sufferin' in the world
like you.

--Jagger and Richards

CHAPTER VII
The World Today--A Warning

Throughout the course of this study I have scrupulously avoided the use of the term *genocide*, using in its place the word ethnocide, by which I have intended to mean the complete (irreversible) destruction of an entire nation. The word is composed of the Ancient Greek root *ethnos*, meaning nation, and the Latin *caedo*, meaning to kill. Genocide is a troublesome word. It is derived from the Latin *gens* or the Greek *genos*, the name for a large family unit of descent, and the Latin *caedo*. The term genocide first appeared around the time of the First Atomic War, and since then has been taken to mean: "the deliberate and systematic destruction of a racial, political, or cultural group."[1] The English words *gene* and *genetics* are also derived from the same complex of Greek root words as genocide.

When it first appeared, the word genocide was primarily applied to the Nazi murder of six million Jews. It was considered somewhat applicable to the Nazi destruction of Slavs and political dissidents as well. However, although Jews have protested since the War that they are not a "race," as Nazi dogma insisted they were, the term genocide seems to be the *most* closely associated

---

[1]

See for example: *The New Merriam-Webster Pocket Dictionary* (New York: Pocket Books, 1971), p. 210.

with the Nazi program of Jewish extermination--the Nazi "Final Solution" to the 'problem' posed by the existence of the Jewish "race." Curiously, however, although the word genocide arose in the context of concentration camps and human extermination, it was not applied, immediately following the War, to existing concentration camps, "racial" ghettoes, "homelands," reservations, "autonomous regions," or reserves, anywhere else in the world outside of Germany or formerly Nazi-occupied regions.

In the chapters above, we have seen from *several* perspectives that there are no such things as "races" of human beings. Viewed in terms of what we now know about the "race" idea, the word genocide seems to very strongly imply, after the manner of the various "racial" hypotheses, that culture, or nationality, is transmitted genetically. Yet we have also seen in the chapters above that throughout the Modern Epoch, key political figures have understood "perfectly well" that culture is not a matter of "blood." This is precisely why, throughout the Modern Age, master practitioners of ethnocide have not stopped at merely defeating an enemy. They have proceeded, fully-aware that culture is acquired by learning, to raze the cities and towns of the vanquished, to destroy all literature and written records of those they defeated, to separate young children from their families and culture and transport them to the heartland of the victor for 'education', to declare illegal the national religion, language and culture practices of their victims, and to program the mentality of the losers regarding their memory of their own history, often going so far as to convince them that they previously were illiterate, nomadic, and savage. Inasmuch as the word genocide implies a genetic transmission of culture, it is a spurious, false word. Inasmuch as the word genocide implies a genetic transmission of culture, it is a word which bears hidden evil intentions.

Over the past four decades, however, the word genocide has gradually become rather commonplace around the world. Nations have been accused of committing genocide upon other nations or "minorities" in the distant or recent past. Nations are accused of actively pursuing genocidal policies, or of planning them. However, there *is* but one possible meaning for the word genocide, and in light of it, all of the recent glib talk about genocide may be seen and understood as an intricate expression of Modern mentality; it is at once the avoidance of the unthinkable, and the preparation for the unimaginable. The unthinkable is the foundation upon which the Modern state rests: ethnocide. Hundreds of nations of the Ancient world have been coldly, ruthlessly, brutally exterminated so that Modern nations could exist. Hitler was not the first, nor did he invent anything new. He was simply among the clumsier Modern practitioners of ethnocide. The unimaginable is the only thing which the term genocide could possibly mean.

There is just one single unique combination of genes which can produce human beings. This unique human genetic code-- borne within the human reproductive cells, and having nothing whatsoever to do with "blood" in the "racial" sense--can carry the message to form a human being of any size, shape, skin color, or sex which is possible for our species. But to repeat: there is but one basic and unique human genetic code. Alter the genetic matrix just slightly, and the code will be that for a chimpanzee, orangutan, or some other species closely related to--but not quite-- human. There is, in the crude sense of the term genocide, but a single human "gene." This is why all of the fast and loose talk about genocide in our own time represents a dangerous preparation for the termination of our species "gene." And this has paralleled and supplemented another dangerous debate in our present age: the debate about the potential threat of nuclear War. *That* debate has focused upon the pending horrors of nuclear War, preparing the public mind for what is to come, while carefully avoiding impressing upon public consciousness the ugly, terrible fact that the First Atomic War has already been fought and won (and lost). Together, the nuclear War debate and genocide question have generated a Modern twentieth century apocalyptic mentality which is preparing our entire species for its own extinguishment.   The longer these discussions are continued--in their present style of avoiding the realities of ethnocide and the First Atomic War--the more prepared the Modern mind will be to accept the unimaginable. And that end need not come with a blinding flash and deafening roar of thunder--if the Modern mind is properly prepared, human species death might just as probably creep up on us subtly, incrementally, silently.

But how possible *is* 'real' genocide?

The answer to this lies in the field of relationships, particularly in the special field of inter-human relationships. It has very much to do with the entire issue of "race," and the human willingness to become self-alienated through the use of "racial" classification. There are currently several means of self destruction available to our species. Some of them even offer the possibility of total annihilation.

Nuclear weapons offer the most obvious means.   The stockpiles of these held by the United States and the nations of the former Soviet Union are large enough to completely destroy life in much of the world should they be subject to uncontrolled use. Although an all-out nuclear exchange between superpowers today seems unlikely, a consortium of concerned scientists from the United States and Russia has pointed out that even a limited atomic War could trigger a global climatic effect known as "nuclear winter." Such an effect could grip the earth in an unrelenting sub-zero degree climate for perhaps as long as six months. A winter of that sort--especially if it should commence during the spring or summer months--would be disastrous in its consequences for plant and animal life around the globe.

But the United States and the nations of the former Soviet Union are not the only nations which possess nuclear weapons or the capacity to build them. The list of nuclear weapons-possessing nations also includes Britain, France, China, India, Israel, and probably South Africa. Among the nations with advanced weapons building capacity are: Canada, Brazil, Argentina, Germany, Iraq, the Netherlands, Sweden, Finland, Belgium, Switzerland, Italy, Pakistan, South Korea, North Korea, Japan, and 'nationalist' China. As this list grows longer--especially due to the global dispersal of highly-trained nuclear scientists which was a result of the breakup of the Soviet Union--and more and more nations join the nuclear 'club'--as they surely will--the real danger of another nuclear War will grow exponentially. The practical danger here is that a conflict between two nations besides the 'superpowers'--or perhaps some turmoil within a single nation--will escalate into the use of atomic weapons, and that then, the U.S. and perhaps China, or maybe even Russia, choosing sides, will be drawn into a general nuclear War. It has also been pointed out that such a disaster could be precipitated by the crash of a large meteorite into one of the less-developed nations which possess nuclear weapons, for the blast caused by such an event would be almost indistinguishable from a nuclear detonation, and the less-developed nations do not possess sophisticated enough radar equipment to distinguish an incoming meteorite from an incoming missile.

The greatest possibility for another nuclear War, however, is probably offered though a third route: the use of nuclear weapons by terrorists. For example, terrorists possessing nuclear weapons could--for their own devious reasons--detonate atomic devices in the United States, or Israel, and then disseminate the information that some nation not aligned with the terrorists had been responsible for the detonation. This is not at all an unrealistic proposition, primarily because of the ease with which homemade nuclear bombs can be constructed. For over a quarter of a century the danger posed by the possibility of homemade nuclear weapons--produced either by a terrorist nation, a terrorist gang, or by an individual--has been a special concern of theoretical physicist Theodore B. Taylor.

Taylor is a man who knows what he is talking about. For seven years--from 1949 to 1957--he was a leading nuclear weapons designer at the Los Alamos Laboratory in New Mexico. He began his career firmly believing in nuclear deterrence as the best means to world peace. He now believes otherwise. In his own words:

> I thought I was contributing to a permanent state of peace. I no longer feel that way. I wish I hadn't done it. The whole thing was wrong. Rationalize how you will, the bombs were designed to kill many, many people. I sometimes can't blame people if they wish all scientists were lined up and shot. If it were possible to wave a wand and make fission impossible--fission of any kind--I would quickly wave the wand. I have a total conviction--now--that nuclear weapons should not be used under any circumstances. At any time. Anywhere. Period. If I were king. If the Russians bombed New York. I would not bomb Moscow.[2]

Taylor is a very worried person. He is worried by the rapid growth of plutonium stockpiles--estimated to reach more than a million kilograms by the year 2000.[3] He is worried by the often lax, careless transportation of plutonium and uranium 235 in trucks and airplanes to reprocessing centers where it is made into fuel for nuclear power reactors. He is worried by the lax security at the storage facilities for these fuels. He is worried by the

---

[2]

John McPhee, *The Curve of Binding Energy* (New York: Farrar, Straus, and Giroux, 1974), pp. 120-121.

[3]

Ibid., p. 46.

incredible toxicity of plutonium oxide--one gram, if used as a poison could kill as many as one million people.[4] He is worried because plutonium or uranium 235 stolen either in an armed hijacking of a shipment, or covertly taken from a processing site, could easily be made into a nuclear device. Very easily. And already, checks of stockpiles of these deadly materials have shown several kilograms of plutonium to have turned up missing and unaccounted for over the past few decades. The missing amount is more than enough to make a few bombs.

John McPhee, a journalist, accompanied Theodore Taylor on a visit to Stanislaw Ulam, inventor of the U.S. hydrogen bomb, in the early 1970[s]. Ulam is also a person who shares Taylor's interest in safeguards for nuclear materials. McPhee listened as Taylor told Ulam:

> ...about the attempted blackmailing in 1970 of a city in Florida. The blackmailer promised not to bomb the city out of existence in return for a million dollars and safe custody out of the United States. A day later, the threat was repeated, and with it came a diagram of a hydrogen bomb. Taylor described the diagram to Ulam--a cylinder filled with lithium hydride wrapped in cobalt, an implosion system at one end of it--and nothing in Ulam's face or Taylor's manner indicated that such a diagram might not be credible. The threat, though, had been a hoax, perpetrated by a fourteen-year-old boy.[5]

A fourteen-year-old boy?

This is precisely why Taylor is so worried. There have been a few other highly-credible nuclear 'hoaxes' in past years. They were also accompanied by accurate diagrams of less-powerful fission bombs. How can this be?

---

[4]

Ibid., p. 69.

[5]

Ibid., pp. 118-119.

The reason is that all of the pertinent information on nuclear bomb construction is now in the public domain. Drawing from the *Encyclopedia Americana*, the *Rare Metals Handbook*, *The Effects of Nuclear Weapons*, the *Sourcebook on Atomic Energy*, and *The Los Alamos Primer*, all sources which are readily available, any potential back yard bomb-builder would have the requisite data to complete such a project. Necessary equipment such as glove boxes and crucibles could be easily obtained from any chemical supply firm.

Yet nuclear terrorists may not need to go to the trouble of hijacking a plutonium or U 235 shipment and then building their own atom bomb from scratch. Nuclear weapons decay, or lose their potency with age, and hence, old weapons of all sorts are quite continually being shipped to a small number of recycling plants in the weapons-possessing nations from locations all over the world where they have been deployed. Given the volume of such business, the theft of ready-made nuclear weapons by terrorists becomes a real possibility. Not all nuclear 'devices' are large and cumbersome. Intercontinental ballistic missiles with multiple warheads contain varying numbers of small, relatively portable nuclear bombs. Atomic artillery shells are also comparatively small and compact. Then there is the "backpack nuke" first developed for the U.S. army (but also 'counter-developed' by the Soviet Union). Designated the special atomic demolition munition, this 58 pound atomic bomb is designed to be carried by one person, and is powerful enough to destroy, for example, the Golden Gate Bridge. The United States has approximately 400 of these powerful little atomic bombs, scattered about in military bases in Europe, South Korea, Guam, and the United States. A former general in the Red Army of the old Soviet Union has recently asserted that since the breakup of the Soviet Union, scores of these kinds of bombs have come up missing in Russia and neighboring countries. Russian authorities deny this. Who *really* knows?

Theft is not the only possible means of acquiring such weapons. Most people in the Modern world are extremely sensitive to money. This, in fact, is the primary threat which has arisen with regard to the enormous stockpile of nuclear weapons left over after the dissolution of the Soviet Union. Throughout Modern history, military organizations have harbored a small number of individuals--officers and enlisted persons alike--who out of a desire for money have been exceedingly willing to engage in the theft and black market sale of all sorts of military equipment, including munitions. The case of Edwin Wilson--the fifteen-year veteran U.S. Central Intelligence Agency operative-- who turned terrorist and sold 21 *tons* of C4 plastic explosive to the Libyan regime of Colonel Khadafy, underscores this point. Espionage, spying and treason--*for money*, rather than for a cause--is a Modern custom. In past decades intelligence services and state departments of the major (that is to say, powerful) Modern nations have over and over again been made aware of this fact. The question is not *whether* terrorists will eventually be able to buy nuclear weapons, but *when* a well-endowed terrorist group (or nation) will find the right price of the right person.

But nuclear War is only the most obvious means of our species' self-destruction--our suigenocide--it is not the most likely means. The end is much more likely to come as a result of some sort of "environmental" oversight or accident resulting, in all probability, from someone's (or some corporate "entity's") haste to make a quick money profit as easily and as inexpensively as possible. There are hundreds of dangerous possibilities, and combinations of dangers. I shall mention just a few of them here.

The generation of electricity by nuclear reactors presents a variety of problems at all stages of the process. Since no one has as of yet conclusively proven what the worst effects of the "meltdown" of a nuclear reactor core would be--whether negligible or catastrophic--the danger of such a mishap must be taken very seriously. Perhaps the potential seriousness of such an incident is indicated by the great lengths to which the U.S. nuclear energy industry went in order to deflect public attention from fixing firmly upon how close the 1979 nuclear 'accident' at Three Mile Island in Pennsylvania actually came to a meltdown.

There are a number of scenarios for the precipitation of such a disaster. Terrorists could disable the controls of a reactor, causing a meltdown. Acts of conventional, non nuclear War could sufficiently damage a reactor to cause a meltdown. Much more likely, however, would be a greed-related incident. In the U.S. alone, work of a number of nuclear power plants has had to be halted in mid-construction because the contractors building them were discovered to be in gross violation of plant construction safety standards. Violating these safety standards was making the contractors a *lot* of money, for free; but it was also likely to lead to a finished product which would be unsafe to operate.

This very sort of greedy cost-cutting is precisely what led to the largest nuclear reactor 'accident' to date, the meltdown at Chernobyl, in the U.S.S.R., on April 26, 1986. (Note, however, that in the case of a non-capitalist nation such as the Soviet Union, this greed is not manifested as a desire for free, unearned profit, but rather, as a desire to possess something which the nation's economy is not strong enough to provide for.) The Soviets, though, greatly improved upon the cost-cutting greed of their U.S. counterparts, going so far as to eliminate the expense of constructing shielding containment buildings around their reactors. The results of eliminating this safety feature would be difficult to calculate in terms of the Chernobyl disaster, for there has been a great deal of equivocation on *all* sides regarding the long-term effects of that catastrophe. In the U.S., an estimate was released from the Los Alamos lab--then quickly retracted--asserting that the Chernobyl 'accident' released as much radiation into the environment as the cumulative total of all previous atmospheric nuclear tests. Some medical experts have predicted that as many as 100,000 persons in the territory surrounding Chernobyl, and in Western Eurasia will die prematurely from cancers caused by the escape of radiation there. The immediate effects of the meltdown at Chernobyl were, however, more obvious: the death of over thirty people and the despoliation and evacuation of sixty square miles of land north of the city of Kiev.

Proponents of the nuclear power industry in the U.S. have of course denied that such a disaster could ever occur in the United States. Before Chernobyl went awry, the Soviets also made their own denials. Months before the 'accident', the Ukrainian power minister boasted that "the odds of a meltdown are one in 10,000 years."[6] Opponents of nuclear power estimate that given the proliferation of nuclear reactors, the odds are more like one in twenty years. But the effects of the ultimate disaster--a full-scale meltdown--as yet remain unknown.

U.S. supporters of nuclear power proclaim that the excellent safety record of domestic nuclear power plants justifies their use. "No one has ever been killed in an accident in a civilian U.S. nuclear power plant," they argue. That's technically true. Barely. But in addition to the Three Mile Island and Chernobyl 'accidents', there have also been half a dozen serious nuclear mishaps around the world. In 1952, there was a partial meltdown of a reactor core at a plant near Ottawa, Canada. A reactor fire at the Windscale Pile north of Liverpool, England, contaminated 200 square miles of countryside in 1957, before it was extinguished. Thirty three deaths were attributed to that incident. A mishap of unknown type and origin occurred near the city of Kyshtym in the Ural Mountains of the Soviet Union sometime in the winter of 1957-1958. What *is* known about that incident is that as much as 400 square miles of that countryside was ruined by nuclear

---

[6]

Quoted in John Greenwald, "Deadly Meltdown," in *Time* (New York: Time Inc., May 12, 1986), p. 50.

contamination, and thirty towns and villages within the region were deleted from the Soviet map. Three workers were killed in January of 1961, in a fatal steam explosion at an experimental military reactor near Idaho Falls, Idaho. It was impossible to remove the bodies of these first victims of a fatal U.S. nuclear 'accident' because of the high level of radiation in the containment building. Radioactive waste water leaked into the Pacific Ocean for several hours at a power station in Tsuruga, Japan, in 1981. On January 4, 1986, when radiation escaped from a uranium processing plant in Gore, Oklahoma, one worker was killed, and one hundred persons were hospitalized.

    The most likely cause for a greed-related nuclear accident remains the *subtlest* form of greed. This is the very selection of nuclear energy as a source for electricity production over other technologies which are now available. In capitalist economies solar and geothermal energy have for example largely been dismissed by utility companies because they are "economically unfeasible." Such economic infeasibility consists of this: a well-designed, thoughtfully-engineered solar or geothermal power plant is, compared to a nuclear power plant, relatively maintenance-free. This means that it can eventually pay for itself, and that the cost of the electricity it produces will continually decrease. Conversely, nuclear power plants are extremely costly to build, and they require continuous maintenance and large staffs to run them. Such start up and operating costs (even when partially defrayed by governmental grants) can easily be doubled or trebled, and then 'justifiably' passed on to consumers. Most importantly, largely due to the continually high cost of plant operation, the price of the electricity which a nuclear power plant produces can remain high, and might even have the potential of increasing in cost.

    So, nuclear power plants have sprung up all over the face of the earth, in complete ignorance--or perhaps defiance--of the dynamic and powerful life force of that composite living being which most Ancients used to call "Grandmother," or "Mother." It is strange that such as-yet unpredictable power can be so forcibly denied. But still, people seem to be determined to forget that the earth is subject to very violent movement. When confronted with an event such as the July 28, 1976 earthquake at Tangshan, China, which killed over 240,000 persons in that city alone, people seem determined to believe that such a thing could not possibly happen where they live. Perhaps the Ancient populations of Santorini or Atlantis can be excused for creating their settlements on top of the very source of their doom-- presumably their earth sciences were not quite as well-informed as our own. But we Moderns have no such excuse.

To be sure, in the United States, thousands did protest the opening of the Diablo Canyon nuclear power plant in California. Great numbers were even arrested in that cause. (The problem with the Diablo Canyon plant, located near San Luis Obispo, is that it sits nearly astride a major branch of the San Andreas Fault, and at any time in the future could be subject to a severe earthquake.) However, over assurances that the plant is "earthquake proof," the facility has been opened. Apparently the engineers and scientific experts in charge of the project were able to convince the proper authorities that they were completely certain that no earthquake could ever possibly damage the containment building, or sever and disable the electrical control cables and backup systems, or rupture emergency cooling conduits. Considering contemporary scientific skepticism toward clairvoyance, that must have been a prodigious feat of prognostication.

What is truly remarkable, however, is what environmentalists and nuclear plant design engineers alike have failed to take into account--what they have not considered to be a threat. The old nuclear plant at San Onofre, California, for instance, is a scant twenty miles from the Elsinore Fault. As residents of Mexico City found out in September of 1985, one need not be at the epicenter of a temblor in order to feel a maximum effect from it. Scores, or even hundreds of miles can be a negligible distance when the earth is shaking. Thus there is also the unknown danger posed by the proximity of the nuclear reactors near Sacramento, California, and the Mammoth Lakes region--about one hundred and fifty miles distant from each other as the crow flies. Mammoth Lakes is an active volcanic region. Geologists predict that a caldera eruption may occur at Mammoth Lakes at any time within the next century. We may be wise to recall here that the devastating explosion of Thera (Santorini) was a caldera eruption, and we would do well to remember how widespread the damage caused by that event was. However, the area of the earth's surface *directly* involved in the Thera explosion (or even in the much more recent Mount Saint Helens or Soufriere eruptions) was less than one square mile. The surface area of the Mammoth Lakes volcanic activity is one hundred square miles--more nearly equivalent to the one hundred and fifty square miles of earth which sank to a significantly lower level very suddenly indeed during the Ancient caldera explosion which formed the Yellowstone basin. The caldera eruption of such a vast area in this age of human occupation would by itself present a natural disaster of unimaginable dimensions. But it is impossible to say whether survivors would be capable of dealing with the additional 'complication' of a related nuclear accident at a nearby reactor.

Earthquake faults and active volcanic areas are, however, not found only in California; they exist all over the world and pose an ever present, subtle, and utterly unpredictable threat to nuclear power plants.

There are other dangers inherent in the use of nuclear power. We have already considered the threat posed by the production, storage, and transportation of fissionable materials which could be stolen and used by terrorists to manufacture homemade nuclear bombs. And the worldwide effects of Modern human arrogance and greed are not limited to flaws in reactor design as in the old Soviet Union, or flaws in reactor site selection as in the U.S. As a byproduct of their operation, nuclear power plants produce all sorts of refuse contaminated by low-level, long-lasting radiation. Up until 1970, these materials were periodically collected up, sealed in metal drums, and routinely dumped into the oceans at numerous disposal sites. In 1970, most nations--excluding Great Britain and a few others--banned this practice, but nothing was done to clean up the existing undersea nuclear waste dumps. Now, the metal barrels have begun to rust through, and at some sites, such as the one off of the Faroe Islands near San Francisco, radioactively 'hot' fish have been snagged up off the sea bottom. Such radioactive pollutants, it seems, have a tendency to become concentrated in the body tissues of the larger animals--such as game and commercial fish--which are at the end of the food chain which is the closest to our human species. So, it is likely that the Geiger counter will eventually become a necessary piece of equipment for commercial and sport fishermen at some time in the future. At any rate, the nuclear waste which has been dumped on the sea bed at various locations around the globe is likely to remain dangerously radioactive for thousands of years to come. The use of nuclear energy also poses other uncomplicated dangers. There are, for example, 'nuclear-powered' satellites which are energized by the radioactive decay of plutonium. Should the launch vehicle carrying one or more of these satellites into orbit explode or somehow fail on or shortly after launch (an amply demonstrated possibility for both manned and unmanned rockets), the area below and downwind could be subjected to a lethal dusting of plutonium. Then there is the matter of the nuclear powered naval vessels sailing the world's oceans. The scores of such submarines, cruisers, and aircraft carriers existing today are all powered by small nuclear reactors. Even if we pretend that a second atomic War will never be fought, we must recognize that such ships would be tempting, or actually *mandatory* targets in a conventional War, or in an undeclared conflict between a small nation and a superpower. In the case of the latter sort of a conflict, suicide missions by the air corps (or perhaps by commandos) of a desperate "third world" nation could pose a serious danger. The effectiveness of such tactics were certainly demonstrated by the Japanese Kamikaze pilots of the First Atomic War. Since the safety of seagoing atomic reactors has never been tested under actual combat conditions, the unknown danger of nuclear powered naval vessels is that in a wartime situation they confront us with a worst case scenario of several reactor meltdowns occurring simultaneously at sea. On the other hand, should the worst not occur, there is always the possibility that the sinking of a number of nuclear powered vessels will 'merely' release a large amount of radioactive waste and radioactive debris into the ocean.

It seems as if--from the Modern perspective--the air, water and soil of the earth--the Mother being of all life species we know--is a garbage dump of infinite, unending capacity. And yet, Modern scientists really know that this is not so. Over the past few decades a variety of scientific minds have set about to investigate the "greenhouse effect"--the gradual warming of the earth's climate as a direct result of the human production of carbon dioxide gas in industrial processes, and by the use of internal combustion engines. Now a majority of responsible scientists of all sorts concur that the greenhouse effect is a real phenomenon, and some suggest that with climatic warming, global coastlines will once again change as they did following the last ice age. As the polar ice caps shrink, more water will be released into the world's oceans, causing sea levels to rise. These scholars have pointed out that by the next century, faced with such a rising sea level, coastal cities will have to be abandoned or relocated. (Then there is the matter of the mysterious holes in the earth's atmospheric ozone layer, which have been observed recurring first over Antarctica every October, and which eventually appeared over the northern hemisphere as well. Scientists seem uncertain about what the *exact* effects of the ozone holes will be--possibly an increase in skin cancers, or disruption of plant growth cycles--should they worsen. But they are in agreement that the situation *is* worsening, and that the ozone layer is being disrupted by a chemical reaction caused by an infusion of man made chemicals.)

Of course, the greater portion of the "greenhouse" problem could be eliminated by the widespread adoption of a new, already-invented internal combustion engine which draws its power from the energy contained within the combination of Oxygen and Hydrogen atoms which constitutes the water molecule. This engine gives off water vapor as exhaust. Yet how much *profit* could be derived from an engine powered by such cheap, abundant fuel? The 'hybrid' motor which employs alternations of electric and gasoline internal combustion power which was introduced by the Toyota motor company late in 1997, stands a much better chance of success, because it can greatly extend the life span of the powerful oil companies. We have again returned to *greed*, the prime motivator behind Modern societies, and a large part of the reason why our Grandmother, the earth, is now treated as nothing else but a bottomless trash pit.

The pell-mell, freestyle dumping of humanity's industrial excrement upon the earth because it is cheap--"economically feasible"--to do so, and therefore represents a large 'free' money profit, indeed presents a fine means of our species' possible self-extinguishment. Countless tons of deadly toxins have been dumped into the earth's living space in scores of manners over the past few centuries. In some regions acid rain is a serious perturbance of aquatic life spaces, in others acid fog has a severe negative effect upon land life; both phenomena may ultimately be traced to the habitual Modern practice of cheapening short-term industrial expenses.

What is known as "land disposal" has over the years consistently been viewed as the "cheapest alternative" for the containment of a variety of toxic wastes. Every year in the U.S. alone, an estimated one million tons of toxic waste are produced. The refuse of years past is often simply left strewn about, unaccounted for. Tailings of asbestos, lead, mercury, and uranium might be found here and there at abandoned mine sites. Some tailings (uranium, to be precise) have even been used as landfill for housing projects.

Among the more potent industrial poisons slopped into the life sphere are dioxin, PCB^s, the fumes of burning PVC, the solvent TCE, and certain pesticides and herbicides. Then there is petroleum. Oil is known to have lethal effects upon marine and terrestrial life. It is constantly being shipped in vulnerable pipelines and tankers which have a demonstrated ability to fail. Large areas of Ocean have already been found to have been seriously damaged by the oil pollution of past years. And so too have large areas of land. Following the rout of Iraqi forces in the recent Gulf War, the retreating Iraqis ignited the oil fields of Kuwait in a last-ditch attempt to destroy that land. Although the fires were eventually extinguished, meteorologists asserted that the enormous plumes of smudge resulting from the fires caused a cooling effect upon global climate in the following year. If nothing else, this unprecedented event of purposeful despoliation of the earth has demonstrated that in their madness, terrorist nations and tyrants of the Modern age will stop at nothing in order to 'make a statement'.

Although the human species has altered the face of the earth--has tampered with the environment--for hundreds of millennia, there is a vast *qualitative* difference between traditional human and Modern human activity in this area. The Ancient practice of burning off savanna grasslands to stampede game herds into a deadfall or an ambush cannot, for example, compare with the Modern possibility of the total elimination of the Amazonian rain forests. Although our species has dumped its refuse upon the surface of the planet earth for hundreds of millennia, a hillock of clam shells or flint flakes cannot compare with a one kilogram mound of plutonium oxide dust, or a million gallon lake of PCB[s]. Perhaps the greatest danger of these Modern toxins in our life space lies in their cumulative and combinative effects.

Acting singly, various agents appear to affect only certain limited areas at a time. There is just enough dioxin to force the evacuation of Times Beach, Missouri, there are just enough PCB[s] to poison Love Canal, New York. There is just enough Agent Orange to defoliate thousands of acres of Vietnam, just enough phosgene gas in Skull Valley, Utah, to kill a few thousand sheep. There is just enough poison gas in Bhopal, India, to kill 2,000 persons, just enough radiation to burn out hundreds of square miles of countryside in the immediate vicinity of Kyshtym and Chernobyl. However, as cumulatively more and more land becomes unavailable for habitation by a steadily-growing human population, the nature of the problem will clarify.

But the list of arrogant or stupidly greedy human-made dangers threatening our species has not yet been exhausted. There are plenty of other threats to human species life here on the planet earth in these Modern times. For example, military, scientific and industrial interests continue to join together in developing new agents for use in chemical and biological War. Perhaps something--a biological agent of some sort, let us say-- which 'works' to near perfection, might be devised somewhere, and perhaps it might be released (accidentally or intentionally) into the planet's unprotected life space. On a planet now populated by billions of human beings, the effect of such a plague could make the first wave of bubonic infection in Medieval Eurasia look insignificant. (*That* first sweep of the plague from India to Iceland claimed roughly 25,000,000 lives--one out of three persons.)

Then there is the new scientific-industrial focus upon techniques of recombinant DNA life forming and cloning, or "genetic engineering." The danger inherent in this new life technology (which at the outset holds the beneficial promise of cures for previously unmanageable diseases) is unlikely to emerge in its initial developmental phases. But such danger may emerge with greater clarity, as the technology involved in genetic engineering becomes more familiar and routinized, such as occurred in the U.S.' N.A.S.A. space shuttle program. Furthermore, such a laboratory-based technology is difficult to monitor, and as popular knowledge in the field of genetic engineering grows, uncontrolled experimentation represents a real source of danger.

At the bottom of each of these lethal fields of human endeavor lies an obsessive interest in capital--in the acquisition and disposal of it. The ebb and flow of capital, whether Columbian (bullion), or Keynsian, or Marxian, seems to be the prime concern of all Modern times. The cheapness with which capital may be generated appears to be the secondary concern.

It is indeed true, as Ronald Reagan quipped in Madrid on May 6, 1985, that: "Christopher Columbus was one of the original entreprneurs." For he, along with the other original entreprneurs Isabella of Castile, Ferdinand of Aragon, and the Borgia Pope, Alexander VI, by inventing "race" and "discovery," brought into the world much more than just fully Modern Rhetoric. By throwing the western hemisphere open to plunder, first by Spain, and then by other Modern nations, Columbus and his co-entrepreneurs had formed the essence of Modern economic theory. That essence was recently summed up in the poetic lyrics of a popular Modern song. (As has often been the case from Ancient to Modern times, popular music is frequently a very accurate reflection of social life in any given society at a particular point in time.) Ostensibly about the lifestyle of contemporary musicians, the lyrics proclaim:

Hey! That ain't workin', that's the way you do it.
You get your money for nothin', and your chicks for free.[7]

Look where we may, we cannot escape the conclusion that such is the essence of Modern economic theory. Whether we consider the Spanish armed robbery of gold and silver from Peru and Mexico, and the Conquistadores subsequent appropriation of the noblewomen of those countries; whether we consider the Puritan annexation of gardens, forest game preserves, and trade routes already worked by others for thousands of years; whether we consider the King Cotton plantations tended by the hands of slaves in the Antebellum South of the U.S., or the high-rolling entrepreneurs of England and the northern U.S. during the same period--supported in all of their activities by the slave-like labors of industrial workers; or whether we consider the privileged life of luxury of the Soviet Politburo elite (who so pridefully bragged about their small annual salaries--while at the same time receiving most of the necessities of life and many luxuries free of charge, as perks of their office)--the inescapable fact appears to be: "That ain't workin', that's the way you *do* it..."

And yet, within every system, in every Modern nation--free or tyrannical, socialist or capitalist--the mass of common (lower and middle class) people work, and work *hard*, clinging to the unrealistic dream that perhaps some day they too might have *their own chance* to get their money for nothing. This is how the first corruption of most souls occurs. And so it is, that *by the masses*, is defended and perpetuated a most vicious system of relation which is deadly and degrading to human and other earthly life. So it is, that by the masses, is defended a system which has *always and only* functioned to the direct benefit of the elites which it supports.

---

[7]

Dire Straits, 1985.

As I suggested above, the answer to the possibility of our species' genocide lies in the field of relationships, in our human relationships with other life forms on the planet earth--including the planet-being herself--and *most* importantly, *in our relationships with each other*.

At the moment when Modern society was chartered and the human species' Ancient sibling relation was sundered to be replaced by "race" relations, it is doubtful that the founders of Modernity realized the full magnitude of what they had done. In destroying the Ancient law of humanity's sisterhood and brotherhood, they had done much more than merely overturn a timeless spiritual mandate. By turning human beings into depersonalized commodities to be exploited and "wasted," they had done nothing less than to deflect major components of our common species' nature which over countless millennia had been *expressed* as a spiritual law.

Every animal life form on this planet possesses a unique combination of physical and behavioral attributes which adapt it suitably to life upon the earth Grandmother.

Physical anthropologist Ashley Montagu puts it this way:

> An animal becomes adapted to its environment by evolving certain genetically based physical and behavioral traits....[8]

Human beings, he asserts,

> ...are the product of a unique evolutionary experience, in that they, far more than any other creature has even remotely approached, have escaped from the bondage of the physical and the biological into the complex and even more challenging social environment. This remarkable development, this movement into the learned part of the environment as their principle mode of adaptation,

---

[8]

Ashley Montagu, *Growing Young* (New York: McGraw-Hill Book Company, 1981), p. 70.

introduces a third dimension, a new zone of adaptation, which many biologists in considering human evolution have tended to neglect. The most important setting of human evolution has been and continues to be the human social environment, human culture, the learned way of life, the human-made part of the environment.[9]

In *Growing Young*, his essay into the "third dimension"--the "new zone" of human adaptation--Montagu intricately describes the function of a number of the most important, uniquely-human, behavioral-cultural adaptations. To the present day, all of these adaptations are universally manifested in human children. However, upon the achievement of adult 'maturity', many of them--in all but the most 'primitive' of societies--simply cease to operate. By contrast, in Ancient societies, the rule was that these adaptations functioned throughout the entire course of human life. I now list here those adaptations which have been the most severely perverted by the "race" idea, the underpinning of all Modern societies. These damaged human adaptive capacities are: cooperation, interdependency, the giving and receiving of love, the establishment of friendships, compassionate intelligence (a deep sympathy coupled with the desire to help alleviate the suffering of others, and an intelligent ability to respond *appropriately*--all tempered with 'something' of pity), mental flexibility, the need to think soundly, the need to know, and not least, the need to learn.

These human species characteristics may seem of little import to those Modern people who have long ago lost their fullest potential, and who have happily watched them being progressively educated out of their own children. It is not so with Montagu, however. He compares damaged Reason (which he calls the need to think soundly) with another vital body function:

---

[9]

Ibid., pp. 69-70.

Strangely enough, it is not generally understood that the ability to think soundly is almost as vitally necessary as the ability to breathe soundly. There are untold numbers of individuals who do not breathe normally, who are shallow breathers, much to the detriment of their health. Nevertheless they survive, even though they suffer from various deficits as a consequence. Unsound thinking leads to unsound conduct; unsound conduct adversely affects health, especially mental health, and results in human as well as socially destructive effects. Thinking soundly leads to the understanding of the necessity of feeling soundly. In the greater part of the civilized world men [and women] have long been bent on a course of self-destruction largely as a consequence of the trained [*conditioned*] inability to think soundly.[10]

But perhaps this is not a blunt enough description of how some of the most important of our human species characteristics have been disabled by the "race" idea. We have seen above, in Chapter III, that upon its inception, the "race" idea was intended to imply a species difference between artificial groupings of human beings. This is why the word mule (*mulatto*) was given as a name for the children of "racially-mixed" sexual unions. This latent, but highly important meaning of the word "race" remains in full force to this day. Common, ordinary people (whatever they hold their own "race" to be) have numerous preconceptions about basic *anatomical, physiological, spiritual,* and *mental* differences which distinguish them from other "races."

At this point, present-day ideologists who adhere to what is known as liberalism, will protest vigorously: "But all races are equal." Political equality, however, is a very difficult concept to pin down. It carries none of the built-in constraints of sisterhood and brotherhood. Here I must beg your forgiveness for sinking

---

10

Ibid., p. 139. *My* additions in brackets.

into a coarse vernacular, but I do so good-naturedly, and I believe it conveys my point more forcefully.　In a mentally and spiritually-healthy family, siblings--*brothers and sisters*--do not fuck with one another, nor can they be expected to murder one another.　There are simply certain rules existing in a healthy sibling relationship which are never broken.

The same, however, cannot be said of the relationship between 'equals' in this post-Machiavellian era. *Any* deception, *any* ploy is considered *reasonable*.　After the most brutal competition, the most ruthless combat, victors may be found literally standing over the corpses of the vanquished chanting: "They had an equal chance. It was a *fair* fight." Or, as equality was paraphrased after the Vietnam War's *My Lai* massacre: "They [the unarmed women and children] could have killed *us*." Or more simply: "They [those "Gooks"] were the enemy." It is in the Modern context of equality that we find Islamic Jihad radicals and contract killers planting time bombs destined to blow up persons they have never known, or teenagers from the United States machine-gunning children in the rice paddies of Vietnam, *or now*, pre-teens in the inner cities of the United States machine-gunning the members of their own communities in battles over gang and drug turf.　Hence, in Ancient times, when the influence of the sibling relationship was generalized, there was the possibility of honor in warfare.　Now, in Modern times, Total War-- a contest between 'equals'--is most often characterized by the seemingly-random spilling of human viscera.

Perhaps political equality refers to the biological fact that all humans are composed of equal portions of carbon, hydrogen, oxygen, nitrogen, phosphorous, and sulphur.　Perhaps it refers to the fact that all human blood is the same color, or that all human blood is mostly made up of salt water.　Perhaps it refers to the fact that in this age of medical organ transplants and blood transfusions, organ tissues and blood types may be matched and donated across "racial" lines.　These, however, are trite forms of equality, for they imply nothing of love, or of compassion, or of pity. And they imply no constraints whatsoever in the relations between human beings.

On the other hand, consider a family of say, four siblings, two brothers and two sisters. One is a philosopher, one is a musician; one is a physician, one is a carpenter. On what Procrustean bed shall the philosopher, the musician, the physician, and the carpenter all be made 'equal'? The physician may save one hundred human lives, the carpenter may build one thousand storage cabinets; but how shall the two be rendered '*equal*'? The philosopher may fill lecture halls with blasts of hot air, the musician may fill great amphitheaters with beautiful sounds; but what is their 'equality'? And yet, if they are mentally and spiritually-healthy siblings, their lifelong relationship will be characterized by love, cooperation, and compassion. There will always be certain brutal or exploitative acts which, *as siblings*, they will be prohibited from practicing upon one another.

As treasured members of the social order, the contributions of the four siblings may be *compared*. Some may indeed be found to be roughly-comparable, and others not at all, but the four shall never be *genuinely equal*.

Should the four live in a Modern culture, in the kind of place which knows nothing but "race," then they will be radically unequal in the eyes of the law--regardless of what the laws say about equality. They will be unequal as males and females, for Modern societies do not make a trivial, merely-human distinction between male and female. Perhaps the females will not be the equal of the males because the laws (as is so often the case in a Modern nation run by fundamentalist Islamic clerics) say that must be so. Perhaps the *males* will be unequal because the system of the laws has been caught perpetuating an injustice upon females, and in self-defense (in defense of the entrenched males who actually run the system) has shifted the blame which *it* deserves upon the lower classes of males in the society.

If the four live in a democratic state, then they will be unequal as voters, as participants in politics. Think about this: if one of them sells a vote, if one of them votes for a friend only because the person voted for is a friend, if one of them votes purely out of self-interest, and if one of them votes with an utmost concern for what might be best for the state; *how* shall these four be '*equal*'?

So maybe equality means that all are equally-treasured in the eyes of that mysterious spiritual force often known as "God." However, one merely needs to recall the "racial" interaction between Catholic Spaniards and "Indians" in the sixteenth century to be disabused of that notion. Nothing has changed since those days. Nothing *will* chance until certain Christian sects cease insisting that those persons who do not recite the formula "I love you, Jesus," according to *their* idea of the correct manner, are condemned to eternal damnation, or until certain Islamic denominations cease insisting that those who do not follow *their* path are "devils."

Thus when we consider assertions of "racial" equality forwarded by contemporary liberal ideologists, we would be better off focusing on the liberalism of the speakers, rather than on their assertions of equality. At the present time, liberalism is a sub-ideology of a larger ideology known as democratic capitalism. The compliment of liberalism is conservatism. In this day, the two cannot exist without each other, and both function to support the ideology of democratic capitalism. Each offers a segment of a democratic capitalist nation a view of what is politically correct, and what is politically wrong. Because they compliment one another so well, the function of both ideologies can easily be understood to be to support the conduct of 'business as usual' under democratic capitalism. With regard to racism, conservatives tend to be rather directly racist--at least *in private*. Liberals, however, profess to be different, to be free of racism. But nothing could be further from the truth. In asserting that:

"All races are equal," liberals employ a most subtle rhetorical defense of racism and the "race" idea which lies at the core of all Modern societies, for as we have seen, *the origin of all racism* is *the very idea that "races" are real human categories.*

However, I must now return to the explanation of how the "race" idea has disabled some of our most important human species characteristics. With but a single exception, depending upon what "race" an individual considers her or himself to belong to, the "race" idea deflects the possibility of *cooperation* with individuals of other "races," and replaces it with a feeling of *aversion* toward a majority of the human beings on earth.[11] The "race" idea destroys the potential for *interdependency* between individuals of differing "races," and replaces it with *rivalry*, or at best, *detachment* (the watchword here is: "Stick with your own kind"). For most persons, the "race" idea blots out the possibility of *giving love to* and *receiving love from* individuals of other "races," and instead creates *animosity* and *suspicion* between supposed groups (again: "Stick with your *own* kind," or "Be *proud* of what you *are*"). Because of the influence of the "race" idea, the *formation of friendships* between persons of allegedly-differing "races" is equally difficult; *ill will*, or at the least *complete indifference* between perceived "races" is much more common.

The "race" idea plays complete havoc with *compassionate intelligence*. What is found in its place is perhaps best illustrated by an all too common situation on "Indian" reservations. This is the repeated, predictably periodic appearance of "white" 'saviors'. These are persons (usually ones who consider themselves to be members of the "white race") who suddenly arrive in reservation

---

[11]

Obviously, since the "yellow race" is by far the largest of such artificial groupings, comprising at least one half of humanity's numbers--depending upon what system of accounting for "race" membership is used--'*their*' common disdain is held toward a *minority* of the earth's human population.

country with little or no knowledge of North America's Ancient nations' histories, and even less knowledge of their present life. But they are rescuers, who have elaborate programs in their minds about how to save "the Indians" from themselves. Their actions may be called *compassionate ignorance*, or perhaps because their ignorance is often very stubborn, they might be considered to be indulging in *compassionate stupidity*. The result of the activities of these rescuers is the enlargement of their own egos. There is another side to this coin too. Some individuals see the suffering of other "races," and understanding exactly what is going on, choose to exploit the situation for the sake of their own personal gain. The best recent example of this is a former U.S. Secretary of the Interior. After leaving his government job, this individual began making the circuit of U.S. reservations, hyping a number of 'economic development' schemes. By utilizing a very clear understanding of what is happening on reservations, he has increased his personal fortune by some millions of dollars over the course of years through *intelligent exploitation*.

Need I explain the manner in which the "race" idea has destroyed *mental flexibility*? Is it not obvious how the *compulsory* division of our human family into four or five supposedly-homogeneous groupings into one of which *each and every human individual* must be fit promotes *mental rigidity*?

Consider next *the need to think soundly*. Since, as we have seen,"race" is not at all real, but is instead *an instrument of political rhetoric--a device by which to control the thoughts and behavior of masses of people*--it is necessary to face the consequence of the fact that the great majority of the earth's human population *does* see "race" as a reality-based system of human classification. That consequence is this: the human species' *need to think soundly* has been supplanted--*via* "race" belief--with *mass delusional thinking. The need to think soundly* has been replaced by: "a false conception and persistent belief, unconquerable by reason, of what has *no existence in fact.*"[12]

Many individuals, under the influence of "race" belief, go a step further. Looking outside of their own supposed 'group', they may see all "white" people as blue-eyed, or all "Blacks" as having dark brown eyes. Such an individual may, for example, look upon an "Indian" with green eyes, chestnut hair and a mustache, and see a person having black hair, a beardless face, and dark eyes. This is *hallucination*: "an extremely projected image or belief which has no corresponding reality to warrant it."[13] Chronic delusional thinking and hallucination, we must recognize, are among the major criteria of insanity.

Certain individuals--usually including some of those who number among the heroic figures of Modern societies--go even further under the influence of "race" belief. Think of the career of Francisco Pizarro--an obsessively devout Roman Catholic and murderer of the Inca dynasty--in terms of the American Psychiatric Association's definition of *Schizophrenia, paranoid type*:

> This type of schizophrenia is characterized primarily by the presence of persecutory or grandiose delusions, often associated with hallucinations. Excessive religiosity is sometimes seen. The patient's attitude is frequently hostile and aggressive, and his behavior tends to be consistent with his delusions.

---

[12]

This particular definition is drawn from Isaac K. Funk, editor in chief, *Funk & Wagnalls New Standard Dictionary of the English Language* (New York: P.F. Collier & Sons Corporation, 1938), p. 676. The *emphasis* is mine. Any common dictionary of the English language would, however, yield the same definition of *delusional thinking*.

[13]

Ibid.

In general the disorder does not manifest the gross personality disorganization of the hebephrenic and catatonic types, perhaps because the patient uses the mechanism of projection, which ascribes to others characteristics he cannot accept in himself.[14]

This description of a *psychosis*, for example, would also apply equally well to certain members of the Mather family from seventeenth century Puritan New England, or to the nineteenth century 'mountain man' known as Liver Eating Johnson.

Finally, the "race" idea has replaced *the need to know* with *the fear of knowledge*, and has substituted *prejudice* for *the need to learn* in the field of human relations.

The point of all this destruction of our human species' adaptive characteristics is related very directly to genocide--the human species extinction potential. To many observers, the present challenge facing humanity appears to consist of a variety of specific, unconnected technical difficulties arising between humanity and the environment as a result of certain human activities. The solution seems to them to lie in taking particular scientifically viable, well-engineered corrective measures designed to address each successive or distinct problem. This may indeed help to some degree--for example an international moratorium on logging and deforestation in the earth's tropical rainforests may in part insure that some breathable atmosphere is conserved on this planet well into the next century--but it is no real solution. The real problem lies in the very manner in which many ecologists and other scientists state the problem: it is seen as the environmental challenge facing humanity. In short, the problem lies in the conception of the planet earth and the human

---

[14]

The Committee on Nomenclature and Statistics of the American Psychiatric Association, *DSM-II: Diagnostic and Statistical Manual of Mental Disorders*, Second Edition (Washington, D.C.: American Psychiatric Association, 1968), p. 34.

species as separate and distinct forces which are sometimes in hostile opposition. It is a relationship problem which consists of the alienation of the human species from the literal ground of its being, the planet earth.

This is a most curious separation, as a moment of reflection will convince almost anyone of. Think of it this way: every molecule, every particle of matter constituting the body of every human being living on this planet has come quite directly from nowhere else but the planet being herself. This we share with every other form of life on this earth: we are all literally living compositions of earth elements.

We should not be surprised to find, as the work of Lynn White, Jr. and other thoughtful and creative Medieval historians has indeed shown, that the alienation of humanity from the earth shares the same general developmental time frame and heartland as the alienation of humanity from itself.[15] Hence it might appear evident that the attempt to "fix" the environmental conditions which threaten our species is literally putting the cart before the horse. How can our species *possibly* reestablish a healthy, life-promoting relationship with our Mother--Grandmother being, the earth--*unless* we first reestablish such a relationship among ourselves? Until all human beings are seen by all human beings as being human, until our species abolishes all "races" and begins to regain the full use of the species characteristics which have been bestowed upon us by hundreds of thousands (if not millions) of years of existence upon the earth being, we shall undoubtedly continue to be confronted by a series of various environmental 'problems' until at last something, or some combination of things

---

15

There are some fascinating collections of historical essays addressing this subject which have been edited by professor White. See for example: *Machina Ex Deo: Essays in the Dynamism of Western Culture* (Cambridge, Massachusetts: The MIT Press), and *Medieval Religion and Technology: Collected Essays, op. cit.*

overcomes us. (Here I must point out that all of the 'ecological catastrophes' facing our species *seem* at this point of their and our development to be possibilities, or at worst, probabilities, not *certainties*. So far, they represent situations which *appear* to be amenable to correction. But one thing *is* certain. *No one* knows *for sure* the *exact* extent of the danger which we have created for ourselves, and that by itself is very troubling.)

There is one more thing, one more danger--albeit a highly abstract and speculative one--which our species has created for itself, and it too is related to what we have already considered. Eulogizing the seven astronauts of the failed *Challenger* space shuttle mission, Ronald Reagan--the most quotable of recent U.S. presidents--said on January 31, 1986, that: "Man *will* continue his conquest of space." Reagan was right, provided our species manages to escape the consequences here on earth of the self-destruction of our own species nature through the use of "race" rhetoric. (*And* presuming that the infinite is amenable to conquest by the finite.)

Reagan's *Challenger* eulogy may be placed into an intriguing context. Somewhat earlier--in November of 1985--on the eve of his Geneva summit conference with the last of the Soviet Premiers, Mikhail Gorbachev, Reagan made a most curious remark. He said (I am paraphrasing him as closely as my memory allows) that if some species not born of this earth were to come to our planet and menace us, we would all soon enough forget our various differences and join together to face the new external threat. One odd facet of Reagan's remark is that it succeeds decades of strenuous U.S. government attempts--*via* such ploys as Project Blue Book--to end public curiosity, debate, and investigation into U.F.O. (unidentified flying object) sightings.

As I have said, this is a highly speculative area, so consider my entry into this topic to be merely the continuation of a line of inquiry which has been opened up by no lesser a figure than president Ronald Reagan himself. Thousands upon thousands of sightings of this class of objects have occurred worldwide since the days of the First Atomic War. While about ninety percent of such sightings have or can be proven to be attributable to human activity and earthly environmental phenomena, a hard core of unexplainable encounters remains. This ten percent (or less) is composed of sightings made by law enforcement officials, airline and military pilots (as, for example, a well-publicized June, 1986, pursuit of unidentified airborne objects by a squadron of Brazilian jet fighter planes), and even U.S. astronauts. (Although our present-day electronic news media bombards us with sufficient information to more than adequately promote oblivion, astute news watchers will recall that during the early days of the U.S. space program, one astronaut returned to earth and blithely reported that his orbiting capsule had been visited--but not entered--by another vessel. Current N.A.S.A. procedures have safeguarded against such casual disclosures by instituting lengthy and secret 'debriefing' sessions for returning astronauts.)

The U.F.O. question is further complicated by a worldwide rash of mysterious livestock dissections which began around 1970. A few thousand such dissections have occurred over about one third of the United States, and in Canada also, all to the complete bafflement of law enforcement agencies. Often such events have occurred within hundreds of yards of human habitations, yet *no person or group has ever been apprehended* in the act, or even *been actively suspected.* Frequently there have been nearby U.F.O. sightings before or after such events have occurred. These dissections have been accomplished with a surgical precision which appears to be beyond human capacity--in one case it was discovered that tissue was removed following the contour of cellular walls, and not by cutting through cell structures. The tissues which have been selected for removal appear to be calculated to provide a genetic readout on the cattle, and a check on local environmental conditions. Often the anus and lower intestines, gonads, and udders have been 'cored out', and although this is done without causing bleeding, the corpses are often drained of blood. Eyeballs have been removed, as have tongues, samples of hide, bone or cartilage, and lip. Most of the dissected cattle show multiple pyramid fractures, which could have only been caused by their having been dropped to the ground from a height of at least ten feet.[16]

Still more complication is added to the U.F.O. queston by the insistence of a handful of quite respectable scientists that high resolution, computer-enhanced photographs taken of the planet Mars by fly-by N.A.S.A. spacecraft show clear evidences of an abandoned civilization there. Whether this is a fanciful replication of a nineteenth-century fantasy, or reality itself, will probably have to wait until that planet is directly investigated by a manned expedition from earth--if it ever is.[17]

The real question is the possibility of life--of intelligent life-- elsewhere than just on earth. Such life, however, is in actuality a probability, statistically speaking, that probability is likely to be overwhelming. The elements which promote and support life on our blue (water) planet earth are common throughout the entire universe. Astronomers are as of yet unsure how many galaxies-- clusters of billions of stars such as our own Milky Way--might exist in the universe, but the number of stars--of life-giving suns-- existing in creation is surely beyond counting. The number of planets is bound to be even greater, and of those, more than a

---

[16]

David Perkins, "The Phantom Cattle Surgeons of the Plains," in *Boulder Monthly* (Boulder, Colorado: Boulder Monthly, Inc., January, 1979), pp. 20-23, 40, 42-43, and 47-49. Also, Lance Beswick, "Mystery Deepens," and Mary Tortosa, "Mutilations move nearer," in *The Edmonton Sun* (Edmonton, Alberta: Edmonton Sun, Inc., November 13, 1979).

[17]

Richard Hoagland, "Metropolis on Mars," in *Omni* (New York: Omni Publications International, Ltd., March, 1985), pp. 64-66, and 82.

handful *are certain* to possess the conditions necessary to nurture life *as we know it.* The possibility of life based on molecular structures unknown to us is another matter altogether. It is statistically inevitable that more than a few life-sustaining planets have nourished civilizations well in advance of our own. What apparently is as-of-yet unknown, is whether they would deign to actively appraise us of their existence.

Then there is the matter of technology and science, specifically of a technology and science sufficient to permit practical travel over the enormous interstellar and intergalactic distances of the universe. Consider here the case of our own recent history. In well under a century, we have discovered and mastered the technique of mechanical atmospheric flight, and then we have gone on to travel through space to our planet's moon. We have just discovered the 'genetic engineering' techniques of recombinant D.N.A., gene splicing, and cloning. Physicists have recently discovered the existence of forces and particles of anti- or counter-gravity. Einstein revolutionized science's concept of space and time with his theory of relativity. But does all of this achievement mean that we have come to the end of scientific inquiry, the fulfillment of knowledge, the completion of understanding? Surely the answer to that question is no. For if it were not, scientific questioning would just smugly come to a halt. But think for a moment of this: what would be the technology and science of some other species on some other place other than earth which had hundreds of years more development than our own? Or thousands of years more development? Or tens of thousands of years more?

Just as it is our own arrogant ignorance which prompts us to confidently proclaim that on only *one* planet out of trillions upon trillions did only *one* intelligent life form--humanity--emerge, so too it is our own arrogant ignorance which prompts us to confidently proclaim that others who might be living in places we do not yet know of, could not possibly know things which *we* have as yet not even dreamed of. However, it is very unlikely that such beings should ever take an actively hostile interest (or for that matter, even a friendly one) in creatures such as us. We are better off left alone. Unless...

We now stand upon the threshold of what we call the "invasion" of space. How have we equipped ourselves--prepared ourselves--for such an almost godlike undertaking? By making ourselves *mad*, it would appear. On earth, since the beginning of the Modern Age, we have proven incapable of recognizing the intelligence--or the humanity--of members of our own species. We have even denied the humanity and the accomplishments of our own ancestors, creating grunting brutes out of people who scholars such as Alexander Marshack have actually found to have been quite the opposite.[18] We have been equally callous--no, even more so--in our interaction with other intelligent species on this planet. This begins to become apparent as we consider the implications of the possession of a sign language vocabulary by Koko, a female lowland gorilla now living in California. Koko has mastered a vocabulary of some one thousand words in American sign language. She uses her vocabulary to communicate with human beings about her feelings, her wants, her fears, about past events, and about trivial everyday matters--and she also uses sign language to communicate with another gorilla.[19] Koko understands spoken English perfectly.

---

[18]

See Chapter IV, above, pp. 109-111.

[19]

See: Francine Patterson, "Conversations With a Gorilla," in *National Geographic* (Washington, D.C.: National Geographic Society, October, 1978), pp. 438-465, and Jane Vessels, "Koko's Kitten," in *National Geographic* (Washington, D.C.: National Geographic Society, January, 1985), pp. 110-113.

Consider the shame of humanity's recent brutal interactions with the highly-intelligent Cetacean family, the whales and porpoises. Finding them to be abundantly easy to kill in the mechanized Modern age, and therefore taking them to be stupid creatures, humanity has pushed a number of their species to the very brink of extinction.

All of this is why Reagan implied a great error--the greatest of errors--when he said that our species would pull together in the face of an external threat. For one thing, it would surely by then be too late. For another thing, such an event could never occur without the severest of provocations, the very kind of provocation which human beings stripped of their human species animal nature are perfectly capable of. To put this in another way, only if humanity "invades" the vastness of outer space in the manner of Roman legionaries, equipped with such venal, pecuniary concepts as Roman-style law--the very condition in which we persist to this day--only then will we be in trouble. For then, it is inevitable that we will commit the gravest of errors, the greatest of crimes--in all likelihood without even knowing it--and thus have ourselves diagnosed by others we may not even be aware of, as a dangerous "cancer." Our trail will lead directly back to our home, the earth, and should the crime be great enough, the penalty might well be planetary cauterization.

But why have I made such an obvious fool of myself by venturing to discuss so absurd a subject as the possibility of an external threat to humanity posed by some unknown space-borne species? It has been an exercise in imagination. It is yet another way of pointing out that *there are no external threats* to humanity. If, for example, venal business people and their hired scientists become so divorced from reality that they utterly ignore the simple fact that everything which the human species dumps upon the earth, the species is quite literally *putting into itself,* then our species is not being faced by an "external threat" when, as a result of this stubborn ignorance of the business people, an environmental breakdown ensues. It is a purely *internal* problem. It is a problem of human consciousness. If, or when the planet earth becomes provoked into becoming our diagnostician-- if, or when the planet's life-promoting shield of ozone is irrevocably sundered by intolerable doses of "profitable" chlorofluorocarbons--if, or when the wound called Modern humanity is thereby cauterized (along with millions of [but not *all*] other species), in the end, *nothing* will have "happened to" us. *We* will have *destroyed ourselves*.

"Hostile invaders" from space, "environmental" crisis, another nuclear War--in these, as in all extinction 'threats' facing our species, the source of greatest danger to us is nothing other than humanity stripped of its human nature. *This* is the difference between Antiquity and Modernity. Antiquity respected and loved, and *understood* the ground of all human existence--the planet being called the earth--because people in Ancient societies began with the understanding that *all human beings are indeed human*. This is why Antiquity never stood a chance against the onslaught of Modernity. This is why *we* will never be worthy of the stars until we first regain our lost human nature.

Wash away my troubles, wash away my pain,
with the rain in Shambala.
Wash away my sorrow, wash away my shame,
with the rain in Shambala.

--Three Dog Night

EPILOGUE

Dear Brothers and Sisters:

The Invention of "Race" has been a difficult essay into human consciousness to set down on paper. The process has entailed more than eight years of library and experiential research, and an additional two years of literary composition. It has taken over a decade to bring it into publication. But this process, although painful, has also included a joyful discharge of obligation. Let me explain.

Twenty years ago I stood alone in a certain place for a certain number of days and nights. In the manner of the spiritual traditions of the nation to which I belong, I was there to pray, to communicate with the mysterious spiritual force which is all--to communicate with "God" as (he-she-it-them is/are) known in the English language. As I stood there alone and nearly naked, hungering and thirsting, wet and cold from nightly rainstorms, too hot from the sun by day, *annoyed* by swarms of mosquitoes at dawn and dusk, fearful above all of the cold and *discomfort* which more rain would bring, I harbored a secret prayer, something which I felt was too great to ask for.

And yet, when the time came for me to confess my failures in the year-long discipline of my preparations for that moment, and again later, when I asked for a favor for myself--to be a good teacher--a small miracle, the smallest of miracles, showed me that I had been heard; that in fact, I was *not* alone. Within months I realized that my secret prayer had been heard as well. That simple prayer was this: I wanted to know what things had *really* been like before the great calamity which had destroyed the now weak and helpless nation to which I belong. I wanted to know *how* the great disaster had occurred.

Although I have long been interested in the conflict between *philosophia* and ideology, I had never been particularly curious about "race" relations, Central and South American archaeology, Roman history, Medieval history, or the Spanish conquest of the Americas. With contempt I had scoffed at the notion that Phoenicians could have ever visited the Americas. But in the year following my prayer fast I found myself drawn to works by Lewis Hanke and Lynn White, Jr., I 'accidentally' discovered Alexander von Wuthenau's ...Art of Terracotta Pottery..., and I became open to investigating the epigraphic studies of Barry Fell, and the archaeology of Thor Heyerdahl. I became open to learning things I did not want to learn; I found myself weighing the merits of these scholars' arguments *by the weight of the evidence they presented* and the fullness of their reasoning, *rather than by the strength of my own prejudiced opinions*. And this is how I knew the prayer in my heart, the words I had been afraid to utter, had been heard.

From then on, the library research portion of this project was simple: I knew--or could easily find out--where to look for information I needed with little trouble. But after a few years of work, a problem arose. As my research continued and my understanding of the past increased, I became filled with a smouldering rage which was visible to all but myself. I was angry about the great murderous injustices of the past, I was angry with those of my friends and colleagues who did not *seem* to understand the importance of or the implications of the project which I had embarked upon, I was angry with *everyone* (including myself) for having been 'brainwashed', I was angry with the 'brain washers'. The cure was soon to come.

A few years later I left a secure job in Hawaii and took a teaching position in a small community college on a reservation in northeastern Montana. For six months everything went very well. I was quickly given a raise and promoted to the position of Chair of the Social Sciences and Humanities Division. In the classroom, things went splendidly. I was delighted to discover how eager college students on a reservation are to learn material such as is included in this study. I was surprised by how popular what and how I taught made me with the student body.

But I had attracted the attention of earthly powers much greater than myself. More quickly than I could believe possible, I found myself accused of a crime of which I had never before been suspected, arrested, tried, or convicted. Suddenly I was purged from the system; I found that recourse to the law was completely unavailable to me, and that somehow my name had become anathema throughout the entire eastern Montana higher education community. I was embarked upon a five and a half year trial of unemployment, or more specifically, sporadic underemployment. In a social order made mad by "race," I was now to feel the effects of that madness all the more directly. Making hundreds of applications for university work outside of the region, I found myself stigmatized either as an "Indian," and therefore academically irrelevant, or by my given name and surname, as a "whitemale," and thereby unworthy of being considered on the merits of my previous academic record. For a brief time, I descended into a life on the streets.

However, I was by no means alone during this ordeal. Looking back from where I now stand, I can see that my loved ones, my friends and family, had never abandoned me, and that they too were abiding the trials I faced with a patience that was formidable. And on that long and lonely-seeming road I walked, I carried with me a sacred pipe, made in the image of an Ancient gift--a symbol and tool of prayer--brought to the nation to which I belong by a holy woman on behalf of all humanity. By the time, over twelve years ago, when my--let us say *daemon*, whispered in my ear that *now* was the time to commence with the composition of the results of my research, I realized that the fire smouldering within me had been extinguished. Throughout this period of great difficulty I had learned a supreme lesson. Reflected in those about me, and in the love of a power much greater than any human being, I had discovered the virtue of patience.

Then I slipped into an even greater pitfall. Shortly after this manuscript was completed, I once again began teaching, this time at a small community college in Central Wyoming. During those same few years I was in and out of negotiations with several publishing houses, both academic and commercial. Nothing ever seemed to come of this, however, and I found myself drifting away from this project as I fell into the comfort of the work-a-day world. This became deeply intrenched in me when, in 1991, I secured the position of Training Director at the State of Wyoming's only publically-supported facility for individuals with developmental disabilities.

During this period the temptation to forget this work was overwhelming. Life was very comfortable. I was teaching almost every day. And I had discovered a new "race"--the developmentally disabled. Here, I had been forced to confront and overcome my own prejudices in this area. I made powerful new friendships with a few people who showed me directly that having a serious involvement with developmental disabilities by no means makes an individual mentally retarded. I was also continuing my study into the dysfunction of governmental bureaucratic institutions and the endless prevarication and dissembling engaged in by high-level administrators and directors, as well as that of middle management functionaries, or for that matter, *anyone* who was *afraid of their job* (afraid of losing their job) in such a setting.

When, in 1993, I signed a contract with a large publishing company in Germany to write a new, original work, I remembered *The Invention of "Race"* once again. However, in the excitement of writing a new manuscript on politics, that thought quickly drifted away. I had, however, purchased a personal computer in order to execute that other project. I had also continued to attend the annual sun dance which my family held on the Pine Ridge reservation, and I had continued to carry my sacred pipe, and to partake of the purification rite whenever the opportunity offered itself. The intervening years were difficult in many ways. The death of my mother, father, and older sister in Pine Ridge, the continuing degenerative progress of a deadly disease possessed by both of my younger brothers, and a difficult divorce, all took a toll upon my will power.

The greatest drain of all, however, was the satisfaction and comfort afforded by my position as director of training. In coming to this place in my life and in the struggle to bring *The Invention of "Race"* into public view, I had come under the influence of *laziness*, perhaps the most powerful of temptations to face any human being. But I had never let go of the sacred pipe, and I had never forgotten the promise I had received about this work in the purification lodge over a decade ago. And so it came to pass through the will of that Great and Mysterious Spirit, that my comfortable position at the Training Department was among fifty others in the facility which were selected for a Reduction In Force (a RIF).

It was at last, and only in this moment, when faced with the end of my ever-so-comfortable employment as a mid-level bureaucrat working for the State, and braced by the reassurance of my new bride, that I realized that my prayers had been answered, and that *The Invention of "Race"* would indeed be published. This I would do myself, in founding Agathon Press.

Please do not misunderstand me. I have not mentioned the spiritual path which I follow merely to pique your curiosity, or in search of converts. The spiritual paths of the *Lakota oyate* are not suited to the bored curiosity of upper class Moderns, or the hyper-kinetic attention of middle class Moderns. The ways associated with the sacred pipe are an integral part of an entire national culture, and are best practiced using the national language of that culture. Taken out of their cultural context, they are of little use to anyone.

Spirit, however, *is universal.* Although many nations express their attention to the spiritual aspect of existence in as many ways as there are distinctive national cultures, the object of their attention remains ever the same. And this is my point. If one accepts the presence of the mysterious spiritual force often known as "God," one cannot deny this fact: everything in the universe, *everything* on this earth--even the very stones--have been filled with spirit (shot through, as if by X-rays), by the touch of "God." To be filled with spirit is to be spiritual. On the spiritual Grandmother being we call the earth, the spirit of "God" is continually about us, manifested in everything which surrounds us. This we may all the more easily see when we observe that miraculous spark of motivation--of movement--which we call *life*.

But look what "race" has done. Our species has become so alienated from the earth Mother that, in the view of many, a reconciliation now seems nearly impossible. How could it be otherwise? At the dawning of the Modern Age, the age of "race," mass-states allied with mass-religions commenced to invade and conquer the entire world. Looking upon other, militarily weaker nations, they proclaimed: "These people do not worship God, they are scarcely human--if they are human at all," and they went on to exterminate them. All of this, we must now have the courage to recognize, was done purely for the sake of easy money. It would be impossible to deny that the Universal Church enriched itself by something much more concrete than "souls" during the period of the Spanish conquest of the Americas.

This is not, however, to devalue the importance of "souls" thus acquired. Without the sometimes blind devotion of its citizens, the Modern mass-state could not long endure. In many ways the measure of a nation-state's power is the degree to which its citizens indulge it with their blind obedience. Can it be any other way with Modern mass-religions? Let me state this otherwise. Was it a mere coincidence that the first Modern nation-state and the Universal Church commenced upon the invasion of the western hemisphere *together*?

I have already said that in my opinion one of the most terrifying prospects facing our species is the specter of one world government. Why? Because we--our species--humanity have already lived through five centuries of covert and overt attempts at achieving this. In that period our species has been subject to unprecedented slaughter at the hands of its own kind--we have suffered cannibalism as cannibalism has never been known before. In that period human life has been disvalued as never before. Besides the rank slaughter and butchery, there are two further measures of this disvaluation of human existence: the population explosion--there is more human suffering amassed on this earth than ever before at any other time; and the importance of money--the meaning of human life has been reduced to the individual pursuit of money to a degree which would have been utterly unimaginable to such holy beings as the Buddha or the Christ. As we consider the way in which universalization affects our humanity, dare we suppose that the danger posed by a universal world religion would be any less than that posed by a universal world government?

If we are to rediscover our own human species nature, which means discovering the full measure of each other's humanity, we must not be afraid of discovering the appropriate spiritual expression which is culturally best suited to each one of us. We must cease threatening other cultures with eternal damnation and then following up those threats with ethnocidal war, simply because they do not worship "God" in our own language, or through our own prophets and holy persons. We must cease being intimidated by such accusations when they are leveled against us. The great spiritual truths brought forth by the many holy persons who have graced our earth over the ages bear a remarkable similarity to one another. Surely we can see that just as the denial of other persons' humanity denies our own humanity, so too the denial of others' spirituality denies our own.

Do not be surprised to find me speaking of spirituality and of "God" here. The alienation of *philosophia* from spirituality is-- like the alienation of humanity from itself, or the alienation of humanity from the earth--a very recent phenomenon. In the Ancient, poly cultural tradition of *philosophia*, the conjunction of spirituality with the love of wisdom is completely in context, and normal.

As I have said, *The Invention of "Race"* has been most difficult to compose and to bring forth into the world. Given the length and breadth of the material which I have discussed, this manuscript is of necessity incomplete. I have had to selectively omit and gloss over some subjects. At the same time, I have been ever aware of the necessity of presenting the strongest possible argument against the notion that the "race" classification of human beings *can ever be taken as being benign*. Perhaps the best way to understand this essay is as an *outline*. It is an outline of a different direction of thought than that one which now prevails. It is a different direction for *philosophia*, for historical understanding, and for social understanding. You might think of it this way: I have set up a road sign indicating: "The light, the Truth, lies somewhere in *this* direction." The road map I have provided is, I know, sketchy at best. Surely it will be found to contain errors. In part, this is due to my conviction that the apprehension of Truth, while an urgently public concern, is an individually personal matter. Unless one has earned one's own glimpse of the light through one's own efforts, the memory of what has been seen will quickly fade.

My intention has been to raise questions, many more, I trust, than I have answered. My intention has been to provoke thought, to stimulate creative thinking. I have written *The Invention of "Race"* so that *any* interested and thoughtful person could follow it through and consider the ideas contained therein. I have written *The Invention of "Race"* so that specialists in the fields I have touched upon will consider what may seem a new point of departure. I am sure that honest intentioned scholars will view any mistakes I have made simply for what they are--correctable errors--and not as a basis for dismissing the entire body of this work. My wish is that scholars more worthy than I will pursue investigations in the direction in which I have pointed, and that they will enrich our constructive understanding of the human past.

Some persons may be tempted to classify *The Invention of "Race"* as 'history from the loser's side'. It occurs to me that such a view might stem from a not too clearly reasoned argument. In the Modern Age we have tended to overlook, dismiss, or forget much of the achievement of Ancient times. This is to the detriment of all of us. We have lost much, and it is therefore in all probability we who are the losers.

Dear sisters, dear brothers, ultimately there are no winners in the "race" system. Are you tempted to think that "your group" is at last rising to the upper ranks of the social system, or at least 'getting even'? Do not be fooled. You are witnessing the *continuation* of the very system which has caused so much suffering in the past. *Nothing* can guarantee that in the future "your group" will not again be the recipient of merciless persecution so long as the "race" system stands intact. Do you harbor resentment against "other races" which seem above "your own," or which are granted unfair governmental advantages against "your kind?" How shall your hatred contribute to the downfall of a system which is based upon the fostering of hatred? Do you feel exempt from, or outside of the system, perhaps because you have immigrated to a nation which bestows great opportunity upon newcomers? Then you must tremble with fear for the sake of your children and grandchildren. For unless you become the wealthiest of the wealthy, *nothing* can guarantee that they will not be cast into some "minority" or "majority" "race," and be persecuted thereby.

Listen. *No one* is exempt from the pain, the anguish caused by the "race" idea. It is indeed true that Christopher Columbus, principle inventor of "race," died rich and famous at Valladolid on May 20, 1506. But that by no means meant that he died a happy man. In the last years of his life, Columbus spent a large portion of his personal fortune helping one hundred and fifty thousand Jews escape from deadly, intolerant, racist Spain. Their flight was absolutely necessary because of the 1492 law which had banished all Jews from Spain. And the law of banishment had been absolutely necessary to Columbus' proposed invention-discovery of "Indians," because Spain--which during the time it was under Islamic rule in the Middle Ages, had been among the most tolerant of nations--now had to learn a new intolerance; and at the time, the connection between "race" and religion was inextricable. But Columbus felt badly, felt guilty about what he had done for the sake of riches and fame. Why? Although it remains a historical speculation, there are those who insist that although Columbus was a Christian--a fanatical Christian--his ancestors were Jewish. If this was so, in his position of richest among the rich, he was never subject to the Decrees of Purity of Blood which controlled the lives of other Jewish and Islamic converts to Christianity in Spain. He never had to be a "*Marrano*"--a Jewish-Christian "pig," but nothing could save him from the guilt which crept into his soul.

The ablest of minds--both good and evil--have been severely disabled by the "race" idea. The maleficent Dr. Mengele of Nazi Germany held degrees in both medicine and anthropology. If not as a medical doctor, then as an anthropologist (or even as an observant human being) he should have known that there are Jews with all colors of skin and all colors of eyes--including blue. But under the sway of propaganda which the equally nefarious Dr. Goebbels surely did not himself believe, Mengele performed inhumanly cruel 'experiments' upon Jewish subjects taken from his concentration camp. He attempted to turn "brown Jewish eyes" into "blue Aryan" ones. This was to be accomplished by ocular injections. And this was by no means the fullest extent of his vile 'experimentation'.

Conversely, Eric Voegelin, twentieth century servant of *philosophia*, made a most serious error in his 1940 anti-Nazi article, "The Growth of the Race Idea." Attempting to account for racism, he wrote:

With the age of discoveries the racial varieties of mankind became known gradually, and travel accounts furnish an increasing wealth of information on the physical, institutional and characterological differences of races.[1]

This is a remarkable statement coming from a historian such as Voegelin who could read the manuscripts of the Ancients in the original Greek in which they often appeared. The Columbus dogma had somehow made him forget that Mediterranean peoples such as the Egyptians, Carthaginians, Macedonians, Greeks, and even Romans (to name just some) had long been familiar with the human complexion colors which we now "racially" classify as "Red," "Black," "white," "Yellow," and "brown."

---

[1]

Eric Voegelin, "The Growth of the Race Idea," in *The Review of Politics, op. cit.*, p. 295.

Since the "race" idea enables human beings to selectively view some members of the species as sub- or non-members, the Modern perspective on 'stone age' humanity is also seriously distorted. Describing a cache of 9,000 year-old artifacts (including the oldest-yet discovered painted mask and fragment of woven cloth) on display at Jerusalem's Israel Museum, prehistory curator Tamar Noy asserted: "These objects are so exquisite that they give us a new view of what our ancestors were like."[2] Had Noy, a highly trained archaeologist, simply *forgotten* Alexander Marshack's detailed investigation into Upper Paleolithic humanity's use of symbolic notation or proto-writing? Had Noy forgotten the widespread, vividly-colored paintings made in western Eurasian caves, some perhaps as early as 20,000 years ago? Had Noy forgotten the much older elaboration of culture by our *neanderthalensis* 'cousins', which included funerary practices, and the erection of structures such as the bone hut at Moldova in Moldavia?

In this Modern age, ostensibly objective scientists are often surprised by what should not be surprising at all, befuddled by data which merely fills in the details of a picture the general form of which is already known. Archaeologists know about the gradual global spread of red ochre use. They know about the poly continental diffusion of Mousterian and Mousteroid culture. They know about the great antiquity of the Lion Cave ochre mine in Swaziland. They know that Australia was settled by seagoing people, most conservatively estimated, no later than 40,000 years ago. They know, in short, of the abundance of evidence which most strongly implies a great antiquity for the human activity of trading.

---

[2]

Quoted in Leon Jaroff, sciences editor, "Cave Cache: Treasures in a hyena's Lair," in *Time* (New York: Time Inc., April 8, 1985), p. 69.

Yet George Bass, a pioneering nautical archaeologist, is perplexed by what has been found at the oldest yet-known shipwreck site, in the eastern Mediterranean. He is bewildered that among the merely 3,400 year-old wreck's varied cargo are goods of Mycenaean, Cypriot, and Canaanite cultures. It is "a mix of goods, that puzzles us no end," says Bass.[3]

"Race" distorts human self-image and image of others. Few people *are* who they or others may *think* they are. Outside of Russia, many people commonly think of Russians as "Slavic" people. Yet the Russian self name is derived from the Ancient *Rus*, a Viking tribal nation's name. Students of "Indian" history are familiar with how in the nineteenth century, George Glass, or Sequoyah, as he was also known, invented the Cherokee syllabary so that 'his' people could become civilized. However, Traveller Bird, Cherokee historian, descendant of Sequoyah, and member of the same Seven-Clan Scribe Society as Sequoyah, explains otherwise. He tells how the Seven-Clan Scribe Society has been the guardian of the nation's history and instructor in its system of writing. He reveals that long before the age of Columbus, a small group of 24 immigrant people were taken in at *Sogwiligigageihiyi*, a village of the Cherokee. They were refugees from the southwest of the continent who had traveled for a year to get to that place. In their homeland, thousands had perished in a great drought which had afflicted the land. Creeks and springs had dried up, crops had failed, game had left the area, and a new nation of hunters and thieves had come into the region.

---

[3]

Quoted in Richard Stengel, "Bounty from the Oldest Shipwreck: The Mediterranean yields a vessel sunk perhaps 3,400 years ago," in *Time* (New York: Time Inc., December 17, 1984), p. 74.

At last, the survivors--following a person of vision--had traveled to the east. With them they brought the gift of their writing, preserved at that time on tablets of gold lamina.[4]

Jewish people are usually thought of as being "Semitic" people. But as Arthur Koestler has shown in his 1976 study, *The Thirteenth Tribe: The Khazar Empire and Its Heritage*, the majority of Western Jews are descended from the Khazars, a medieval warrior empire of central Eurasia, north of the Caucus Mountains.[5] This large and powerful nation converted *en masse* to Judaism, contributing mightily in numbers to the total Jewish population.

There is found in Japan a certain prejudice against Koreans. *However*, "...a good percentage of the Japanese are descendants of Koreans who migrated to Japan en masse in ancient times."[6] Most of the rest are descendants of Ancient Chinese emigrants. (And in Japan there is also a certain prejudice against Chinese.)

Brothers and sisters: together we have just completed a most difficult journey from past to present. If you feel an urge to weep for the past--for what has been lost (as you must know I have done)--do not feel ashamed. Let your tears flow freely and cleanse the sorrow from your spirit. Take heed of this advice as well: now is *not* the time for recriminations, for anger, for guilt. The perpetrators of "race," those greatest of criminals--Christopher Columbus, the Borgia Pope, Alexander VI (the father

---

[4]

See Traveller Bird, *The Path to Snowbird Mountain* (New York: Farrar, Straus and Giroux, 1972), pp. 84-87.

[5]

Arthur Koestler, *The Thirteenth Tribe: The Khazar Empire and Its Heritage* (New York: Popular Library, 1978).

[6]

"For many Japanese, those 'roots' are Korean." excerpted from *Japan Times Weekly*, in *The Honolulu Star Bulletin and Advertiser* (Honolulu: Hawaii Newspaper Agency, Inc., Sunday, February 12, 1978), p. F-1.

of his own grandchild), their Majesties Isabella and Ferdinand--have all been dead for nearly five hundred years. Anger and revenge cannot possibly touch them, but it can twist and deform our own spirits, and that would be a crime. Guilt shall not be ours if we can only open ourselves up to our innate species' ability to learn.

When we do this, we will find that some persons--because of the deadly efficiency of rhetoric--will *seem* incapable of grasping the simple fact that "race" is unreal. We must meet them with patience and love, for eventually they *will* follow along. Certain other persons will be found to understand the workings of the "race" idea--especially its economic imperatives--all too well. They will do all in their power to buttress the system of "race," to stand against Love, and they must be shunned. Now, sisters and brothers, is the time for each and every one of us to reach deeply within ourselves and firmly grasp *what is there*. Now is the time for us to bring forth what has lain dormant for a half a millennium; now is the time for us to bring forth from ourselves what is good. I shall return to this subject in a moment.

I must first acknowledge that a critical inquiry such as *The Invention of "Race"* will seem to be incomplete without the inclusion of some suggestions for remedial action. These I now propose here. Expect no "manifesto" though. What I present here is not an exhaustive plan, nor shall I suggest any action which does not emerge--rather self-evidently--from the information we have already considered.

Beginning on the international level, there is the elimination of the word "race," and all supportive terms (such as "mulatto") associated with the "race" idea. We have seen how this language complex first gained introduction to the speech of our entire species beginning in the Iberian peninsula in the sixteenth century. There is no reason why we *must* believe that what has been made cannot be undone. Remember that although the Romans called their torture of captive persons "the games" for over 670 years, their language usage was unable to ever *really* make that torture into a game, and in the end they abandoned the practice of that torture all together. Five hundred years of "race" language and the 'selective breeding' it fosters has similarly failed to make "race" genuinely real, nor is "race" language any less immune to abandonment than was gladiatorial language. Remember that languages are continually changing, that words are always coming into and passing out of usage. English speakers, for example, no longer drumble in the dingle-- acclumsid and sloomy--and gaze upon the glory of the scrow at sparrow-fart, as they might have in the sixteenth century.[7]

Withdrawal of the concept of "raciality" and such supportive words as "Negroid," "Mongoloid," and "Caucasoid" by no means implies refusing to see or acknowledge the rich and wide variation which exists in human complexion color and body structure. The elimination of the concept of "races" will in fact be very likely to enhance the appreciation of our remarkable species' beauty among *all* members of our species.

There is much which organizations of international scope can do to promote the abandonment of the "racial" concept. As it now stands, the United Nations' statement on "race," issued through U.N.E.S.C.O. in 1950, is weak and flaccid. It asserts that:

a.   In matters of race, the only characteristics which anthropologists have so far been able to use effectively as a basis for classification are physical (anatomical and physiological).

b.   Available scientific knowledge provides no basis for believing that the groups of mankind differ in their innate capacity for intellectual and emotional development.

---

[7]

To decipher this passage see: Susan Kelz Sperling, *Poplollies and Bellibones: A Celebration of Lost Words* (New York: Penguin Books, 1977), pp.89-113.

c.   Some biological differences between human beings within a single race may be as great or greater than the same biological differences between races.

d.   Vast social changes have occurred that have not been connected in any way with changes in racial type....

e.   There is no evidence that race mixture produces disadvantageous results from a biological point of view....[8]

This is a most peculiar pronouncement. It seems to strongly suggest that "race" is not real, or at the least, that racism is wrong and unjust. At the same time it employs the very language which supports the proposition that the "race" idea is an expression of reality. *If* the United Nations honestly wishes to erase the misery caused by racism and the "race" system of class, then the United Nations will issue a simple and straightforward statement: "Race" is not a physical or natural reality, it is a rhetorical instrument devised to separate human beings into artificial color groupings for the purpose of exerting political control over them.

There is one international organization which bears a particular obligation. We now know the parties who stood at the scene when the "race" idea was promulgated. The Roman Catholic Church could go a long way toward eliminating the suffering generated by racism by issuing a formal Papal declaration renouncing and denouncing the concept of "race." Do not mistake the intention of the historical investigation we have just completed. I have not, in forthrightly discussing the lethal behavior of individuals and institutions *in the past*, intended to present an attack upon Catholicism. I have not intended to reject the virtue of any religion to its faithful, or to impugn the sincere faith of individuals who make up the body of any church. One does not throw Mother Teresa out with Vicente de Valverde or

---

[8]

Quoted in E. Adamson Hoebel and Thomas Weaver, *Anthropology and the Human Experience* (New York: McGraw-Hill Book Company, 1979), p. 75.

Ignatius Loyola. To do so would be insane. Conversely, if we truly seek to know reality, then we must courageously admit that what is or has been, *really* is or has been, whether we like what we see or not. There can be no other way for us to continue to learn. The Catholic Church has undergone many changes over the past several centuries. It presently proclaims itself a champion of humanity and defender of human dignity. So now, then, let it denounce the great tormentor of humanity, the concept of "race."

Perhaps Spain should formally denounce the concept of "race," and so too might every other nation which claims in its national charter that human life is something to be treasured. Beyond this, all nations, all human beings face the impossible-seeming task of renouncing the use of rhetoric for self-justification. There must be other worthy grounds for self-explanation than concatenations of half-truths. And yet we now have so many words for the *same* thing: rhetoric, grammar, dogma, cant, ideology, hyperbole, hype, propaganda, conditioning, brainwashing, disinformation. In the English language, every word ending with the suffix *ism* can be connected with rhetorical half-truths: capitalism, communism, conservatism, liberalism, socialism, Catholicism, Protestantism, environmentalism, feminism, male chauvinism. People can easily see the errors of the *isms* of others, but never of their own. There are so many terms with which to express jealousy, meanness and hatred, and yet we have so few words for Love. This is a problem of staggering individual as well as national and international dimensions. It surely must be impractical for me to suggest this, but again, the Catholic Church could point the way for our species by renouncing the principle of church *dogma*. Individually, each and every nation must ask itself this question: Is its ground of existence so shaky that it can *only* be supported by the body of half-truths known as the national ideology? That it can *only* exist by inviting its members to disable their thinking faculties?

Bonded with the entire question of rhetoric is the relation between the profession of the bar and the abstract concept Justice. Lawyers have existed for a long time. For example, Phoenician trading companies found it necessary to have lawyers draw up shipping liability contracts between themselves and captains in their service. This was especially necessary in cases of long and dangerous voyages such as those to the Americas. But with the advent of the Roman Republic, and later the Empire, something about the profession of the law began to change. The legal profession began to be placed ever more at the defense of propositions such as those that human torture was actually a well-regulated "game," that the Carthaginian and other ethnocides-for-profit were expressions of Justice, or that emperors were "gods." Presently almost every nation in the Modern world acknowledges the lineal descent of its own legal profession from the Ancient Roman model. Now, in the present-day Modern world we are at a curious impasse. What shall we do? We all live within complex frameworks of laws--often regarded as being almost sacred--which seem capable of only being interpreted by lawyers. The laws themselves are for the most part the product of the efforts of lawyers, and the profession of the bar is itself exclusively policed and controlled by lawyers. One does not often hear of such a thing as a lawsuit brought for legal malpractice. We must remember that Justice had been served long and well before the advent of Roman law. We must be able to understand that Justice has even been served most finely in nations without even a single lawyer.[9] We must not forget that lawyers sat at the table from which the "race" idea was served up. What *shall* we do? The

---

[9]

For an excellent anthropological-legal investigation of this proposition, see Llewellyn and Hoebel, *The Cheyenne Way, op. cit.*

quest for Justice--to understand it, to grasp it--should become a passionate concern for all. But in reevaluating where we now stand, we must be fair, open minded, and forgiving.

Nothing save the "race" idea with which it is associated, has so demeaned human existence as the current "population explosion." All nations must somehow join together in the cause of radically reducing our planet's human population. Such a project must be undertaken in a humane manner, and must, by its very nature, take *centuries* to accomplish. There are a variety of means available, all of them involving forms of what we call birth control. Since Ancient times birth control through the use of contraceptive devices has been practiced with varying degrees of success. The practice in some cultures of banning sexual intercourse for a specified length of time between a couple who has just had a child born to them is another form of birth control. So too are forms of marriage other than Christian monogamy. In Ancient times, polyandry and polygyny were effective in limiting population growth. (It *is* true that at one point during the Middle Ages when western Eurasia's population had been terribly devastated by the Plague, Christian churches encouraged polygyny as a measure to increase population. However, in other Ancient contexts this has been a *limiter* of population growth.) In economically and spiritually-healthy Ancient societies, such forms of group marriage--in addition to restricting population growth in the obvious manner--have strengthened family economies, empowered the individual contracting members, and enriched the developmental environment of children. These Ancient forms of marriage relation cannot, however, be judged by comparison with their Modern Age perversions such as found in Arabian Islam, Mormonism, or the mistress relationships common to western Eurasia--all of which are (or have been) lawfully-defined exploitative relationships. Such non-Modern contracts would only prove workable in nations which aggressively nurtured a particular kind of health in their internal economies and mental and spiritual health among their citizens.

We have considered the interaction between the Modern world's terrible, grinding poverty, and overpopulation. At this very moment there is enough food, enough money in this world to feed, shelter and clothe every human being now living. There is enough so that none should have to suffer the misery of Modern poverty. How can this be accomplished? This, it is not my place to say. The solution of this dilemma is the responsibility of the wealthy--of the wealthiest persons of this world. It would appear from a close examination of the past as if there *is* one thing which "always was:" a mixture of those who are wealthy and those who are poorer in human societies. That is to say, there seems to have been rich and poor as long as there has been politics among our species. But in the Modern Age, human beings have come to live more unlike one another than the Ancient generations of their ancestors had ever done. Probably at no time since the age of the God Kings has the wealthy-impoverished gap been as great as in the present Modern span between billionaires and paupers. Yet look at the difference. The primary--and sometimes it seems the sole--obligation of billionaires is ever and always the acquisition of more wealth, and the preservation of what they already own. The primary living obligation of the God Kings was to govern, and to look after the welfare of those whom they governed. And on through the ages of Antiquity, this remained the *obligation* of the privileged and the powerful, be they lesser monarchs, tyrants, oligarchical councils as those of the Carthaginians, or aristocracies. In Ancient times wealthy persons forthrightly acknowledged that they were living in the midst of--that they were *connected to*-- their communities. In the Ancient past, the wealthy were grateful to those who were the ultimate source of their riches. And so, they were not afraid to expend sometimes vast portions of their personal fortunes for the sake of that which they were a part of. If today's wealthy and quasi-wealthy "political" elites do not act soon and forcefully enough, they may some day awaken to find that there is nothing left for them to squeeze money out of any more. The donation which Ted Turner made to the United Nations in the summer of 1997, sets a healthy precedent.

Another matter of international concern which I can think of is in what might generally be known as the field of historical scholarship. We--as a species--have lost and forgotten enormous portions of our human past. If one-tenth of the amount of the annual international expenditure for space exploration was devoted to historical investigation, we might stand a chance of learning who we really are. There are presently thousands upon thousands of incised clay tablets laying about undeciphered in museum storerooms the world over. There are countless epigraphs on rocks all over the earth, there are gold and lead laminae, there are numerous inscribed tablets, all begging for decipherment. There are Ancient Codices and Papyri, there are books forgotten and unread for a half a millennium. All of these must be more readily available to honest scholars. Nations and powerful institutions can do much to encourage this. Resources can be made much more readily accessible. Such resources include the likes of the Spanish Naval Archives, the Vatican Library, the Imperial Library in Beijing, and similar hoards.

But scholarship *must* be honest. Let there be no further attempts to deform the past into 'an arrow of historical meaning' which points directly toward the Modern "West," or any other contemporary culture. Let there be no further "proofs" that the human past demonstrates the "correctness" of communism. Let scholars see the intricacy of the past, its give and its take, its advances and retreats, its stagnations and blind alleys, its sameness, its differences.

Honest scholarship could also become a concern for religious organizations and sects. More than only Christian persons could be very interested in the contents of the suppressed--but recently-rediscovered--gospels now known as the Gnostic Gospels. Persons who wish to follow the Way of Jesus might want to absorb as much information as possible about his life and teachings. Or so one would surmise. Surely the more they know about him, the more closely they would be able to follow his wisdom. Some Christian groups appear to have lost, at various points of their histories, certain parts of the picture. If what *he* said about himself is credible, then Jesus was a Nazarine Jew, who founded The Way, which is symbolized by a fish. *He* did not name his spiritual movement after the Ancient Roman criminal charge of *christianus, he* did not choose for its symbol an Ancient Roman instrument of execution.

In roughly the middle of this century--in 1945--two events occurred which may be taken as symbolizing two widely divergent possible futures--two possible roads--for humanity. These were the detonation of the first atomic bomb, and the rediscovery, at Nag Hammadi, of the "Gnostic" Gospels. One of these roads points to destruction, the other points to a resurrection--a resurrection of the lost human capacity for lifelong learning. (The very importance of the Nag Hammadi discovery is that it reopens the investigation of a subject about which the book has *long* been considered to have been closed.)

My sisters, my brothers, I was born in the year before the detonation of that first terrible nuclear fire. All of my life I have lived in an environment filled with the varieties of propaganda designed to convince all of us that further nuclear War is practical, inevitable, survivable, and winnable. I *remember* the "drop drills" we practiced as grade school children in the late 1940^s and early 50^s. At any time during the school day the teacher might yell "drop," and we well-conditioned children would scuttle under our desks, making sure our backs were to the windows so as to avoid the coming shower of glass shards, and being careful to shield our eyes in our folded arms from the brilliant blinding light of the blast. We even learned how to huddle alongside the curb, next to the sidewalk, should we be caught by "the bomb" while out in the street. I remember the countless civil defense advertisements on television in those early days of the 50ˢ, repeating that dismal message over and over again.

Because I *do* remember this conditioning of my early childhood, I have been able to make it a part of my life. I have *chosen* to reject the dismal path, the way of destruction. My choice has been for the path of the open heart, the open mind. What, dear sisters and brothers, shall be *your* choice? Some nations among us have now carried our species to the edge of a journey among the stars. Do you suppose we might conceive of how to best be worthy of such a place? Could we be facing the possibility of *not* surviving until the time when such a journey might commence?

When we look at the splendor of Modern life, when we consider the positive side of our artificial environment, there are still many questions we must ask ourselves. Is it not now possible that the power of Modern economies is so developed; that the strength, the craft of Modern technologies is so refined; that the knowledge and information of Modern sciences is so extensive; that the control of Modern national political regimes is so firm; that the trade and exchange between Modern nations is so rich, that the great nations no longer need prey upon the small, that the strong no longer need captivate the weak in order to survive? Can there any longer be any excuse or explanation for the existence of any "minority" group within *any* nation? Should not every nation now let all within be citizens--*fully* citizens--or let those who wish to be, be free to be themselves?

Not long ago, the South African nation was the worst of all with respect to the issue of citizenship. It was not only unjust and tyrannical, it was absurd as well. It was a shame upon humanity.

But now all of that has changed. Now Nelson Mandela, the once-imprisoned enemy of the regime of apartheid, is the President of South Africa. South Africa was not the only shame upon humanity. There were other such shames, and there still continue to be. It is a shame upon humanity that China still holds Tibet; that Russia holds the Siberian nations; that Northern Ireland still suffers English occupation; that the United States holds the nations it calls "the Indians;" that there are so many tiny, weak nations in thrall within the nations of Central and South America, and in Canada, and in Australia. The shame upon humanity is in fact still too great and numerous to recount. So why not let the weak at last be freed from their chains? Are not the strong at last strong enough to cease their torment of the weak? Are not the strong at last strong enough to learn the virtue of generosity? Can they not now acquire through negotiation and honorable agreement what in the past has been acquired by force and guile? The fact that there is now the existence of an incipient Palestinian nation, that Scotland and Whales have been granted limited independence as of the fall of 1997, and that there has been a settlement in the War between Chechnya and Russia, shows that the answer to these questions can be "*Yes!*" This represents *the promise* of the return of our humanity.

I think that there is another thing which all nations could do in order to banish the mentality of "race." Jews commemorate May 6, as Holocaust Day. Should not our entire species establish such a memorial? There is no longer any reason for the multi national celebration of October 12 as Columbus Day to continue. Why shouldn't we honestly admit exactly what sort of an undertaking Columbus' "enterprise" was? Perhaps the nations should instead commemorate a great memorial on October 12. Perhaps the day should be a day of international mourning for the greatest human suffering of all time. Perhaps if that is done, no one will ever forget what must never again be done, *anywhere*, for *any* reason.

Each and every nation individually can do a great deal to delegitimize and destroy the "race" idea, and thereby eliminate racism.   Consider the United States as an example.   The Constitution, the basic national law of the United States, presents the "race" idea four times: "Indians" are mentioned three times, in Article I, Sections 2 and 8, and in Amendment XIV, Section 2; and in Amendment XV, the concept "race" is given recognition. The framers of the Constitution knew exactly what they were doing by mentioning "Indians not taxed," and "commerce...with the Indian Tribes."   They were explicitly delineating the proposition that the original nations of North America were not nations at all, but that they were simply an unorganized, backward "racial" entity (and simultaneously, they brought forth the position that the people of North America's first nations should have no U.S. citizenship).   These passages can do nothing other than reinforce the "racial" classification of human beings, and thereby induce racism.

Many persons, however, who have been reduced to "Indians" by United States' law, still continue to preserve important portions of their Ancient national cultures, and persist in thinking of themselves as members of nations other than the United States. The amendment of Article I, Sections 2 and 8, and Amendment XIV, Section 2, to simply delete the word "Indian," would go a long way toward eliminating the sanction in favor of racism which now stands embodied in Unites States' law.   The amendment of Section 1 of Amendment XV, to expunge the word "race," would complete the elimination of racism from the fundamental body of United States' law.

But much more needs to be done.   No city, county, state, or federal law should be allowed to legitimize the "racial" concept *if* the United States cares to claim as its goal the elimination of racism, and of all forms of discrimination based upon "race." To this end, a further constitutional amendment is in order.   Its wording might be *something* like this: "All forms of discrimination, public or private, governmental or institutional, based upon the spurious concept of human "racial" divisions, shall forthwith and forever be deemed illegal...."

The passage of such a measure would entail a preparedness to face massive social and governmental institutional transformations aiming toward the Just. Every law at every level of government which negatively or positively recognizes a "race," or some "races," would be nullified. This would include everything from affirmative action statutes to annual budget funding for the Bureau of Indian Affairs. Indeed, there could be no Bureau of Indian Affairs. Neither could the spurious field of "Indian law"--a field which has made millionaires out of many greedy individuals who have no other connection to North America's Ancient past than the desire to make money--continue to exist. Relations between the United States and the earlier nations of the land it now holds would be placed squarely where they belong: in the field of international relations.

The elimination of the Bureau of Indian Affairs would present an immediate problem: the disposition of the "Indian" reservations. The solution to this is simple and straightforward, and is one which has often been followed in cases where colonialism has come to an end in other parts of the world. Each reservation community could be offered a plebiscite vote on its national future. Each voter on each reservation could be presented the fullest imaginable range of choices: total absorption of the reservation into the surrounding counties, the conversion of the reservation into a new county, the conversion of the reservation into a new state, the consolidation of several small reservations into a larger unit composed of culturally-affiliated groups, the establishment of independent national status in commonwealth relation with the United States, or the establishment of total national independence.

All of these voters must be enabled to understand that they shall never again be able to levy or have levied upon them, benefits or liabilities according to "race." There is no reason to expect an easy transition to national independence for those who choose to do so. The post Atomic War end of colonialism, beginning in the late 1940^s, has proven this point. And the reason for this is not because of the innate incompetency of the people of the former colonies, but because the function of Modern colonialism was to utterly destroy the institutions--the capacity-- for self-government of the nations which it conquered, nations which had been self-governing for hundreds of even thousands of years. At the point of liberation from colonialism, there is nothing which the former colonizer--the former destroyer--can do except stay out of things. Sometimes a newly-freed nation must even go through a bloody and shameful period of revolutions in order to rediscover its national self-identity.

In the case of those nations seeking full, or even commonwealth independence, the United States does have a particular obligation (in addition to offering food and economic development aid such as it has so generously spread about other parts of the world). Many U.S. citizens have land holdings on reservations. While the assumption of genuine national sovereignty will mean the adoption of the full range of activities of independent sovereign nations, including immigration and naturalization, it is to be expected that some U.S. citizens will decline to become members of these newly-reestablished nations. Such persons might remain where they are as resident aliens, fully-subject to the laws of the nation within which they reside, or they might choose to leave their homes and businesses behind. In these latter cases, the U.S. government has the responsibility of fully compensating those persons for the ensuing loss of their property. U.S. citizens living on reservations are in the position they are in just as much as a result of U.S. government policy and procedures, as are the persons whom the government has labeled "Indians."

Despite the events of the past, there are very good feelings on the part of persons who have been labeled as "Indians" toward the United States of America. There is no reason to expect 'hard' borders between the U.S. and any of the nations which might be recreated by the plebiscite votes. Furthermore, it would be absurd to conceive of hostilities occurring between these small nations and the overpowering might of the United States. It is entirely conceivable that a number of individuals in the newly-recreated nations might--for a variety of reasons--wish to retain their U.S. citizenship, becoming holders of genuine dual citizenship. However, unlike the former relationship between the U.S. government and "Indians," such dual citizenship would be constituted of *real* citizen duties--a *full* liability to the laws of appropriate jurisdictions, and, in all probability an increase in tax liabilities--rather than being a means of avoiding citizen obligations as it now is.

An onus of proof lies squarely upon the United States to show whether it truly is a nation which upholds law, honor, and the virtue of human life. For example, for scores of years the United States bought gold at the going market price from the old apartheid regime of South Africa. The United States, however, did not do this at home. If the U.S. wants gold from the mountain of that metal in the Black Hills, must it still continue to take it by force from the *Lakota* nation? Is the United States still so mean and stingy a power that it will not do in North America what it has been willing to do in southern Africa? Would not negotiation and purchase at the fair market value be a healthier, more Just, more mature means of acquisition?

Since the writing of the *Constitution*, the United States has developed an elaborate body of legal rhetoric to defend the proposition that the existence of Ancient North American nations *as* nations would be "impossible." In the early 1830s, in the case of *Cherokee Nation v. Georgia*, the U.S. Supreme Court Chief Justice John Marshall characterized North America's Ancient nations as "domestic dependent nations." But since an accurate view of the past shows that not a few of those nations actually enjoyed perfectly adequate independence for a few thousand years (quite the opposite of dependency), we may now perceive that Marshall's statement was simply an oily legalistic lie (and utterly arrogant one--coming as it did from a nation which had only existed for fifty-four years).[10] So too was the decision of Judge Taylor of the Supreme Court of Alabama in the 1832 case of *Caldwell v. The State of Alabama*. Taylor wrote:

> ...the Creek Indians, may establish and maintain a separate government forever, and the State of Alabama would have within its borders another and a distinct sovereignty; an *imperium in emperio*.

> Where such consequences would ensue, something must be wrong, and the error would be in the decision producing them.[11]

Taylor's statement was, in fact, *palpably* false. It was false for the Ancient past, it was false for Taylor's present, and it is still false in our own day and age. Consider these nations of our present world: Lesotho is completely surrounded by South Africa, the nation of Gambia is within the nation of Senegal, San Marino is within Italy, the Vatican is within Italy, Monaco is within

---

10

Is this really so surprising? Did not the laws of the United States make "racial" slavery legal until the mid-1860s? Did not Supreme Court Justices uphold the "justice" of that great injustice? Did not the Supreme Court of the United States then uphold the lawfulness and "justice" of "racial" segregation up until the 1950s?

11

Quoted in Vine Deloria, Jr., editor, *Of Utmost Good Faith* (New York: Bantam Books, Inc., 1972), p. 48.

France, the Cabinda province of Angola is totally separate from that nation, and Argentina's Tierra del Fuego lands are surrounded by those of Chile.

There will never be an end to racism in the United States until the legal promotion of the "race" idea is completely removed, until the laws no longer recognize the existence of any "race," be it "Indian," "Black," "Asian," "brown," "white," or *whatever*, and until the nation-rebuilding consequences of such a change are followed through with. And in so doing, in following through with such an act of wisdom and generosity, the United States could firmly regain the position of world preeminence which now seems to be slipping away from it.

But how must the United States look to the community of nations up to this point? Not all of the citizens of the United States--who are in the habit of calling themselves Americans--have yet reached full unequivocal citizenship. Many of those whose ancestors were forced to migrate to New England in the early seventeenth century--long before the United States' Revolution--are still not simply "Americans." They are hyphenated-Americans, they are Americans with qualification, they are "Black"-Americans. How must it also look to the community of nations that within the United States there *still exist* the prisoner of War camps--the concentration camps--'innocently' known as "Indian" reservations?

There have, however, already been the beginnings of a change. In 1985, Dr. C. Everett Coop, the U.S. Surgeon General, declared that it was his department's finding that the time had come to recognize "violence as a health issue." Pointing out that in most cases of violence, "the victim didn't deserve it," Dr. Coop exhorted his fellow citizens to "support the victim of violence." Perhaps in the near future Dr. Coop will come to recognize how great a measure against violence the elimination of the "race" system would be, for that pernicious system of class has generated more violence in the human past than any other single factor.

   Dear brothers and sisters, in *The Invention of "Race"* we have struggled together to gain a clearer, more honest understanding of the human past. We have made a *beginning*. Can you not guess what each and every individual who has *begun to understand* may do to end the scourge of "race?" Shall you ever again stand ready to accuse another human being of having a "racial" identity? And what of yourself? Has not the "group" into which you have been impressed been accused of innate craftiness and greediness? Or of being cold and unfeeling? Or of being born to mystic, spiritual abilities? Or of having an ingrown musical talent? Of or indwelling stupidity and laziness? Are you now still willing to imprint these lies upon others, or upon *yourself*? Shall you not now choose to be *truly* proud of who and what you are? There are hundreds of variations in the texture and color of human complexion. Human beings come in the greatest variety of shapes, sizes and weights. Shall you any longer be willing to participate in the denial of the phenomenon of our species' beauty by compulsively attempting to force each and every human being into one of four or five unreal "racial" boxes? If your ancestors have suffered a great injustice because of the "race" idea, are *you* going to be the one who keeps that idea alive?

   The secret to paradise, to tranquility, to harmony and love right here on this earth, lies deeply embedded within each and every one of us. It is at the core of our very species' nature. While it *is* true that behavioral conditioning is a *terribly* awesome and effective instrument of mass-control, ultimately it remains but a thin veneer, an opaque coating which each and every one of us can strip away if only we are willing to turn upon ourselves the light of self-understanding. This is an act of courage. A simple human act such as any of us is capable of. Like the courage of

Malcolm X to allow himself to be touched and moved by a Power greater than any person while he was in Mecca. Like the courage of George Wallace's confession delivered to the congregation of the Dexter Avenue Baptist Church. Like the courage of Martin Luther King, Jr. delivering his *I Have A Dream* speech in the face of his own impending murder. And like the anonymous, self-effacing passion of Lenny Skutnik, who dove into the icy waters of the Potomac River to save the struggling victims of an airplane crash.

Be proud of what you are, of who you are. If you choose to do so, treasure the national culture(s) of your ancestors. But have the courage to realize that this has nothing to do with "race." If the national heritage--the ethnicity--of your ancestors has been destroyed by centuries of the "race" system's operation, and still you seek to find it, to understand it, then you must dig deeply to do so. But in the end you will find a nation--*some* nation (be it small or large)--from which they came. And, in the end you will discover that ultimately, for your ancestors, "race" had nothing to do with their sense of self. Accept the beauty of yourself as it is revealed to you in a mirror. Then, will you not accept as well, the beauty of yourself as it is reflected to you in the faces of others-- even those others who you *think* do not "look like" yourself?

The key to the best of what we are lies within our human species' nature. Look upon your own children--their friendliness, their love, their quickness to learn, their desire to know, their creative thoughtfulness. Look upon your children--especially before they have begun to have their humanity 'schooled' out of them--and remember what you have been. Think of what you might yet become again.

The holy persons, prophets, seers and visionaries who have graced this earth for the past few thousand years have repeated the message again and again. "Know yourself" were the terms which Socrates used for it, and *he* got them from the Oracle at Delphi. The Christ phrased it thus:

If you bring forth what is within you, what you bring forth
will save you. If you do not bring forth what is within you,
what you do not bring forth will destroy you.

Is this really so hard to understand? Is it really that difficult
to express our love of "God" and of ourselves by recognizing the
brotherhood and sisterhood of all of our species? Shall we not
now be willing to discover if there can be a Post Modern Era, an
even better age than our own, in which we may all veer away from
that form of contempt for all of that which is sacred, that form of
hatred, that cannibalism which we know as the "race" idea? Dear
sisters and brothers, may we not at the least do what we can to
learn to think more clearly on such matters?

So now, *what* shall be *your* "race?" The time is come for *you*
to choose, for *I* shall give you none. What is my "race?" I will
have *none*. After all, that, and *that alone* is what *will* bear up
under the purest light of Reason.

In the spirit of Love, I remain your obedient servant,

The tragedy of life
is what dies inside a man
while he lives.

--A. Einstein

BIBLIOGRAPHY
A List of References Cited

Alperovitz, Gar. *Atomic Diplomacy: Hiroshima and Potsdam: The Use of the Atomic Bomb and the American Confrontation With Soviet Power.* (New York: Simon and Schuster, 1965).

Armstrong, Virginia Irving, compiler. *I Have Spoken: American History Through the Voices of the Indians.* (Chicago: The Swallow Press Inc., 1971).

Bacon, Francis. *The Advancement of Learning, and New Atlantis.* (London: Oxford University Press, 1974).

Berkhofer, Robert F., Jr. *The White Man's Indian: Images of the American Indian from Columbus to the Present.* (New York: Vintage Books, 1979).

Beswick, Lance. "Mystery Deepens." *The Edmonton Sun.* (Edmonton, Alberta: Edmonton Sun, Inc., November 13, 1979).

Blainey, Geoffrey. *Triumph of the Nomads: A History of Ancient Australia.* (Melbourne: Sun Books, 1976).

Bordaz, Jacques. *Tools of the Old and New Stone Age.* (Garden City, New York: The Natural History Press, 1970).

Borden, Morton, editor. *Voices of the American Past: Readings in American History.* (Lexington, Massachusetts: D.C. Heath and Company, 1972).

Brennan, Louis A. *American Dawn: A New Model of American Prehistory.* (New York: The Macmillan Company, 1970).

Brown, Dee. *Bury My Heart at Wounded Knee: An Indian History of the American West.* (New York: Bantam Books, Inc., 1972).

Caesar, Julius, Hanford, S. A., translator. *The Conquest of Gaul.* (New York: Penguin Books, 1951).

Canby, Thomas Y. "The Search For The First Americans." *National Geographic.* (Washington, D.C.: National Geographic Society, September, 1979).

Catlin, George. *Letters and Notes on the Manners, Customs, and Conditions of the North American Indians Written during Eight Year's Travel (1832-1839) amongst the Wildest Tribes of Indians in North America.* (New York: Dover Publications, Inc., 1973).

Ceram, C. W. *The First American: A Story of North American Archaeology.* (New York: Mentor Books, 1972).

_____ *Gods, Graves, and Scholars: The Story of Archaeology.* (New York: Bantam Books, 1972).

Clark, Grahame. *The Stone Age Hunters.* (New York: McGraw-Hill Book Company, 1967).

Committee on Nomenclature and Statistics of the American Psychiatric Association. *DSM-II: Diagnostic and Statistical Manual of Mental Disorders.* (Washington, D.C.: American Psychiatric Association, 1968).

Commoner, Barry. "How Poverty Breeds Overpopulation (and not the other way around)." *Ramparts.* (San Francisco: Ramparts, Inc., August/September, 1975).

Cowgill, Genevieve A. "Salvaging Lives After Torture." *The New York Times Magazine.* (New York: The New York Times, August 17, 1986).

Crick, Bernard. *The American Science of Politics: Its Origins and Conditions.* (Berkeley: University of California Press, 1967).

de las Casas, Bartholome, Collard, Andrée M., editor. *History of the Indies.* (New York: Harper Torchbooks, 1971).

Deloria, Vine, Jr., *Of Utmost Good Faith.* (New York: Bantam Books, Inc., 1972).

Díaz, Bernal, Cohen, J. M., translator. *The Conquest of New Spain.* (Baltimore, Maryland: Penguin Books Inc., 1972).

Diddlebock, Bob. "Archaeological team theorizes early Celts left mark in Colorado." *Rocky Mountain News.* (Denver: Rocky Mountain News, June 2, 1985).

Dobyns, Henry F. "Estimating Aboriginal American Population: An Appraisal of Techniques with a New Hemispheric Estimate." *Current Anthropology.* (Volume VII, Number 4, October, 1966).

Drinnon, Richard. *White Savage: The Case of John Dunn Hunter.* (New York: Schocken Books, 1972).

Eastman, Charles A. *Indian Boyhood.* (New York: McClure, Phillips & Co., 1902).

_____ *From the Deep Woods to Civilization.* (New York: McClure, Phillips & Co., 1916).

Eddy, John A. "Probing the Mystery of the Medicine Wheels." *National Geographic.* (Washington, D.C.: National Geographic Society, January, 1977).

Esposito, Vincent J. "Korean War." *The Encyclopedia Americana.* (New York: The Americana Corporation, 1962).

Fanon, Frantz. *The Wretched of the Earth.* (New York: Grove Press, Inc., 1968).

Fell, Barry. *America B.C.: Ancient Settlers in the New World.* (New York: Quadrangle/The New York Times Book Co., 1976).

_____ *Saga America.* (New York: Times Books, 1980).

_____ *Bronze Age America.* (Boston: Little, Brown and Company, 1982).

_____ "Christian Messages in Old Irish Script Deciphered from Rock Carvings in W. Va." *Wonderful West Virginia.* (Charleston: State of West Virginia Department of Natural Resources, March, 1983).

Fey, Harold E., and McNickle, D'Arcy. *Indians and Other Americans: Two Ways of Life Meet.* (New York: Harper & Row, Publishers, 1970).

Gallo, William. "Tall teepees illustrate housing shortage." *Rocky Mountain News.* (Denver: Rocky Mountain News, July 16, 1985).

Greenwald, John. "Deadly Meltdown." *Time*. (New York: Time Inc., May 12, 1986).

Groueff, Stephane. *Manhattan Project: The Untold Story of the Making of the Atomic Bomb*. (New York: Bantam Books, Inc., 1968).

Hamilton, Alexander, Madison, James, and Jay, John. *The Federalist Papers*. (New York: The New American Library, Inc., 1961).

Hamilton, Edith. *The Roman Way to Western Civilization*. (New York: Mentor Books, 1957).

_____, and Cairns, Huntington, editors. *The Collected Dialogues of Plato Including the Letters*. (Princeton: Princeton University Press, 1971).

Hanke, Lewis. *The First Social Experiments in America: A Study in the Development of Spanish Indian Policy in the Sixteenth Century*. (Cambridge: Harvard University Press, 1935).

_____ *Aristotle and the American Indians: A Study in Race Prejudice in the Modern World*. (Bloomington: Indiana University Press, 1959).

Hapgood, Charles H. *Maps of the Ancient Sea Kings: Evidence of Advanced Civilization in the Ice Age*. (Philadelphia: Chilton Company, 1966).

Hermann, Paul, Bullock, Michael, translator. *Conquest by Man*. (New York: Harper & Brothers, Publishers, 1954).

Heyerdahl, Thor. *American Indians in the Pacific: The Theory behind the Kon-Tiki Expedition.* (New York: Rand McNally & Company, 1953).

_____, and Skjölsvold, Arne. "Archaeological Evidence of Pre-Spanish Visits to the Galápagos Islands." *American Antiquity.* (Salt Lake City, Utah: The Society for American Archaeology, Volume XXII, Number 2, Part 3, October, 1956).

_____ *Early Man and the Ocean: A Search for the Beginnings of Navigation and Seaborne Civilization.* (Garden City, New York: Doubleday & Company, Inc., 1979).

_____ *The Tigris Expedition: In Search of Our Beginnings.* (Garden City, New York: Doubleday & Company, Inc., 1981).

_____ *The Maldive Mystery.* (New York: Ballantine Books, 1986).

_____, Sandweiss, Daniel H., and Narváez, Alfredo. *Pyramids of Túcume, The Quest for Peru's Forgotten City.* (New York: Thames and Hudson, Inc., 1995).

Hilger, Sister Mary Inez. "Japan's 'Sky People', the Vanishing Ainu." *National Geographic.* (Washington, D.C.: National Geographic Society, February, 1967).

Hoagland, Richard. "Metropolis on Mars." *Omni.* (New York: Omni Publications International, Ltd., March, 1985).

Hoebel, E. Adamson, and Weaver, Thomas. *Anthropology and the Human Experience.* (New York: McGraw-Hill Book Company, 1979).

Hyde, George E. *Indians of the Woodlands, From Prehistoric Times to 1725.* (Norman: University of Oklahoma Press, 1962).

Japan Times Weekly. "For many Japanese, those 'roots' are Korean." *The Honolulu Star Bulletin and Advertiser.* (Honolulu: Hawaii Newspaper Agency, Inc., Sunday, February 12, 1978).

Jefferson, Thomas. *Notes on the State of Virginia.* (New York: Harper & Row, Publishers, Incorporated, 1964).

Jennings, Francis. *The Invasion of America: Indians, Colonialism, and the Cant of Conquest.* (Chapel Hill: The University of North Carolina Press, 1975).

Jones, Douglas C. *The Treaty of Medicine Lodge: The Story of the Great Council As Told by Eyewitnesses.* (Norman: University of Oklahoma Press, 1966).

Jordan, Winthrop D. *White Over Black: American Attitudes Toward the Negro, 1550-1812.* (Baltimore, Maryland: Penguin Books Inc., 1969).

Kappler, Charles J., editor. *Indian Treaties:* 1778-1883. (New York: Interland Publishing, Inc., 1973).

Kennedy, Emmet. *A* Philosophe *in the Age of Revolution: Destutt de Tracy, and the Origins of "Ideology."* (Philadelphia: The American Philosophical Society, 1978).

Kinney, W.A. *Hawaii's Capacity for Self-Government all But Destroye*d. (Salt Lake City: Frank L. Jensen, Publisher, 1927).

Kinsman, Robert S., editor. *The Darker Vision of the Renaissance: Beyond the Fields of Reason*. (Berkeley: University of California Press, 1974).

Kiste, Robert C. *The Bikinians: A Study in Forced Migration*. (California: 1974).

Koestler, Arthur. *The Thirteenth Tribe: The Khazar Empire and Its Heritage*. (New York: Popular Library, 1978).

Landes, Ruth. *The Mystic Lake Sioux: Sociology of the Mdewakantonwan Santee*. (Madison: The University of Wisconsin Press, 1968).

Leo, John. "Salvaging Victims of Torture." *Time*. (New York: Time Inc., February 18, 1985).

Lessner, Christian. "World War II." *The Encyclopedia Americana*. (New York: The Americana Corporation, 1962).

Levathes, Louise E. "The Land Where the Murray Flows." *National Geographic*. (Washington, D.C.: National Geographic Society, August, 1985).

Link, Marion Clayton. "Exploring the Drowned City of Port Royal." *National Geographic*. (Washington D.C.: National Geographic Society, February, 1960).

Llewellyn, Karl N., and Hoebel, E. Adamson. *The Cheyenne Way: Conflict and Case Law in Primitive Jurisprudence*. (Norman: University of Oklahoma Press, 1941).

Locke, John. *Two Treatises of Government*. (New York: Mentor Books, 1960).

Lothrop, S. K. *Treasures of Ancient America: Pre-Columbian Art from Mexico to Peru.* (New York: Rizzoli International Publications, Inc., 1979).

MacNeish, Richard S. "Introduction." *Early Man in America: Readings from Scientific American.* (San Francisco: W. H. Freeman and Company, 1973).

Mallery, Garrick. *Picture-Writing of the American Indians.* (New York: Dover Publications, Inc., 1972).

Marble, Dr. Samuel D. *Before Columbus: The New History of Celtic, Phoenician, Viking, Black African, and Asian Contacts and Impacts in the Americas before 1492.* (New York: A. S. Barnes and Company, 1980).

Marinatos, Spyridon. "Thera, Key to the Riddle of Minos." *National Geographic.* (Washington, D.C.: National Geographic Society, May, 1972).

Marshack, Alexander. *The Roots of Civilization: The Cognitive Beginnings of Man's First Art, Symbol and Notation.* (New York: McGraw-Hill Book Company, 1972).

Marx, Karl, Bottomore, T. B., translator. *Early Writings.* (New York: McGraw-Hill Book Company, 1964).

_____, Padover, Saul K., translator. *On America and the Civil War.* (New York: McGraw-Hill Book Company, 1972).

_____ *Surveys from Exile: Political Writings, Volume II.* (New York: Vintage Books, 1974).

McDonald, William. "How Old Is American Man? Artifacts Hint He Was Here Far Earlier Than Archaeologists Had Thought." *The National Observer.* (Washington, D.C.: The National Observer, May 31, 1975).

McKeon, Richard, editor. *The Basic Works of Aristotle.* (New York: Random House, 1941).

McPhee, John. *The Curve of Binding Energy.* (New York: Farrar, Straus and Giroux, 1974).

Means, Philip Ainsworth. "The Incas, Empire Builders of the Andes." *National Geographic on Indians of the Americas: a Color-Illustrated Record.* (Washington, D.C.: National Geographic Society, 1955).

Merk, Frederick. *Manifest Destiny and Mission in American History: A Reinterpretation.* (New York: Vintage Books, 1966).

Mertz, Henriette. *Pale Ink: Two Ancient Records of Chinese Exploration in America.* (Chicago: Henriette Mertz, 1953).

_____ *Atlantis: Dwelling Place of the Gods.* (Chicago: Henriette Mertz, 1976).

Montagu, Ashley. *Man's Most Dangerous Myth: The Fallacy of Race.* (New York: Oxford University Press, 1974).

_____ *Growing Young.* (New York: McGraw-Hill Book Company, 1981).

Morley, Sylvanus Griswold. "The Maya of Yucatan." *National Geographic on Indians of the Americas: a Color-Illustrated Record.* (Washington, D.C.: National Geographic Society, 1955).

Nash, Gary B. *Red, White, and Black: The Peoples of Early America.* (Englewood Cliffs, New Jersey: Prentice-Hall, Inc., 1974).

Nevin, David. *The American Touch in Micronesia.* (New York: 1977).

Pagels, Elaine. *The Gnostic Gospels.* (New York: Random House, 1981).

Paris, Edmond. *The Secret History of the Jesuits.* (Chino, California: Chick Publications, 1975).

Patterson, Francine. "Conversations With a Gorilla." *National Geographic.* (Washington, D.C.: National Geographic Society, October, 1968).

Pellegrino, Charles. *Unearthing Atlantis: An Archaeological Odyssey.* (New York: Vintage Books, 1993).

Perkins, David. "The Phantom Cattle Surgeons of the Plains." *Boulder Monthly.* (Boulder, Colorado: Boulder Monthly, Inc., January, 1979).

Pohl, Frederick J. *The Sinclair Expedition to Nova Scotia in 1398: A pre-Columbian crossing of the Atlantic definitely dated to year, month, and day of landing.* (Pictou, Nova Scotia: Pictou Advocate Press, 1950).

Poliakov, Léon, Howard, Edmund, translator. *The Aryan Myth: A History of Racist and Nationalist Ideas in Europe.* (New York: Basic Books, Inc., Publishers, 1976).

Porteus, Stanley D., and Babcock, Marjorie E. *Temperment and Race*. (Boston: Richard G. Badger, Publisher, 1926).

Pyle, Robert L. "A Message from the Past." *Wonderful West Virginia*. (Charleston: State of West Virginia Department of Natural Resources, March, 1983).

Quimby, George Irving. *Indian Life in the Upper Great Lakes: 11,000 B.C. to A.D. 1800*. (Chicago: The University of Chicago Press, 1960).

Reed, Nelson. *The Caste War of Yucatan*. (Stanford, California: Stanford University Press, 1964).

Rights, Douglas L. *The American Indian in North Carolina*. (Winston-Salem, North Carolina: John F. Blair, Publisher, 1957).

Romer, Alfred S. *The Vertebrate Story*. (Chicago: The University of Chicago Press, 1959).

Rosenblatt, Roger. "A Nation Coming Into Its Own." *Time*. (New York: Time Inc., July 29, 1985).

Rowdon, Maurice. *The Spanish Terror: Spanish Imperialism in the Sixteenth Century*. (New York: St. Martin's Press, 1974).

Sandoz, Mari. *Cheyenne Autumn*. (New York: Avon Books, 1964).

Schofield, John. "Christopher Columbus and the New World He Found." *National Geographic*. (Washington, D.C.: National Geographic Society, November, 1975).

Schoolcraft, Henry Rowe, LL.D. *History of the Indian Tribes of the United States: Their Present Condition and Prospects, and a Sketch of Their Ancient Status.* (Philadelphia: J. B. Lippincott & Co., 1857).

Shaw, L. Earl, editor. *Modern Competing Ideologies.* (Lexington: D. C. Heath and Company, 1973).

Shevchenko, Arkady. "Breaking With Moscow: Part II, The Reluctant Spy." *Time.* (New York: Time Inc., February 18, 1985).

Sperling, Susan Kelz. *Poplollies and Bellibones: A Celebration of Lost Words.* (New York: Penguin Books, 1977).

Stebbins, Ray, editor. "Custer, He Wanted Glory but Found Death Instead." *Colorado.* (Denver: Colorado Magazine, Inc., July-August, 1972).

Steiner, Stan. "China's Ancient Mariners." *Natural History.* (New York: American Museum of Natural History, December, 1977).

Stengel, Richard. "Bounty from the Oldest Shipwreck: The Mediterranean yields a vessel sunk perhaps 3,400 years ago." *Time.* (New York: Time Inc., December 17, 1984).

Terasaki, Nancy. "Who Gives a Damn?" *The Asian American Journey.* (Los Angeles: Agape Fellowship, February, 1980).

Tortosa, Mary. "Mutilations move nearer." *The Edmonton Sun.* (Edmonton, Alberta: Edmonton Sun, Inc., November 13, 1979).

Traveller Bird. *The Path to Snowbird Mountain.* (New York: Frarrar, Straus and Giroux, 1972).

Trinkaus, Erik. "Hard Times among the Neanderthals." *Natural History.* (New York: American Museum of Natural History, December, 1978).

United Press International. "Note authorizing the first atomic bomb is uncovered." *Honolulu Advertiser.* (Honolulu: Honolulu Advertiser, Inc., May 18, 1979).

Van Sertima, Ivan. *They Came Before Columbus.* (New York: Random House, 1976).

Vessels, Jane. "Koko's Kitten." *National Geographic.* (Washington, D.C.: National Geographic Society, January, 1985).

Voegelin, Eric. "The Growth of the Race Idea." *The Review of Politics.* (Notre Dame, Indiana: The University of Notre Dame, July, 1940).

_____ "Reason: The Classic Experience." *The Southern Review.* (Baton Rouge: Louisiana State University, Volume X, Number 2, April, 1974).

Vogel, Virgil J. *This Country Was Ours: A Documentary History of the American Indian.* (New York: Harper & Row, Publishers, 1972).

_____ *American Indian Medicine.* (New York: Ballantine Books, 1973).

von Puttkamer, W. Jesco. "Man in the Amazon: Stone Age Present Meets Stone Age Past." *National Geographic.* (Washington, D.C.: National Geographic Society, January, 1979).

von Wuthenau, Alexander. *The Art of Terracotta Pottery in Pre-Columbian Central and South America.* (New York: Crown Publishers, Inc., 1969).

White, Lynn, Jr. *Medieval Technology and Social Change.* (New York: Oxford University Press, 1962).

_____, editor. *The Transformation of the Roman World: Gibbon's Problem after Two Centuries.* (Los Angeles: University of California Press, 1966).

_____, editor. *Medieval Religion and Technology: Collected Essays.* (Los Angeles: University of California Press, 1976).

_____, editor. *Machina Ex Deo: Essays in the Dynamism of Western Culture.* (Cambridge, Massachusetts: The MIT Press,).

Willey, Gordon R. *An Introduction of American Archaeology, Volume One: North and Middle America.* (Englewood Cliffs, New Jersey: Prentice-Hall, Inc., 1966).

Wrone, David R., and Nelson, Russell S., Jr., editors. *Who's the Savage? A Documentary History of the Mistreatment of the Native North Americans.* (Greenwich, Connecticut: Fawcett Publications, Inc., 1973).

X, Malcom. *The Autobiography of Malcom X.* (New York: Grove Press, Inc., 1966).

The Invention of "Race" *is set in 10 point News 702,
and printed on acid-free, neutral pH paper.
Typesetting and book design by A.A. Huemer,
Cover artwork and* Agathon Books *logo by
Belinda B. Huemer.
Printed in the United States of America by
Gilliland Printing, Arkansas City, Kansas.*